Philosophy of Education

Introductory Readings

Second Edition

William Hare
and
John P. Portelli

Editors

Detselig Enterprises Ltd.
Calgary, Alberta, Canada

William Hare
John P. Portelli

Mount Saint Vincent University
Halifax, Nova Scotia

Canadian Cataloging in Publication Data

Main entry under title:

Philosophy of education

Includes bibliographical references.
ISBN 1-55059-136-3

1. Education – Philosophy. I. Hare, William. II. Portelli, John
P. (John Peter)
LB1025.3.P53   1996   370'.1   C96-910236-4

©1996 by Detselig Enterprises Limited
1220 Kensington Road NW, Unit 210
Calgary, Alberta, Canada T2N 3P5

Distributed by:

Temeron Books Inc.
P.O. Box 896
Bellingham, Washington 98227

Temeron Books Inc.
1220 Kensington Road NW, Unit 210
Calgary, Alberta, Canada, T2N 3P5

Printed in Canada   SAN 115-0324   ISBN 1-55059-136-3

To
Niki, Andrew, Antony, Stephen
and
Anna, Julian, Cecilia

Preface

The material gathered here has been edited to achieve a measure of consistency with respect to spelling, gender neutral references, and format. If these changes have produced any awkwardness, the editors are responsible not the authors. Minor deletions have been made of material which would have been inappropriate outside the original context. We are grateful to the contributors for making their material available for this collection.

Anna Portelli and Niki Hare have given valuable assistance with typing and proofreading.

In every respect, this project has been a joint effort of both editors.

Finally, our sincere thanks to Ted Giles and Detselig enterprises for supporting this second edition and for assistance at various points along the way.

William Hare
John P. Portelli

Halifax, Nova Scotia
August, 1996

Contents

Contributors

Sharon Bailin is Professor of Education at Simon Fraser University, Burnaby, British Columbia.

Joyce Bellous is Assistant Professor, McMaster Divinity College, Hamilton, Ontario.

Eamonn Callan is Professor of Education at the University of Alberta, Edmonton, Alberta.

David Carr is Reader in Education at the Moray House Institute, Heriot-Watt University, Edinburgh.

Charles Clark was formerly at Goldsmith's College, London, England.

Robert F. Dearden was formerly Professor of Education at the University of Birmingham, England.

Elliot W. Eisner is Professor of Education and Art at Stanford University, California.

Harold Entwistle is Professor Emeritus of Education at Concordia University, Montreal, Quebec.

Paulo Freire was formerly Professor of Philosophy and Education at the University of Recife, Brazil; Consultant for World Council of Churches in Geneva; and Secretary of Education for Sao Paulo.

Maxine Greene is William F. Russell Professor Emerita of the Foundations of Education at Teachers College, Columbia University, New York.

Amy Gutmann is Professor of Politics and Laurance S. Rockefeller University Professor at Princeton University, New Jersey.

William Hare is Professor of Education at Mount Saint Vincent University, Halifax, Nova Scotia.

Sheva Medjuck is Professor of Sociology at Mount Saint Vincent University, Halifax, Nova Scotia.

Nel Noddings is Lee L. Jacks Professor of Child Education at Stanford University, California.

John P. Portelli is Professor of Education at Mount Saint Vincent University, Halifax, Nova Scotia.

Richard Rorty is Kenan Professor of Humanities and University Professor at the University of Virginia, Charlottesville, Virginia.

Ann Margaret Sharp is Director of the Institute for the Advancement of Philosophy for Children Graduate Programs, and Associate Director of I.A.P.C. at Montclair State University, New Jersey.

Jane Roland Martin is Professor Emerita of Philosophy at the University of Massachusetts, Boston.

Harvey Siegel is Professor of Philosophy at the University of Miami.

Basil R. Singh is Reader in Education at the University of Sunderland, Sunderland, England.

Barbara Thayer-Bacon is Assistant Professor of Education at Bowling Green State University, Ohio.

Max van Manen is Professor of Education at the University of Alberta, Edmonton, Alberta.

Baroness Warnock is a Fellow and the former Mistress of Girton College, Cambridge, England.

P.S. Wilson was formerly at Goldsmith's College, London, England.

Introduction

In this second edition, it remains our intention to offer a collection of essays in philosophy of education which will provide students in teacher education programs with a lively and accessible introduction to some of the central debates and issues in the field. In addition, teachers, administrators, and graduate students should find this collection a valuable resource. As with the first edition in 1988, and given our intended readership, we have selected discussions which establish a connection between philosophical reflection and pedagogical practice, in the belief that philosophical understanding is a vital aspect of professional development. We have chosen work which will challenge student teachers to formulate their own views on matters which remain controversial and problematic, and which are intended to provoke them into a thoughtful engagement with assumptions which influence contemporary schooling.

The relationship between philosophy and teaching is an instance of the more general relationship between theory and practice, and this connection is one which, notoriously, generates suspicion and puzzlement. Since teaching is patently a practical endeavor, why would training and practice not suffice? Why the need for theory at all? Recent developments in some countries would suggest that many are inclined to take the view that an apprenticeship model of teacher training is precisely what is required. In the present climate of opinion, we would do well to recall Dewey's warning that "unless the practice is based upon rational principles, upon insight into facts and their meaning, 'experience' simply fixes incorrect acts into wrong habits."[1] The collection begins, therefore, with a section dealing with theory and practice in which the prevailing scepticism about educational theory in teacher education is critically examined.

Running counter to a fashionable view which regards teaching primarily in terms of technical expertise, the opening essays present a certain conception of excellence in teaching which involves among other things: having a heightened sense of what the problems of education and teaching are; an awareness of, and concern about, the way in which ethical values inevitably permeate one's practice as a teacher; and an appreciation for what fitness for teaching, at a deep level, might mean in terms of the central qualities and virtues a teacher ought to possess. These themes, which raise the issue of what it means to be a good teacher, turn up in subsequent essays, for example in the interview with Paulo Freire, in Maxine Greene's discussion of the principled teacher, and elsewhere. The invitation to student teachers is to think seriously about the notion of teaching to which they implicitly subscribe in order to assess its appropriateness in the light of the complexities and challenges of the role.[2]

Theory can also be linked with practice through the consideration of detailed examples and cases which force one to articulate general principles which might explain or justify the experience or issue in question. Many of the essays in this collection are rich in such examples: Jane Roland Martin's thoughtful examination of Richard Rodriguez' autobiographical reflections; John P. Portelli's account of a grade 6 class discussing the "revised" version of "The three little pigs," told from the wolf's point of view; the many examples from literature introduced by Maxine Greene in her discussion of multicultural-ism. Two essays are entirely devoted to an inquiry into recent, controversial incidents in Canadian education which ultimately led to the teachers involved being removed from their teaching positions. Students might also usefully supplement the readings in this collection with discussion of case studies where theoretical and practical issues are fruitfully engaged.[3]

Such an emphasis on student teachers thinking critically about educational issues itself reflects what has become one of the most keenly contested notions in contemporary educational discourse, critical thinking. A number of essays address questions of meaning and justification related to critical thinking, and raise the question of what teaching in a critical manner might entail and what problems are associated with such an aim.[4] Moreover, recent contributions, written from feminist and postmodernist perspectives, have raised serious questions about what is seen as the taken-for-granted possibility and desirability of critical thinking, assumptions which are now openly challenged. Clearly we need to ask whether or not the ideal of critical thinking can survive these objections.[5]

Controversy over critical thinking is indicative of the way in which any educational aim or proposal is potentially problematic and divisive. Several essays present perspectives on the matter of controversy: the various ways in which curriculum materials can be controversial; the role of teachers in dealing with controversial material; the limits placed on teachers who maintain contro-versial views, whether in public or in private life. The Keegstra and Ross cases took a tortuous path through the legal system all the way to the Supreme Court; and the various decisions and reversals showed, as did editorial commentaries in the media, just how divided Canadian society was about these matters. Student teachers need to ask what useful lessons emerge from these events.

Before considering how to educate, Bertrand Russell observed, it would be wise to be clear about the result we hope to achieve.[6] A number of essays raise fundamental questions about the overall conception of education which teachers ought to adopt. Should student teachers, for example, think of educa-tion at school as primarily socialization, as Rorty suggests? Is it true, as Jane Roland Martin contends, that what would quite naturally be described as a highly successful education might be more accurately described as a process of alienation? Is Nel Noddings right to claim that a renewed commitment to moral education, based on the perspective of caring, is the orientation to education which is now desperately needed?

Student teachers preparing to enter the classroom at the end of the twentieth century must examine their educational aims in light of the fact that the student population they will encounter reflects the pluralistic, multicultural society which has now emerged. Is it possible, as Maxine Greene asks, to affirm difference and yet create community? Can we, in Eamonn Callan's words, cultivate a shared reasonableness which will promote mutual respect? Are there, indeed, any common principles which can be appealed to, and how are these to be determined? Or must we succumb to the prevalent relativism which would suggest that all values and beliefs are little more than the dominant prejudices of the day?

Questions about values immediately raise concerns about imposition. If moral education is vital, and if certain shared values are to be cultivated, how is the danger of indoctrination to be averted? Are there ways we can find to avoid the coercive practices which Joyce Bellous describes, and to promote practices which empower children? Is there any reason to think that parents are exempt from the general prohibition against indoctrination? Should children in general be allowed simply to pursue their own interests at school? And what would such a policy mean in terms of educational standards?

There is a wealth of material here for discussion and debate. This collection will have served its purpose if it helps to promote reflection and inquiry among student teachers, and if it demonstrates that there is an important philosophical dimension to questions about educational practice and policy.[7]

Notes

[1]See "What psychology can do for the teacher," in Reginald D. Archambault (ed.), *John Dewey on Education: Selected Writings* (New York, NY: Random House, 1964), 201.

[2]See also William Hare, *What Makes A Good Teacher* (London, ON: Althouse Press, 1993).

[3]See, for example, William Hare and John P. Portelli, *What To Do? Case Studies for Teachers* (Halifax: Edphil Books, 1993).

[4]For a consideration of critical teaching in the context of philosophy for children, see John P. Portelli and Ronald F. Reed (eds.) *Children, Philosophy, and Democracy.* (Calgary, AB: Detselig, 1995).

[5]For further relevant discussions, see John P. Portelli and Sharon Bailin (eds.), *Reason and Values: New Essays in Philosophy of Education* (Calgary, AB: Detselig, 1993).

6. Bertrand Russell, *On Education* (London: Unwin Books, 1971), ch. 2. (Originally published, 1926).

[7]Students interested in contemporary debates about the nature of philosophy of education and topics related to the ones represented in this collection, should consult Wendy Kohli (ed.), *Critical Conversations in Philosophy of Education*, (New York: Routledge, 1995).

Acknowledgments

The Editors are grateful to the following journals, publishers and institutions for permission to reprint in this collection those articles or chapters, or versions therof, which have been previously published.

Oxford Review of Education, 18, 3, 1992: 241-51, for "Practical Enquiry, Values and the Problem of Educational Theory" by David Carr.

The Robert W.B. Jackson Memorial Lecture Series, for "Fit for Teaching" by Max van Mannen (originally published under the title "Childhood Contingency and Pedagogical Fitness"); and for "The Role of Reasons in (Science) Education" by Harvey Siegel.

McGill Journal of Education, 29, 2, 1994: 137-51, for "The Challenge of Teaching for Critical Thinking" by John P. Portelli.

Informal Logic, 9, 1, 1987: 23-30, for "Critical and Creative Thinking" by Sharon Bailin.

Thinking: The Journal of Philosophy for Children, 8, 2, 1991: 31-7, for "The Community of Inquiry: Education for Democracy" by Ann Margaret Sharp.

Inquiry: Critical Thinking Across the Disciplines, 10, 2, 1992: 3-7, and **Philosophical Studies in Education** (Proceedings of the Ohio Valley Philosophy of Education Society), 1992, for "Is Modern Critical Thinking Theory Sexist?" by Barbara Thayer-Bacon.

Journal of Curriculum Studies, 13, 1, 1981: 37-44, for "Controversial Issues and the Curriculum" by R.F. Dearden.

The Royal Institute of Philosophy, for "The Neutral Teacher" by Mary Warnock, published in S.C. Brown (ed.), **Philosophers Discuss Education** (London: Macmillan, 1975).

Canadian Journal of Education, 15, 4, 1990: 375-89, for "Propaganda in the Classroom: The Keegstra Case" by William Hare. (Originally published under the title "Limiting the Freedom of Expression: The Keegstra Case").

University of New Brunswick Law Journal, 41, 1992: 285-94, for "Re-examining the Meaning of Freedom of Expression: The Case of Malcolm Ross" by Sheva Medjuck. (Originally published as "Rethinking Canadian Justice: Hate Must Not Define Democracy").

Language Arts, 62, 1, 1985: 15-21, for "Reading the World and Reading the Word: An Interview with Paulo Freire."

Wadsworth Publishing Company, for "Teacher as Stranger" from **Teacher as Stranger**, 1993, by Maxine Greene.

Dissent, 36, 2, 1989: 215-30, for "Education without Dogma: Truth, Freedom, and our Universities" by Richard Rorty.

Journal of Education, 167, 3, 1985: 71-84 for "Becoming Educated: A Journey of Alienation or Integration?" by Jane Roland Martin.

American Journal of Education, 96, 2, 1988: 215-30 for "An Ethic of Caring and Its Implications for Instructional Arrangements" by Nel Noddings.

Educational Researcher, 22, 1, 1993: 13-18 for "The Passions of Pluralism: Multiculturalism and the Expanding Community" by Maxine Greene.

Canadian Journal of Education, 20, 3, 1995: 251-71 for "Common Schools for Common Education" by Eamonn Callan.

Teachers College Record, 92, 1, 1990: 7-20 for "Democratic Education in Difficult Times" by Amy Gutmann.

Educational Review, 47, 1, 1995: 11-24 for "Shared Values, Particular Values, and Education for a Multicultural Society" by Basil R. Singh.

Interchange, 23, 1 & 2, 1992: 63-9 for "Culture, Democracy, and the University" by Sharon Bailin.

Phi Delta Kappan, 76, 10, 1995: 758-64 for "Standards for Schools: Help or Hindrance?" by Elliot W. Eisner.

Educational Philosophy and Theory, 7, 1, 1975: 41-54 for "How to Base Your Curriculum on Children's Interests" by Charles Clark and P.S. Wilson.

Paideusis: The Journal of the Canadian Philosophy of Education Society, 8, 2, 1995: 3-14 for "Should We Teach Students to Resist?" by Joyce Bellous.

The Philosophy of Education Society, for "Indoctrination and Parental Rights" by Eamonn Callan, published in **Philosophy of Education 1985**: 97-106.

Detselig Enterprises Ltd. appreciates the financial assistance for its 1996 publishing program from the Department of Canadian Heritage and The Alberta Foundation for the Arts, a beneficiary of the Lottery Fund of the Government of Alberta.

Part One

Theory and Practice

The essays in this section deal with the issue of theory and practice – an issue that has for a long time troubled those who are concerned about the nature of professional activities as well as the preparation of those who will be working in the professions such as law, medicine, and education: Do professional activities deal only with practical matters? What is the nature of practical matters? Do practical matters simply involve the application of skills? What is the best or most appropriate way to prepare people to become competent professionals? Should the emphasis be on theoretical concerns or practical concerns? Can the two be separated? The replies to these questions will vary according to how one views the nature of theory and practice, and the relationship between the two. And, in turn, such views will determine how one conceptualizes the discipline or disciplines (for example, philosophy of education) that underlie a certain profession (for example, education). More specifically, then, the nature of philosophy of education and the role of philosophers of education will vary according to one's perspective about the relationship between theory and practice.

In the first essay, David Carr challenges the popular view that teacher education is dominated by theory oriented courses, and argues that several problems and misconceptions arise from misunderstanding what the relationship between theory and practice in education ought to be. While agreeing that education and teaching are primarily practical activities, he cautions us that this does not preclude any function for deliberation and rational discussion. Contrary to popular beliefs, he argues that educational matters are not to be resolved solely by taking technical matters into account, for educational issues are inextricably connected with values issues. Carr contends that the popular view is still based on the belief that education is primarily a technical matter and hence we can have a science of education that can, on the basis of empirical research, provide universal solutions to educational problems. According to Carr, such a narrow perspective creates (i) disillusionment for practioners who expect theories to solve their day-to-day practical problems and (ii) disempowerment of teachers who are not encouraged to think reflectively on their practice. From Carr's perspective, then, the problems of the lack of correspondence between theory and practice are created by the sharp division between the technical and moral, and misconceptions about the role of theory. The rigid, traditional notion of theory that assumed neutrality and is expected to provide

1

detailed, specific, secure, universal prescriptions or solutions is rejected by Carr.

The second essay by Harold Entwistle explicitly discusses the following questions: What causes the gap between theory and practice? Can this gap be lessened? How ought theory and practice be related? Should we expect or demand a one-to-one correspondence between theory and practice? To what extent can or should theory "guide" practice? How could a theory be applied? Entwistle is in agreement with Carr's position for he believes that educational theory (including philosophy of education), of its nature, does not offer and is not meant to offer specific knowledge and skills "applicable to a given practical situation." For Carr the role of theory is to "generate problems more than to solve them" and encourage "professional autonomy." For Entwistle the role of theory is to "evoke judgment rather than rote obedience." He argues that, if done well, theory does offer the opportunity for teachers to develop new perspectives which help them to analyze, question, be aware of the complexities in the teaching context, and resolve problems that arise from practice. Nonetheless, Entwistle argues that although "learning the art of compromise" will help teachers to reduce the gulf between theory and practice, in the final analysis the gap is inevitable. However, Entwistle contends that struggling with this fact will help us refine both theory and practice!

To what extent can reflective deliberation help teachers become "fit for teaching"? Can they afford to do otherwise? "How does one prepare to be pedagogically fit?" These are the kind of questions dealt with in the third essay by Max van Manen. Van Manen contends that while teaching is necessarily contingent in nature, the fracturedness, intensity, contradictions, and uncertainties of the modern world increase the complexities of teaching and highlight the importance and inevitability of making choices. And he asks: "If childhood is the experience of contingencies, what then is our professional educational responsibility?" The direct and short answer he offers is that we need to be able to handle change, to be more reflective on the pedagogical relationship between the child and adult, "to be able to act thinkingly," and "to be 'outfitted' with tact."

Although van Manen does not explicitly criticize the narrow, technocratic view of theory, his emphasis on the importance of being sensitive to the contingent (whether it is childhood contingency or situational, classroom contingencies) and the inevitability of the contingent, indicate that he does not adhere to the reductionist notion of theory. As he warns us, it is only the inexperienced teacher who thinks that one could teach well as long as "you knew [the subject] well, and as long as you used the right instructional technique to express it all." What is missing in this framework is the notion of "pedagogical tact" which is at the core of pedagogical fitness. Van Manen defines pedagogical tact as "the active readiness, sensitivity, and flexibility that educators demonstrate when they are dealing with young people in everyday educational situations." Tact is not a matter of implementing theory. Tact as "an oriented mindfulness" is more like a disposition or way of being that combines theory and practice or perhaps even goes beyond theory and practice. For van Manen "tact is not simply some kind of mediator between theory and practice," it is "a kind of practical normative intelligence that is governed by insight while relying on feeling," and is based on "a certain kind of reflection, or better on an active intentionality of thoughtfulness." And hence he concludes that "the essence of tact is that it cannot be separated between theory and practice . . . tact as pedagogical fitness overcomes the theory-practice split and retains a wonderful quality of ambiguity."

The renowned Canadian philosopher, George Grant, remarked that "whatever the relation between the theoretical and the practical life there is bound to be some division, and so there is something nonsensical about giving immediate advice to people who have to carry it out practically." From this it doesn't follow that we should not be concerned with theory or that anything in the practice is acceptable. But it does follow that there is something faulty or nonsensical with the view that the role of theory is to give immediate advice. Hence educators and teachers, as professionals, need to be careful what to expect or demand from theory whether it is a theory developed by them or others. To avoid the nonsensical, professionals need to constantly remember the unending dynamism or dialectic that exists between the educational and moral realms, professional autonomy and empowerment and critical judgment, and the contingent and ambiguous and the desire for certainty and stability. From this perspective, while theory and practice are conceptually distinct, they are inseparable, very much like the two sides of a coin.

Further Readings

Wilfred Carr, *For Education: Towards Critical Educational Inquiry*. Buckingham, U.K.: Open University Press, 1995.

John Elliott, "Educational Theory, Practical Philosophy and Action Research," *British Journal of Educational Studies*, 25, 2, 1987: 149-169.

B. Fay, *Critical Social Science: Liberation and Its Limits*. Cambridge: Cambridge University Press, 1987.

Richard D. Hansgen, "Can Education Become a Science?" *Phi Delta Kappan*, May 1991: 689-694.

4 Theory and Practice

William Pinar and Madeline Grumet, "Socratic Caesura and the Theory-Practice Relationship," in W. Pinar (ed.), *Contemporary Curriculum Discoursess*. Scottsdale, Arizona: Gorsuch Scarisbrick, 1988.

Susan Ohanian, "On Stir-and-Serve Recipies for Teaching," *Phi Delta Kappan*, June 1985: 696-701.

Donald A. Schon, *Educating the Reflective Practioner: Toward a New Design for Teaching and Learning in the Professions*. San Francisco: Jossey-Bass Publishers, 1987.

John Smyth (ed.), *Educating Teachers: Changing the Nature of Pedagogical Knowledge*. Philadelphia: Falmer Press, 1987.

John Smyth, "A Critical Pedagogy of Classroom Practice," *Journal of Curriculum Studies*, 21, 6, 1989: 483-502.

Ronald Sultana, "Towards a Critical Teaching Practice: Notes for the Teacher Educator," *Journal of Further and Higher Education*, 14, 1, 1990: 14-30.

R. Winter, *Learning from Experience: Principles and Practice in Action Research*. Lewes: Falmer Press, 1989.

Practical Enquiry, Values and the Problem of Educational Theory

David Carr

The Alleged Preponderance of Theory Over Practice

In a recent feature for BBC's *Public Eye*[1] concerned with current debates on the nature of the professional education and preparation of teachers, we were informed – once again – that there is a problem about the place of theory in pre-service teacher education. Apparently there is currently too much theory in most higher education courses concerned with such professional education and not enough practice. Despite the fact that an entire battalion of distinguished contemporary professors of education was assembled apparently to concur (in one way or another) with this view and to try to come up with ingenious strategies whereby all this putative theory might be more practically applied (or better still dispensed with) there are questions to be asked – or aired anew – about the nature and extent of this alleged preponderance of theory over practice.

An initial question – one for the empirical researchers into education perhaps – might be: is there any hard evidence for the truth of this view that teacher education is theory dominated? As a professional colleague in another institution observed to me in a discussion of the *Public Eye* feature – he wished he knew where all these theory dominated colleges were so that he might go and teach in one. In point of fact there has been a steady and systematic erosion of studies of an academic or theoretical kind in most institutions concerned with teacher education in recent years and for quite some time now the general trend in education has been towards more practically based or vocationally orientated patterns of professional preparation at B.Ed and other levels. So, although one can easily picture people taking to heart from the *Public Eye* program the moral that the trouble with young people today is that their teachers have had too much theory and too little practice in their professional preparation, I suspect that this might be hard to substantiate in terms of solid evidence.

What troubles me rather more about the general level of discussion of the educational theory-practice problem in the television program in question, however (and in other "serious" documentary coverage of this kind on television) is the conspicuous failure to address any questions about what might be *meant* – of the many *different* things which might be meant – by talk of educational theory and its relations to practice. Surprisingly, not one of the learned contributors to the program paused to raise any of the conceptual issues which might have effectively obviated many of the subsequent practical proposals – and it is precisely to these conceptual questions that I have thought it appropriate to address this essay, primarily to the question – what is the problem of the relationship of theory to practice in education supposed to be?

Before we set out to criticize the so-called theoretical input of teacher education courses, then – to say that there is too much theory or how that theory ought to be integrated into professional practice – we need to be clear about the nature of theoretical discourse and about the goals it is concerned to achieve. For it would certainly be unfair to criticize such discourse for failing to achieve goals which are inappropriate to it and it is therefore a matter of some urgency to discern its true nature; only then can we see how the issues which it is concerned to raise might enter into the professional preparation and practice of apprentice and other teachers.

The Logic of Practical Discourse

Let us begin with a very large note of agreement with the severest critics of educational theorising and its role in teacher preparation – that education and teaching *are*, to be sure, matters of practice more than theory. In fact, I think that it is quite essential, for a proper understanding of these issues, to grasp the point that education as a practical activity is in a very real and crucial sense *opposed* to theory. That sense and the contrast on which it depends is precisely coincident with that which was marked by Aristotle 2000 years ago between the different logical natures of theoretical and practical inquiry. Aristotle's observation in the *Nicomachean Ethics* that moral enquiry is concerned primarily with the problem of how to *become* good rather than with that of arriving (in the manner to which Plato aspired) at some formal or quasi-scientific definition of goodness or justice rested squarely and soundly on his original discovery of a distinction between theoretical and practical enquiry, from which it follows that there cannot be the sort of precise, strict and formal definitions of moral and other evaluative notions that there might be in the theoretical studies of science and mathematics.[2] For Aristotle, ethics as a form of practical inquiry is concerned with the world of what is particular and contingent by contrast with the scientific world which aspires to the discovery of general and (more debatably) necessary truths. Thus, theoretical and practical inquiries and activities have quite different characters and aims – and education is clearly a branch of *practical* inquiry in Aristotle's sense.

Of course, this distinction between theoretical or truth-seeking inquiries like science and practical or good-seeking activities like art or morals does not presage the end of all ethical discussion; on the contrary, it signals the beginning of an inevitably endless debate about the true nature of human benefit or flourishing and the conduct which is most conducive to it. Whilst it is true enough that morality is not a theoretical business in one particular sense, then, that of being concerned with the discovery of truths about the natural order of things, it is nevertheless the case that moral conduct *is* a matter for genuine enquiry – perhaps the highest of all enquiries in which human agents can be engaged – that of how to live well. Moreover, the enquiry in question is rational in character and is of a kind for which clear, careful and consistent thought is a *sine qua non*. This point is sometimes missed by those who think that logic and rationality are relevant only to the sphere of scientific or truth-theoretical activities and not at all to the realm of practice and action; but we can reinforce it by reference to two indispensable features of sound human conduct – practical consistency and rational values.

First, it is easy enough to show that considerations of logical coherence and consistency *do* enter into our practical affairs as much as they do into the realm of theoretical knowledge and belief. Just as we are enjoined by theoretical reason to eschew simultaneous subscription to two conflicting propositions (for example, that dolphins are fish and that they have lungs), so we are also required by practical reason to avoid promulgating inconsistent prescriptions or attempting to engage in self-defeating conduct. If, for example, a mother instructs her child to go to the shop by the shortest route but not to go by the canal – though the shortest way *is* via the canal – then the mother has required the child to do what it is not within his or her power consistently so to do. Or, if I contribute to two different charities, one which aids a particular kind of medical research and the other which supports efforts to alleviate animal suffering, then I have clearly given with one hand and taken away with the other if the medical research in question involves painful experimentation on animals. It is also plain enough to see that in the absence of proper rational reflection about the overall aims of our efforts in such respects as these, it is easy for us to fall into inconsistent and ineffective conduct of one sort or another.

These very considerations, however, may also serve to draw to our attention that voluntary deliberate human action and conduct are expressly directed towards the achievement of goals and purposes which enshrine *values* which may be consistent or inconsistent. Indeed, a value is quite generally a preference for one sort of human goal over another in the light of the fact that such goals are often not simultaneously achievable or, at least, may conflict with one another in various ways. Thus the mother is concerned both that the shopping chores should be done as expeditiously as possible and that her child's safety should be reasonably well safeguarded. The contributor to charity is concerned to relieve the human suffering that the medical research might alleviate and also to spare the animal suffering which such research often seems to entail. Where it is not possible to achieve all these aims simultaneously we are required to evaluate and order them in terms of relative importance and, perhaps, to relinquish entirely the pursuit of some goals in favor of others.

Precisely, then, we are frequently required to *prefer* some practical goals or courses of conduct over others – and many of these preferences may be regarded as *values*. Of course, not *all* human preferences would naturally be called values; choosing the apple strudel over the raspberry yoghurt might be done according to preference, but it would be strange to include strudel eating as one of my values. Again, though getting the shopping done quickly is something a mother might prefer, it is hardly a value of hers – or, at any rate, not a moral one – whereas a degree of reasonable concern over her child's welfare and safety clearly is. Wanting to relieve human suffering and wanting to spare animal suffering are, of course, easily describable as values – and moral ones at that. Quite generally, then, values are choices or preferences which are rooted in rational principles and considerations of a kind that have distinct ethical implications – principles, that is, which have reasonably serious consequences (moral, prudential, utilitarian, aesthetic, hedonistic, and so on) for the good or ill of human and other sentient creatures.

This gloss on values as *principled* preferences is of quite considerable importance here since it underlines the fact that unlike other sorts of preferences which are based merely on personal taste or natural disposition, values are standardly a consequence of something approaching intelligent deliberation and are thus, in principle, susceptible of rational appraisal and re-appraisal. Notoriously, this has been from time to time denied by those moral philosophers[3] who have tried to insist that values are neither cognitive, rational nor objectively grounded – but this claim sits extremely ill with the crucial role which values *do* clearly play in the rational conduct of human practical life. Thus it seems that a parent who preferred to get the shopping done promptly, even if this put his or her child's life at serious risk, would be guilty as much of irrationality as of callousness – especially if the child's favorite breakfast cereal featured prominently on the shopping list. Granted that the actual demise of the child might in certain exceptional circumstances be exactly what a cruel parent wants, it is clearly irrational for a normal caring parent to prefer expeditious shopping to his or her child's safety. (Here, then, it is rational to let the moral value override the prudential one.)

In the case of the clash between the values concerned with the relief of suffering which lie behind giving or withholding aid to medical research, it is clearly much more difficult to decide what should be done than in the case of the parent's conflict between moral and non-moral imperatives, but it is nevertheless also an occasion for a rational response more than one of mere taste. Both values concern, after all, the relief of suffering and raise problems of practical rationality about the significance of suffering. Animal experiments may well lead to less human suffering by causing more widespread suffering among sentient creatures in general, but someone might be inclined to accept this cost on the grounds that the pain of rational human beings is qualitatively worse or more deplorable than that of non-rational or unselfconscious creatures. My concern is not to take sides on this issue, only to show that we are here faced with a conflict of principle more than personal inclination – one which requires to be addressed in terms of what is ethically or morally right rather than through some kind of instinctive or conventional response. In short, questions about what to do arising from conflicts of values – especially those which spring from conflicts of *moral* values – are occasions for serious rational reflection and deliberation and are not to be decided in advance of a profound consideration of the principles and evidence which bear on the circumstances of the particular case. For the moment, it must suffice to say that many questions about what to do in education are clearly questions which are implicated in value conflicts of this kind.

The Difference Between Moral and Technical Reasoning

Of course, not all questions about practice – about what we should do – are questions of this sort. With respect to a wide range of practical problems, there are only really questions about what means to adopt to achieve a given pre-determined purpose which need not give rise to any particular difficulties about values. Leaving aside the environmentally aware car owner's problems of conscience about whether he or she should have his or her vehicle modified to take unleaded gasoline or whether he or she should own a car at all, once he or she does own a car his or her main concern may well be simply that of how to keep it on the road by means of basic maintenance. This, the owner or the garage mechanic contrives to do not by recourse to anything like practical reflection of a moral sort but with the help of the mechanical knowledge contained in the maintenance manual together with some basic scientific knowledge of physical properties and chemical reactions. The problems raised in this and many other cases of human practical uncertainty are relatively straightforward (even if complex) problems about the adoption of scientific knowledge of one sort or another to a range of practical or instrumental dilemmas in the light of certain goals or purposes. Though they are practical matters, they are not moral but *technical* difficulties.

The crucial question for educationalists with respect to this important distinction between kinds of human practical inquiry – the moral and the technical (basically Aristotle's *phronesis* and *techne*) – precisely concerns whether problems of educational practice should be construed as primarily moral or technical in nature. I am in no doubt that they are actually of both kinds and that serious confusion between the two lies at the heart of the purported problem of understanding the relationship between so-called educational theory and educational practice. For there are undoubtedly many relatively straightforward educational problems concerning pedagogy, class management, departmental and class administration, stocktaking, and so on, which are of a largely technical kind that require to be dealt with by means of a rationalization or streamlining of existing procedures. On this model of educational practice, education, like car maintenance, proceeds according to certain pre-established goals – the effective delivery of the optimum curriculum (whatever that is) to the education clientele (whoever they are) – and teachers are simply the technicians whose job it is to provide the appropriate service for the consumer. The educational goals themselves are defined and set by the designers and policy makers of education with the assistance and guidance of the expert advisers on practical management, administration and pedagogical science who are engaged at the cutting edge of educational theoretical research in the universities and colleges.

This general idea of education as a more or less straightforward and value-free technical exercise is quite widely subscribed to in an explicit or implicit theoretical or pre-theoretical way both inside and beyond professional education circles. It is certainly evident in the administrative and policy-making strategies of governments and politicians who persistently require teachers to comply with and implement centrally determined initiatives regarding education, more often than not without any sort of democratic consultation of the professional workforce who are to bear the burden of such initiatives. It is also exhibited in the attitudes of the college and university students of education who often expect to be told what to do both in college and on teaching practice – to be handed the information and skills necessary for immediately effective practice – by those placed in authority over them. Conversely, it is also revealed in the doctrinaire attitudes and practices of those university and college lecturers who are foolish enough to allow themselves to be cast in the role of "super-teachers" with all the answers to problems of educational practice – even those in circumstances which may be unfamiliar to them.

The view is also well-entrenched in the role that many university departments of education seem to have established for themselves as empirical research-based faculties of educational science. It is a remarkable fact that seems hitherto to have gone largely unremarked that, in many if not most university departments of education in the UK, educational research is synonymous with *empirical* research of the kind that is conducted in the largely "soft" sciences of psychology, sociology, economics, management, and so on (with the cultural-conceptual disciplines of history and philosophy of education largely on the decline) – all of which is devoted to the frantic gathering of information, data and evidence which is allegedly necessary to correct and improve the current practice of teachers in schools. In short, it is widely assumed that the main problems of education, like those of car maintenance, raise issues of a mainly technical kind which can be solved via pursuit of the sort of empirical research into the operations of human learning, group interaction, the economic functions of institutions and so forth which, so it seems to be believed, will facilitate the development of effective techniques of pedagogy, class control and school management.

This view of the nature of the relationship between theory and practice in education – that of educational theorizing as a kind of quasi-scientific enterprise which serves to inform a technology of teaching – is thus quite widespread both within and without professional educational circles; but it takes only a little mature reflection to see that it is at once a deeply flawed and a seriously impoverished view of the bearing on educational practice of intelligent theoretical discourse about education. It is easy to see in the light of this idea, however, why even well-intentioned students and teachers become seriously disillusioned with their educational theory courses when what has been presented to them under the guise of practical science fails to deliver the results for practice which would seem to have been promised. For whilst there are, to be sure, practical educational problems of a more or less technical nature about effective lesson preparation, organization, presentation and the control of groups, these are normally of a very specific nature which relate to circumstances of resources, current discipline practices and curricular traditions in particular schools and they are not issues to which the higher level and more general researches of social scientists into cognitive development, attitude formation, group dynamics or personnel management can provide much in the way of direct practical solutions without considerable critical and evaluative reinterpretation and adaptation to particular circumstances. The sort of craft knowledge and skill (*techne*) which is required for efficient and effective everyday practice is in truth best learned on the job and it is probably not greatly or immediately assisted by general meditation on the empirical findings of social scientists. This is not to say that social scientific observations on human behavior are of absolutely no relevance to practising teachers – they are an important part of their professional education – it is only to say that it is a mistake to regard them as feeding into the immediate solution of a teacher's technical educational problems in his or her specific circumstances as a car maintenance manual might lead directly to the diagnosis and remedy of that faulty carburetor.

Teachers will often become disillusioned with so-called educational theory, then, when, having been led to believe that such theoretical speculations as they encounter in it represent a body of quasi-scientific knowledge which underpins an effective technology of pedagogy or control, they recognize that the generalization of a Piaget or Bruner are of little help in sorting out the particular practical problems they are immediately faced with – of, say, how to teach *this* dull child X or how to control *that* unruly child Y. It must also be acknowledged, however, that the teacher will often feel doubly betrayed or short-changed, not only when he or she finds that the promised technological solutions to his or her problems have not been delivered, but also because he or she has been encouraged in an undue reliance for professional salvation on the authority and advice of others – the alleged theoretical expertise of his or her academic tutors in university or college. Professional training has fostered not a real confidence in his or her own educated judgment, initiative and personal resources, but an impotent dependence on the assumed wisdom of others who nevertheless appear persistently to fail to provide the sort of advice that is relevant to his or her current problems; the idols have feet of clay.

The Moral Roots of Educational Discourse

The practising teacher's feeling of disillusionment with the so-called educational theory he or she was taught at college is, however, based on a substantial confusion about the nature of educated educational discourse, the way in which theoretical or academic studies impinge on that discourse *and* about the contribution which such educational studies have to make to the professional development of teachers – a mistake in which students, teachers and university and college lecturers all too often collude. Put simply, the mistake is that of taking the essence of educational problems to be of a predominantly technical nature when they are at heart, if not exclusively, ethical or evaluative in character. One of the direct implications of this is to recognize that debates and discussions about education in universities and colleges are properly concerned, paradoxical as it sounds, to *generate* problems more than to solve them – to alert students precisely to those serious ethical and evaluative issues concerning the proper conduct of education about which they may have hitherto had not the faintest suspicion. It is also the job of those who raise these debates and conduct these discussions to assist student teachers to develop the professional resources which might enable them to deal with these complex ethical and evaluative problems in as informed, mature, principled, civilized and decent a way as they possibly can. From this point of view it is not the job of university and college lecturers, nor is it within their power, to provide students with tailor-made answers to their particular practical difficulties; rather it is to help them explore in the context of a wider *education* about education, schooling and their contributions to social and individual flourishing, the different available rational conceptions of and perspectives on education as a human moral practice. The proper task of academic or theoretical educational studies in universities and colleges is not that of training classroom technicians to perform routine functions but that of the education of individuals in the kind of professional autonomy which will assist them to make wise and principled decisions on complex moral and evaluative issues.

It is a sad reflection, moreover, on the general state of our system of education – a system which is all too often focused on the acquisition of information and closed skills – that college students often find the open-ended and inconclusive character of rational education discussion and debate rather hard to engage with. In a recent seminar in which I attempted to question the sense and internal coherence of a student's account of the nature of curriculum activity X and how it should be taught, I encountered the defensive response that she "had been told" she could teach it in this way. My own reply to the effect that the proper approach to teaching should proceed via her own critical and considered reflection on the rational integrity and meaning of a subject rather than on the uncritical adoption of someone else's half-baked idea of how to teach it, was greeted merely with further obvious resentment. Likewise, in relation to a recent episode of (generally favorable) student monitoring of a course designed to explore the curricular rationale and educational justification of activity Y, I replied to the mild criticism – "the trouble is we weren't given the answer" – by saying that I would not have given it to them even if I had the answer myself; once again, this provoked obvious incomprehension and consternation.

What precisely such student teachers find difficult to grasp is that genuine professional maturity as an educationalist cannot be based on the casual acceptance of simple, final and conclusive answers to complex questions such as those about the significance and contribution of forms of knowledge and understanding to healthy individual growth and flourishing; that any teacher who has ceased to think further about such matters and is no longer able to see the entire enterprise or education as – in a variety of ways – inherently problematic, is no longer properly functioning or progressing as a mature professional. Thus the very greatest disservice is done to student teachers by those who are ready with trite solutions to complex educational problems and who reinforce a most common attitude among pre-service students that educational debate and discussion involving theoretical speculations comes to an end when they have finally sat their end-of-course examinations. (Sadly, of course, for many of them it does.)

As we have already indicated, the crucial reason why questions about education are essentially open-ended questions – questions which raise further questions rather than ones which invite straightforward and unequivocal answers or solutions – is that education is at heart a moral practice which is deeply implicated in values and conflicts of values, more than a technological enterprise directed towards the optimum or efficient achievement of predetermined or agreed ends. Again this is a much missed point which is nevertheless not hard to see. If my car comes to a dead stop because of a broken timing chain, it may be a lengthy, complex and expensive business to dismantle the car and replace it, but given that I need that car and want it repaired, there are no real problems about what I should do other than *how* to get it done. But, on the other hand, if I want to exercise discipline over an unruly class and have discovered that wiring the children's desk seats to the national grid and administering short sharp shocks to recalcitrants secures the necessary order, the discovery of this straightforward pragmatic solution to a practical educational problem hardly concludes matters but rather raises considerable further problems about what I am up to in educational terms at all. This rather outlandish and overdrawn illustration of the point does at least serve to bring into focus what is really at issue in the debates that have actually raged – and still from time to time resurface – about the point and justification of physical and other sorts of punishment in schools. Far too many teachers have assumed that because the strap or the cane has seemed to be a working practical solution to a range of discipline problems in many schools, the matter is actually settled in favor of its continued use. This is precisely a case of mistaking a moral or evaluative issue for a technical one and of seeing further educational discussion and debate as terminated rather than occasioned by the discovery of a particular instrumental means to a given educational end.

But, someone might say, isn't the means in this case – the just flogging of offenders – justified by the reasonable and rational end of the establishment of good order for learning in the classroom, just as the means – the dismantling of my car engine – is justified by the reasonable and rational goal of establishing the good running order of my car? The proper reply to this is again in the negative because the analogy is predicated, once more, on the mistaken idea that means are related to ends on the discipline issue in a technical rather than a moral way. Roughly, then, whereas the means are related to the ends of car maintenance *externally* or as cause to effect, the means to moral ends – such as the effective discipline of children – are related *internally* or constitutively; moral means contribute qualitatively to the very character – in this case of human discipline – of the goals which they produce. Some years ago I found myself on a school visit in the company of a teacher who was roundly chastising a student for some minor misdemeanor in terms which I would have considered hardly appropriate to a dog. After the child had been dismissed he turned to me and remarked that it was necessary to speak to the students in the school like that so that they might learn proper respect. But, of course, there are crucial questions to be asked about the quality and value of "respect" that is learned in such cases.

The point, then, is that in case of a moral practice like education our aims and goals are not logically separable or distinct from the procedures we adopt for their achievement. Presumably we do not just require *any* order of discipline in the classroom but a particular sort of order and discipline. We ought not (as good liberal democrats, at any rate) to want order and discipline which is based on fear, resentment and discourtesy, because presumably, and amongst other things, confidence, trust and courtesy are some of the qualities that we do want children to acquire – and it seems that these qualities as well as their opposites are often acquired by children through example. Discussions of physical and other punishment in education have thus all too often been vitiated by a failure to distinguish within the logic of practical discourse, the moral from the technical. The advocates of physical punishment will say that it works and their opponents will say that it doesn't and they rest their respective cases on empirical evidence one way or another. Such arguments and the evidence to which they apply clearly cannot conclude matters, however, since it is quite intelligible to maintain that even if beatings do serve in every case to deter or control (or whatever) offenders, the practice should nevertheless be avoided because it teaches children that it is appropriate or permissible in the last resort to enforce one's will or get one's own way by the exercise of violence. It is also intelligible to argue, of course, that even if corporal punishment does not deter or reform in all or even the worst cases of maleficence, it ought to be used in the interests of justice understood in terms of simple tit for tat reciprocity. This is to my mind a dubious argument, but it is at least the *right* sort of argument to engage in when discussing matters of educational procedure because it is addressed fairly and squarely to the moral and evaluative dimensions of the issue.

Conclusion:
Theoretical Studies and the Educated Professional

The principal moral of this essay, then, is that educationalists are widely mistaken about the contribution of theoretical and academic studies to the practice of education – for such studies are only in a small part concerned with the development of directly vocational skills, a technology of pedagogy and with the discovery of pragmatic solutions to problems of teaching, organization and management. They are in a much greater part concerned to raise in a disciplined and rigorous way questions about the larger goals and purposes of education in relation to wider considerations about human moral, social and political life and the meaning of human growth and flourishing. The contribution of so-called theoretical studies to professional educational practice is to locate the teachers chalk face work within a broader context of significance informed by a rational appreciation of what education ought to be aspiring to achieve with respect to the ethical complexities of individual development and human association. This is the reason, by the way, that the cultural, evaluative and conceptual questions raised by educational philosophers and historians are not merely peripheral or ornamental to educational studies, as has sometimes been supposed, but absolutely central to them. The main task of those who have usually been called educational theorists, then, is not primarily to develop craft skills but to promote the sort of professional consciousness which is able to discern in an educated way the true character of the moral and evaluative complexities to which the conduct of education inevitably gives rise. Moreover, it is not their concern to give simple, final and conclusive answers to such questions, but to bring their problematic nature to life for students.

Yet why should we trouble prospective teachers and other educational professionals with unanswered and probably (this side of eternity) unanswerable questions, when they have so much else on their plates with respect to teaching and administration? Again, this objection fails to grasp the point that education is not a technology or a craft but a form of moral conduct. The tradespeople can apply their technology or craft to the solution of routine problems of plumbing or car maintenance because their operations are relatively value-free, but the teacher can do hardly anything in the classroom which is value-free in the same sense. To employ behaviorist learning techniques is essentially to acquiesce in the view that manipulating others, regardless of their will in the matter, is a morally appropriate way to treat them; to employ physical punishment is essentially to legitimize the use of violence and force in certain circumstances; and so on. The difference between the teacher who has rote-learned (by, say, apprenticeship) certain strategies for survival and the one who has come to discern the larger professional questions through wider inquiry may also appear, in the short term, to the credit of the former, since he or she seems to get things done – giving short shrift to the miscreant to get on with the lesson, for example. In the long run, however, we may have reason to be more grateful to the reflective teacher who recognises that a given child's indiscipline is not just an irritating impediment to his or her professional task but a *part* of that professional task and who takes the longer, wearier and more patient way around to promote that true respect for discipline which must be one of the central goals of education.

In any event, there can be hardly any doubt that whether or not a given teacher does take the trouble to reflect on questions of value, he or she will teach according to *some* set of values – be they his or her own prejudices or the beliefs of those who are set in authority over him or her; the mere avoidance of serious questions of educational value by no means implies neutrality with respect to such questions. (The ostrich does not, as it were, sit on the fence.) Moreover, if teachers do not try (or are not provided with proper occasions and opportunities) to develop duly informed professional perspectives on the wider human, social and political implications and education practice through engaging with something like the traditional academic educational disciplines, they run a real risk of becoming mere instruments of others' wills – unreflective pawns in the political games of those set in power over them. Herein lies the real danger of mistaking the discourse of so-called educational theory for technical rather than moral discourse. The technical mentality is all too often the servile mentality; waiting to be told what to do by others is a handy excuse for abdicating ultimate responsibility both for our own personal and professional lives – and for the lives and development, if we are teachers, of those entrusted to our care.

The recent *Public Eye* debate on the preparation of teachers which set out to air and illuminate issues of professionalism in education only succeeded in being grossly misleading with respect to the vexed question of the balance of the theory and practice in such professional preparation. Both the two main solutions to the so-called problem of the relationship of theory to practice which emerged in the course of the program – that theory might be dispensed with altogether in favor of some sort of craft apprenticeship or that it might somehow be integrated with such apprenticeship – presupposed a fundamental assumption on the part of most, if not all, contributors, that discourse of a theoretical nature about education is essentially of a technical nature and can have no real relevance to educational practice if it lacks a direct practical application. At no point was any attempt made, of the kind I have made here, to distinguish conceptually between the different ways in which relationships between theoretical and practical educational discourse – moral and technical – might be construed. Even to suggest that the "problem" of educational theory might be solved by taking it out of the colleges and into the schools is to miss the point that the purpose of much of such theoretical discourse is not to assist pragmatically in the direct functioning of immediate practice, but to educate more widely about the rational and moral nature of such practice; from this point of view it does not much matter whether the initiation into such discourse is done in the schools or in the lecture theatre – as long as it *is* done. In fact the *real* issue – again hardly acknowledged in the *Public Eye* feature – is not that of the relevance or otherwise of theoretical educational discourse to immediate practical concerns, but of whether the professional preparation of teachers is properly to be construed as a matter of *education* or some rather more low grade *training* in craft skills. The argument of this essay rests on the view that in the absence of a wider perspective – which takes the professional preparation of teachers to entail an educated and disciplined understanding of the moral and evaluative roots and complexities of educational discourse – there cannot be much real hope for the proper future education of our children.

Notes

[1]"Teacher Training – Back to the Classroom" introduced by Peter Taylor and shown on BBC2's *Public Eye*, Friday 7th June, 1991. Among those who appeared in the program to air their views were Professors Alan Smithers, Anthony O'Hear, David Hargreaves and Richard Pring.

[2]Aristotle, *The Nicomachean Ethics* translated by Sir David Ross (Oxford: Oxford University Press, 1925). For the nature of the relationship between morality and practical inquiry see Book I, and for the distinction between practical and theoretical discourse see Book VI.

[3]See, for example, David Hume, *A Treatise of Human Nature*, E. C. Mossner (ed.), (Harmondsworth: Penguin, 1969), Part III, Section 1; A.J. Ayer, *Language, Truth and Logic* (London: Victor Gollancz, 1976), chapter 6.

2

The Relationship between Educational Theory and Practice: A New Look

Harold Entwistle

Why a new look at educational theory and practice? I have been troubled by the problem of the relationship between the theory and practice of education for almost forty years. As a student doing my teacher training in an English college of education (or training college as it was then called) I remember writing an article for the college newspaper denouncing the theoretical component of my course as being utterly irrelevant to conditions in the school as I found them on teaching practice. As a qualified teacher I would experience similar frustration when inspectors, advisors and other people who were no longer practitioners would come to my classroom and offer me unworkable advice. When I eventually went to do graduate work in education, I recall wanting to do my thesis on the relationship between theory and practice. My supervisor warned me off it – I think I now know why. Then I became a teacher trainer (or teacher educator) and found myself in the peculiar position of being accused by my own students of offering advice that was "alright in theory but no good in practice." I suspect that most of what I have to say is the result of my efforts to come to grips with the fact that I had now become just another starry-eyed theorist.

So, for me, this is a new look at an old problem.[1] But I make this point about my own changing experience and changing perspective on the problem in order to suggest that whatever the solution is, it is far from simple. Indeed, I think that in terms of the way that the problem is usually posed, there probably is no solution. On the one hand, I believe practitioners have a perfect right to take theorists to task for what often is quite unrealistic advice about the practice of teaching. On the other hand, when you see it as a theorist from the other side of the fence, even when you have had practical experience of the problems of teaching yourself, the theory-practice problem has a new dimension, and the discrepancy invites a different kind of explanation. And I think this fact that when experienced and successful practitioners become theorists, even they become vulnerable to the charge of being unrealistic about practice, is salutary. It is sometimes suggested that the gap between theory and practice would be bridged if only we had the sense to fill colleges of education with practicing

19

teachers. It may be a good thing, other things being equal, that teachers of educational theory should actually have taught in schools. But on the basis of my own experience, and the experience of colleagues and friends with whom I have discussed the problem, ex-practitioners can look as unrealistically theoretical to their students as anyone else.[2]

To come to my major points. I want to argue that there are two main reasons for the gap between theory and practice. On the one hand, from the side of the practitioner, I believe it often follows from a misunderstanding of what theory is. This is to say that practicing teachers are apt to demand of educational theory what it is not in the nature of theory to deliver. I am suggesting that, in part, the theory-practice gap is the "fault" of practitioners. I will come back to this point later.

On the other hand, I am also convinced that a gap between theory and practice frequently exists because theory is often quite inadequate. Practitioners who criticize theory are sometimes kind enough to say "That's alright in theory but it won't work in practice," implying that there is really nothing wrong with the theory – that as theorists we have done our job well enough – but that practice is simply just a different world. I want to suggest, to the contrary, that the theory is often not alright; it is misleading and inadequate theory which practitioners have a perfect right to dismiss.

Let me give my reasons for saying this.

First I believe that educational theory is often unacceptably utopian. An example of this would be in the conception of the child which dominates liberal educational theory. We assume the existence of a perfect learner – essentially innocent, insatiably curious and intrinsically motivated. We rarely entertain the possible truth contained in Shakespeare's characterization of the second age of man as a period when the child inevitably goes "unwillingly to school." What follows from this Shakespearean assumption is that teachers will often be faced with an uncooperative learner, and will need to have recourse to extrinsic motivational devices. Teachers, even good teachers, experience this problem daily in the classroom and I believe that they are right to distrust a sentimental model of the child which fails to take account of the reality of childhood.

This utopian assumption of original student perfection derives from one or the other of two sources. On the one hand, it is often a metaphysical fiction without any empirical basis; that is, it is a model of what we would like children to be or, perhaps, a moral conclusion about what they ought to be. On the other hand, when it does have a basis in the real world, the perfectionist model is derived from child study which is conducted in privileged circumstances – indeed, in conditions which are near utopian from the standpoint of the typical classroom – in private schools, or with small groups of learners, or even, as with a good deal of Piagetian research, with individual children. In this connection, it is also worth noting that old-fashioned learning theory based on the study of animal behavior was derived from the study of individual rats or pigeons.

This brings me to a second reason why educational theory is often inadequate. It is almost universally true that the institutional unit in which pedagogy has to be conducted is the class, a social group; occasionally, as in the graduate seminar, a group of half a dozen, but often in large lecture groups of several hundreds or, if you are lucky, with a group of around fifty. In elementary school, you may be lucky enough to have as few as twenty children, more likely to have around thirty, but even there classes in excess of forty are not unknown. Yet, despite this institutionalization of learning in the class grouping, liberal educational theory is overwhelmingly individualistic in orientation. Theory urges us to remember that each child brings a unique personal history to school, which peculiarly affects his or her motivation, which defines his or her idiosyncratic needs, interests and preferences. We are even asked to entertain the view that each learner has a unique learning style and pace, such that the only adequate pedagogy would really be based on individualized instruction.[3] And logically, as is sometimes asserted, what this really adds up to is an individualized and personalized curriculum for every child. But the reality is that we do not, we cannot, teach children as individuals in schools, except occasionally and marginally. It is not even clear that it would be desirable to completely individualize instruction even if we could, for it is not only the existence of economic constraints which leads us to group students together in classes. The wealthy in society who can well enough afford to buy individual tuition for their children, choose to send them to schools, on the assumption that education is a social process requiring a social pedagogy. Yet teaching a group a common subject matter poses its own special problems to which few educational theorists address themselves, except for notable exceptions like John Dewey whose embryonic project method was essentially a social pedagogy. What I am arguing here is that the educational individualism of liberal educational theory inevitably opens up a gap with practice because the context of institutional practice is inevitably a social one, the class.

Thirdly, context of another kind is often ignored in a way which also serves to drive a wedge between theory and practice. It is a legitimate criticism by practitioners that educational theory often ignores the bureaucratic context of classrooms and schools. Here I am not using the word pejoratively; I take it that in the modern world bureaucracies are necessary to providing a public service like schooling or health care and so on. But just as it individualizes the learner, educational theory often also implicitly individualizes the classroom and the school, in the sense that it assumes both to be autonomous associations in which the teacher is able to function independently, without bureaucratic constraints upon one's professional judgment and competence. But in classrooms, teaching and learning have to be accomplished subject to legal, economic and other constraints, as well as with an eye on the competing (and often contradictory) claims of interest groups of various kinds, and the expectations of parents which are not always in accord with academic realities or the norms of a liberal education. The result is that teachers often cannot avoid performing in a manner which their better judgment tells them is not exactly pedagogically sound. An obvious example of this would be the pressure to resort to rote teaching and learning in order to achieve success in external examinations.

One of the things which is implicit in the three points I have made about the responsibility which theorists have for the existence of the theory-practice gap, is that practitioners know their work frequently involves compromise, but they believe that theorists refuse to recognize the inevitability that successful human action is full of compromise. We almost always use the word in a pejorative sense: compromise is associated with betrayal of principles, with untrustworthiness or want of integrity; it almost carries the implication of moral turpitude. In fact, compromise is part of the stuff of which successful and harmonious relationships are made. Husbands compromise with wives, parents with children, doctors with patients, law enforcement officers with offenders, politicians with other politicians and their constituents, even perhaps, clergy-men with parishioners. And most teachers would hardly survive in the class-room without compromising with bureaucrats, with colleagues, with students, with parents, between the competing claims of individuals and of the individual student and the group, and between pedagogical and bureaucratic imperatives. Compromise is a fact of classroom life. The fact that compromise is necessary in applying theory to practice ought to be treated as an aspect of educational theory itself. That is, maybe the successful marriage of theory with practice is consummated, in part, by learning the art of compromise.

This brings me to my alternative explanation of the gap between theory and practice: the practitioner's misconception about the nature of theory. If part of the fault lies in inadequate theory, I believe it also follows from the unrealistic expectations which practitioners often have of theory, and their failure to recognize that even the best of theories has to be applied with discrimination to the practical situation. It is in the nature of what a theory is that there can never be an exact, neat, one-to-one fit between theory and practice. Theories are generalizations about practice, whilst practical situations are particular, peculiar, and widely varied. A theory draws its relevance and cogency to every conceivable situation which it seeks to explain only by being an exact description of none of them. There never can be a one-to-one correspondence between theory and practice, if by this we mean theory that predicts accurately every contingency in a practical situation. As Donald Schön puts it in *The Reflective Practitioner*: "An overarching theory does not give a rule that can be applied to predict or control a particular event, but it supplies language from which to construct particular descriptions and themes from which to develop particular interpretations."[4]

This means that educational theories have to be applied by practitioners in an active, thoughtful, creative sense, not passively as though applying pre-digested instructions or advice. The application of theory to practice, instead of being an exercise in carrying out good advice, is rather a matter of learning to ask a variety of questions about practical situations with the guidance of relevant axioms or generalizations. The philosopher, Kant, put it this way: "A set of rules presented in a certain generality and with disregard of particular circumstances is called a theory . . . the practitioner must exercise his judgment to decide whether a case falls under a general rule."[5] That is, the job of a theory is to evoke judgment rather than rote obedience. The application of theory to practice means bringing critical intelligence to bear on practical tasks rather than merely implementing good advice. We have to learn not only rules, theories and principles, but also how to interpret and apply them appropriately. That is, some initiative is required from the practitioner in discovering the pertinence of theory to his or her own peculiar practical situation. But if practitioners do not do this, or do not know how to do it, this may also be a fault that we have to lay at the door of teachers of theory. Too often, educational theories are taught not as analytical tools, but as ideologies or dogmas which brook no argument. I suggest that just as teacher educators should confront teachers with the fact that compromise is a fact of life in classrooms, they should also accept the fact that part of the teaching of educational theory must consist of teaching exactly what a theory is, what it can and cannot be expected to do for practice, and the various ways in which theories have to be applied.

What I have just said about the practitioner's responsibility for actively applying theories, exercising judgment or critical intelligence, can be summed up in Schön's notion of the reflective practitioner in his book of that name.[6]

With reference to schooling, the notion of the reflective practitioner is the idea of a professional in a practical situation, confronting the problems and the opportunities it poses, asking intelligent, well informed questions about the situation, acting in a manner suggested by the answers to these questions, evaluating the results, reflecting again on the implications of these, and so on. The result of this interpenetration of theory and practice is to develop what is sometimes referred to as *praxis*. Out of this continuous reflection on practice, one develops one's own practice-relevant theory, one's own characterizations of what one is trying to do in the classroom, why one succeeds or sometimes fails, and what has to be done to accommodate the failure, either by improving one's practice or, perhaps, by redefining the situation. This raises the question of what it is that causes the practitioner to reflect critically, on his or her practice and, especially, what it is, if anything, that academic educational theory contributes to intelligent reflection on practice.

One answer to this last question about the relevance of educational theory for reflective practice is that it contributes nothing, or very little. This is a point of view which might be expected from the cynical or disillusioned practitioner who feels that he or she has been left to work it all out alone. But the view that educational theory does little to inform educational practice, that it has no impact upon the teacher's reflection on practice, is one that one hears, occasionally from educational theorists themselves.

I have in mind here the view that when it gets down to the bare boards of the classroom floor, the only relevant guides to practice are common sense and worldly wise axioms or aphorisms like 'Praise is better than blame,' 'Don't expect them to sit and listen for too long,' 'When they get restive give them something to do,' 'Test them at fairly regular intervals,' 'Give them feedback as soon as possible,' 'Spare the rod spoil the child,' 'Open the windows,' 'Never turn your back on them,' 'Start tough and then you can afford to relax' and so on. I remember spending some time several years ago with an American educationalist on sabbatical leave at the university's Department of Education where I worked. He spent most days sitting at the back of a classroom at the local primary school. A good deal of his time at recess, lunch break and at the end of the school day was spent discussing with the class teacher how she had seen the lesson or the day. Inevitably, he argued, her account of how things had gone consisted of observations on individual children, wondering if a particular child had been unwell, or feeling the strain of family breakdown, or was watching too much television for too long; or how much the class had been distracted by interruptions from outside, perhaps a change in the weather; or how some of them did Math last year with Miss Smith who really drills them in the fundamentals, and some of them with Mr. Jones who is a super teacher when it comes to the Language Arts but who is bored to distraction by Math and does not do much more than go through the motions.

These kinds of reflective comment on the successes and failures of the teacher's day may be more or less subtle and insightful but, according to my American friend, they seem to depend hardly at all on a knowledge of academic educational theory. Evidently, what the teacher reflecting on his or her day does not do is to wonder what Piaget would have said about these things; or whether Plato or R.S. Peters might throw some light on his or her problems; or whether, like so many other things, they do it better in Sweden; or whether, according to Bernstein, it is all a matter of direct and elaborated language codes; or whether it all really comes down to the correspondence principle and, like Bowles and Gintis claim, the point is that we will never get schooling right until we get rid of capitalism. I do not know which discipline from educational theory I have omitted from that list, but if there is one, the reflective practitioner does not draw on that either in order to explain his or her day and to plan for a better tomorrow.

Now it may be that in reflecting on practice, the teacher rarely makes explicit or conscious reference to academic educational theory. But the fact is that not all homespun reflection on the practical situation in the classroom is equally relevant, equally cogent, or equally sensitive to moral standards and interpersonal relationships. And mere reflection from out of a teacher's own untutored cognitive resources may fail to come to grips with the complexity of a practical situation or to explore the wide range of alternative explanations of classroom phenomena, or alternative solutions to educational problems. Nor is all folk wisdom equally sensitive to the moral issues arising in the classroom. After all, Jim Keegstra was presumably a reflective practitioner, according to his own lights.[7] And he may be unique; but, on my own experience of staffroom reflection, rednecks, racists, sexists and chauvinists are not unknown, nor are practitioners who expect nothing of children and whose conception of what it means to be an educated person would make a Dickensian schoolmaster look like a liberal do-gooder.

I want to suggest that intelligent, well-informed, critical reflection on practice can be the outcome of familiarity with academic educational theory, however tacitly this theory may enter into thinking about practice. In fact, I would make much the same claim for the practical outcomes of a knowledge of academic educational theory that Peters does for the influence of the academic disciplines of the school upon the education of the person. As Peters suggests, the point of a liberal education is not that one arrives at a destination but that one travels with a different point of view. One of the things which I take this to mean is that the educated person is not merely satisfied to acquire a repertoire of relevant skills, and knowledge which satisfies one's needs, ministers to one's interests and assists one in solving problems in the here and now. In Peters' sense, a liberal education transforms one's perception of what the problems are, what opportunities are offered by life, what new interests might enrich one's daily experiences. Being educated, one is aware of new needs and interests, and the relevance of knowledge has to be tested with reference to the possibility of a changing and developing, not a given, static way of life. It seems to me that theory of education – psychology, comparative studies, philosophy, history and sociology of education – does not provide knowledge and skills which are applicable to a given practical situation: it provides new perspectives such that one confronts educational problems and opportunities from a different point of view. Educational theory can provide a liberal education, such that the teacher's reflection on practice becomes intelligent, morally sensitive, capable of making finer conceptual distinctions, and more subtle analyses of educational problems, and well-informed about the various relevant contexts of educational practice. The justification for educational theory is the same as the justification for liberal education itself. The teacher reflecting upon teaching equipped with more subtle educational theory, is much like the liberally educated citizen reflecting intelligently upon public affairs.

To look for an educational theory which eliminates the gap between theory and practice is to chase a will o' the wisp. Indeed, it is arguable that good educational theory which sensitizes the teacher's capacity for reflection will inevitably widen the gap. In order to elaborate this point I want to give a brief account of what Schön says about the reflective teacher.[8]

First, it is interesting that Schön assumes that the teacher will carry on his or her reflective activity in terms of the individual model of education to which I referred earlier. The teacher's reflection is never about problems of teaching the class or the group, but always in terms of the individual learner, his or her needs, interests, strengths and weaknesses. What will inevitably emerge from this reflection is a curriculum and teaching strategies defined entirely by reference to individual need.

Secondly, the teacher's reflection (which amongst other things will give rise to a completely new conception of the nature of curriculum) will inevitably bring him or her into conflict with bureaucratic norms and requirements. Things like timetabling, required syllabuses, objective testing, uniform student records, and many of the disciplinary and control mechanisms of the school will all seem to stand in the way of ministering to the individual student's educational needs.

Thirdly, the teacher will conclude that reflective practice is hardly compatible with the kind of student-teacher ratio which is common in the public schools.

Notwithstanding these pessimistic conclusions that the reflective practitioner will inevitably discover a widening gap between one's increasingly sensitive theory and the given, objective conditions of classroom life, the teacher must choose between two options which offer themselves at this point. He or she may choose to abandon the role of reflective practitioner, concluding that reflective practice is just another example of those things which look good in theory but, because of the bureaucratic and economic contexts of teaching, do not work in practice. One can reject the notion of the reflective practitioner as one of those utopian fantasies which do not fit the real world: something which looks good in theory but which will not work in practice.

Or we can settle for half a loaf and see reflective practice as one of those things about which we have to learn to compromise. Indeed, one of the things which reflective practice would entail is thinking about the compromises which are necessary and possible and justifiable in the classroom. This amounts to repeating what I concluded earlier – that part of teacher education in both its theoretical and practical aspects is learning the art of compromise.

My conclusion is that the gap between theory and practice is probably inevitable, and that attempts to bridge the gap may even make it wider. Perhaps this conclusion is all that has come out of my new look at the problem. But far from this conclusion being regrettable or a source of disillusionment with theory, it seems to me to constitute rather an opportunity. I have argued that one of the things which educational theory has to do is to give an account of why the discrepancy between theory and practice is there, and how one might learn to live with it, not as a blemish or something which disfigures the educational enterprise, but as something which nurtures both theory and practice. The continuous process of interrogating our practice with theory and refining our theory in the crucible of practice is the condition of our growth as both theorists and practitioners.[9]

Notes

[1]See my "Practical and Theoretical Learning," *British Journal of Educational Studies,* 17, 22, 1969: 117-28; *Child-Centred Education* (London: Methuen, 1970) Ch. 11; "The Relationship between Theory and Practice," in J.W. Tibble (ed.), *An Introduction* to the Study of Education (London: Routledge and Kegan Paul, 1971), 95-113.

[2]In speculating on the reasons for this, I recall a comment made by my own education lecturer in response to the critical article in the college newspaper to which I earlier referred. This was along the lines of: "What you are pointing out is not a gap between theory and practice but a gap between my theory and practice and your practice." Implicitly, it was not only the theory he taught which differed from my practice; his practice (which he believed to be quite consistent with his theory, since he had hammered out his theory from reflection on his practice) also differed from mine: he had been an experienced practitioner, I was merely a tentative, vulnerable, inexperienced novice. Reflecting on his wise observation over the years, I have concluded that one reason why experienced practitioners appear to give unrealistic advice to novices, is that their theory is a reflective account of their long, experienced and successful practice. When experienced practitioners become theorists they probably give an honest account of their own reflections on practice, practice refined by familiarity with educational theory and tested through trial and error over the years. It is this description, explanation and analysis of their own work as experienced teachers which students are apt to reject as unrealistic when applied to their own practice. In fact, it is unrealistic only in their own circumstances, inexperienced and differently contexed in time and place. But, in turn, the reflective practitioner will fashion his or her own theory from

his or her own experienced practice; as such, it may well seem unrealistic to an inexperienced colleague.

[3]For the argument that personal learning styles probably differ much less than our individually-oriented educational theory suggests, see Brian Simon, "Why No Pedagogy in England," in his *Does Education Matter?* (London: Lawrence & Wishart, 1985), 94-5.

[4]Donald A. Schön, *The Reflective Practicioner* (New York: Basic Books, 1983).

[5]See Kant's essay "On the Saying 'That may be all right in theory but is no good in practice,'" in G. Rubel, *Kant* (Oxford: Clarendon Press, 1963).

[6]Although Schön makes passing reference to teaching, he does not analyze the notion of the reflective practitioner in relation to teaching at anything like the length which he does for some other professions. So what I want to say about the teacher as a reflective practitioner does not necessarily closely correspond with the brief observations which he makes on the subject.

[7]Keegstra was a history teacher in Alberta found guilty of fomenting racial hatred through teaching, amongst other things, that the Holocaust never happened. See further, chapter eleven in this collection.

[8]See Schon, *The Reflective Practitioner.*

[9]This is a slightly modified version of a paper presented at Mount St. Vincent University, Halifax, Nova Scotia, March 27th, 1987.

3

Fit for Teaching

Max van Manen

As most teachers will tell you, the everyday life of teaching and bringing up children requires a certain fitness.[1] We may call it "pedagogical fitness." Pedagogical fitness does not only mean the physical stamina and mental reserve that teachers need sometimes to get through hectic days. More particularly, pedagogical fitness refers to the educators' readiness of knowing just how to deal with young people and what to say or do when facing children. In their daily conduct with children, teachers, just like parents, are expected to act immediately, thoughtfully, and in a pedagogically appropriate manner with children. They constantly have to be able to distinguish between what is appropriate and what is not (or less) appropriate for children. The question is, how does one prepare to be pedagogically fit? One may be a specialist or scholar in some educational discipline, but we all know that scholarly training is no guarantee of pedagogical fitness. There are experts in educational psychology, authors of books about child development who are quite awkward with children. There are specialists in reading theory who are strangely ineffective in the classroom or in helping children with reading problems. Professional educators, such as teachers too may have learned all the techniques of teaching and yet be pedagogically unfit.

The point is that the actual process of teaching and parenting children is so difficult because we are forever dealing with children in situations of contingency. To be pedagogically fit is to be able to deal with situations or predicaments that are uncertain, unpredictable, sensitive, unique, personal. We may distinguish between two kinds of contingencies that are especially characteristic of modern educational environments: the contingent nature of modern childhood and the contingent nature of the pedagogical moment. Children's lives and the pedagogical situations in which we find ourselves with children is, comparatively speaking, more contingent than in previous decades.

To Be Fit for Teaching is to Be Able to Handle Change

Most of us recognize that, compared to their parents and grandparents, young people today live in a severely fractured world. Families are less stable

29

and divorce has become commonplace. Many children now live in single parent families, in families where the parents are both working and frequently absent, in blended families, or in families in different states of disintegration. Neighborhoods tend to be in flux more and less community-minded, schools are less personal and more competitive, and peer groups demand conflicting loyalties. While the family in North America in the last hundred years has always been weaker than the family structures of, for example, Western Europe or Asian countries, at present there is even less permanence, preserve, and provision associated with the child's experience of family life. Even children living in more stable and traditional settings experience the break-up and disintegration of family and community life vicariously through the experiences of their friends, peers, and through the portrayals of modern family life on television.

Children are living in a hyper-reality, a reality experienced in an extreme intensity. Television, radio, newspapers, video, computers, and other communication media rush images of adulthood into the living space of young children – vivid images beset with violence, mature sexuality, drugs, pornography, global crises, warnings, and conflict. Many parents and educators feel uneasy, for example, about the frenzied, intensely-eroticized, delirious icons of music-videos on the developing minds and bodies of young viewers. They believe that children prematurely "see" too much and "experience" too much in our consumer-oriented, information-based, and advertising driven culture. Aspects of adult life that previously remained secret from children until they had mastered more sophisticated reading levels and until they had obtained access to more mature literature now have become dominant themes of the lifeworlds of children. This has led educators such as Neil Postman to suggest that the boundaries between childhood and adulthood are eroding and that childhood itself may be disappearing.[2]

Of course, ever since the beginning of the industrial revolution young people have lived, like their elders, in a world of change. But change itself seems now to be structured and experienced differently. Unfortunately there are few if any sound scientific studies on the attitudes and values of the generations of the eighties and nineties. But from journalistic and impressionistic accounts an unsettling picture emerges.[3] Where the previous generation of the babyboomers could still idealize change, work for change, and see change as progress, as a positive promise, there is the impression that the younger generations tend to feel out of control, paralyzed, displaced, and strangely passified by the enormity of global crises, technologically-induced disasters, and human suffering brought on by overwhelming natural forces, and political-economic powers. Of course there are those who are more actively optimistic but even these young people are living in rough times of crises and doom about the viability of the human race and the questionable survival of the earth it populates.

In this hyper-reality of changed change, plurality, complexity, fragmenta-tion, conflict, and of contradictory beliefs, values, faiths, living conditions, aspirations, and life-styles, the lives of young children today turn into an experience of contingency. Contingent life is indeterminate, unpredictable, uncertain, subject to chance, impacted by events and unforeseen circumstances. The Canadian youngster born into the modern social world often must respond personally to early pressures and premature expectations; these are pressures to grow up faster than seems possible or advisable.

More than in times when you knew, by virtue of being born in a certain social niche, what you were expected to become, what you could count on, what you could do, present day children must live with contingency. What does this mean? It means that they must make active choices in their lives for fear of not becoming anything or anyone. The modern child must actively realize that he or she is born into a condition of possibilities. He or she *is* this body of possibilities. To become a person, to grow up and to become educated, is to transform one's contingency into commitment and responsibility. One must choose a life.

To be a contingent person can be seen negatively and positively. Negatively it means that many present-day children are growing up in an uncertain world, a world in which their own parents often seem unwilling or unprepared to make deep or lasting commitments to each other, to their children, and to their community; a world with too many conflicting views, values and aims. This predicament can mean that children drift into (self)destructive lifestyles. The positive meaning of contingency is that each young person must make choices and commitments in life, that they must come to terms with their possibilities. The child is, in a real sense, the agent of his or her own destiny – at both the individual and the collective social level.

For educators childhood contingency means that they must know how to stand in a relation to children and young people; that is, a relation of respon-siveness to contingency rather than an outdated relation governed by yesterday's social norms, traditional beliefs, worn values, old rules and fixed impositions. The pedagogy of living with children must be an ongoing project of renewal in a world that is constantly changing around us, and that is continually being changed by us. And the vocation of pedagogy, of being educationally involved with children, is to empower children to face and give active shape to life's contingencies.[4]

While living at the turn of a new millennium poses unforeseen and unforeseeable challenges to parents, teachers and other professional educators, this does not mean that we should dismiss or abandon every valued cultural construction that appears presently under siege. For example, just because, in a new age of commercialized social mores and more fluid interpersonal relations, the family has difficulty maintaining its former cohesiveness does not mean that the more close-knit familial structure is or was wrong and that we should give up on the idea that children need, if possible, a mother and a father, as well as other extended communal and familial relations, all playing active roles in the child's journey to adulthood. A new pedagogy must face the challenge of change but also be prepared to defend, or reconstruct in new forms, inherited norms and value frameworks that growing up seems to require.

Life into the twenty-first century will be carried by new realities and new visions. Some of these realities will be exciting and positive experiments in human living. But we must recognize also that increasingly spheres of human intimacy come under duress from seductive consumer, economic, bureaucratic, corporate, and political technologies and ideologies. The notion of education, conceived as a living process of personal engagement between an adult and a young person, may well disappear in an increasingly managerial, corporate and technicized environment. We need to ask how educating and bringing up children can remain a rich human and cultural activity?[5]

If childhood is the experience of contingency, what then is our professional educational responsibility? Even in these times of eroding parental and family influence, parents carry the primary responsibility for the child's well-being and the child's growth. Yet, today educating and bringing up children seems to have become so much more difficult than it was for parents of previous generations. It seems that just about every development in modern society conspires to disable parents in carrying out their parental responsibilities. Does anybody have a right to diminish the rights and abilities of parents to be responsible for their children's welfare and growth?

The implication of childhood contingency for teachers is that they must avoid taking a narrow view of their vocation, that they are constantly being reminded to be mindful of their status *in loco parentis*. Professional educators always need to realize that, if possible, they must try to assist the parents in the fulfillment of their primary pedagogical responsibility. And they also need to see that what is relevant for the pedagogical relation between parents and children may be informative for the pedagogical relation between teachers and students. As schools and other childcare institutions have taken on more and more responsibilities which previously were dealt with within the domain of the family, professional educators need to become more reflective about what the notion of *in loco parentis* entails.

There exist deep connections between the nature of teaching and the nature of parenting, yet these connections are rarely explored. In the North American educational literature the parent is remarkably absent. It is as if in the minds of educational theorists the education of children is cut off from the whole process of growing up. Even the English language reflects this separation between education (which is largely an institutional process of teaching-learning in schools) and childrearing (which is usually considered the process of parenting in and around the home). In contrast, in my native Dutch language the common term *opvoeding* and the more academic term *pedagogy* are both concepts that equally describe the inseparable efforts of school education as of parenting.

The school, as cultural-political institution, also needs to come to terms with its *in loco parentis* responsibilities. The *in loco parentis* responsibility of the adult resides in the needs of children for a protective and safe sphere in which they can supportively develop a self-responsible maturity. The school as institution also possesses *in loco parentis* responsibility which is legally drawn. The school's boundaries were commonly considered as a transitional space between the secure intimacy of the family and the more risky public openness of life in the outside world.[6] On the one hand, it is questionable whether schools still offer such transitional space to young people. And on the other hand, we can no longer take for granted that this secure family intimacy exists for the child; and to the extent that it exists it cannot be assumed that this family "intimacy" grows out of the right kind of love for the child. And so, the *in loco parentis* responsibility of the school does not only consist in the academic preparation of the child for the larger world, it also consists, for example, in the responsibility of protecting the child from the risks of neglect and of mental, physical and sexual abuse of the "intimate" sphere of the family.

Some have argued that the increasing selfishness and greed of adult society requires that professional educators develop caring school environments, for the sake of the children and ultimately for the sake of society.[7] Similarly, we see schools struggle with the task to prepare children, not only for the challenges and dangers of the larger world, but also for the demands of the relations of intimacy and moral responsibility that a successful family life presupposes but that families find increasingly difficult to pass on to their children. In other words, the institution of the school needs to orient itself increasingly to the norm of *parere* that parents themselves seem to have "forgotten" as it were. While the parents are excused, the schools are often accused of improperly preparing children for the responsibilities of parenthood. And thus we see the development of Family Life, Life Skills, and Career Development courses becoming mandatory accessories to the curriculum.

To Be Fit for Teaching is to Be Able to Act Thinkingly

The second kind of contingency I would like to discuss is situational contingency. Life in classrooms is incredibly busy as every teacher knows.

Some researchers have suggested that teaching consists in an ongoing process of reflective decision making; teachers make a dozen or more decisions every five or ten minutes.

Indeed it is the reality of these pedagogical moments that much existing literature has been trying to grasp and clarify under the labels of "reflective teaching," "teacher thinking," "the teacher as reflective practitioner," "teacher as problem solver," "teacher as decision maker."[8] But we need to question this image of teaching. The interactional space of teaching is much too crowded to allow for reflective decision making. The usual case is that teachers (and parents too) do not have time to sit back and deliberatively decide what to do in concrete situations. And even when there is time to reflect critically on what several alternatives are available and what best approach one should take, in the pedagogical moment itself one must act (even though that action may consist in holding back).

Teaching is not a constant making of decisions and choices. If it were, then my wife, a junior high school English teacher, would be totally inadequate to the task. She has a hard time making up her mind about anything that requires choice. When she goes shopping for a new coat, a dress, or shoes, she more often than not will eventually return home empty-handed. She simply could not decide. Yet, at home as mother and in the classroom as teacher, she acts confidently in situations that constantly require her to do something.

Let me sketch a series of situations that are mere instances of pedagogical life as we might recognize it in our own everyday experience:

• Sue complains that Jack broke her pencil.

• Sandra has completed her work and she hands it with visible pride to her teacher.

• While reading out loud during the class reading lesson, Billy mispronounces several words.

• Mark is learning about environmental awareness in grade five at school, but at night he can't sleep, and he confides about all the problems and dangers of the world to his father.

• Chen reads her poem to the class in a way that is so powerful that it deeply stirs the teacher.

• Emmy fails to understand when the teacher is trying to get something new across to the students.

• In class Jan challenges the teacher's competence in a caustic tone that borders on effrontery.

• Rob refuses to participate in the science lesson since he feels repulsed at killing and dissecting a living creature.

• All the children are applying themselves to their work in class, but David persistently does not seem to be able to concentrate.

• After ten years of music lessons Erin announces that she no longer wants to take or practise the violin.

• Mary is in tears, she comes to the homeroom teacher and confides that she feels that nobody in class likes her.

• Mother sees her seven year old son John taking money from her purse.

• Twelve year-old Sook asks his father if he can go to a movie, that many of his friends have seen, even though the rating is "mature."

We could go on indefinitely drawing pedagogical incidents from everyday life. The *in loco parentis* situation of teaching is structured as a never-ending series of contingent moments. But what is the pedagogical nature of each incidence? Let us first notice that each situation is pedagogically charged because something is expected of the adult, the parent, or the teacher. In each situation an action is required even if that action may be non-action. That active encounter is the pedagogical moment. In other words, a pedagogical situation is the site of everyday pedagogical practice. And the pedagogical moment is located at the centre of that praxis.

So in our daily living with children, we often must act on the spur of the moment. No matter how well we have prepared our language arts unit or our science lesson, if we are approaching our teaching in an open and responsive manner (rather than in an overly structured, aloof, and authoritarian manner) then the actual experiences of teaching-learning in the classroom are inherently unpredictable and contingent. How the learning in classrooms proceeds and is experienced by the students is given by the mood of the moment, the atmosphere of the class, the chemistry of personalities, the temper of interchanges, the tone of reflections, the speech climate, the pathic quality of the subject matter, the ambience of trust, and concretely by the kinds of things that are said and done. In other words, the true pedagogical fitness of the teacher is constantly tested in the ongoing rush of school life and classroom events.

Imagine for a moment that you have just begun block three with a grade ten class on Monday morning. You would like to engage the class in some discussion on a theme that is relevant to the poetry material that they are to learn. You have settled down the initial chatter and activity that accompanies changing classes. Now you are making some comments in order to focus on the nature of the poem. However, you are uneasily aware that most students are not attuned to the material. Do they seem uninterested? You must somehow create a tone for the lesson.

If you were an inexperienced or naive teacher, then you might have thought that you could just walk in and teach poetry. As long as you knew it all, and as long as you used the right instructional technique to express it all, then the task would have been done. The measure of how well it would have been done would have depended on how carefully you would have thought through what you would need to say and do, and on the extent that the students caught on to what you were trying to do. But now you know that it is not enough to just walk in and expect the students to be ready for poetry.

As you walk into the classroom, you implicitly gain a sense of where these kids are coming from. You know that some of them have been working part-time during the weekend, others have had good or bad experiences on Saturday and Sunday, some have been up late nights and they are not necessarily looking forward to another week of school. Yet all these kids have managed to get on the bus or somehow arrive at school, and they have all managed to sit in their seats at eight forty-five this morning. Right now they may care little about poetry. So as you walked into the classroom you are sensitive to the atmosphere and dynamics of the group.

To find the right tone is a subtle but important feature of a lesson for any teacher (young or old) who tries to engage a class in a genuine manner. You ask a question and call on this or that student. "But," said one teacher, "as you stand there in front of the class you get the uneasy feeling sometimes of artificiality. You are standing there and the students are looking at you. The result is that you cannot let yourself go. You feel like a poor stage actor, who is saying the lines but cannot forget the audience. While you are trying to get the lesson underway you sort of wonder to yourself: Are they really attentive? Do these kids want to be here? Does what I am saying or doing mean anything?"

One of the students is offering a response to your question. You nod encouragingly. But the student's words do not seem to flow from a live source. Meanwhile some other students are obviously preoccupied with a private matter. Gesturing admonishingly for their attention, you try to open up a real discussion but the conversational atmosphere in the class is flat, lifeless. You are still uncomfortably aware of yourself standing there in front of those kids. Are you objectifying yourself? Are you being self-conscious? Or is it just that you feel the contrivedness of the situation? You feel aware of your face, your posture, where your hands are. You feel the eyes of the students on you. Until at least half a dozen students have become animated by the topic of the lesson, the right tone is not strong enough to warm the atmosphere. You struggle on. You add some drama to your voice.

Then, after a few minutes, usually, it happens. You have roused some students, made contact. And almost like wildfire, the spark travels from one student to the next. It is as if the whole class is stirring, waking up. As teacher, you are now beginning to lose your self-consciousness. You start to feel more naturally in touch with both the topic of the lesson and the spirit of the students' interest. It is not until this special tone and relation have been established that the pedagogical life takes shape.

Interest is probably one of the relational meanings that is somehow caught up in the atmosphere or tone that the teacher is able to create at the onset of a class. You cannot just say "Show interest!" to students who seem to lack motivation or willingness to participate in the lessons. Interest is not a state of mind that can be requisitioned or produced upon request. "Interest" is rather a word that describes a person's way of being in the world. To be interested in something is to maintain a caring relation to something, to be intensely present to something or somebody. By being intensely present to something I experience the subject of my interest in a focussed way. My focus allows me to concentrate, to be attentive, to gain an awareness of the possibilities, the indefinability, the openness of the subject. In contrast, the subject matter of the school often has only didactic significance; it interests neither the teacher nor the students. The difference between didactic questions and animated questions is that didactic questions are closed, lack possibilities, do not matter to the teacher who already knows the answers and to the students who know that the answers are predetermined.

Unfortunately, disinterestedness, boredom, indifference are often prevailing conditions among many school children and youth, especially those who have left the primary grades. Yet, interest is one of the most fundamental aspects of the relation between person and knowledge, reflection and life. Without interest, genuine interest, everything that happens in school is in danger of turning into empty pretence, illusion, sham, and feigned importance. The teacher's command to "show interest!" may really be a request to the student to fake it, to cooperate in a game of illusion. When the teacher asks for a "show" of interest, students may feel that they are required to simulate, to feign a certain behavior – to put on a show, a front that covers their real feelings. The problem is that neither the educator nor the students are willing to admit to the grand illusion.

Attentiveness that is coerced, and not prompted by the impulse of interest, is only fleeting attention. Effort extorted, and not energized by the thrust of interest, is only half-hearted effort. Striving that is the effect of someone's pushing, and not lured by the fascination stimulated by interest, is unauthentic striving. Discipline that is imposed by threats, and not taken on in the desire to follow systematically the path of interest, is mutiny-raising discipline. Concentration compelled from without, and not an internal response to the inner pulse of interest, is likely to be an absent-minded concentration. Achievement purchased at the cost of tedium, not the outcome of engaged interest, is likely to be shallow, short-lived achievement.

What happens when we no longer understand or fail to presume that there exists a primordial connection between learning and interest? In schools and classrooms where learning now must be pushed in the absence of interest, one replaces the power of desire and interest with the extrinsic motivation of hidden seduction or coercive compulsion. This means that we come to expect and demand from the child industriousness, diligence, good work habits, a willingness to apply oneself obediently to lesson assignments and activities that students tend to experience as dreary, dry, tedious, and tryingly boring. Of course there seems much to recommend in the positive moral values of diligence and hard work. When children no longer relate to a subject matter and a teacher with interest, there may be little alternative for teachers than to stress forced effort, industriousness, work-habits, and artificially generated goodwill. Yet it seems wrong to assume that we must routinely substitute the instrumental value of work and achievement evaluation for the natural value of desire that accompanies real interest in learning. My point with this digression about the value of interest is to suggest that teachers who are preoccupied with the importance of finding the right tone at the beginning of each lesson have an implicit understanding that to speak of the tone of a classroom is a complex, intriguing phenomenon.

Not all teachers, of course, are so preoccupied with finding the right tone at the beginning of each lesson. Teachers who tend to be more aloof, distant, impersonal, overly routinized may not be sensitive to the tone or atmosphere of a class. But I am less intrigued with the question of the incidence than with understanding the meaning of this practical sensitivity. Teachers tend to speak of certain classes, the 8Bs as compared to the 8Cs, as having a certain character or quality that makes it easier or more difficult to establish or maintain a tone conducive to teaching and learning.

I have used the example of tone first to illustrate the contingent nature of classroom life. Interest is just one aspect of the tone of a lesson. When we speak of a good tone we do not only refer to something that makes teaching more effective. It also is a normative or moral notion. A good tone is good because it describes a desirable human experience, a positive climate for teaching and learning. As teacher educators we sense intuitively that the tone of teaching is not something that can easily be conceptualized or managed with trainable behavioral techniques.

Here, I believe, lies the practical profit of human science (such as phenomenology and critical hermeneutics) for education. It lies in the significance of pedagogical tact. I would define pedagogical tact as the active readiness, sensitivity, and flexibility that educators demonstrate when they are dealing with young people in everyday educational situations. The practical importance of the study of "the formation of tact" lies in its direct relevance to teacher education by offering a more experience based interpretation of pedagogical reflection on the one hand, and of the nature of the practical pedagogical moment of teaching on the other hand.

In general, tact implies sensitivity, a mindful, aesthetic perception. *Webster's Collegiate Dictionary* defines tact as "a keen sense of what to do or say in order to maintain good relations with others or avoid offense." But the essence of tact does not just inhere in the simple desire or ability to get on well with others, to establish good social relations with them. Tact has interpersonal and normative or moral properties that appear especially suited to our pedagogical lives with children. Of course, what I am getting at is that tact is the unique ability to deal with the contingent nature of children's lives and that tact is eminently suited to deal with the situational contingencies of pedagogical moments. Indeed, we speak of tact as instantly knowing what to do, an improvisational skill and grace in dealing with others. Someone who shows tact seems to have the fitness to act quickly, surely, confidently, and appropriately in complex or delicate circumstances.

To Become Fit for Teaching is to Be "Outfitted" with Tact

Before relating the idea of tact to pedagogical fitness, I first need to say something about tact in general.[9] Philosophically and linguistically the social concept of tact appears closely related to the concept of tone. Tact, like tone, derives from music. It is thought that around 1769 Voltaire imported the notion of tact from the musical domain into the social sphere.[10] In music, *Takt* is German for the "beat," the unit of musical time; baton is *Taktstock*, the stick that beats time. The musical notion of beat refers to the pulse underlying a musical work – this rhythmic beat is the heart of music. Music can be without melody, as in percussion ensembles or in African drum traditions, but melody cannot exist without rhythm. Initially the conductor's baton or *Taktstock* was shaped like a cane or walking-stick. Well, Jean-Baptiste Lully, the French composer and conductor, died of blood poisoning in 1687 when he accidentally stabbed himself in the foot with his stick while banging the beat during a musical performance at the court of the French King Louis XIV.

When later conductors stopped banging the beat with a stick, in favor of swinging a small baton, this may have had something to do with the changing function of *Takt* in music. Periodically shifts are occurring in the application of rhythm to music. Such a shift took place between the Baroque and Rococo period on the one hand, and the Classical and Romantic turn that followed them on the other hand. With the strong body rhythms of Baroque musicians – such as Bach, Vivaldi and Handel – the beat was quite vigorous or even mechanical, not unlike the role of the rhythm section in Jazz. With the Classical composers – such as Haydn, Mozart, and the early Beethoven – and with the Romantic masters – such as Chopin, Schuman, Liszt, and Brahms – the beat that organizes the music became more subtle, retreating somewhat and less everpresent to the ear. This shift of *Takt* from the regular, mechanical, vigorous mode to more subtle and restrained forms may have contributed to Voltaire's application of the notion of tact to the social sphere, where it acquired the meaning of subtle sensitivity and of restraint or holding back in human relations and interactions.

The Germans, Dutch, and English adopted this usage of tact from the French. For example, the English poet Christina Rossetti described tact as a gift and a grace:

Tact is a gift; it is likewise a grace.
As a gift it may or may not have fallen to our share;
as a grace we are bound either to possess or to acquire it.

Only in German educational theory has there been an articulation and discussion of tact in a pedagogical sense.[11] Moreover, the German *Taktgefühl* expresses a more subtle sentient quality than the English "tactfulness." The term *Gefühl* means feeling, sensitivity: the sentient quality of having a "feel" for something. Thus, to be tactful with another person one must be able to "hear," "feel," "respect" the essence or uniqueness of this person. While the English "tactful" means the quality or being full of tact, the German word *Taktgefühl* has the additional connotation of having a feeling for tactfulness. There is a hint here that the quality of tact is somewhat like talent. We often think of talent as a fortuitous gift – either you are or you are not blessed with a "feel" or talent for the violin, the canvas, or the stage. But, of course, talent must be recognized, developed, nurtured, and disciplined. Similarly, pedagogical tact, although a gift in some sense, needs to be prepared and practised as a special "feel" for acting tactfully.

While thinking about processes of teaching it is helpful to avoid confusing tact with tactic. A *tactic* is a method for accomplishing an end. There is a calculating, planning meaning to tactic while tact is essentially situational. In fact, tactic and tact are etymologically unrelated. Tactic is derived from early Greek, where it referred to military science, the strategic talents of a general in moving his troops in battle. Someone who approaches teaching by way of tactics thinks of maneuvers, stratagems, masterminding a program of directives and objectives. To be good at tactics means that one is good at getting an organization to execute some plan of action. Thus, tactics also connote superintendency, supervision. The tactics of teaching are strategies, schema, ways and means that one draws up like a master plan, scenario, outline, blueprint, timetable, schedule, or design for the preparatory processes of teaching. However, in the interactional sphere of teaching it is often the unsteady, unstable, variable moment that requires tactful action of a sort that is essentially unplannable. And yet, this unstable moment is not an accident of teaching, but rather it belongs to teaching essentially.

It may be helpful as well to distinguish tact from associated behaviors such as "diplomacy," "address," "poise," "savoir faire," or "finesse." These are terms often provided as synonyms of tact. For example, a diplomat is "diplomatic" for the purpose of manipulating perceptions for political ends. This does not necessarily mean that a diplomatic person would lie or be deceitful, but while diplomacy may not involve telling untruths it may involve withholding truths that should actually be told. A diplomat is ultimately motivated by self-interest or by the interest of the party the diplomat is representing. Tact, in contrast, is always in the service of the person toward whom the tact is directed. Thus, tact avoids the political motivation and conciliation of "diplomacy."[12]

To this point I have given you a brief sketch of the origin and meaning of tact. And I have hinted that tact may be the basic component of pedagogical fitness. Now, what does the fitness of tact consist of? I would distinguish four abilities with which the teacher needs to be outfitted:

First, a tactful educator has the sensitive ability to interpret inner thoughts, understanding, feelings, and desires from indirect clues such as gestures, demeanor, expression, and body language. Tact involves the ability to immediately see through motives or cause and effect relations. A tactful teacher is able as it were to read the inner life of the young person.

Second, tact consists in the ability to interpret the psychological and social significance of the features of this inner life. Thus, tact knows how to interpret, for example, the deeper significance of shyness, frustration, interest, difficulty, tenderness, humor, discipline in concrete situations with particular children or groups of children.

Third, an educator with tact appears to have a fine sense of standards, limits, and balance that makes it possible to know almost automatically how far to enter into a situation and what distance to keep in individual circumstances. It is an essential feature of pedagogical intentionality that teachers and parents always expect more and more from children. Yet, most parents and teachers realize that they should not have expectations that, when challenged, children cannot manage to live up to. So, paradoxically, tact consists in the ability of knowing how much to expect in expecting too much. Similarly, in their relations with children educators often must get close to children such as when challenging them, sparking an interest, or setting a tone in a class; again, paradoxically, they must know how far to go in going too far.

Finally, tact seems characterized by moral intuitiveness: A tactful teacher seems to have the ability of instantly sensing what is the right or good thing to do on the basis of perceptive pedagogical understanding of children's nature and circumstances. This moral intuition is predicated on the practical requirement of pedagogy in everyday life where the teacher must constantly be able to distinguish between what is good and what is not good for a child or a group of children.

So to act tactfully as an educator[13] may mean in a particular situation to be able to see what goes on with children, to understand the child's experience, to sense the pedagogical significance of this situation, to know how to act and what to do, and to actually do something right. To act tactfully may imply all this, and yet, tactful action is instantaneous. The perceptiveness needed, the understanding or insight required, the feeling for the right action are not necessarily separate stages in a sequential process. Somehow, insight and feeling are instantly realized in a mode of acting that is tensed with a certain thoughtfulness or thinking attentiveness. We may say that tact is a kind of practical normative intelligence that is governed by insight while relying on feeling.

The etymology of the Latin *tactus* also contains terms such as "touch," "thoughtfulness," "effect."[14] Tact is associated with physical touch, tactile or material things that you can touch or feel with your body. And yet, tact carries also the ambiguous sense of a nonphysical influence or effect of one human being on another. Tact possesses the mindful quality of reflection, perceptiveness, thoughtfulness. In tactful pedagogical action the adult orients concretely and thoughtfully to the child. Often tact involves a holding back, a passing over something, which is nevertheless experienced as influence by the person to whom the tactful action is directed. So the epistemological relation between thoughtfulness and tact is such that thoughtfulness incarnates itself in tactful action. Tact is the embodiment, the body work of thoughtfulness.

With this I would like to suggest that tact is not simply some kind of mediator between theory and practice. Rather tact possesses its own epistemological structure that is based on a certain kind of reflection, or better on an active intentionality of thoughtfulness. Thus, the essence of tact is that it cannot be separated between *theory* and *practice,* so that the issue of the relation between knowledge and action would be turned into an epistemological and educational problem of application in the preparation of teachers with instructional skills or competencies. In this sense, tact as pedagogical fitness overcomes the theory-practice split and retains a wonderful quality of ambiguity.

Of course, as teachers our actions are always governed by certain in-tentionalities – for example, we are busy at restoring order, or we are involved explaining a difficult concept, or we are trying to create a tone at the beginning of a lesson. And yet, as I argued earlier, the reflective component in our immediate interacting with others is usually limited.[15] When a child "misbe-haves" in class, the teacher usually does not have time to reflect on the situation in order to decide what is the best thing to do. A teacher who was to pause and deliberate at some length about alternatives and about what action to take with respect to a rude comment of a difficult child may already be interpreted as being hesitant, wishy-washy, or spineless. As a teacher you simply have to do something with it, even if your acting consists of ignoring or pretending that you did not notice the rude remark.

Similarly, when during a lesson a child asks a question which shows misunderstanding then the teacher usually does not have the luxury to consult a teaching text in order to deal with this question in the way that is just right for this child (a teaching text would not likely be able to provide advice like this anyway). The same is true for parents and for other adults who have pedagogical responsibilities. When the child falls and hurts himself or herself, or when a child protests the parent's reminder that it is bedtime, then there is *decision* no opportunity to sit back in order to figure out what to do in this situation. In *on* situations where tact is required there is no chance to reflect in a deliberative *feet* or planning manner. Tactful acting is always contingent, immediate, situational, improvisational. And tact as a form of human interacting means that we are in a thinkingly active manner in a situation: emotionally, responsively, thought-fully.

From my discussion it may seem that pedagogical tact is an elusive and slippery notion. What does tactful acting look like when we see it in the classroom? What does pedagogical tact do? How does pedagogical tact do whatever it does? Indeed there is no technology to tact. But we may compose some narrative answers to these questions that may help place tact on a surer and imitable footing. Here I can only outline such narrative answers.[16]

First, what does pedagogical tact look like? How or where can we see pedagogical tact at work? Naturally these are difficult questions. It may not always be easy to tell genuine tactful actions from artificial, pretense, feigned and false forms of behavior that do not seem motivated by an authentic interest in children's welfare. Children often can tell the difference quite accurately between teachers who are "real" and caring and those who are "fake" and not truly interested in the children's welfare.

Pedagogical tact manifests itself primarily as a mindful orientation in our being and acting with children. This is much less a manifestation of certain observable behaviors than a way of actively standing in relationships. Nevertheless, there are ways of describing how tact manifests itself as a showing in our pedagogical being and acting. Tact shows itself as holding back, as openness to the child's experience, as attunement to subjectivity, as subtle influence, as situational confidence, and as improvisational gift.

Second, what does pedagogical tact do? Pedagogical tact does what is right or good for the child. But how do we know what is the right or good thing to do? If one cannot go up to the abstract level of moral or critical theory to answer this question in a general manner then one needs to go down to the concrete level of everyday experience to observe what tact does in specific situations or particular circumstances. We know from our experience of living with children what kinds of actions lie in the sphere of pedagogical tact. Pedagogical tact preserves a child's space, protects what is vulnerable, prevents hurt, makes whole what is broken, strengthens what is good, enhances what is unique, and sponsors personal growth.

Third, pedagogical tact does what it does by exercising a certain perceptive sensitivity as well as by practising an active, expressive, and caring concern for the child. On the one hand, pedagogical tact relies on our ability to "see" and "hear" (sense) what the needs are of children and also what the possibilities are of these children or of any particular child. This means that pedagogical tact can only do its work when the eyes and ears are used for searching in a caring, open and receptive manner what is the potential of a child, what this or that child can become, in other words what is the "essence" or "excellence" of this child. This then requires a perceiving and listening that is oriented to the otherness of the child and that uses a multiplicity of perspectives, considerations, and vantage points to try to gain a vision and pedagogical understanding of a child. It is important to contrast the openness of this sensitive capacity of tact to the inclination to see and hear only what one wants to see and hear about a child. The latter orientation leads to inflexible judging, stereotyping, classifying – to seeing only the external behaviors of children and not their inner lives and their personal intents and projects.

On the other hand, the sensitive eye of tact mirrors back its caring glance. Tact does what it does by using the eyes, speech, silence, gestures, etc. as resources to mediate its caring work. Again, by using the eye as an example, we compare the analytical and detached glance which coolly observes and judges from above as it were with the sympathic glance which establishes contact and searches for pedagogical understanding in a dialogical relation with children. The eye that is only observant of the behavior of children objectifies whereas the tactful eye subjectifies. The tactful eye makes contact, makes personal relationship possible. We know the difference in these two types of glances when we think about occasions when in our interaction with another person we gained the feeling that the other person was not really conversing with us but was studying us, as it were. In the latter case the other person is not looking at me but looking at my body, at my hands, at my face, at my legs – the other is "looking me over" and thus "overlooking me" who *is* my body. The objective glance cannot mediate my tactful action, and similarly the objective ear cannot ask the mouth to mediate the thoughtful response of its hearing in tactful speech. If I cannot hear the undertones of the inner life in the child's speaking then I cannot produce tactful speech myself. Just as tact can be mediated through speech, so it can be mediated through silence, through the eyes, through gesture, through atmosphere, and through example.

I would like to say briefly something about the exercising of pedagogical thoughtfulness and tact. We learn pedagogical thoughtfulness and tact through the practice of teaching, but not only through the practice of teaching itself. We come to embody tact by means of past experiences coupled with thoughtful reflection on past experiences. And we reflectively acquire sensitivities and insights in various ways – such as through literature, film, stories by children, stories about children, and childhood memories.

In my book *Researching Lived Experience: Human Science for an Action Sensitive Pedagogy,*[17] I have shown how thoughtful pedagogical tact can be sponsored through a research program of reflective writing. Thoughtful reflection is an experience that gives (or perceives) significance to the experience on which it reflects. And so the significances that we acquire in thoughtful reflection on past experience leave a living memory that is no less a body knowledge than are the physical skills and habits we learn and acquire in a less reflective manner.[18] However, this thought engaged body knowledge of tactful acting attaches an attentive or thinking quality to our ordinary awareness of our everyday actions and experiences.

The preparation of professional educators tends to rely heavily on bookish approaches in institutions of higher learning. But vicarious experiences provided by texts tend "to get to our heads" and do not speak to our bodies. Especially books that mostly offer mere information, abstract concepts, and theoretic explanations and classifications may often be poor substitutes for the lived experiences provided by life itself. Pedagogy requires more embodied rather than mainly intellectualistic forms of knowledge. The processes of systematic and thoughtful reflection on experiences must carefully mediate between universal and particularistic understandings, between what is far and what is near, between the ideal and the real, the essential and the incidental in teaching and living with children. A more experience based human science approach is what can make pedagogical theory a theory of the unique, suited to the particular case. Thus, educational scholars need to produce textual bodies of knowledge that can turn into body knowledge by edifying a reflective thoughtfulness and a sense of improvisational tact. "Pedagogical fitness" is a cognitive and emotional and moral and sympathic and physical preparedness. Tactful acting is very much an affair of the whole embodied person: heart, mind and embodied being.

Finally, to talk or write about pedagogical thoughtfulness and tact courts the dangerous presumption that one claims to know how to behave with moral superiority. By definition pedagogy is always concerned with the ability to distinguish between what is good and what is not good for children. Many educational thinkers are uncomfortable with this assumption, they try to pursue educational problems and questions in a value neutral or relativistic manner. It is wrong, however, to confuse pedagogical discourse with moral preaching. Preaching is an act of moral exhortation on the basis of some unquestioned dogma. But pedagogy does not aim to deliver sermons. On the one hand, educators need to show that in order to stand up for the welfare of children, one must be prepared to stand out and be criticized. On the other hand, pedagogy is a self-reflective activity that always must be willing to question critically what it stands for.

It is not possible here to explore more deeply the question what pedagogical fitness requires of teachers. As a closing thought I would propose that the following qualities are probably essential to pedagogy: a sense of vocation, a love of and caring for children, a deep sense of responsibility, moral intuitiveness, self-critical openness, thoughtful maturity, sensitivity toward the child's subjectivity, an interpretive intelligence, a pedagogical understanding of the child's experiences and needs, improvisational resoluteness in dealing with young people, a passion for knowing and learning the mysteries of the world, the moral fibre to stand up for something, a certain understanding of the world, active hope in the face of prevailing crises, and, not the least, humor and vitality.

Moreover, teachers who are pedagogically outfitted should know what they teach, and should take responsibility for the world and traditions which they share; and they need to know how gradually to hand over this world to children so that they can make it their own world. In other words, to be a fit educator is a multifaceted and complex requirement – a tall order for any human being. And yet underlying this suggestion is a crucial question: Does a person who lacks any of these qualities or abilities possess the pedagogical fitness required for educating young people?

Notes

[1]This text was first presented as *Childhood Contingency and Pedagogical Fitness*, the 1990 Robert Jackson Memorial Lecture, Halifax, Nova Scotia.

[2]Neil Postman, *The Disappearance of Childhood* (New York: Vintage Books, 1994).

[3]For example, see the cover story "Twentysomething" of *Time* magazine, July 16, 1990. On the cover it writes, "Laid back, late blooming or just lost? Overshadowed by the baby boomers, America's next generation has a hard act to follow."

[4]I am not taking an existentialist philosophical position here. There are obvious limits to human freedom in our social and political culture. However, it would appear to me that more so than in the recent past young people live in contexts punctuated by conflicting worldviews, competing norms for living, contrasting interpretive frameworks, antinomous values, discordant local and larger philosophies and other influences that tend to have decentering, fragmenting, rupturing, and itinerant effects. Thus, young people stand in more uncertain, ambivalent, reflective and critical relations to their own traditions at the familial, social, ethnic, and cultural levels.

[5]In spite of the changing nature of the life experiences of young people, in spite of the fact that the primary experiences of growth in the family and in the community pose challenges to young people that we as adults have hardly begun to acknowledge and understand, schools go about their business as if nòthing has changed. The interest of curriculum workers largely remains centered on never-ending curriculum innovation and achievement evaluation, and educational researchers have for several years now been preoccupied with overcoming the damages of deskilling teachers as a result of forcing on them narrow technological models of instruction, and from approaching the administration of schools by means of top-down business models governed by performance objectives, and growth output measures. Similarly, the present trend among university based researchers seems to focus on investigating – empirically, conceptually, ethnographically, or narratively – what it is that teachers do when they teach. Something is lacking in these research and development perspectives. What is lacking is the acknowledgement that at the heart of education lies the pedagogical relation between the child and the adult that must sustain all processes of teaching and learning.

[6]See, for example, Hannah Arendt, *Between Past and Future* (Harmondsworth: Penguin Books, 1978), 173-196.

[7]See, for example, Jerome Bruner, "Schooling Children in a Nasty Climate," *Psychology Today*, 16, 1, 1982: 57-63.

[8]See, for example, Donald A. Schön, *The Reflective Practitioner: How Professionals Think in Action* (New York: Basic Books, 1983); and Donald A. Schön, *Educating the Reflective Practitioner* (San Francisco: Jossey-Bass, 1987). For a discussion of this literature see also James Calderhead, "Reflective Teaching and Teacher Education," *Teaching and Teacher Education*, 5, 1, 1989: 43-51.

[9]For a more detailed treatment of the idea of pedagogical tact see also Max van Manen, *The Tact of Teaching: The Meaning of Pedagogical Thoughtfulness* (London, Ont.: Althouse Press, 1991).

[10]*The Oxford Dictionary of English Etymology* (Oxford: Oxford University Press, 1979), 899.

[11]The person who introduced the notion of tact or tactfulness into educational discourse is the German educator Johann Friedrich Herbart (see Jacob Muth, *Pädagogischer Takt* (Essen: Verlagsgesellschaft, 1982)). In 1802, during his first lecture on education, Herbart told his audience that: "The real question whether someone is a good or a bad educator is simply this: how has this person developed a sense of tact?" Herbart posited that tact occupies a special place in practical educational acting. The main points of his speech pertaining to tact were that (a) "tact inserts itself between theory and praxis;" (b) tact manifests itself in everyday life in the process of "making instant judgments and quick decision;" (c) tact forms a way of acting which is "first of all dependent on *Gefühl* [feeling or sensitivity] and only more remotely on convictions" derived from theory, etc; (d) tact is sensitive to "the uniqueness of the situation;" and (e) tact is "the immediate ruler of praxis."

In spite of this early fluid conceptualization, Herbart's later writings, and especially that of his followers, assumed a more instrumental relation between educational knowledge and practical acting. Even in the above paraphrases from Herbart's speech there is evident a somewhat mechanistic conceptualization of the mediating role of tact between theory and practice. Rather than see tact as a device for converting theory into practice we may see tact as a concept that can help us to overcome the problematic separation of theory from practice. And rather than understand tact as a process of making instant "decisions" we may reconceive tact as an oriented mindfulness that permits us to act thoughtfully in our living with children and young people.

Herbart was not the first who used the notion of tact in order to refer to a special form of human interaction (see Van Manen *The Tact of Teaching*). Hans-Georg Gadamer refers to the work of a contemporary of Herbart, the physiologist Wilhelm Helmholtz, to bring out two aspects of tact: tact as a form of human interaction and tact as a human science facility which Helmholtz had elaborated (H.-G. Gadamer, *Truth and Method* (New York: Seabury Press, 1975, 17)). In the first sense tact is commonly understood as "a particular sensitivity and sensitiveness to situations, and how to behave in them," but for which "we cannot find any knowledge from general principles."

In the second sense, tact is moreover a kind of scholarship or *Bildung* – such as a sense of the aesthetic or the historical – that the human scientist uses to do his or her interpretive work. The scholar demonstrates the measure of his or her tact by the insights that he or she is able to produce with respect to the meaning of a text or a social phenomenon. In making this distinction Helmholtz had suggested that tact is not simply a feeling or unconscious inclination, but rather that tact is a certain "mode of knowing and a mode of being" which encompasses the important human science notion of *Bildung* (forming or education). There is an implication here that tact is not a simple affect or learnable habit, but that it can be fostered through the more profound process of humanistic growth, development and education. In passing, we should note that the notion of "tact as scholarship" is exercised in a different modality than tact as a form of human interaction. Tact as scholarship is usually practised while reading or writing texts. This is a highly reflective human activity. In contrast, tact as human interaction is usually practised in the spur of the moment where one is required to act in an instant or immediate fashion.

[12]Similarly, tact does not stress the idea of dexterity and preoccupation with success in trying circumstances as does "address," tact lacks the calculating cleverness of "being savvy," tact is not self-conscious of its own social bearing and self-possession as is "poise," tact does not emphasize worldly experience and a sure awareness of expediency as does "savoir faire," and tact is more concerned with what is appropriate or good than with refinement of approach like "finesse."

[13]The image of tact as a special contact or relation between people may be most relevant for education or pedagogy. However, there is an outstanding distinction to be made between general social tact in the interaction between adults on the one hand, and the more specific form of pedagogical tact in the interaction between adults and children on the other. And this distinction harkens back to the nature and structure of pedagogical relations. General tact in the lives of adults is symmetrical while pedagogical tact is asymmetrical. Among adults we expect tactful behavior to be reciprocal, in keeping with the nature and circumstances of the situation. And similarly we teach children to practice general social tact towards other children and towards adults. To be tactful in a general sense means that we respect the dignity and subjectivity of the other person and that we try to be open and sensitive to the intellectual and emotional life of other people whether they be young or old.

But as adults we do not have a right to expect from children pedagogical tact. Pedagogical tact is an expression of the responsibility we are charged with in protecting, educating and helping children grow. Children are not charged with the pedagogical responsibility of protecting and helping their parents or teachers grow and develop. Children are not there primarily for us. We are there primarily for them. This does not mean of course that children do not teach us and do not show us new ways and possibilities of experiencing and being in the world.

[14]Tactful means "having the quality of tact, full of touch," and it also means "to be able to have an effect." To be tactful is to be thoughtful, sensitive, perceptive, discreet, prudent, judicious, sagacious, perspicacious, gracious, considerate, cautious, careful. Would any of these notions speak badly of an educator? In contrast, someone who is *tactless* is considered to be hasty, rash, indiscreet, imprudent, unwise, inept, insensitive, mindless, ineffective and awkward. In general to be tactless means to be disrespectful, ill-considered, blundering, clumsy, thoughtless, inconsiderate, stupid.

[15]Thoughtfulness and tact are not identical to skills and habits and yet they are not unlike this constellation of body skills and habits which have become our second nature and which determine to an extent who we are, who we have become, what we are able to understand, perceive and do. Indeed the word "skill" is related to the term *skilja* which refers to the ability to discriminate, to distinguish, to separate between things that make a difference. Etymologically *skill* means "to have understanding," "to make a difference." And so the notion of body skill is an unexpected ally in our exploration of the nature of thoughtful pedagogical perceptiveness.

When I teach a group of children and I notice that some children experience a certain shyness, exuberance, frustration, animation, boredom, wonderment, curiosity, puzzlement, confusion, or sense of insight, then what I "see" is less given by a "technical instructional skill" that I may have learned in a teacher-effectiveness workshop than by a more embodied "orientational pedagogical skill" that I have acquired in a more experiential-reflective manner. However, this skill of perceptiveness (of sensing, for example, what a situation means for a child) is something I cannot practise in the same way that I may be able to practise a skill such as lesson planning, classroom management, or even story-telling.

Pedagogical perceptiveness relies in part on a kind of tacit or intuitive knowledge that the teacher may learn from personal experience, or through apprenticeship from a more experienced teacher. Most human activities, that depend on knowledge and skills, involve tacit or intuitive complexes that constitute a kind of body knowledge or body skill. For example, medical doctors confronted with certain symptoms may intuitively sense what is wrong with a patient on the basis of such tacit understandings – even though the symptoms may not have been that easy to pinpoint or articulate. Just so, a teacher who senses that a child has certain difficulties in dealing with a problem may not be able to identify exactly on what clues the perceptive understanding was based. The tacit or intuitive nature of our body skill and body knowledge is learned in subtle ways by attuning ourselves to the concrete particulars of situations.

[16]For a more extensive treatment see van Manen, *The Tact of Teaching.*

[17]M. van Manen, *Researching Lived Experience* (London, Ont.: Althouse Press, 1990).

[18]Tact is a kind of body knowledge that resembles body skills and habits. We all know how the human body acquires or learns certain bodily skills and habits which become like second nature to our practical living. When I am thirsty I take a cup from the usual place, I turn the tap and "thoughtlessly" close or tighten the tap. In a way I leave this routine behavior almost blindly to my skilled and habituated body. This does not mean that I am not aware of what I am doing, but that I can do bodily habituated things without having to do them attentively and consciously. Only when the tap won't open or when the water smells unusually bad would we probably break our routinized behavior.

For many things in life we rely on the doxic knowledge of our bodies to perform certain tasks. Where is the light-switch? How do you tie a knot? Which way does the tap turn to open? We may have to simulate the gesture to discover what our skilled body already "knows." A variety of intellectual tasks too rely on this kind of body skill: how do you spell "lieutenant"? Sometimes we may have to write the word on paper to discover what our fingers already know. Our body skills also permit us to perform tasks and actions that require flexibility and spontaneity, as when we drive a car or a bike across town. Once at our point of destination we may remember little of all the stops we made – our skilled body guided us through the hectic traffic.

Part Two

Critical Teaching

Recognition of the importance of critical thinking in education is sometimes thought to be a recent insight. The enormous interest in critical thinking in the contemporary literature on philosophy of education creates the impression that modern educators have identified an aim which somehow eluded their predecessors. This is quite mistaken. Some of the earliest recorded reflections on learning and knowledge show unmistakably that the ideal of critical thinking was clearly recognized as central. Confucius, for example, observed that learning without thought is labor lost, and added that thought without learning is perilous. Socrates suggested that life itself was wasted if it were lived in an unreflective, unexamined manner. These early philosophers had no doubt that, in addition to acquiring knowledge and information, it was vitally important for human beings to adopt an inquiring, questioning attitude with respect to those ideas.

The germ of the ideal had been identified but it proved, and continues to prove, difficult to keep alive in the context of schooling. Critical thinking must be exemplified in an approach to teaching which itself merits the label critical if there is to be any real hope of fostering the spirit of critical thought in students. Critical teaching, however, exists precariously even when teachers acknowledge the importance of critical thinking. The pressure to communicate information, for example, tends to lead away from what Dewey called the most worthwhile knowledge, namely knowing why something deserves to be thought of as knowledge at all. This kind of knowledge, however, demands the critical ability to assess the evidence and the reasons which separate knowledge from dogma, opinion and guesswork. A healthy balance between gaining familiarity with what is now regarded as knowledge and learning to judge and assess the various beliefs and opinions one encounters is extremely hard to achieve, and harder to maintain, as the current debate between proponents of cultural literacy and critical thinking illustrates.

Success also requires that teachers manage to retain a clear and viable conception of critical thinking itself. Here, however, there is always the possibility that critical thinking will be reduced to something which is only a pale imitation of the real thing. For example, critical thinking may come to be identified with the acquisition of various skills, or distinctions, which are themselves not thought about critically. They are taken for granted, and no longer viewed as problematic. Once, of course, these may have represented lively, innovative ideas, but over time they have settled into that inert form which Whitehead rightly derided. Interesting suggestions and possibilities have a way of turning into inflexible rules and procedures about which critical thinking is not encouraged or even thought to be needed. Inner attitudes, such as open-mindedness and impartiality, tend to be neglected in the search for instructible skills.

In the readings in this section we find illuminating discussions of the relationship between critical thinking and critical teaching. John P. Portelli presents a conception of critical teaching inspired by the philosophy for children movement and its central assumption of the class as a community of inquiry, and he illustrates the many challenges which such an approach must deal with: the threat of nihilism and cynicism; resistance from conservative forces; the retreat to teacher neutrality and the drift towards relativism; the potential divorce of reason and emotion; and the need for personal courage in the face of hostile responses. The discussion reveals complexities involved in critical teaching which are not readily apparent in the customary fanfare.

Related issues and concerns are taken up in the succeeding chapters in this section. Sharon Bailin is concerned to emphasize that the traditional dichotomy between critical and creative thinking is one which deserves careful reconsideration. Rethinking the connections between creative and critical thinking, and recognizing that critical thought has an imaginative and constructive dimension, have implications for the way in which we conceptualize critical teaching as our view of knowledge itself begins to shift. Ann Margaret Sharp enlarges on the idea of a classroom as a community of inquiry and develops the notion of dialog as crucial to critical teaching, where the teacher fosters, sustains and contributes to the common quest for understanding. Barbara Thayer-Bacon proposes a revised model of critical thinking, identified as constructive thinking, which is free of what she sees as the sexist aspects of the dominant conception of critical thinking, a conception which tends to omit consideration of feelings, caring, cooperation, and the inner voice. Harvey Siegel offers a conception of critical thinking which has rationality and reasons assessment at its heart, and he explores the implications of this conception for critical science education where teachers strive to engage students in the active consideration and evaluation of scientific theories.

The discussion as a whole suggests the need for a close look at the ideal of critical thinking, since our interpretation of this ideal is certain to influence what we do in the name of critical teaching.

Further Readings

Mary Jane Aschner, "Teaching the Anatomy of Criticism," *School Review,* 64, 7, 1956: 317-22.

Stephen D. Brookfield, *Developing Critical Thinkers.* San Fransisco: Jossey-Bass, 1988.

Nicholas C. Burbules, *Dialogue in Teaching.* New York: Teachers College Press, 1993.

Neil Cooper, "The Intellectual Virtues," *Philosophy,* 69, 1994: 459-69.

Susan Haack, "Knowledge and Propaganda: Reflections of an Old Feminist," *Partisan Review,* 60, 4, 1993: 359-72.

William Hare, "Content and Criticism: The Aims of Schooling," *Journal of Philosophy of Education,* 29, 1, 1995: 47-60.

Matthew Lipman, *Thinking in Education.* Cambridge: Cambridge University Press, 1991.

Deanne Kuhn, *The Skills of Argument.* Cambridge: Cambridge University Press, 1991.

John Passmore, *The Philosophy of Teaching.* London: Duckworth, 1980.

Israel Scheffler, *Reason and Teaching.* Indianapolis: Bobbs Merrill, 1973.

4

The Challenge of Teaching for Critical Thinking

John P. Portelli

In the dialogue *Charmides,* Socrates says to Critias, who is eager to know what Socrates' view is: "You come to me as though I professed to know about the questions which I ask . . . whereas the fact is that I am inquiring with you into the truth of that which is advanced from time to time, just because I do not know; and when I have inquired, I will say whether I agree with you or not. Please then to allow me time to reflect."[1] Unlike the Sophists, Socrates was unwilling to rush to conclusions. Following Socrates' tradition, Robin Barrow reminds us that the aim of this kind of reflection is "to rid our minds of hazy generalizations, ambiguous slogans, inarticulate ideas and half-truths . . . to enable us to resist and see through the catch-phrase, the advertisement playing on our emotions, package-deal thinking or ideology, unnecessarily or meaningless coined jargon . . ."[2] When we reflect on critical thinking we need to keep these cautionary remarks in mind, for it is unfortunately the case that "critical thinking" has become yet another slogan in educational discourse. The original meaning of the word "slogan," which is derived from Gaelic, is "army cry." A slogan, then, is meant to urge one to rally for battle; it encourages one to rush to action. And while, indeed, there are times when we do need to act quickly and spontaneously, regular uncalculated actions can impede progress, create frustration and myths. I do not want to be misunderstood. I want to argue for the ideal and value of critical thinking. But I want to point out at the outset that the biggest danger to the ideal arises from (i) misunderstandings of what is involved in the ideal itself and (ii) the variety of things, at times, contradictory ones, that are claimed to be done under the catch-phrase "critical thinking." While it has become quite convenient and common to defend what we do simply by describing it as critical thinking, and while several documents published by government departments of education seem, at face value, to have endorsed the notion we need to ask: Do our teaching and work in schools really reflect the ideal? Is the spirit of such documents really consistent with that of critical thinking?

The aim of this essay is to offer some clarification as to what is involved in the notion of teaching for critical thinking. In section one I clarify the notion of teaching for critical thinking by focusing on and analyzing the assumptions and practical implications of two contrasting teaching situations. In section two I identify and briefly comment on some of the common challenges that face those who take the ideal of critical thinking seriously.

At this stage I should note that I do not mean to propose the ideal and practice of critical thinking as a panacea to all educational ills. To do so would assume that there is only one direct way how to resolve educational problems. Such an approach would also assume that if we make changes here and there within the educational institution itself, irrespective of what happens outside the schools and in other institutions, we would be able to achieve the educational aims in a democracy. Education is a political activity – that is, one that involves power relations between individuals such as teachers and students, parents and administrators, curriculum supervisors and teachers and so on.[3] As Paulo Freire has argued, educational activities are either for humanization or dehumanization.[4] There is no neutral stance in between. Educational activities within educational institutions are, of course, influenced by, and hopefully influence, activities in other institutions. It would be naive for me, therefore, to argue that all we need to do is make sure that we attempt to follow the ideal of critical thinking. Yet, on the other hand, I equally believe that taking critical thinking and the practices that flow from it seriously, is necessary for the sustenance and reconstruction of the democratic way of life – a way of life , which as Bertrand Russell put it, requires that we "encourage independence, initiative, thinking for [oneself], and the realization that anybody may be mistaken."[5] Or as John Dewey put it, a way of life whose foundation depends on the "faith in human intelligence and in the power of pooled and cooperative experience"[6] – an experience that fosters certain attitudes, dispositions and skills, such as, the development of "intelligent judgment and action," free discussions and inquiry, the trust and support that is needed for self-correction, "allowing differences a chance to show themselves because of the belief that the expression of difference is not only a right of the other persons but is a means of enriching one's own life-experience. . . ."[7]

Section One:
The Meaning of Critical Thinking in Relation to Teaching

In the western world – a "eurocentric" world – the ideal of critical thinking (referred to in a variety of terms such as, rationality, critical judgment, reflective thinking etc.) has been promoted at least since the time of Socrates.[8] References to this ideal are found in the work of almost all of the major educationists. At the end of the 19th century and the beginning of this century, Dewey revived the ideal by giving it a central role in the sustenance and continuous reshaping of a democracy and education in a democracy. He also linked the ideal with "the problem solving method," "the scientific method" and the disposition of "open-mindedness." Following and developing on Dewey's work, in the 1960s, philosophers of education (with differing philosophical perspectives) such as Israel Scheffler, John Passmore, Robert Ennis and Maxine Greene, explicitly attempted to connect the ideal of critical thinking with the teaching context. The following are some of the questions they focused on: How does critical thinking relate to moral education and reasonableness? What does "teaching to be critical" really mean and imply? What kind of dispositions and skills are involved in developing critical thinking? And why is the critical spirit crucial in analyzing and enhancing the encounters between teachers and students?

Since the 1960s, interest in critical thinking has developed into a world-wide movement. And hence: (i) differences of interpretation of the ideal became more explicit and controversial; (ii) several programs aiming to foster critical thinking have been developed; (iii) critiques and limitations of the ideal based solely on rationality have emerged;[9] and (iv) more attempts have been made to explore the connection between the ideal of critical thinking and a variety of teaching contexts. And, of course, the questions have increased and have moved beyond those related to the meaning of the term. Some of these questions include: Is critical thinking to be analyzed in terms of various skills and abilities? Can critical thinking be taught? Is critical thinking generalizable or is it directly related to specific subjects? Should it be taught on its own or incorporated throughout the entire curriculum? When should it be taught? Are children capable of dealing with critical thinking situations? How can critical thinking be evaluated? What are some of the justifications for critical thinking? Are critical thinking and teaching critically the same? What is the relationship between critical thinking, teaching critically and democracy? Should critical thinking be based on problem-*solving* or on problem-*seeking*? Are the critical and creative opposed or two sides of the same coin? Why is critical thinking deemed important for teaching? What practical issues emerge when critical thinking is incorporated into one's own teaching? For example, how will this influence or change the role of the teacher? To what extent can critical thinking help resolve ethical and political issues which arise in teaching?

Scenario one

I will now move to an analysis of a teaching context: the one provided in the first two chapters of *Hard Times* by Charles Dickens.[10] What are some of the assumptions the teacher makes with regard to teaching, his role and the role of the students? What do the children learn? Why is this not an example of teaching that fosters critical thinking? The teacher believes that there is a sharp distinction between facts and imagination or "tastes" or values and that teaching is exclusively concerned with facts. Actually his claim is stronger than that. He believes that all one needs is to know facts. Knowledge is reduced exclusively to acquiring facts; teaching is a matter of imparting facts. He also assumes that children are incapable of contributing anything to the learning process since they are "empty vessels." Since they have nothing to contribute, the teacher, the one with all the knowledge, has no consideration at all for the views of the children, no respect for them as individuals. Quite clearly, given these assumptions, there will be no room for imagination, no consideration of subjective views, no discussion of anything (including value issues), no consideration for alternate views. The only view that counts is that of the teacher which is correct since it is allegedly based on facts.

What do the children learn from this situation? The children learn the following: to give the teacher what he wants; that their ideas are not important; that if they voice their ideas they will be crushed; that everything has to be reduced to facts, that there is nothing of worth beyond facts; to accept facts as presented by the teacher or the text; not to question anything; to memorize definitions for the teacher's view of knowing implies that to know something you have to know its definition; that learning is stressful; to dislike school.

The kind of learning identified above is contrary to the skills and dispositions that teaching for critical thinking ought to foster. One may retort that this is an extreme and outdated case. Although it may be hard to find this very specific kind of situation, one still encounters teaching which seems to operate on the assumptions of the teacher in the case.[11]

Scenario two

I will now focus on another teaching situation – one that exhibits qualities associated with the ideal of critical thinking. A grade 6 class of 26 students in an ordinary public school. As part of the language arts and social studies (and possibly even in other subject areas), the teacher explicitly encourages discussions on topics that are of interest to the students. Sometimes she provides them with a reading that may trigger discussion, on other occasions the students themselves now have learned to identify issues that they would like to discuss in an organized, civilized manner as a community of inquirers – that is, a community in which a group of individuals share a common aim and a commonly accepted procedure of inquiry, one in which individuals of the community exchange and share ideas and information with one another, clarify views, respect each other's views, offer reasons for their views, are willing to consider alternatives, and attempt to construct together a reasonable position.

On one occasion, the teacher provided them with *The True Story of the Three Little Pigs! By A. Wolf.*[12] After the reading the teacher asked for the children's reactions and together, as a group, they identified the following "leading ideas": Was the wolf really sick or was he pretending? Had the wolf intended to eat the pigs? How is it possible to know who was telling the truth, who was right? Why did he want to make a cake for his granny? Why didn't the pigs want to give him some sugar? Why didn't he just do a postcard? Why did the third pig tease the wolf about his granny? Why was the wolf imprisoned? Why didn't the wolf buy some sugar? Why did people lie about the wolf? Is this really the true story? Why did the wolf assume that the pig in the straw house is not intelligent? Should we always believe what is reported in newspapers?

The point of the leading ideas is to construct the agenda for the discussion. The teacher is aware that there are different kinds of talk that can take place in a class. In this instance the purpose is to develop a critical/philosophical discussion (in contrast to a traditional debate or mere chit chatting or an exposition of the teacher's interpretation of the issues). This is something the teacher had introduced in the beginning of the year and gradually with her input helped develop further. Initially the teacher asked questions eliciting opinions or views. The teacher was aware that to develop a critical/philosophical discussion more than a mere expression of an opinion was needed. So gradually she introduced questions that encouraged them to clarify and provide reasons for their views, to consider the implications of and alternatives to their views, as well as the appropriateness of their reasons.

The aims of the teacher include (i) developing the class into a community of inquiry and (ii) helping the children to think well for themselves. She believes that the two aims have to develop concurrently. The teacher is aware that in order to fulfil these aims there will be some practical implications for both the classroom and wider level. At the classroom level, the power relation between teacher and students and students themselves ought to be more cooperative, open and less threatening than the one found in traditional classrooms. The role of the teacher will no longer be viewed as the purveyor of all the "truth," mechanically implementing a totally preplanned curriculum irrespective of context. Teaching will no longer be viewed as the execution of a set of reductionist and behaviorist goals. Mere teacher didactic talk will give room to the give-and-take of open yet constructive discussions in which the students' own views will be taken seriously and at times even determine the nature of the curriculum. In a nutshell, an executive/behaviorist approach to teaching will have to be abandoned in favor of an interactive or constructivist approach to teaching which takes democratic procedures in education more seriously; while the teacher retains the ultimate responsibility, the students are realistically and prudently invited to share in this responsibility.

The teacher, therefore, is aware that she will have to assume a different role. She is aware that in the initial phases, the teacher, as the leader of the group, will have to model for the students by keeping track of the points made, intervening by asking questions that move the discussion forward, making occasional comments in order to help clarify the difference between a critical perspective from other perspectives with regard to the issue at hand, encouraging them to compare differing points of views, carefully demanding clarifications and reasons when these are lacking. She is also aware that she will have to learn to balance her interventions while allowing and encouraging the students to express their views, question one another's ideas and those of the teacher. This is a very crucial point especially if students are not used to engaging in any form of discussion. Eventually students will get used to this approach and they will ask to lead discussions themselves. In those instances the teacher, as a participant or member of the community of inquiry, will still have the responsibility to guide the discussion as necessary, but not to a predetermined or fixed point. The direction of the inquiry ought to be determined by the nature of the questions asked or the problems posed and by the kind of replies and further questions that arise in the inquiry. If a determinate or pre-established path channels the direction of the discourse in the sense that the teacher will only allow or expect one kind of reply, the one she really wants to hear, then of course, no discussion has really taken place. Part of the role of the teacher is (i) to create a non-threatening environment so the students will comfortably express their views and questions even if these differ from the accepted norm, (ii) to make sure not to hinder the children's thinking, and (iii) to ensure that she does not manipulate the discussion in order to force the students to accept her views. But it is also the role of the teacher to ensure that the critical/philosophical procedures are being followed: to learn to tease out assumptions of views expressed, to patiently and caringly offer justifications for their views, to examine the plausibility of reasons and examples offered and so on. Obviously, this teacher believes that children are good at doing certain things (which in the past has not been assumed) such as seriously engaging in critical/philosophical discussions. But she also believes that they need nurturing and that these kinds of discussions will be successful only if the children are provided with a rich context which relates to them and the children are given the opportunity to discuss issues that interest them.[13]

The approach exhibited in this scenario is heavily based on the "philosophy-for-children" approach. Although "philosophy for children" is the name of a critical thinking program developed by Matthew Lipman and his associates at the Institute for the Advancement of Philosophy for Children, it also refers to a movement which aims to encourage and develop philosophical discussions in schools.[14] To achieve the aims of helping children to think well for themselves[15] and develop the class into a community of inquiry,[16] it is argued that philosophical inquiry/critical discussions need to be incorporated into the school curriculum rather than acquiring a skill or skills in isolation. Lipman suggests that "thinking skills . . . should be taught in the context of a humanistic discipline . . . ."[17] This quality distinguishes the philosophy-for-children approach from the approach promoted by other popular "thinking skills" programs. In short, philosophy for children attempts "to introduce children to ideas drawn from the philosophical tradition"[18] through discussions that are reasonable and connect to the children's lives. It is important to note that this approach does not necessarily lead to naive relativism or subjectivism or an anything goes mentality. While it is true that the community of inquiry, which is "central both to Philosophy for Children and to the general thrust of teaching for better thinking and reasonableness,"[19] is based on open-mindedness, as Dewey warns us, open-mindedness is *not* equivalent to empty mindedness, and as William Hare argues, open-mindedness calls for fairness and a certain amount of impartiality.[20] Trying to achieve a community of inquiry requires that the teacher and the students evaluate the views and arguments expressed in discussion. There has to be an evaluation of the discussion on philosophical grounds (for example, cogency, appropriateness, and coherency) if one claims that one can determine whether or not philosophical progress was made in a discussion. Hence, the participants have the responsibility to intervene and point out fallacious arguments, misinterpretations, or any other inadequacy. One needs to insist, however, that the intervention, which could take the form of a criticism, has to be made in a respectful and supportive manner. According to Henry Perkinson, Socrates failed to create a supportive environment – "a caring environment, one in which pupils recognize that they are trusted, prized, accepted, even loved."[21] The philosophy-for-children approach should be able to create such a supportive environment by the formation of a community of inquiry. In this respect, this approach not only follows but improves the Socratic one.

Section Two: The Challenges

In section one I offered a clarification of the notion of teaching for critical thinking by focusing on and briefly analyzing two contrasting teaching contexts. Teaching for critical thinking is a demanding endeavor that faces a variety of challenges. In this section I will consider five challenges that face those who take teaching for critical thinking seriously: (i) the challenge of misunderstanding what is involved in being critical and teaching for critical thinking; (ii) the challenge of the conservative educational ideology; (iii) the challenge of "the soft liberal position"; (iv) the challenge of critical and feminist pedagogy; and (v) the challenge of risk-taking.

Challenge No. 1: The challenge of misunderstanding what is involved in being critical and teaching for critical thinking

". . . the Western habit of critical thinking means that first we must find faults and then seek to put them right, so anything without faults is impossible to improve."[22] De Bono's notion of critical thinking in this instance is very similar, if not identical, to the popular usage of the term "criticism" in the sense of finding a fault or a mistake in something. This usually has negative connotations as this sense of "critical" implies some element of destruction. This usage assumes that one cannot be critical unless one has found a mistake or weakness in something. This is not what "critical" means in the phrase critical thinking. This is a crucial point that needs to be emphasized for the major resistance to critical thinking may perhaps rest on this misunderstanding. It is not unusual for parents to misinterpret the intent of developing critical thinking in children, and hence they complain that children will start objecting to anything. This, however, is not the intent or meaning of developing critical thinking. The misunderstanding arises because critical thinkers are seen as "cynical people who often condemn the efforts of others without contributing anything themselves."[23] Of course, if this were the case then critical thinkers would be rightly seen as being arrogant and anti-social. But, as Brookfield argues, the opposite is really the case. For "when we think critically we become aware of the diversity of values, behaviors, social structures, and artistic forms in the world. Through realizing this diversity, our commitments to our own values, actions, and social structures are informed by a sense of humility. . . ."[24] There is a difference between (i) finding fault with something and (ii) fair-mindedness. Of course, the latter may at times call for identifying possible problems in a position. This is different from the negative ring associated with being critical just for the sake of being critical. The *manner* and *intention* of the critical element becomes crucial.

Another popular misinterpretation holds that critical thinking is identical to "effective thinking," or "creative thinking," or "imaginative thinking" or "problem solving" or "decision making" or simply thinking. For example, the psychologist Robert Sternberg writes that critical thinking "is the mental processes, strategies and representations people use to solve problems, make decisions and learn new concepts."[25] (quoted in Splitter 1991, p. 90). While not denying the connection between critical thinking and effectiveness, creativity, imagination and solving problems, the point that needs to be made is that critical thinking is not just these things. It is not hard to envisage cases where one is effective or creative or imaginative or has solved problems without being critical. And one can foresee situations in which in order to be effective one has declined questioning anything at all from the status quo position. As Freire reminds us critical thinking contrasts with naive thinking.[26] One can be very creative, imaginative and effective and yet be very naive. Likewise one may be excellent at solving specific problems which someone else provides and yet be unable to identify problems or even consider the worthwhileness or appropriateness of the solutions one is providing.

Challenge No. 2: The challenge of the conservative educational ideology.

As I mentioned earlier in section one, there are attitudes, beliefs, and practices associated with a conservative or traditional position that are still influential today. In a sense the problem is more dangerous today since those who still adhere to the beliefs associated with this conservative position have camouflaged or softened the tone of these beliefs by making reference to popular slogans such as, excellence, equality of opportunity, access, self-esteem, cooperative learning, problem solving, relevance, needs, and basics. We need to look beneath the surface terminology and ask: What is included as basic? Whose basics? Whose needs? What criteria are used to determine excellence? Does access without support really create equality? Relevant to whom? And in whose interest? When such slogans are analyzed in context several contradictions may emerge. In a recent document published by the Government of Canada, it is stated that prosperity depends on "the willingness of Canadians to develop a renewed sense of partnership" yet the document is entitled "Prosperity through Competitiveness"[27]; and the contradiction is more blatant in the document "Learning Well . . . Living Well":

> Canada's Future Prosperity, and our ability to provide all citizens with a high quality of life, depends on our ability to compete successfully both at home and abroad. Our ability to compete – to produce and provide high quality goods and services – depends in turn on the willingness of Canadians to cooperate, to develop a renewed sense of partnership. (p. v).[28]

In some provinces the contradictions are more acute since while still promoting holistic learning, in the same breadth traditional modes of evaluation are being reintroduced.[29]

Challenge No. 3: The challenge of "the soft liberal position"

I am here referring to the danger arising from the excessive individualism, arising from an extreme liberal position.[30] This position, as Fred Inglis puts it, holds:

> ... that nobody has any right to tell anybody else what to think, but that, since the central good of human life is individual freedom, which is exercised in the making of choices, the good life is best organized by clearing as large a space as may be cleared for the choosing activity, compatible with not infringing the choosing space of others, and validated by more or less optimistic trust in the innate goodness of people. If, however, that trust turns out to be misplaced, liberalism still upholds as a paramount good the freedom of individuals to go to the bad, as long as that is their choice.[31]

When taken to an extreme, as I am claiming it has been done in some educational circles, this position leads to the illusion that freedom has no limits, that individual choice ought not to be influenced by other individual choices, that individual choices do not influence others, that somehow there is the possibility of making choices in a neutral context, and that any individual choice is acceptable. It is exactly this kind of view that leads to extreme relativism or extreme scepticism or an anything goes mentality: open-mindedness becomes empty-mindedness; objectives or plans become unacceptable because they limit the students' choice; suggestions from teachers become non-natural since they do not arise from the students; student participation becomes student domination; sharing on the part of the students turns into control by the dominant few in the group. Any intervention or correction on the part of the teacher is seen as an imposition of the views of the teacher, or to use the latest catch-phrase, to intervene is to be judgmental. The assumption here is that any judgment is necessarily judgmental or demeaning. But, then, should a teacher not intervene if the students exhibit racist or sexist or classist attitudes? Should they not be made aware of a variety of differing views? The critical spirit calls for a respectful intervention or an attempt to increase one's awareness. Allowing an expression of differing views and respecting other's views is not the same as accepting any view whatsoever. Emphasising the importance of the process does not imply that the process exists in separation from the content, or that any conclusion one arrives at is acceptable since what we should be concerned about is simply the process. Thinking is always about something, and what that something is makes a big difference. As Douglas Barnes warns us:

> Schooling must not become merely 'technical' but should help young people to engage in ethical and social issues both at a personal and political level. The idea of substituting 'process' for 'content' is nonsensical: understanding

is impossible without knowledge. Academic curricula have been at fault not in celebrating knowledge but in teaching it as if it were monolithic and unquestionable.[32]

Challenge No. 4: The challenge of critical and feminist pedagogy[33]

I consider the challenge of the critical and feminist pedagogs to be positive for in essence these pedagogs are concerned about the limitations of the notion of critical thinking associated primarily or exclusively with logic or rationality. This notion, it is argued, does not necessarily lead to the kind of awareness and action that is needed. From this perspective, the dominant view of critical thinking is deemed to encourage a detachment between the agent and the object of investigation: the popular view of critical thinking still assumes that to be fair the critical thinker has to dissociate the emotions from reasons, thought from action, and the researcher from the object of investigation or else objectivity will not be achieved.[34] How is critical thinking defined from this perspective? Let me offer three examples:

> 1. True dialogue cannot exist unless the dialogers engage in critical thinking – thinking which discerns an indivisible solidarity between the world and men and admits of no dichotomy between them – thinking which perceives reality as process, as transformation, rather than as a static entity – thinking which does not separate itself from action, but constantly immerses itself in temporality without fear of the risks involved. Critical thinking contrasts with naive thinking . . . only dialogue which requires critical thinking is also capable of generating critical thinking. Without dialogue there is no communication, and without communication there can be no true education.[35]

> 2. [A critical inquiry is one that] takes into account how our lives are mediated by systems of inequity such as classism, racism, and sexism.[36]

> 3. All of these current theories presented function under the dominant paradigm that critical thinking is a process based in logic where facts are separated from opinion; the model being used is the scientific method, in which the critical thinker remains objective, distancing herself from what she is examining. . . . My desire is to encourage self-awareness as a part of the development of critical thinking skills, with the understanding that one cannot divorce oneself from one's own point of view. Instead of viewing the self's contribution (subjective knowing) as something that is distracting or prejudicial to critical thinking, I am arguing that what one contributes is necessary (impossible to remove) and adds contextually to the knowing.[37]

These are very serious claims and should not be taken lightly; for in essence, if we do not take heed of them, we may end up making the same kind of assumptions made by the teacher in *Hard Times,* who dissociated facts from opinions, reason from emotions, facts from values, knowledge from imagination and subjectivity. Unless we encourage our students to apply the kind of analysis, investigation and critique associated with critical thinking to their own contexts and beyond in order to act accordingly when faced with injustices, we will remain at the level of the teacher's concern in *Hard Times* of whether it is alright to imagine flowers on our carpets or horses on our wallpaper! As Jane R. Martin has eloquently argued, a democratic society is not well served by having merely spectator-citizens: ". . . an education that favors spectatorship over participation – that is devoted almost exclusively to the former – is not an appropriate one for the young of any society, certainly not ours."[38] To achieve this kind of participation, however, we will need to do more than merely provide students with choices or feed them with problems to solve. We need to encourage them also to find alternatives and then choose, and to find problems themselves. And, more importantly, we need to make them more aware of the political and moral dimensions of their choices. As Martin concludes: "The best thinking in the world is of little avail if a person has not acquired the will, the ability, the skill, the sensitivity, and the courage to act on it."[39, 40]

Challenge No. 5 The challenge of risk taking

Taking critical thinking in its entirety seriously will make us teachers have to face delicate and controversial situations, which at times, create conflicts and tensions. Critical teaching may at times lead to an "unquiet pedagogy."[41] John Passmore warned us that any teacher who takes critical thinking seriously, as democracy requires, "must expect constantly to be embarrassed . . . to be harassed, by his [her] class, by his [her] headmaster, by parents."[42] Are we as teachers and teacher educators prepared to take this needed risk? Or, are we, as Russell put it "tempted to set ourselves up as little gods"[43] within the haven of institutional bureaucracy?

Concluding Remarks

The aim of this essay has been to clarify the notion of "teaching for critical thinking" by inquiring into (i) what is implied by this concept, (ii) some of the common misinterpretations and the kind of practices, policies and visions that hinder the realization of this kind of teaching, and (iii) current educational positions that urge us to go beyond traditional perspectives of critical thinking. The aim has not been to offer a succinct, precise definition of critical thinking. I have argued elsewhere that attempting to do so with certain concepts will create further myths and illusions.[44] The same, I contend, applies to the notion of critical thinking. However, my discussion does indicate (i) some qualities (such as those identified in the brief analysis of scenario one) that are inconsistent with teaching for critical thinking, and (ii) some qualities (such as those identified in my analysis of scenario two and the criticisms of popular views dealt with in section two) that are consistent with critical thinking and ought to be encouraged if the notion of teaching for critical thinking is taken seriously.[45]

Notes

[1]Plato, *Charmides,* 165c. In *The Dialogues of Plato Vol.2: The Symposium and Other Dialogues* (B. Jowett, Trans.). London: Sphere Books Ltd., 1970.

[2]Robin Barrow, *The Philosophy of Schooling* (Brighton: Wheatsheaf Books, 1981), 16.

[3]"Power" is not used interchangeably with force. I am here referring to a certain relationship which arises from the inescapable nature of human beings as social beings. Harvey Siegel makes a similar point when he argues that "educational institutions and practices which are informed by ideals, being social, inevitably impact the body politic in multifarious ways and are in that sense inevitably political." (*Educating Reason: Rationality, Critical Thinking, and Education,* New York: Routledge, 1988, 69).

[4]See: Paulo Freire, *Pedagogy of the Oppressed* (New York: Seabury, 1970); "Reading the World and Reading the Word: An Interview with Paulo Freire," *Language Arts,* 62, 1, 1985: 15-21; Paulo Freire, *The Politics of Education: Culture, Power and Liberation* (Westport, Conn.: Greenwood, Bergin-Garvey, 1985); Paulo Freire and Ira Shor, *A Pedagogy for Liberation: Dialogues on Transforming Education* (Westport, Conn.: Greenwood, Bergin-Garvey, 1987); and Paulo Freire and Myles Horton, *We Make the Road by Walking: Conversations on Education and Social Change* (Philadelphia: Temple University Press,1990).

[5]Bertrand Russell, "Education for Democracy," *National Education Association,* 77, 1939: 533.

[6]John Dewey, "Democracy and Educational Administration," in Dewey, *Philosophy of Education: Problems of Men* (Totawa, N.J.: Littlefield, Adams, 1958), 59.

[7]John Dewey, "Creative Democracy: The Task before Us," in M.H. Fisch (Ed.), *Classic American Philosophers* (New York: Prentice Hall, 1951), 393.

[8]Molefi Kete Asante argues quite convincingly by providing evidence that the notion of rationality in ancient Greek philosophy was inherited from the Egyptians. See, *Kemet, Afrocentricity and Knowledge* (Trenton, N.J.: Africa World Press, 1990).

[9]See for example, some of the work in "critical pedagogy," "feminist pedagogy and "postmodernism": Barbara Thayer-Bacon, "A Feminine Reconceptualization of Critical Thinking," *Journal of Thought,* 27, 3 & 4, 1992, and "Caring and Its Relationship to Critical Thinking," *Educational Theory,* 43, 3, 1993; J.M. Fernandez-Balboa, "Critical Pedagogy: Making Critical Thinking Really Critical," *Analytic Teaching,* 13, 2, 1993; and Jane R. Martin, "Critical Thinking for a Humane World," in S. Norris (Ed.), *The Generalizability of Critical Thinking: Multiple Perspectives on an Educational Ideal* (New York: Teachers College Press, 1992).

[10]I am assuming that the reader is familiar with the scenario in these two chapters.

[11]For examples that support this claim see I.J. Baksh and W.B.W. Martin, *Teaching Strategies: The Student Perspective* (St.John's, NFLD: Memorial University of Newfoundland, 1986); Frank Smith, *Insult to Intelligence* (New York: Arbor House,

1986); Kenneth Sirotnik, "What Goes on in Classrooms? Is this the Way We Want It?," in L.E.Beyer and M.W.Apple (Eds.), *The Curriculum: Problems, Politics and Possibilities* (Albany, N.Y.: S.U.N.Y. Press, 1988); Peter McLaren, *Life in Schools: An Introduction to Critical Pedagogy in the Foundations of Education* (Toronto,Ont.: Irwin Publ., 1994); Patrick Shannon, *Broken Promises* (Granby, MA: Bergin and Garvey, 1989); Michael Apple, *Official Knowledge: Democratic Education in a Conservative Age* (New York: Routledge, 1993); Donaldo F. Macedo, "Literacy for Stupification: The Pedagogy of Big Lies," *Harvard Educational Review*, 63, 3, 1993; Sandro Contenta, *Rituals of Failure: What Schools Really Teach* (Toronto: Between the Lines, 1993); and Kathleen Shannon, *At Home At School: A Child's Transition* (Bothell, WA: The Wright Group Publ., Inc., 1995).

I will provide three anecdotes in support of this claim. First, my children still ask: Is this really the correct answer that will make the teacher happy? Second, a journal entry from a high school student I know:

> School has *ruled* my life for twelve years now, and I still do not know how I feel about it. School is a place where kids are supposed to learn and grow as individual people but I do not think that is what the school system is doing for all the students.
>
> I look at school as the basic training for adulthood and our future jobs. As I sit here and think I try to put together what it has taught me for the future. I'd like to think that it taught me discipline, but I don't think it has. Some might say that I do all my homework because I'm disciplined enough to make myself do it even though I'm busy or I want to go out. I know that it is not true. The only reason why I do that work is because it gets me higher grades.
>
> Grades is what school is about. I go, I sit, I listen, I take notes, I memorize and then give back what I'm told for tests. If I memorize correctly I get high grades and told that I learned a lot. I could not tell you what I studied in English in Grade 9, or my History for that matter.
>
> I know I do not like the schools system. It does not allow you to think, be creative, explore the world by experience. That is what children need for today's world. But I have no idea how to get it into the system. I want them to get rid of the grades. How can they judge one person's knowledge with numbers. Children should be allowed to be creative and to think and learn but it cannot be done only in the classroom. It is impossible to do all this in just rooms.
>
> I feel that I have lost my creativity. My imagination is disappearing and I do feel it is a great loss. Sometimes I wish I was a pioneer going across the prairies when children were not in front of the TV day and night. But I like technology and I enjoy it. Right now I'm using technology, my computer. It is wonderful help for my work and makes everything a lot easier.
>
> School is a place were I learn from my mistakes with my friends. I learn some things, like how to interact with people and respect them. But I can't help feeling like people from the past have destroyed me from becoming what I want and becoming what society wants.

And the last anecdote: An elementary teacher with twenty years of teaching experience in one of my graduate classes wrote in her weekly comment which the teachers share with each other at the beginning of each class: "I see a major part of the curriculum problem today stemming from the teaching profession's widespread lack of critical questioning of what we must do and why. But the public school education system we grew up in did not encourage us to ask questions, just to accept and perform as requested. How do we go about changing something that is so ingrained in us?" (January, 1993). And in the discussion that followed she explained an incident that made her write this comment: She was talking to her colleagues during lunch break. As teachers usually do, they spoke about things that had happened in their classes during the morning. She mentioned how a grade 5 boy wonderingly asked her why they were doing that particular math activity. Janice told her colleagues that she took some time to explain why, and in the process of doing so, other children asked more questions and at the end of this 10-15 minute explanation/discussion the children cheerfully continued the activity. She was concerned about the reaction she got from her colleagues who sort of reprimanded her for first, allowing the children to ask those kind of questions, and second, for taking time to reply to the questions.

I want to make it clear that my aim in offering these references and anecdotes is not to engaging in teacher bashing. My point is simply that the attitudes found in scenario one still exist. Scenario two will hopefully show that there are other possibilities and hope!

[12]Jon Scieszka, *The True Story of the Three Little Pigs! By A. Wolf* (New York: Viking, 1989).

[13]This last point does not necessarily imply that the teacher should never introduce issues or points which the students have not explicitly identified. There is a difference between simply pursuing or following interests and developing interests. From an educational point of view, the latter cannot be abandoned.

[14]For information about the Philosophy for Children Program contact the I.A.P.C., Montclair State College, Upper Montclair, New Jersey, U.S.A., 07043. For a detailed account about Lipman's work and his contribution to philosophy for children and philosophy of education, see, Ronald F. Reed and Ann E. Witcher, "Matthew Lipman: Restoring the Connection between Education and Philosophy," in James J. Von Patten (Ed.), *Academic Profiles in Higher Education* (Lampeter, Dyfed, Wales: The Edward Mellen Press Ltd., 1992), 203-228. For information about the philosophy for children movement throughout the world, check the web site on philosophy for children at Deakin University, Australia (http://www.deakin.edu.au/arts/SSI/PStud/p4c.html). There are three main journals that publish articles on philosophy for children: *Thinking: The Journal of Philosophy for Children* (published by the I.A.P.C.); *Analytic Teaching* (published by Viterbo College, La Crosse, Wisconsin, U.S.A., 54601); and *Critical and Creative Thinking: The Australian Journal of Philosophy for Children* (Available from Deakin University-Warrnambool, Warrnambool, Vic 3280, Australia). The literature on philosophy for children is extensive. The following are a few recent major publications in the field: Gareth Matthews, *The Philosophy of Childhood* (Cambridge, Mass.: Harvard University Press, 1994); John P. Portelli and Ronald F. Reed (Eds.) *Children, Philosophy, and Democracy* (Calgary, AB.: Detselig Ent. Ltd., 1995); and Laurance Splitter and Ann Margaret Sharp, *Teaching for Better Thinking: The Classroom Community of Inquiry* (Melbourne: The Australian Council for Educational Research Ltd., 1995).

[15]Thinking well for oneself is not taken to mean that any kind of thinking will do. The purpose here is to prevent unreasonableness or to promote reasonableness which include a better understanding of something, looking for and properly relating evidence

and reasons, being creative and imaginative, being sensitive to other points of view, and forming a coherent and plausible perspective.

[16]For more information and discussion on the community of inquiry see Ann Margaret Sharp's essay in this collection as well as the following: Ann Margaret Sharp, "What Is a Community of Inquiry?" *Journal of Moral Education*, 16, 1, 1987: 22-30; Matthew Lipman, "Educating for Violence Reduction and Peace Development: The Philosophical Community of Inquiry Approach," in J.P. Portelli and R. Reed (Eds.), *Children, Philosophy, and Democracy*, 121-138; David Kennedy, "Philosophy for Children and School Reform: Dewey, Lipman, and the Community of Inquiry," in *Children, Philosophy, and Democracy*, 159-178; Paul Bitting, "Philosophy in the Democratic Multicultural Community of Inquiry," in *Children, Philosophy, and Democracy*, 179-190; Laurance Splitter and Ann M. Sharp, "Thinking: The Classroom as a Community of Inquiry," in Splitter and Sharp, *Teaching for Better Thinking: The Classroom Community of Inquiry*, 5-31.

[17]Matthew Lipman, "Philosophy for Children and Critical Thinking," *Phi Kappa Phi Journal*, 1985: 20.

[18]Lipman, "Philosophy for Children and Critical Thinking," 21.

[19]Splitter and Sharp, *Teaching for Better Thinking*, 2.

[20]See John Dewey, *Democracy and Education* (New York: The Free Press, 1966), 175, and William Hare, *Open-mindedness and Education* (Montreal: McGill-Queen's Press, 1979) and *In Defence of Open-mindedness* (Montreal: McGill-Queen's Press, 1985).

[21]Henry Perkinson, "The Socratic Approach to Education Today," in W.Hare and J.P. Portelli (Eds.), *Philosophy of Education: Introductory Readings* (Calgary, Alb.: Detselig Ent. Ltd., 1988, 1st ed.), 237.

[22]Edward de Bono, *I Am Right You Are Wrong: From This to the New Renaissance: From Rock Logic to Water Logic* (Harmondsworth, Middlesex: Penguin Books, 1990), 167.

[23]Stephen D. Brookfield, *Developing Critical Thinkers: Challenging Adults to Explore Alternative Ways of Thinking and Acting* (San Francisco: Jossey-Bass Publishers. 1987), 5.

[24]Brookfield, *Developing Critical Thinkers,* 5.

[25]Quoted by Laurance Splitter, "Critical Thinking: What, Why, When and How," *Educational Philosophy and Theory*, 23, 1, 1991, 90.

[26]Freire, *Pedagogy of the Oppressed,* 81.

[27]Government of Canada. *Prosperity through Competitiveness.* Ministry of Supply and Services Canada, 1991, iii.

[28]Government of Canada. *Learning Well . . . Living Well.* Ministry of Supply and Services Canada, 1991, v.

[29]See, Gerry Carty, "An Open Letter to the Minister of Education," *The Teacher* (Nova Scotia Teachers Union), 31, 8, 1993: 8; and Maude Barlow and Heather Jane Robertson, *Class Warfare: The Assault on Canada's Schools* (Toronto: Key Porter Books, 1994).

[30]See, Jesse Goodman, *Elementary Schooling for Critical Democracy* (Albany, N.Y.: S.U.N.Y., 1992).

[31]Fred Inglis, *The Management of Ignorance: A Political Theory of the Curriculum* (Oxford: Basil Blackwell, 1985), 156.

[32]Douglas Barnes, "Knowledge as Action," in M. Lightfoot and N. Martin (Eds.), *The Word for Teaching Is Learning* (Portsmouth, NH: Heinemann: 1988), 31.

[33]Although critical pedagogy and feminist pedagogy are not identical, they will be treated as representing a common perspective since their concerns about critical thinking are very similar. Moreover, their major thrust as a pedagogy is very similar if not identical. Peter McLaren, for example, writes that "critical pedagogy examines schools both in their historical context as part of the existing social and political fabric that characterize the dominant society. . . . Critical pedagogy does not . . . constitute a homogeneous set of ideas. It is more accurate to say that critical theorists are united in their *objectives*: to empower the powerless and transform existing social inequalities and injustices." (*Life in Schools*, 167-8). And Linda Briskin, a feminist pedagogue, writes: "[The] emphasis on social change recognizes feminist pedagogy as a form of feminist practice having its roots in the women's movement, and firmly situates feminist pedagogy in the traditions of critical and radical pedagogies that see education as a form of empowerment and a tool in social change." (*Feminist Pedagogy: Teaching and Learning Liberation*, (Ottawa, Ont.: Canadian Research Institute for the Advancement of Women, 1990), 33.

[34]See, Jane R. Martin, "Critical Thinking for a Human World," and Barbara Thayer-Bacon, "Constructive Thinking: Personal Voice," *Journal of Thought*, 30, 1, 1995, 55-70.

It is important to note that this stance does not deny the role of reason. As Thayer-Bacon states, the aim is "to integrate the inner voice (the subjective, intuitive, believing voice) and the voice of reason (the objective, critical, doubtful voice)." ("Constructive Thinking," 56).

[35]Paulo Freire, *Pedagogy of the Oppressed*.

[36]Patti Lather, "Critical Frames in Educational Research: Feminist and Post-structural Perspectives," *Theory into Practice*, 31, 2, 1992; 87.

[37]Barbara Thayer-Bacon, "Is Modern Critical Thinking Theory Sexist?" *Inquiry: Critical Thinking Across the Disciplines*, 10, 2, 1992, 6-7.

[38]Jane R. Martin, "Critical Thinking for a Humane World," 175.

[39]Jane R. Martin, "Critical Thinking for a Human World," 178.

[40]For other examples of this kind of challenge, see: Ira Shor, *Empowering Education: Critical Teaching for Social Change* (Chicago: The University of Chicago Press, 1992); Jesse Goodman, *Elementary Schooling for Critical Democracy*; and J.M. Fernandez-Balboa, "Critical Pedagogy: Making Critical Thinking Really Critical."

[41]E. Kutz and H. Roskelly, *An Unquiet Pedagogy* (Portsmouth, NH: Heinemann, 1991).

[42]John Passmore, "On Teaching to Be Critical," in R.S.Peters (Ed.), *The Concept of Education* (London: Routledge & Kegan Paul, 1967), 219.

[43]B. Russell, "Education for Democracy," 532.

[44]John P. Portelli, "On Defining Curriculum," *Journal of Curriculum and Supervision*, 2,4, 1987: 354-367.

[45]Earlier (Febrary, 1993) versions of this essay were read as a keynote address at Teachers College in Truro, N.S., and at the conference on Critical Thinking and Problem Solving at Mount Saint Vincent University, Halifax, N.S. (May, 1993). Special thanks to my colleagues, Ann Vibert and William Hare, who offered helpful comments and suggestions on this essay.

5

Critical And Creative Thinking

Sharon Bailin

Introduction

A central goal of contemporary education is to improve the thinking skills of students, and the notions of critical thinking and of creative thinking provide focusses for this effort. As educators we would like our students to be better critical thinkers. This implies thinking more effectively within curricular subject areas – understanding the reasoning employed, assessing independently and appropriately, and solving problems effectively. It involves, as well, improved thinking skills in dealing with real life problems – in assessing information and arguments in social contexts and making life decisions. We also want students to be more creative – not simply to reproduce old patterns but to respond productively to new situations, to generate new and better solutions to problems, and to produce original works.

These goals of fostering critical thinking and of fostering creativity are generally considered to be quite separate and distinct. Critical thinking is seen as analytic. It is the means for arriving at judgments within a given framework or context. Creative thinking, on the other hand, is seen as imaginative, constructive, generative. It is what allows for the breaking out of or transcending of the framework itself. There is, however, disagreement among theorists as to the relationship between the two types of thinking. Some view them as different but complementary. Edward Glaser, for example, states, "creativity supplements critical thinking. It may not be an essential ingredient in critical thinking."[1] Other theorists such as Edward de Bono believe that there is a tension between critical and creative thinking, that breaking out of a prevailing framework requires an abandonment of the logic and standards for critical assessment which characterize the framework. Both groups are in accord, however, in the belief that critical and creative thinking are fundamentally different and that they therefore require different pedagogies. The complementarity view usually entails efforts to teach critical thinking skills on their own or integrated into curricular materials plus techniques to encourage flexibility, spontaneity, divergent thinking, etc. The opposition view usually involves the abandonment of some aspects of critical thinking and disciplinary skills in favor of such creativity techniques, on the grounds that the former are inhibiting to the latter. De Bono makes the latter point thus: "Too much experience within a field may restrict creativity because you know so well how things should be done that you are unable to escape to come up with new ideas."[2]

I believe there are serious conceptual and educational problems in this radical dichotomy between critical and creative thinking. I shall argue there are analytic, highly judgmental aspects to generating creative results, and imaginative, inventive aspects to being critical, and that it is exceedingly difficult to neatly separate out two distinctive kinds of thought. Moreover, I will demonstrate the problematic educational outcomes of the view of thinking on which this separation rests – outcomes such as a basic curriculum in the schools which is static and encourages appeal to authority, a consequent picture of knowledge in general as authoritarian, the notion of critical thinking as a set of isolatable add-on techniques, and a downplaying of skills and knowledge in favor of intuition and irrationality in the name of creativity. Finally, I would like to try to give a sense of what difference it might make educationally to view critical thinking and creative thinking as joint and inseparable goals.

The Standard View

The standard view about the nature of critical thinking and of creative thinking which underpins much contemporary psychological and educational theory and practice sets up a sharp separation between the two. According to this view, critical thinking involves arriving at assessments within specific frameworks. It is the means for making reasoned judgments within these frameworks based on the standards of judgment inherent in the framework. It is thus essentially analytic, evaluative, selective, and highly rule-bound. Given the necessary information from within the framework and the appropriate techniques of reasoning, arriving at judgments is almost algorithmic. In thinking critically one is, however, confined to the specific framework. Because it is circumscribed by the logic of the framework, critical thinking cannot provide the means to transcend the framework itself nor to question its assumptions. De Bono puts the point as follows: "Logical thinking can never lead to that alteration of sequence that leads to the 'insight' rearrangement of information ... Logical thinking may find out the best way of putting together A, B, and C but it will not discover that A, B and C are inappropriate units anyway."[3]

Creative thinking, on the other hand, is precisely the type of thinking which can transcend frameworks. It is inventive, imaginative, and involves the generation of new ideas. Because it involves breaking out of old frameworks, creative thinking is thought to exhibit characteristics which are precisely the

opposite of critical thinking. It is essentially generative, spontaneous, and non-evaluative. It involves divergent thinking, rule-breaking, the suspension of judgment, and leaps of imagination. And, instead of being characterized by logic or appeal to reasons, it relies heavily on intuition, and unconscious processes. This dichotomy is evident in Arthur Koestler's contrast between disciplined thought and the creative act: "ordered, disciplined thought is a skill governed by set rules of the game, some of which are explicitly stated, others implied and hidden in the code. The creative act, in so far as it depends on unconscious resources, presupposes a relaxing of the controls and a regression to modes of ideation which are indifferent to the rules of verbal logic, unperturbed by contradiction, untouched by the dogmas and taboos of so-called common sense."[4]

A False Dichotomy

I believe, however, this opposition between critical thinking and creative thinking is false, and that it is mistaken to view them as radically different and unconnected. First, it can be shown that thinking critically plays a crucial role in innovation. Innovation must be viewed in terms of creating products which are not simply novel but also of value, and critical judgment is crucially involved in such creative achievement. In any creative solution to a problem, the initial recognition that there is a problem to be solved, the identification of the nature of the problem, and the determination of how to proceed all involve critical assessment. Initially, the realization that there is a problem to be solved, that there are phenomena in need of explanation or exploration involves judgment. The recognition that a new direction or approach is required is an evaluation based on knowledge and an understanding of the problem situation. And there is judgment involved in determining the general range and form of possible solutions to problems or next moves in creating, the ideas and directions that might be fruitful, and even the ideas that will count as solutions or achieve the completion of a work. Thus the idea that creative thinking is not dependent upon critical thinking will not hold up under scrutiny.

Second, the idea that creative thinking is essentially rule-breaking can also be questioned. It is frequently the case that innovation requires the breaking of a rule or rules of the framework in question, but it is generally only very few rules that are broken. The majority remain intact, rules which give coherence to the activity as essentially rule-breaking largely ignores the background of rules and rule-governed activity against which any creation occurs and the continuity between an innovation and that which precedes it.

This continuity points to the fact that creative thinking is not grounded in irrational processes but is, in fact, a reasonable response to a problem situation.

Creativity is not merely a question of generating new solutions to problems, but of generating better solutions, and is thus not a matter of arbitrary novelty or random invention, but involves change which is effective, useful, and significant. Such change is connected with high-level skills and in-depth knowledge in an area, with a profound understanding of the problem situation and with attempts to solve these problems in ever better ways. This implies highly developed critical judgment. Critical thinking is, thus, intimately involved in creative production.

I think that it can also be demonstrated that critical thinking is not merely analytic, selective, and confined to frameworks, but has imaginative, inventive, constructive aspects. Definitions of critical thinking generally make reference to assessing on the basis of reasons (For example, Robert Ennis: "the process of reasonably deciding what to believe or do"[5]; and Harvey Siegel: "being appropriately moved by reasons"[6]), but such assessments are not generally clear-cut or mechanical. They require an imaginative contribution on the part of the assessor. Even within traditional subject areas which are considered technical, the reasoner must go beyond the confines of the given information, supplying imaginative constructs. David Perkins has made this point with respect to mathematics: "The evident challenge posed by many mathematical problems plainly calls upon the problem solver's powers of invention. To be sure, if a mathematical problem allows a solution by sheer guesswork or systematic computation, with no need to discover a path from given to answer, then imagination need play no role. But virtually all serious mathematical problems do not surrender so easily, else they would not count as serious."[7]

This is all the more true in the case of informal reasoning, where considerable invention is required of the reasoner. Even in the case of assessing individual arguments according to the criteria of informal logic, the procedure is not merely technical or algorithmic. Identifying assumptions, inventing hypotheses, generating counter-examples and constructing counter-arguments are all examples of aspects of informal reasoning which require imagination. As Ennis has pointed out, such reasoning activities as observing, inferring, conceiving alternatives, and offering a well organized line of reasoning are all activities in which "the thinker contributes more than evaluation to the result."[8] And Michael Scriven sums up this point nicely when he states, "the very process of criticism necessarily involves the creative activity of generating new theories or hypotheses to explain phenomena that have seemed to other people to admit of only one explanation."[9]

Moreover, critical thinking involves more than assessing isolated arguments according to clearly-defined criteria and using specifiable techniques, as Richard Paul has pointed out in his critique of "weak sense" critical thinking.[10]

In actual instances of critical reasoning, it is rarely the case that we pass definite judgment on isolated arguments. Rather, we judge between conflicting points of view, and adjudicate among competing arguments. And certainly the criteria of informal logic provide one basis for so doing. Yet such criteria are seldom decisive in and of themselves, and what the reasoner must do is to construct a new view which resolves the problems posed by the conflicting views and synthesizes the soundest aspects of each into a new and coherent whole. Even in those cases where one of the views is, in the end, wholly accepted or rejected, serious assessment must involve an understanding of the strengths of both views, and a "sympathetic reconstruction" of the strongest arguments for each, as Paul puts it.[11] This dialectical aspect of critical thinking is one which has been pointed out by numerous theorists including Paul, Glaser, and Perkins, and it is an aspect of critical thought which clearly requires imagination and invention.

One reason for this dichotomized view of thinking into the critical and the creative might be connected with the notion of frameworks. According to this view, ordinary thinking takes place within rigidly bounded and highly rule-governed frameworks. Within these frameworks, all necessary information is given, and the mode of thinking required is analytic and evaluative, involving judgments made almost mechanically according to the logic of the framework. Given this picture of frameworks, it would seem to follow that a radically different type of thinking is required to transcend frameworks, a type of thinking which suspends the criteria of judgment of the framework, breaks rules, which makes irrational leaps, and which generates novelty. This is the line taken by de Bono, as the following quote demonstrates: "A framework of reference is a context provided by the current arrangement of information. It is the direction of development implied by this arrangement. One cannot break out of the frame of reference by working from within it. It may be necessary to jump out, and if the jump is successful then the frame of reference is itself altered."[12]

I would argue, however, that this view of how frameworks operate is mistaken. In actuality, there are only a very limited number of cases in which we operate within clear-cut, clearly determined, and rigidly bounded frameworks. In most situations which require critical thought, frameworks overlap, shift, and have indefinite boundaries. Even within traditional disciplines, one is not dealing with static and rigid bodies of information. Rather, disciplines are open-ended and dynamic. They involve not merely information, but also live questions and modes of investigating these questions. And even the body of facts is not fixed but is in flux. There are open questions, ongoing debates, and areas of controversy within every discipline, and these furnish the arena for evolution and change. Thus the rigid framework model does not appear to be accurate even within disciplinary areas.

This fluid aspect to frameworks is even more apparent in inter-disciplinary and real life problem contexts. In such situations, relevant considerations are seldom confined to one framework, but involve, rather, information from a variety of perspectives and frames of reference. As Paul states with reference to such real life problems, "We cannot justifiably assume that any one frame of reference or point of view is pre-eminently correct, as the perspective within which these basic human problems are to be most rationally settled."[13] Moreover, even the notion of a clearly defined framework has limited applicability in such contexts. What, for example, would be the framework for thinking about questions regarding war and peace or concerning love and human relationships? Once it is recognized that frameworks have this fluid, indeterminate character, the case for two separate and distinct modes of thinking, one for operating within and the other for transcending frameworks, is considerably weakened.

I would contend, then, that critical thinking and creative thinking are not separate and distinct modes of thinking which operate within different contexts and to different ends. Rather, they are intimately connected and are both integrally involved in thinking well in any area. In all instances in which serious thinking is required, both the constraints of logic and the inventiveness of imagination come into play. There is some degree of creativity evident in all critical thinking, and in some cases, deliberations over what to reasonably believe or do lead one to question presuppositions or break rules – and issue in products which display considerable novelty. This is not connected with irrational leaps, but rather with a broad and in-depth understanding of the problem situation and of what is really at issue. Truly critical thought aims at the best judgments, actions, and outcomes and what is better is necessarily also new. Thus the critical and the creative are inextricably linked and are joint aspects of effective thinking.

Education

This radical separation of critical and creative thinking has its source in a specific picture of thinking and knowledge, namely that ordinary thinking is convergent, analytic, and takes place within rigid frameworks, and that creative thinking requires imaginative leaps to transcend the frameworks. This picture has, I think, held considerable sway in educational circles and has had what I believe to be a detrimental effect on the way we teach in schools. As a product of this picture, the various subject areas are conceived of as defined and fixed bodies of knowledge, static collections of facts to be assimilated and recollected. Students are thus left with a sense that knowledge is complete, definite, and fixed, and that it is based on an appeal to authority – be it of the text, of the teacher, of the unnamed "they" who say that it is so. Theorists and educators have certainly realized the inadequacy of this approach and have attempted to introduce critical thinking into the curriculum, either as a subject on its own, or in conjunction with disciplinary materials. Some theorists have also noted this traditional type of curriculum can be stultifying and deadening to creativity and so have advocated techniques to encourage creative thinking. Thus we see a proliferation of techniques such as brainstorming and the random stimulation of ideas which purport to foster creativity. In the best case, these are seen as an adjunct to disciplinary skills and knowledge and to critical thinking skills. In the worst case, disciplinary skills and knowledge and critical thinking skills are viewed as inhibiting to creativity because they lock one into a prevailing framework and so such skills are neglected or considerably downplayed in favor of irrational processes.

It seems to me that such efforts to counteract the inadequacies of the traditional curriculum are insufficient in the case of critical thinking and sometimes misguided in the case of creativity. They are both supplemental measures which do not attack one root of the problem, namely the picture of knowledge as complete, definite, and fixed. Such measures will remain remedial unless teaching and learning in subject areas begins to reflect the critical and creative nature of knowledge itself. Disciplines are not merely static collections of information but are modes of inquiry, containing open questions, areas of controversy, and ongoing debates. Mechanisms for criticism and thereby for evolution are built right into the disciplines themselves, and students must gain a sense of this in the way subjects are presented or it is unlikely that the hold of the authoritarian picture of knowledge will be broken. Criticism must be understood as part of the subject matter itself, as part of what it means to learn a discipline, as the method whereby inquiry proceeds. And it must be understood that the possibility for evolution and innovation is afforded by the critical and dynamic nature of disciplines and does not require an abandonment of disciplinary skills nor a reliance on irrational processes.

I also suspect this dichotomized view of thinking and this picture of knowledge as definite and fixed, which is created by the traditional school curriculum, extends as well, into thinking in non-disciplinary areas and is one reason why it is so difficult to enhance the critical thinking skills of students. They are accustomed to seeking the right answer according to authority and to accepting algorithmic solutions to problems and this is their mode of proceeding with respect to life problems as well. On the other hand, they may aim for creativity which, they have learned, can be achieved by thinking divergently, relying on subjective personal opinion, and ignoring critical criteria for assessment. I believe it is crucial that students learn that there is a path between dogmatism and ignorance. It is vital that they understand that thinking well in any area is based on knowledge, but is questioning and critical according to sound reasons, and that creativity is an extension of thinking really well about problems. They need to acquire a sense that knowledge is made, developed and advanced, but that this takes place within the constraints of logic and the principles and goals of the relevant area.

What, then, am I suggesting with respect to education? First, I am arguing that the notion that disciplinary knowledge and critical thinking skills are inhibiting to creativity is mistaken, and that, in fact, the possibility for advancement and innovation in any area rests on a thorough and in-depth understanding of the state of the art of the discipline and on highly developed critical judgment. Thus I am advocating that we really emphasize mastery of disciplinary knowledge and skills as a precondition for any creative achievement. This must include, not merely the current body of information, but also the principles and procedures of the discipline, the methods whereby inquiry proceeds, the standards according to which reasons are assessed, and the over-all goals and deep questions which are at issue. Thus the critical nature of knowledge and knowledge growth must be stressed.

In addition, we must communicate a sense that thinking and knowledge are creative. This implies an understanding that disciplinary knowledge is not static and rigidly circumscribed within a fixed framework, but is dynamic, taking place within overlapping and fluid frameworks, and that it grows and develops. Knowledge must be understood not as an authoritative body of facts, but as something made by people who are thinking well about problems. This type of picture of knowledge as dynamic, non-authoritarian and creative would, I think, give rise to a more critical attitude on the part of students with respect to thinking in all areas.

This creative aspect to all thinking must also be taken into account in the teaching of critical thinking. Critical thinking consists in more than isolated technical skills, although such skills are an indispensable starting point. It generally takes place in contexts which are not clearly defined nor totally specified, and in situations which are dynamic, and the reasoners must make an imaginative contribution to the assessment. This points to the necessity to present critical thinking skills within real and dynamic contexts, and to encourage the ability to reconstruct opposing arguments and to develop an independent line of reasoning. The dialectical aspect of critical thinking is thus emphasized by the recognition of the creativeness of critical thinking.

Peter McKellar, in his book *Imagination and Thinking*, gives the following description of the attitude which he feels is most conducive to creativity: "serious receptivity towards previous thought products and unwillingness to accept them as final."[14] This is, I think, a very good characterization of the kind of attitude toward thinking and knowledge which comes out of an understanding of the close interconnection of the critical and the creative. Taking previous thought products seriously implies recognizing the importance of knowledge and skills, of judgment, of in-depth understanding, and of criticism and reasons in creative production. Unwillingness to accept such products as final entails an understanding of the dynamic, lively, evolutionary nature of knowledge and the creative nature of criticism. Both these aspects are crucial in any attempt to improve the thinking of our students both within disciplinary areas and with respect to real life problems. Thus I would advocate the encouragement of critical thinking and of creative thinking as joint and inseparable goals in education.[15]

Notes

[1]Edward Glaser, "Critical Thinking: Education for Responsible Citizenship in a Democracy," *National Forum*, 65, 1, 1985: 25.

[2]Edward de Bono, *Practical Thinking* (Harmondsworth: Penguin Books, 1976), 165.

[3]Edward de Bono, *The Mechanism of Mind* (Harmondsworth: Penguin Books, 1969), 228.

[4]Arthur Koestler, *The Act of Creation* (London: Pan Books, 1975), 178.

[5]Robert Ennis, "Rational Thinking and Educational Practice," in J. Soltis (ed.), *Philosophy of Education* (Chicago: National Society for the Study of Education, 1981), 143-183.

[6]Harvey Siegel, "Critical Thinking as an Educational Ideal," *Educational Forum*, 45, 1, 1980: 7-23.

[7]David Perkins, "Reasoning as Imagination," *Interchange*, 16, 1, 1985: 15-16.

[8]Robert Ennis, "A Conception of Rational Thinking," in J. Coombs (ed.), *Philosophy of Education (Proceedings of the Philosophy of Education Society, U.S.A.)*, 1979, 5.

[9]Michael Scriven, *Reasoning* (New York: McGraw-Hill, 1976), 36.

[10]Richard Paul, "Teaching Critical Thinking in the Strong Sense: A Focus on Self-Deception, World Views, and a Dialectical Mode of Analysis," *Informal Logic*, 4, 2, 1982: 2-7.

[11]Richard Paul, "Critical Thinking and the Critical Person," in D. Perkins, J. Lockhead and J. Bishop (eds.), *Thinking: The Second International Conference* (Hillsdale, N.J. : Earlbaum, 1987), 373-403.

[12]E. de Bono, *The Mechanism of Mind*, 240.

[13]Richard Paul, "Critical Thinking and The Critical Person."

[14]Peter McKellar, *Imagination and Thinking* (London: Cohen and West, 1957), 116.

[15]I am grateful to Harvey Siegel and to Rodney Clifton for their helpful suggestions on the manuscript. An earlier version of this paper was presented at the Fourth International Conference on Critical Thinking and Educational Reform at Sonoma State University, Sonoma California, August, 1986.

6

The Community of Inquiry: Education for Democracy

Ann Margaret Sharp

In this essay I would like to focus on the classroom community of inquiry as an educational means of furthering the sense of community that is a pre-condition for actively participating in a democratic society. Such a community cultivates skills of dialog, questioning, reflective inquiry and good judgment. In the course of the essay, I will attempt to answer the following questions: When I enter a classroom, how do I know a community of inquiry is in formation? What behaviors are the students and teacher performing and what dispositions are manifest? What are some of the theoretical assumptions of these behaviors? And more importantly, what are some of the practical, social, ethical and political consequences of such behavior?

I will assume that a community of inquiry is characterized by *dialog* that is fashioned collaboratively out of the *reasoned* contribution of all participants. Over time, I assume that the classroom discussions will become more disciplined by *logical, epistemological, aesthetic, ethical, social* and *political* considerations that are applicable. In such a community, the teacher monitors the logical procedures but, in addition, philosophically becomes one of the community. Students learn to *object to weak reasoning, build on strong reasoning,* accept the responsibility of making their contributions within the context of others, accept their dependence upon others, follow the inquiry where it leads, respect the perspective of others, collaboratively engage in *self-correction* when necessary and take pride in the accomplishments of the group as well as oneself. Further, in the process, they practice the art of making *good judgments* within the context of dialog and communal inquiry.[1]

There are cognitive behaviors that can be observed: giving and asking for good reasons, making good distinctions and connections, making valid inferences, hypothesizing, generalizing, giving counter-examples, discovering assumptions, using and recognizing criteria, asking good questions, inferring consequences, recognizing logical fallacies, calling for relevance, defining concepts, seeking clarification, voicing implications, perceiving relationships, judging well, standardizing, using good analogies, sensitivity to context, offering alternative points of view, building logically on contributions of others and voicing fine discriminations.

Participants come to regard the production of knowledge as contingent, bound up with human interests and activities and therefore always open to revision. Further, students become more tolerant of complexity and ambiguity and recognize that justification for belief is rooted in *human action*. The human condition often might require that we make a provisional commitment to one belief or one course of action because of the need to act, but this in no way means that the particular belief can be justified as absolute truth. It is this need to act that calls for *good practical judgment* that will only be as good as one has been educated dialogically in making fine discriminations and learning how to do full justice to particular situations. Ultimately this capacity to judge is based on *communal civic sense* that is necessary for making moral and political judgments.[2] Such judgments are intersubjective and appeal to and require testing against the opinions of other judging persons.

Since there is no criterion, independent of various practical concerns, that will tell us when we have arrived at truth, and since knowledge is inescapably linguistic and inseparable from human activity, knowledge is a product of practical reasoning. It is for this reason that the acquisition and retention of knowledge must always be an *active* process.[3]

There are *social behaviors* that can be observed: listening to one another, supporting one another by amplifying and corroborating their views, submitting the views of others to critical inquiry, giving reasons to support another's view even if one doesn't agree, taking one another's ideas seriously by responding and encouraging each other to voice their views. A certain *care* is manifest in the group, not only care for the logical procedures but for the growth of each member of the community. This care presupposes the disposition to be open, to be capable of changing one's view and priorities in order to care for the other. In a real sense to care presupposes a willingness to be transformed by the other – to be affected by the other. This care is essential for dialog. But it is also essential for the *development of trust*, a basic orientation toward the world that accounts for the individuals coming to think they have a role to play in the world, that they can make a real difference. Further, the world is such a place that will receive not only their thoughts but their actions. Trust, in turn, is a pre-condition for the development of *autonomy* and *self-esteem* on the part of the individual participants. Care, then, makes possible a conception of the world as a play in which one can shape outcomes and create beauty where none has existed before.[4]

Participants appear to be capable of giving themselves to others, speaking when they think they have something relevant to say or when they think they have a responsibility for getting the dialog back on track. Students appear to have repudiated the *prima donna* role and seem able to collaborate and cooperate in inquiry. They can hear and receive what others have to say in such a way that meaning and vitality is shared.[5] They are free of the need always to be right. They have the courage and ability to change their minds and to hold their views tentatively. They do not appear defensive but rather delighted to be in a community of inquiry. With respect to the ideas of others, it implies also an openness to emerging truth, a giving of oneself in the broadest sense, even though one realizes that the truth one gains in the end is only provisional. To do this, students must be capable of coming to understand that they do not know many things, if anything at all.

There are *psychological* or *socio-psychological* characteristics that can be observed. These involve the growth of the self in relation to others, putting of the ego in perspective, disciplining of self-centredness and eventually the transforming of oneself. Participants refrain from engaging in extended monologues that preempt dialog or do not really call for a response. They know how to dialog with each other. Dialog implies a certain capacity for intellectual flexibility, self-correction and growth.[6] Have we not all had the experience of submitting a question to the group and then seeing emerge from the painful yet exciting dialog an insight or understanding that is far more profound than that offered by any single contribution? Such an event should not only be evaluated in terms of the product but in terms of the process – the relationships experienced during the course of the inquiry.

Teachers and participants can mute themselves in order to encourage others to speak their own ideas. They have the ability to let go of their positions in order to listen openly, hear and follow the inquiry where it leads. The latter requires letting truth emerge even though one knows it will be provisional and might require that one reconstruct one's own cherished belief-system. In a working community of inquiry, participants will move from considering themselves and their accomplishments as all important to focusing on the group and its accomplishments. They are not only conscious of their own thinking but begin examining and correcting each other's methods and procedures. Once they internalize the self-correcting methodology, they have the possibility of becoming critical thinkers – individuals who are open to self-correction, are sensitive to context and use criteria consciously in the making of practical judgments.[7]

The relationship of the individual to the community is thus inter-dependent. The success of the community is compatible with, and is dependent on, unique expressions of individuality. Yet, each participant accepts the discipline of making his or her contribution in the context of the contributions of others. This means accepting inter-dependence and repudiating an attitude of "knowing-it-all." The community will not function unless the participants can conform to the procedures of that community – logical and social. If one of the procedural principles is brought into question, other procedures must be adopted so that the discussion can proceed. Conformity is also manifest in a growing commitment to the underlying principles and practices that govern the enterprise itself: tolerance, consistency, comprehensiveness, open-mindedness, self-correction, conscious use of criteria, sensitivity to context and respect for all participants as potential sources of insight. Zaniness is tolerated only if it produces progress for the group's inquiry. If not constructive, the group will self-correct and eliminate the behavior. Often this is done with silence – not responding to behavior that blocks dialog or reflective inquiry.[8]

When one observes a functioning community of inquiry, one does not simply see a group nor simply individuals. What one observes is a community in which individual opinions are exchanged and serve as the source for further inquiry. Participants are capable of being fully *present* to each other in such a way that the entire meaning and vitality of the dialog is shared.[9] Participants do not talk about themselves but rather offer meanings to which others may make a response. They can take the risk of communicating. If the trust and care of the community are in place, the individual is far more likely to take this risk. And at times it is a real risk. One is exposing one's beliefs aware that one will probably be challenged and be forced to rethink one's position. This rethinking or restructuring takes time which means that there will be a period during which the individual will feel confused and perhaps insecure and maybe even frightened. I have seen shy students finally muster the courage to express their belief verbally only to have it fall to the floor with a thud of silence. And yet, many were capable of accepting the silence and trying again and again to make some kind of contribution to the on-going inquiry. Participants tend to refrain from voicing their views dogmatically. If one observes closely one sees that individual convictions more often relate to basic character, always in formation, rather than to knowledge claims.

Individuals in a community of inquiry must be able to hear and respond to the *meaning* of the dialog itself. Such meaning comes from two sources: (1) the participants willing to be involved in the inquiry and (2) the subject under discussion in light of the intellectual tradition of which we are all heirs. One must be willing to listen to the question behind the question, the fear behind the bravado, the insecurity behind the pretence, the courage behind the timidity, all of this being an essential component of the meaning of the dialog itself. Further, one must be able to see – to read the faces of the speakers and the non-speakers and to interpret what they are saying and not saying. Some might be silent because they have nothing to say. Others might be silent because they are afraid to voice their views. Others might be shy. Others might be afraid that their views will be challenged – this is a sign that something is wrong.

The breakdown of the community occurs when there is an obliteration of persons. This takes place when one person exploits another, that is, uses the relations that have been formed for any purpose other than its intended one: the pursuit of meaning and understanding and the furthering of the growth of each member of the community. To the extent that individuals engage in monologues, they block inquiry. To the extent that they make assumptions about what the other is going to say before the other has the opportunity to say it they block inquiry. To the extent that they engage in image making when another is speaking, they block inquiry. To the extent that they take it upon themselves to speak for others out of fear or insecurity, they destroy the trust essential for dialogical inquiry.

One purpose of the dialog among participants is to bring *vitality* or life to the *form* of the community of inquiry. Without this vitality, the form is empty or meaningless. Asking questions means nothing if one is not actively involved in the quest for understanding. Tension among members of the group may produce conflict but it is not itself conflict. For example, when violin strings have just the right tension, they can be used to produce beautiful music. Similarly, when a creative tension exists among participants a tension between the vitality of the many relationships and the form of the community of inquiry, the group has the potential for open debate, growth and each participant has the potential for self-transformation. Because tension is painful, we tend to want to get rid of it at any cost. Often we find ourselves choosing instead the mere form of a dialog, the mere form of communal inquiry. The purpose, however, of a community of inquiry is to restore the tension between vitality and form, to bring participants into deeper and more significant relationships, to shake them free of their complacency, their false convictions and to make them available for more comprehensive understanding.[10] Therefore, it follows that dialogical thinking within the community requires a willingness to be disturbed and to be challenged by the ideas of the other, a process of active reconstruction using criteria of comprehensiveness, coherence and consistency, together with sensitivity to the particularity of each situation.

As mentioned before, individuals in a community of inquiry have learned to hold their beliefs tentatively. Given the nature of human knowledge and justification – that is, to justify any belief we have to base our belief on another belief that is language-dependent – it is a matter of finding coherence among our beliefs and correspondence with the world. What I mean here is the world independent of language, perception and human understanding. But there is no such thing as knowledge of the world-as-it-really-is, since we can never be separated from the language and activities of particular groups or communities of human beings. Thus knowledge is always inescapably contingent, open to revision, and a matter of practical judgment. It is not a matter of aiming some mirror that is highly polished at the world as it really is and then passively noting the way things really are, independent of human practical concerns, social and personal. Rather, knowledge is an historical, linguistic and social *activity* and, as such, always open to self-correction as new data or evidence has to be taken into account. There is no ultimate foundation for our knowledge.[11] What we have is reason as a regulative ideal, and even the form of this reasoning process is open to revision within the context of questioning, dialog and *praxis*.

Thus, one could say that the community of inquiry provides a process of communication for the students, a moving back and forth between a narrower and wider framework, which may allow meaning and understanding to emerge and which each participant may be able to actively judge at the end, the dialog of the community itself. When one is actively involved in a community of inquiry, one assumes that subjective individual experience, as an unconsidered given, cannot reveal even provisional truth. It is the starting point of inquiry, not the end result. Further, the meanings that totally subjective experience do reveal are narrow and paltry compared to the meanings one can derive from communal inquiry.

Lastly, there are *moral* and *political* considerations that one must take into account when considering the nature of a community of inquiry. If we assume that the purpose of education is not only to transmit a body of knowledge but also to equip children with the skills and dispositions they need to create new knowledge and make better practical judgments, then the traditional classroom of "telling" is not appropriate. If we further assume that the purpose of education is the bringing into being of persons – persons of responsibility and integrity, persons of moral character who are capable of making wise judgments about what is right and wrong, beautiful and ugly, appropriate and inappropriate, then, if we are correct above, dialog becomes an inescapable instrument or means of education and the community of inquiry becomes a means and an end satisfying and worthwhile in itself, while at the same time giving rise to the traits essential for a morally discriminating person.

The community of inquiry requires not only perseverance and courage but all of the socratic virtues. It calls further for a commitment to stay with the group through its growth and change. It involves persons in a way of being-in-the-world aimed at struggling for understanding and self-knowledge by means of a process that is intersubjective. Further, the end products of such a community of inquiry are also intersubjective. However, in multiplying persons we do not simply multiply intelligences, experiences and perspectives. Rather we aim to produce practical knowledge in the *exchange* of perspectives, opinions, the sharing of experiences and the questioning of the assumptions of the beliefs that we do hold. Note that this is very unlike the working out of an argument. It is more akin to the playing of a quartet in which each instrument has an important role to perform in the production of the music. And, in all likelihood, there will be many quartets and many pieces of music played with integrity and beauty. The ideal of one universal community of inquiry embracing all of mankind is highly unlikely.[12] But this in no way invalidates the vision of many communities in which there is genuine inquiry, genuine participation of all human beings (rather than just white western men) with *open communication* between the various groups.[13]

Thus, the community of inquiry constitutes a *praxis* – reflective communal action – a way of acting on the world. It is a means of personal and moral transformation that inevitably leads to a shift in meanings and values which affect the daily judgments and actions of all participants. One striking characteristic of a community of inquiry over time is that its members change. In time, they will be capable of saying to themselves such things as:

• I find I'm no longer bullied into accepting views that lead to consequences that I think are harmful.

• I think I've always thought that way, but now I can explain why I think that way.

• I am no longer in need of pretending what I feel or what I think.

• My taste in many things is changing.

• I'm beginning to realize what patterns of behavior make more sense in my daily life.

• I can change my mind about matters of importance.

• What other people say can make a difference in what I think.

• I'm beginning to understand how very little I really know.

One can explain such claims as a slow progressive release from subjectivism, intellectual and social isolation, finding the world an alien and confusing place into discovering what it is to participate in a community of inquiry that enables one to live actively, reasonably and responsibly in the world rather than merely accepting it, escaping it or ignoring it. It's as if the process itself of participating *in* such a community becomes a sense-finding enterprise. Participants discover the moral guidelines they want to live by and the moral virtues they want to exemplify in their daily lives. They gain practice in making discriminating, sensitive and appropriate moral judgements. In a real sense they, at one and the same time, discover and create themselves as they inquire together – they discover and create the persons they think they ought to be.

Lastly, the commitment to engage in a community of inquiry is a *political* commitment even at the elementary school level. In a real sense, it is a commitment to freedom, open debate, pluralism, self-government and democracy. Practical reason, reflective inquiry and practical judgment reflected in communal political *praxis* presupposes that the people in the society have a sense of communal dialog and inquiry and a facility with the skills of such inquiry. It is only to the extent that individuals have had the experience of dialoging with others as equals, participating in shared, public inquiry that they will be able to eventually take an active role in the shaping of a democratic society. Shared understandings and experiences, intersubjective daily practices, a sense of affinity and solidarity, together with all the tacit affective ties that bind people together in a community are a *pre-condition* of communal reflection action in the political sphere.[14]

Thus, in answer to the question, "How can we further the type of community participation, dialog, inquiry and mutual recognition and respect that is presupposed in political communities?" one can propose the conversion of educational classrooms into communities of inquiry beginning with kindergarten and extending such a conversion right through graduate school experience. It is only in this way that the next generation will be prepared socially and cognitively to engage in the necessary dialog, judging and on-going questioning that is vital to the existence of a democratic society and the maintenance of the planet earth and survival of the species. In these times when the threat of nuclear extinction and ecological disaster is so very real, it is all the more crucial to try to foster and nurture classroom communities of inquiry at the elementary school level and throughout the educational experience so that the next generation will be able to act in such a way that the human community will not only continue to exist, but to exist in a more reasonable and just manner. Such a conversion of the educational institutional structure moves us beyond arguments and beyond theories into the realm of concrete actions aimed at changing the world for the better.

Notes

[1]See, Hannah Arendt, "Crisis in Culture: Its Social and Political Significance" in *Between Past and Future* (New York: Viking Press, 1961), 197-226. Arendt goes on to say "that the ability to judge is a specifically political ability in exactly the sense denoted by Kant, namely, the ability to see things not only from one's own point of view but in the perspective of all those who happen to be present: even judgment may be one of the fundamental abilities of man as political being insofar as it enables him to orient himself in the public realm, in the common world." (221) See, also Richard Bernstein, "Judging the Actor and the Spectator," in Robert Boyers (ed.), *Proceedings*

of History, Ethics, Politics: A Conference Based on the Work of Hannah Arendt (Saratoga Springs N.Y.: Empire State, 1982.) Also see Michael Dennery, "The Privilege of Ourselves: Hannah Arendt on Judgment," in R. Boyers (ed.), *Proceedings of History, Ethics, Politics*, 245-274; and Hannah Arendt, *The Life of the Mind* (New York: H.B. Jovanovich, 1978) Volume I and II.

[2]This communal civic sense is what John Dewey calls *taste*. See *The Quest For Certainty* (New York: Minton, Balch, 1929), 262. Also for a development of the same idea see John Dewey, *Art as Experience* (New York: Minton, Balch, 1934).

[3]Richard Rorty, *Consequences of Pragmatism* (Minneapolis: University of Minnesota Press, 1982), xii-xxxix.

[4]I am indebted to Monica Velasca from Guadalajara, Mexico for innumerable comments on the importance of care in the community of inquiry contained in her various papers submitted as a requirement for the degree of Masters of Arts in Teaching Philosophy for Children, Fall and Spring, 1988-89. For a philosophical analysis of the status of "Being-As-Care," see Martin Heidegger, *Being and Time* (New York: Harper and Row, 1962), 235-241. And for a psychological analysis of the importance of care in the cultivation of trust, autonomy and self esteem, see Erik Erikson, *Childhood and Society* (New York: Norton, 1950) and *Insight and Responsibility*.

[5]See Martin Buber, *Between Man and Man.* (New York: Norton Press, 1964). In this volume one can find two essays, one on "Education," and the other on "The Education of Character." Both speak to the role of dialog in education.

[6]See, Martin Buber, *I and Thou* (New York: Scribners, 1970) Part I.

[7]Here I am indebted to Matthew Lipman, "Critical Thinking: What Can It Be?" *Educational Leadership*, 46, 1, 1988, 38-43.

[8]Here I am indebted to James Heinegg, "The Individual and the Community of Inquiry," ms. submitted as requirement for the degree of Master of Arts in Teaching Philosophy for Children at Montclair State College, Fall of 1988.

[9]Buber says, "The present exists only insofar as presentness, encounter and relation exist. Only as the You becomes present does presence come into being." (*I and Thou*, 63).

[10]I am indebted to Ronald Reed, who pointed out to me that John Dewey, in "My Pedagogic Creed" (Reprinted in Reginald D. Archambault (ed.), *John Dewey on Education: Selected Writings* (New York: Random House, 1964), talks about vitality in relation to informal education. One could argue that a good classroom dialog is modelled on what one finds in an informal environment, conversations that deal with real problems and real concerns of the participants. Usually such discussions focus on real questions that the participants have a stake in getting it right. However, in the informal environment no one looks askance if one excuses oneself because one is no longer interested in talking. But the child in the classroom cannot do this. Once the child loses interest (if he or she ever had any) he or she tends to be condemned to play the spectator role. Dewey's point is that active participation and involvement in the discussion seems to go together with vitality and mere spectating seems to go together with dry sterility.

[11]When I say that there is no ultimate philosophical foundation for our knowledge, I am relying here on Rorty, in particular. See Richard Rorty, *Philosophy and the Mirror of Nature* (Minneapolis: University of Minnesota Press, 1982). For the argument of reason as a regulative ideal, see Hilary Putnam, "Why Reason can't be Naturalized," *Synthese*, 52, 1, 1982: 1-23. For an argument against complete relativism, see Alasdair

MacIntyre, "Relativism, Power and Philosophy," the Presidential Address delivered before the 81st Annual Eastern Division Meeting of the American Philosophical Association in New York, December 29, 1984, in *Proceedings and Addresses of the American Philosophical Association,* (Newark, Delaware: APA, 1985), 5-22; and his postscript to the second edition of *After Virtue* (Notre Dame, Indiana: University of Notre Dame Press, 1984), 265-272. Also see MacIntyre, *Whose Justice? Which Rationality?* (Notre Dame IN: University of Notre Dame Press, 1988, 1-11, 370-388, and 389-403). Also see: Richard Rorty, "The Contingency of Language," *London Review of Books* (April 17, 1986), 3; Bernard Williams, *Ethics and the Limits of Philosophy,* (Cambridge: Harvard University Press, 1985); and Richard Bernstein, *Beyond Objectivism and Relativism* (Philadelphia, University of Philadelphia Press, 1983).

In my previous article, "What is a Community of Inquiry?," *Journal of Moral Education,* 16, 1, 1987: 37-45, I argued that the community of inquiry is not condemned to relativism and endless self-correction, that some progress can be made and that the concepts of truth and justification cannot be reduced to the conceptual scheme of the tradition. Rorty thinks that all we have is the dialog itself, the endless conversation spoken within the philosophical tradition. Further, he and others think the dialog in connection with the establishment of local communities is sufficient to make the world more reasonable. Other philosophers, like Hilary Putnam, Jurgen Habermas and Alasdair MacIntyre, disagree. Putnam argues that the very fact that we can speak of our different conceptions as different conceptions of rationality posits truth. The very fact that we can agree that some thinkers in the past have been wrong-headed, presupposes that reason can serve as a regulative ideal. (See: *Reason, Truth and History* (Cambridge: Cambridge University Press, 1982), 163-216.)

In this essay, I argue that dialogical thinking and speaking takes courage, letting the truth emerge even if it forces one to reconstruct one's own cherished beliefs. (When I use the word "truth," I mean "warranted assertion" – Dewey's term.) No one captures this idea of the necessary courage more than Alasdaire MacIntyre in his APA presidential address (1984):

> What can liberate rationality is precisely an acknowledgement only possible from within a certain kind of tradition, that rationality requires a *readiness* on our part to accept, and indeed to welcome, a possible future defeat of the forms of theory and practice in which it has up till now been taken to be embodied within our own tradition, at the hands of some alien and perhaps even as yet largely unintelligible tradition of thought and practice; and this is an acknowledgement of which the traditions that we inherit have too seldom been capable.

It is just this disposition of "readiness" that the community of inquiry cultivates in the young child.

[12]As Alasdair MacIntyre contends: "What matters at this stage is the construction of local forms of community within which civility and the intellectual and moral life can be sustained." *After Virtue,* 244.

[13]Here see the works of Hans-Georg Gadamer and Habermas on communication and the need for community. In particular, Gadamer's autobiographical sketch, *Philosophische Lehrjahre* (Frankfurt am Main: Vittoria Klostermann, 1977); *Truth and Method* (New York: Seabury Press, 1975), 306-310, and 278-89; and for a treatment of practical judgment, "Problem of Historical Consciousness," in Paul Rabinow and William M. Sullivan (eds.) *Interpretive Social Science: a Reader* (Berkeley, CA:

University of California Press, 1979), 120-30. And Habermas, "Dialectics of Rational-ization:An Interview," *Telos*, 49, 1981: 7; "A Reply to My Critics," in John B. Thompson and David Held, *Habermas:Critical Debates* (Cambridge, MA: M.I.T. Press, 1982), 263-269.

I am also indebted to a paper, "Community of Inquiry," by Marcello Marer, from San Paulo, Brazil, submitted in requirement for the Masters of Arts in Philosophy for Children, Montclair State College, Spring 1989. In this paper, Marer tries to show the Peircean foundations of the concept, "Community of Inquiry," and the way in which the theory of Habermas plays an important role in the theoretical foundations of the concept, "community of inquiry," as it is used in Philosophy for Children.

[14]See Richard Bernstein, *Beyond Objectivism and Relativism: Science, Hermeneu-tics and Praxis* (Philadelphia: University of Pennsylvania Press, 1983), 171-231. In this section, Bernstein discusses *praxis* and practical discourse as seen in the works of Rorty, Gadamer, Habermas and Hannah Arendt.

7

Is Modern Critical Thinking Theory Sexist?

Barbara Thayer-Bacon

Introduction

The operating paradigm of critical thinking and what is considered intelligent thought can be traced back to Aristotle.[1] It is a paradigm that stresses critical thinking as a process based in logic where facts are separated from opinion, and the process of critical thinking is seen as a sequence of steps in which the critical thinker remains objective, and distanced from what is being examined. Critical thinking, as described, is used as the tool to guide and help philosophers (or others using critical thinking) arrive at Truth and Certainty.

I am developing a model of critical thinking which stresses the impossibility of separating the self from the object, and calls attention to the fact that this impossibility, this objectified illusion, reflects back an image of self as autonomous and severed from the outside world of other subjects as well as severed from one's own subjectivity. The idea that the subject can be detached from the object is the core of the problem with the current paradigm of critical thinking. One can even argue, as I wish to do so here, that the operating critical thinking paradigm is sexist. For, not only does it separate the self from the object and cause one to lose touch with one's own personal voice, in order to try to develop an objectified, expert voice; it has also historically passed judgment on those who tend to try to listen to their inner voice (women) and said such a way of thinking was inferior, for it didn't follow the dominant paradigm of what has been said to constitute knowledge. To separate the self from the object, or attempt to do so, for I have argued elsewhere that it isn't really possible to even accomplish that goal, is very dangerous because it leaves people feeling severed and distant from each other and from the world they depend on for life.[2] Aside from the dangers of attempting such an impossible separating task, are the dangers that result when a dominating paradigm, due to its sheer dominance, silences and marginalizes other ways of thinking. Many feminists have argued that philosophy's traditional epistemology is a form of patriarchal epistemology, which leads to the control of knowledge, and the ways of knowing, by men, and the silencing or devaluing/subordinating of women's ways of knowing.[3] Indeed, the study of women's ways of knowing by Belenky et al.[4] models what has happened to women's thinking, under the traditional patriarchal epistemology: they have been silenced, or taught to refer to other, male, authorities; maybe they have learned to rely on their own "women's intuition" (which has been viewed by others, men, as "magic" or "nonsense"); or they have, if given enough opportunity for education, learned to defer to the male voice of reason. Very few have learned how to be constructive thinkers, able to listen to their own inner voice, as well as their expert, authority voice, with the confidence that they, as thinkers, are able to construct knowledge.

The basic insight about knowing that I am working with is the idea that we need to reclaim the self and attempt to integrate personal knowledge and expert knowledge. My sources for this insight come from work in feminist theory that stresses interrelationships, connections, and that knowledge and all methods we have of obtaining it are human constructions.[5] Other sources for my work come from our American pragmatists, Peirce and Dewey, and our most recent pragmatist/postmodernist, Rorty.[6] Peirce's notion of fallibilism encourages us to think of truth as something that is emerging and evolving, and that we, as knowers, are participating in the construction of truth. Dewey stresses, in his principle of interaction, the interaction between the subject and the object, between the individual and the environment. The principle of interaction "assigns equal rights to both factors in experience – objective and internal conditions."[7] Rorty has added greatly to this work with his sound defeat of the monster, "privileged access to knowledge." He has left us wondering how it is we know, and has encouraged us to look at notions like epistemology, rationality and critical thinking in new ways.

This essay will attempt to make a contribution toward changing attitudes about what constitutes knowledge. I will address how we have thought about thinking in critical thinking theory by taking a look at four current critical thinking theories from a feminist perspective, specifically Robert Ennis, John McPeck, Harvey Siegel, and Richard Paul's theories.[8] I would like to follow the same method Noddings modeled recently in *Women and Evil*[9] when she chose a very old topic, evil, and looked at it anew, from a woman's perspective. With this approach, I hope to show what's sexist about critical thinking theory, and what a feminist would suggest needs to be done to correct the error(s).

The Theories

Robert Ennis

Robert Ennis is usually credited as rekindling the current interest in critical thinking, with an article he wrote for The *Harvard Educational Review* in 1962, titled "A Concept of Critical Thinking."[10] He originally defined critical thinking as "the correct assessment of statements."[11] The focus of this article was to identify twelve aspects, and three dimensions of critical thinking, and elaborate a system of criteria to be applied in this form of thinking. The goal behind identifying aspects of critical thinking, was to help us avoid making errors, and to enable us to correctly assess statements. His list of proficiencies is the most detailed, complex, and useful to be developed. Yet his original definition confused process with product. The assessing of statements is a process, that the assessing is correct is the product of that assessing.

Subsequently, Ennis revised his definition of critical thinking, in response to criticism, to "reasonable reflective thinking that is focused on deciding what to believe or do."[12] This definition is not meant to exclude creative thinking, but, the focus is on critical thinking as a practical activity that has reasonable belief or action as its goal, and Ennis still focuses on listing fourteen dispositions, and twelve basic types of abilities required of a critical thinker. This newer definition includes abilities and dispositions, rather than just abilities, as his earlier article seemed to suggest, to ensure that it is not enough just to have the necessary skills to be a critical thinker, one must also have the tendency to use these skills.

What does Ennis's theory of critical thinking look like, from a feminine perspective? His list of dispositions a critical thinker must have include: seek a clear statement of the thesis or question, seek reasons, try to be well informed, use and mention credible sources, take into account the total situation, try to remain relevant to the main point, keep in mind the original and/or basic concern, look for alternatives, be open-minded (defined as using dispositional thinking, dialogical thinking, and withholding judgment if the evidence and reasons are insufficient), take a position (and change a position) when the evidence and reasons are sufficient to do so, seek as much precision as the subject permits, deal in an orderly manner with the parts of a complex whole, use one's critical thinking abilities, be sensitive to the feelings, level of knowledge, and degree of sophistication of others.

Ennis's list of abilities required for a critical thinker are all of the logical sort: focusing on a question, analyzing arguments, asking and answering questions of clarification and/or challenge, judging the credibility of a source, observing and judging observation reports, deducing and judging deductions, inducing and judging inductions, making value judgments, defining terms and judging definitions in three dimensions, identifying assumptions, deciding on an action, interacting with others (in terms of employing and reacting to fallacy labels, logical strategies, rhetorical strategies, argumentation).[13]

A constructive thinker is someone who has a high tolerance for internal contradiction and ambiguity, one who is able to live with conflict. She moves beyond systems but puts systems to her own service. For the basic insight of a constructive knower is, "all knowledge is constructed, and the knower is an intimate part of the known."[14] The truth is viewed as a process of construction in which the knower participates. Characteristics of constructive knowers are: they open the mind and the heart to embrace the world; they become aware and stay aware of the workings of their minds, this awareness is vital to their sense of well-being; they have the potential to be sympathetic, attentive, caring of people, written word, even impersonal objects; they establish a communion with what they are trying to understand, and use a language of intimacy to describe the relationship between the knower and the known; they use "real talk" instead of didactic talk, where domination is absent and reciprocity and cooperation are prominent, where the goal is to share one's ideas and the process of one's thinking; question posing is central to their way of knowing; and the moral response is a caring response.[15]

I think one can anticipate the problems with Ennis's list of characteristics, versus the one above for a constructive thinker. His focus is on logical skills, and the abilities he mentions are ones most of us would consider to be abilities required of a logical thinker. But where is the mention of the need to know oneself and what one contributes to the knowing? Where is the mention of feelings and relational skills that are necessary to help open not just one's mind, but also one's heart to the world, including objects, and other people? Where is the mention of a need to be caring of others? I suspect Ennis would wonder what caring has to do with critical thinking, but most of us who have been in vulnerable, subordinated, marginalized roles know how hard it is to even submit reasons for consideration in an argument, when we don't feel like the person really cares to hear what we have to say. Caring is value-giving, whereas blind justice (Ennis's judgment) is unwilling to consider context; it is absolutisizing, and silencing. Ennis's theory follows the traditional paradigm for knowing, and leaves no room for subjectivity, feelings, or contextuality. Constructive knowers have no voice here.

John McPeck

For John McPeck, critical thinking is a subset of rational thinking. Rational thinking is "the *intelligent use of all available evidence* for the solution of some problem."[16] Critical thinking occurs only when one encounters a problem in using that available evidence, such as the need to decide what is to "count" as evidence, or the decision to "disregard" some portion of the available evidence. Critical thinking is "the disposition and skill to find such difficulties in the normal course of reasoning."[17] If rational thought is the intelligent use of evidence to solve a problem, and critical thinking is how we determine intelligent use, the judging of evidence, then one can see that for McPeck critical thinking is context and content specific. In order to be able to judge evidence, one must have the know-how of the specific subject area; one must have the necessary information, which may require being an expert in the subject, to be able to determine intelligent use. This is McPeck's argument, and it set up a debate between theorists such as Ennis and Paul, who argued that critical thinking is a general skill, not necessarily subject specific, and that McPeck's approach to critical thinking was atomistic,[18] and theorists such as Siegel, who argued McPeck was right and Ennis/Paul were right, critical thinking was both a general and specific skill.[19]

McPeck has recently published a book, *Teaching Critical Thinking*, in which one can find his general view remains the same, "that specific subject content determines the required ingredients for thinking critically in each case."[20] McPeck's main theoretical points are: that thinking is always thinking about some particular thing or subject; that an effective thinker in one area is not necessarily an effective thinker in all other areas; that critical thinkers are people who think for themselves, and have the relevant knowledge and understanding to help them do so. He argues that critical thinking is not a general ability or a specific skill, but that it contains a knowledge component and a critical component.

In focusing our attention on the point that one needs information, expert knowledge, in order to be able to make judgments of the kind Ennis lists, and in arguing that this knowledge is context specific, a feminist might want to applaud McPeck for at least recognizing the contextuality of knowing. And for that, via the late Wittgenstein's influence on McPeck's view of logic[21] I am grateful. But McPeck's view of critical thinkers as information gatherers, offers no notice to the inner voice, and what the knower contributes to the knowing, as part of the necessary information. Subjectivity, and the idea that we, as subjects, are part of the context the knower specifically needs to know in order to be a critical thinker, is not discussed by McPeck. Therefore, his theory creates no room for a constructive thinker either.

Harvey Siegel

Harvey Siegel has taken Israel Scheffler's notion of rationality, "the ability to participate in critical and open evaluation of rules and principles in any area of life,"[22] and incorporated it in *Educating Reason*.[23] Siegel's argument is that, to seek reasons, one has to recognize and commit oneself to principles, for principles are needed to determine the relevance and strength of reasons: "Because of this connection between reasons and principles, critical thinking is principled thinking; because principles involve consistency, critical thinking is impartial, consistent, and non-arbitrary, and the critical thinker both acts and thinks in accordance with, and values, consistency, fairness, and impartiality of judgment and action."[24]

One can hear warning bells going off from the postmodern philosophical camp, with Siegel's definition, and his obvious essentialistic tendencies. Postmodernists, such as Rorty's central challenge to the modern tradition, have dealt with this claim of being able to accurately represent reality (be impartial, consistent, and non-arbitrary). Rorty, and others such as Kuhn[25] have made us well aware of the fact that we are all contextual knowers, we are all affected by political, social, psychological, and historical forces, and cannot represent ourselves as neutral agents of knowledge. Yes, we have experiences we can test for correspondence, and ideas we can check for coherence, but there is a subjective side to all of this we can never dismiss. We can never get out of our skins, and lose our "I," we can never stop filtering what we know through our contextuality of time and place. Indeed, who we are has been developed through the context of being social beings, who use language and language-based thinking. Due to this understanding, a representational theory of knowledge has been abandoned by many; the "truth" of the text is no longer any more significant as a criterion of adequacy than other contextual variables, such as political, social, psychological and historical variables.

Putting Siegel's strong modernist tendencies aside, he does have more to say about critical thinkers. There are two dimensions to critical thinking, the reason assessment component and the critical spirit component. Siegel believes both components are necessary and sufficient for a definition of critical thinking. He defines the characteristics of critical thinking: "the focus on reasons and the power of reasons to warrant or justify beliefs, claims, and actions. A critical thinker, then is one who is *appropriately moved by reasons*: she has a propensity or disposition to believe and act in accordance with reasons; and she has the ability properly to assess the force of reasons in the many contexts in which reasons play a role."[26] Critical thinking is coextensive with rationality, according to Siegel, not just a dimension of it, "for rationality and critical thinking are both coextensive with the relevance of reasons."[27]

In looking more closely at the two necessary components of critical thinking, the reason assessment component is one that encompasses the fact that a critical thinker must be able to assess reasons and their ability to warrant beliefs, claims and actions properly. In order to do this, Siegel argues that a critical thinker must have a good understanding of both subject-specific and subject-neutral (logical) principles that govern the assessment of reasons, and be able to use them. For Siegel, this means a critical thinker must understand epistemology, for epistemology is the general study of reasons, warrants, and justification. Basically he is agreeing with Ennis and McPeck, and my comments concerning the reason assessment component are the same as what I said about their theories.

What I find interesting in Siegel's theory is the critical spirit component. The critical spirit component of critical thinking means that in order to be a critical thinker a person must have "certain attitudes, dispositions, habits of mind and character traits."[28] It is not enough to know how to assess reasons, a person must also be disposed to do so. Siegel conveys that a critical thinker acts in certain ways and is a certain sort of person. Aside from having a love of reasons, a willingness to conform judgment and action to reasons, even one's most deeply held convictions (which, we will see, is Paul's point in his strong-sense critical thinking) Siegel says "a person who is a critical thinker must be, to the greatest extent possible, emotionally secure, self-confident, and capable of distinguishing between having faulty beliefs and having a faulty character. A positive self-image, and traditionally-conceived psychological health, are important features of the psychology of the critical thinker, for their absence may well present practical obstacles to the execution of critical thinking."[29] It is here that we first find mention of the inner voice of the critical thinker. In Siegel's theory, he acknowledges that people subjectively contribute qualities that can help make them better critical thinkers, or not. One might be able to retranslate what he has said to my constructive thinking description that it is important to become aware and stay aware of the workings of one's own mind. Siegel does acknowledge that subjective knowing is important, but only because if one is not psychologically healthy, it will get in the way of one being able to be a critical thinker. If one doesn't feel good about oneself, or is lacking in confidence, this sickness can become an obstacle to good assessment of reasons. Where at first glance it appeared we were leaning in a feminist direction with Siegel's theory, it turns out there is no acknowledgment that the self, whether healthy or not, is all any of us have to work with, and work with it we must. If pushed on this issue, since he has opened the door a little, it may be that he would agree with me on this matter, and actually open the door wide, to embrace the self, in all her glory, faults and perfections included.

Richard Paul

Richard Paul calls attention to the possibility of degrees/levels of critical thinking, one which is weak and one which is strong.[30] Weak sense critical thinking is "disciplined to serve the interests of a particular individual or group, to the exclusion of their relevant persons and groups," and strong sense critical thinking is "disciplined to take into account the interests of diverse persons or groups."[31] With Paul's distinction between weak and strong sense critical thinking, he makes us very aware that one is not either a critical thinker or not, as other theorists have tended to emphasize. (See Siegel's consistency principle above.) One can use her critical thinking skills just to find fault with others' arguments, and support for one's own, or one can use those same skills to attempt to understand others' points of view more clearly, and to reflect on one's own point of view more critically. Paul is credited by Siegel with pointing out the need for a critical thinker to have a certain disposition, indeed have certain character traits, such as: developing intellectual humility and suspending judgment, developing intellectual courage and good faith or integrity, developing intellectual perseverance and confidence in reason. It's not enough to be adept at critical thinking skills, one must also have the disposition to use those skills. We saw with Ennis's theory, above, that he made changes in his definition to include dispositions, probably in response to Paul's (and Siegel's) point. Central to Paul's theory is the notion that people by nature are egocentric and ethnocentric,[32] and that our tendency is to be irrational; we have to work very hard to be rational, critical thinkers – it doesn't come easy for us.

A problem with Paul's distinction between weak and strong sense critical thinking is that he is confusing about what he means by strong sense critical thinking. Weak sense critical thinking, since it is by definition not consistently being applied to one's own thinking, would not be labelled critical thinking by other theorists such as Siegel. With strong sense critical thinking, at times, Paul stresses a combative approach to critical thinking. At other times he stresses a nurturing, supportive approach to critical thinking. Paul's (stronger) strong sense critical thinking leaves one always feeling like there is a hedging because one does not know if one has ever thought strongly enough. The stronger version of strong sense critical thinking functions best as an ideal we can all attempt to strive for. Paul's (weaker) strong sense critical thinking, in emphasizing the need to understand other people's perspectives and world views, leans in the direction of relationships and caring. It leans toward stressing interconnections and relatedness, and contextual relativism. One can find the possibility of a feminine perspective in Paul's critical thinking theory. This is what drew me originally to his theory, in my own development of a critical thinking theory.

The problem with Paul's theory, and what ends up getting in the way of his recognizing thinkers as constructive knowers, is his notion of the self. Paul recognizes the thinker's subjectivity in a negative way, as did Siegel, above. For Paul, our natural tendency is to be egocentric, meaning self-centred, and to use reasons to score points, defeat others, and make our own point of view look good. The fact that we have perspectives ultimately makes us selfish and just gets in our way. His distinction between weak and strong sense critical thinking focuses on whether the skills of critical thinking are used to support one's own position, and these remain extrinsic to the character of the person, or if these skills become intrinsic to the character of the person, and are used to add insight into one's own affective and cognitive processes. His stress is on removing the self from the critical thinking process, in order to try to fairly understand others' points of views, and to apply the same critical thinking skills on ourselves that we use to judge other positions. It is easy to anticipate a feminist response to Paul's theory, that in trying to remove oneself, and understand others' standpoints, one will end up feeling like a chameleon, able to remove her own voice to understand others', but losing, or at least weakening, her own identity in the process. Also, a postmodernist would add, removing the voice is impossible!

Conclusion

We have seen that in the current field of critical thinking, there are many examples of definitions of critical thinking. Ennis stresses skills, Siegel focuses on rationality, McPeck points to critical thinking being domain specific rather than generally applicable, and Paul calls attention to the possibility of degrees/levels of critical thinking, one which is weak and one which is strong. All of these current theories presented function under the dominant paradigm that critical thinking is a process based in logic where facts are separated from opinion; the model being used is the scientific method, in which the critical thinker remains objective, distancing herself from what she is examining. There is a move, though, amongst current theorists such as Paul, and Siegel, to take more seriously what the critical thinker contributes to the knowing situation. Paul and Siegel have emphasized that critical thinking involves a subject, a person, who needs to use the critical thinking skills gained through education, and learn to apply these skills to her life. But none of them seem to have approached the question, what happens in the process of learning and using critical thinking skills, what does the person contribute to knowledge? Richard Paul comes closest to this question with his focus on people's tendency to be egocentric and use critical thinking skills to bolster their own point of view, rather than critiquing their perspective. But Paul's focus on what the knower contributes to knowledge is a negative focus. His goal is to encourage critical thinkers to remove their own perspective as much as possible so that they can as fairly as possible listen to and try to understand another's point of view. This is not what I am striving for.

My desire is to encourage self-awareness as a part of the development of critical thinking skills, with the understanding that one cannot divorce oneself from one's own point of view. Instead of viewing the self's contribution (subjective knowing) as something that is distracting or prejudicial to critical thinking, I am arguing that what one contributes is necessary (impossible to remove) and adds contextually to the knowing. The alternative model of constructive theory presented here is very important because it opens the doors wide to all people and their different, varied voices. It encourages contribution by all to the conversation on what can be considered agreed-upon knowledge.

This essay I hope is a contribution toward changing attitudes about what constitutes knowledge. We come to know in relation with others, even learning how to use language and developing thought happens because we are social beings in relation with each other. We don't come to know by separating our self and isolating our thoughts, detaching and objectifying our voice. Thinking we can do that and therefore be able to arrive at Truth and Certainty is very dangerous and destructive. Thinking that we all affect each other and that we can arrive at knowledge when we can agree, will lead us to harmony and living together in this world, rather than fighting against each other for a little piece of this world. It will encourage constructive thinking, equality, and the development of responsibility and caring. It should help us continue to grow and work towards peace, which is my ultimate concern.

Notes

[1] M. Horner, "Toward an Understanding of Achievement-related Conflicts in Women," in J. Stacey et al. (eds.), *And Jill Came Tumbling After* (New York: Dell Publishing, 1974), 43-62.

[2] Barbara Thayer-Bacon, "A Feminine Reconceptualization of Critical Thinking," *Journal of Thought*, 27, 3&4, 1992.

[3] Dale Spender, *Women of Ideas and What Men Have Done to Them* (Winchester, MA: Pandora Press, 1982).

[4] Mary Field Belenky, Blythe McVicker Clinchy, Nancy Rule Goldberger, and Jill Mattuck Tarule, *Women's Ways of Knowing: The Development of Self, Voice, and Mind* (New York: Basic Books, 1986).

[5] See: Charlotte Bunch and Sandra Pollack (eds.), *Learning Our Way: Essays in Feminist Education* (Trumasburg, NY: The Crossing Press, 1983); Carol Gilligan, *In a Different Voice* (Cambridge, MA: Harvard University Press, 1982); Jean Grimshaw, *Philosophy and Feminist Thinking* (Minneapolis, MN: University of Minnesota Press, 1986); Belenky, Clinchy, Goldberger, and Tarule, *Women's Ways of Knowing: The Development of Self, Voice, and Mind*; Nel Noddings, *Caring: A Feminine Approach to Ethics and Moral Education* (Berkeley, CA: University of California Press, 1984); Nel Noddings, *Women and Evil* (Berkeley, CA: University of California Press, 1989); and Sara Ruddick, *Maternal Thinking: Toward a Politics of Peace* (Boston: Beacon Press, 1989).

[6]Charles Sanders Peirce, *Values in a Universe of Chance: Selected Writings of Charles Sanders Peirce (1839-1914)*, edited by Philip P. Wiener, (Garden City, NJ: Doubleday & Co, Inc., 1958); John Dewey, *Experience and Education* (New York: Macmillan, 1938); John Dewey *How We Think* (Lexington, MA: D.C.Heath, 1933); and Richard Rorty, *Philosophy and the Mirror of Nature* (Princeton, NJ: Princeton University Press, 1979).

[7]John Dewey, *Experience and Education*, 45.

[8]Robert Ennis, "A Concept of Critical Thinking," *Harvard Educational Review*, 32, 1, 1962: 81-111; Robert Ennis, "A Taxonomy of Critical Thinking Dispositions and Abilities," in Joan Boykoff Baron and Robert Sternberg (eds.), *Teaching Thinking Skills: Theory and Practice* (New York: W. H. Freeman, 1987), 9-26; Harvey Siegel, *Educating Reason* (New York: Routledge, 1988); John McPeck, *Critical Thinking and Education* (New York: St. Martin's Press, 1981); and Richard Paul, *Critical Thinking: What Every Person Needs in a Rapidly Changing World* (Sonoma, CA: Sonoma State University, 1990).

[9]Nel Noddings, *Women and Evil* (Berkeley, CA: University of California Press, 1989).

[10]Robert Ennis, "A Concept of Critical Thinking," *Harvard Educational Review*, 32, 1, 1962: 81-111.

[11]Ibid., 83.

[12]R. Ennis, "A Taxonomy of Critical Thinking Dispositions and Abilities," 10.

[13]See, R. Ennis, "A Taxonomy of Critical Thinking Dispositions and Abilities," 12-15.

[14]Belenky et al., *Women's Ways of Knowing*, 137.

[15]See Belenky et al., *Women's Ways of Knowing*, 141-146.

[16]John McPeck, *Critical Thinking and Education*, 12.

[17]Ibid.

[18]See Richard Paul, "McPeck's Mistakes," in John McPeck, *Teaching Critical Thinking* (New York: Routledge, 1990), 102-111.

[19]See Harvey Siegel, *Educating Reason*.

[20]John McPeck, *Teaching Critical Thinking*, xiv.

[21]McPeck discusses this in *Teaching Critical Thinking*.

[22]Israel Scheffler, *Reason and Teaching* (Indianapolis: Bobbs-Merrill, 1973), 62.

[23]Harvey Siegel, *Educating Reason*.

[24]Ibid., 34.

[25]Thomas Kuhn, *The Structure of Scientific Revolutions*, 2nd. edition, (Chicago: University of Chicago Press, 1970).

[26]H. Siegel, *Educating Reason*, 23. The italics are Siegel's as well as the feminine pronoun, her. Siegel uses feminine pronouns consistently throughout his writings and I do want to thank him for that gesture.

[27]Ibid., 30.

[28]Ibid., 39.

[29]Ibid., 29.

[30]Richard Paul, *Critical Thinking: What Every Person Needs to Survive in a Rapidly Changing World*.

[31]Ibid., 185.

[32]Paul discusses his notion of egocentrism in most of his writings, but a good example can be found in, "Critical Thinking and the Critical Person," in *Critical Thinking: What Every Person Needs in a Rapidly Changing World*, 114-115.

8

The Role of Reasons in (Science) Education

Harvey Siegel

In these days of educational reform – which days seem to be always upon us, either in virtue of our desire to try something new, or to return to practices and aims once rejected but now seen as tried and true – much is made of the notion of critical thinking as a target of such reform.[1] How to understand this notion, however, and how to conceive of its place in education, are more than a little unclear. What is critical thinking? What is it to be a critical thinker? What is the role of critical thinking in education? What is its role in inquiry? Is that role constant across disciplines, or do different disciplines utilize alternative and incompatible critical techniques? If the latter, then how can critical thinking function as a general educational ideal?

In what follows I hope to shed some light on these and other questions concerning critical thinking. I shall present a conception of critical thinking according to which critical thinking is very closely linked to the notions of *reasons* and *rationality*. I shall argue that critical thinking, so conceived, is rightly regarded as an educational ideal which is general and relevant to all disciplines. While not denying that disciplines differ, in their aims, criteria, principles of assessment, or techniques of inquiry, I shall argue nevertheless that critical thinking is rightly conceived as an ideal that transcends disciplinary boundaries, and that unifies and makes sense of the melange of discipline-bound activities and curricula that we know as education. After clarifying the notion of critical thinking and its place in education and as an educational ideal, I shall illustrate its impact on the disciplines by considering its role in science education. I shall conclude, finally, by suggesting that critical thinking, contrary to the familiar distinction drawn at the outset, is an ideal which is both new *and* tried and true.[2]

What Is Critical Thinking?

When we say that we want our students to be critical thinkers, or that we want our educational efforts to foster critical thinking, what exactly do we mean? Any sort of systematic answer to these questions requires that we focus on *reasons* and their role in thinking. To say of an episode of thinking that it constitutes critical thinking is to say something about its responsiveness to relevant reasons or rational considerations. Similarly, to say of a student that she is a critical thinker is to say that her thinking is generally carried out in accordance with, and adequately reflects due and proper consideration of, matters which bear relevantly on the rational resolution of whatever her thinking concerns. Critical thinking is thinking which adequately reflects relevant reasons; a critical thinker is one whose thinking is similarly reflective of reasons. We can say, in short, that a critical thinker is one who is *appropriately moved by reasons*, and that critical thinking is thinking which appropriately reflects the power and convicting force of reasons.

This conception of critical thinking – the "reasons" conception – places reasons at its centre; taking critical thinking as an important educational notion places reasons at the centre of our conception of the nature and purpose of education. We might even go so far as to say that critical thinking is properly regarded as a fundamental educational ideal which informs the entire range of our educational activities and aspirations. On such a view reasons are central to our educational efforts, and those efforts are conceived as having as their ultimate aim the fostering of rationality. But what is it to be "appropriately moved by reasons?" Again, but in more detail: what is it to be a critical thinker? According to the reasons conception, critical thinking involves two essential components: skills and abilities of reason assessment, and the "critical spirit."

Reason Assessment

The first component of critical thinking involves skills and abilities of *reason assessment*. For students to be critical thinkers, they must be able to evaluate the ability of considerations offered as reasons to provide warrant or justification for the conclusions, claims and judgments for which the considerations are offered as reasons. Considerations offered as reasons sometimes constitute genuine reasons for the claims and judgments they are alleged to support; sometimes, however, putative reasons fail to afford support for those claims and judgments. Some genuine reasons offer only weak support; others offer strong or even conclusive justification. For example, the putative reason

(1) The Bible says so

offers no support for the claim

(2) The Bible is the divine word of God

because (1) assumes what it attempts to establish: namely, that the Bible is a reliable source of information concerning its own authorship. If the Bible is not the divine word of God, then the fact that the Bible says of itself that it is the divine word of God offers no warrant at all for the claim that it is – any more than this paper, if it said of itself that it is the divine word of God, would afford any warrant for the claim that the author of this paper is not Siegel, but God. In general, self-declarations of divinity afford no warrant for the divinity of such declarations; if we seek warrant for (2) we must look elsewhere for reasons which warrant (2) – say, to circumstances surrounding the authorship of the Bible that tend to rule out human (or other non-divine) authorship. (1), then, is a putative reason for (2) which fails to provide any reason for believing (2). A critical thinker must be sufficiently adept at reason assessment to recognize the failure of (1) to count as a reason for, or genuinely warrant, (2). This last example illustrates the case in which a putative reason fails to constitute any sort of reason at all, and fails to afford any warrant at all, for the claim it alleges to support. Many putative reasons do offer some support for judgments and claims, however; such putative reasons are genuine reasons. Here the task of the critical thinker is to judge the strength of the warrant afforded by the reason for the conclusion; the degree to which the reason supports the relevant judgment or claim. For example,

(3) Smith, a Nobel Prize winner in physics, teaches at the University of Miami

supports,[3] but only weakly supports,

(4) The University of Miami has an excellent undergraduate program in physics;

but (3) very strongly supports

(5) The University of Miami physics faculty includes at least one Nobel Prize winner.

(3) supports (5) very strongly, although not conclusively: it is possible, for example, that Smith teaches in the chemistry department but that her research overlaps chemistry and physics sufficiently that she won the Prize in physics; similarly, it is possible that a researcher of Smith's stature enjoys a University appointment and has no official tie to the Physics Department. These possibilities (and others like them) are sufficient to establish that (3) does not *guarantee* (5); it is possible for (3) to be true and (5) false. Nevertheless, (3) strongly supports (5): if Smith in fact teaches at the University of Miami and has won the Nobel Prize in physics, then it is quite likely that the University of Miami's physics faculty includes at least one Nobel Prize winner.

The relationship between (3) and (4), however, is different. (3) offers some support for (4): the fact that the University of Miami has such an eminent physicist on the faculty as Smith provides some reason to think that there are other high quality physicists at the University of Miami (if not, why would Smith stay?), and that at least some of them, perhaps Smith herself, teach undergraduates. However, it may be that the University of Miami has neglected undergraduate physics instruction for graduate and post-graduate activity; it may be that an eminent figure such as Smith does not teach at all, let alone teach undergraduates, but rather devotes her time entirely to research. We could embellish the example further if we wished, but such embellishment would be unnecessary for present purposes. The point is simply that (3) supports both (4) and (5), and is a reason for both, but supports them to different degrees. (3) strongly supports (5), but only weakly, or at least less strongly, supports (4). To recognize this, a critical thinker must be able to assess the degree to which a reason supports or warrants a claim or judgment; she must be able, that is, to evaluate the power of reasons to warrant conclusions. She must be able to tell whether a putative reason offers any justification at all for a claim or judgment, and if so, how much support it offers. A critical thinker must, that is, be able competently to assess the power and convicting force of reasons. This is what is involved in the reason assessment component of critical thinking.

What must the critical thinker master in order to be a competent evaluator of reasons? How does she know that (1) does not support (2) at all, that (3) weakly supports (4), and that (3) strongly supports (5)? The short answer is that the critical thinker must master a variety of *principles of reason assessment*. She must know, understand, and know how to apply a variety of such principles.

Principles of reason assessment come in all shapes and sizes. Consider, for example, the judgment that (1) does not support or constitute a reason for (2). (1) fails to support (2) because it begs the question: (1) supports (2) only if one thinks that the fact that the Bible says so (i.e., says of itself that it is the divine word of God) in some measure establishes the truth of what it says (i.e., that it is the divine word of God). But saying so establishes the truth of what is said only if one has some reason for thinking that its utterances are reliable, and the main reason for thinking that those utterances are reliable is exactly that the Bible is alleged to be divinely authored. If divinely authored, then the fact that the Bible says of itself that it is the divine word of God does provide reason – very strong reason indeed, given our conception of God – for thinking that what the Bible says is true, i.e., for thinking that it is in fact divinely authored. But if not divinely authored (or otherwise authoritatively authored with respect to questions concerning the divinity of authorship), then (1) fails to provide any reason for (2). (1) supports (2), then, only insofar as we assume or have reason to think that (2) is true. (1)'s status as a reason for (2) rests, then, on assuming the truth of (2). But then (1)'s status as a reason for (2) depends upon assuming exactly the point (1) is supposed to establish: (1) constitutes a genuine reason for (2) only insofar as we antecedently accept (2). This is exactly the fallacy known by logicians as begging the question: assuming in one's premises the very point at issue that one's premises are supposed to establish, or for which they are supposed to constitute reasons. Here we appeal to a principle of reason assessment to assess the ability of (1) to support (2), and we find, when doing so, that (1) fails to constitute a reason for (2). The principle in question might be stated as

(P): Putative reasons which beg the question, i.e., which assume the very point for which they are offered as support, fail to warrant or to constitute (good) reasons for that point.

Notice that this principle is entirely subject-neutral. It does not presuppose specialized knowledge of any discipline or field, nor is its application restricted to any selected field. Begging the question is as much a fallacy in history as it is in chemistry, in photography as much as in deciding whether to vote for a particular candidate in the next election. Some principles of reason assessment, then, are general and subject-neutral. These are the principles studied by the field of logic – both formal and informal – and constitute one major type of principle of reason assessment.

Other principles of reason assessment are subject-specific. To know that

(6) The battery is dead

counts as a reason for

(7) The car won't start,

one must know something about cars and the workings of internal combustion engines (in particular, that they rely upon energy supplied by the battery in order to start, and that if a battery is dead it cannot supply that energy); similarly, to know that

(8) Her skin is yellow

counts as a reason for

(9) Her liver is not functioning properly

one must know something about human anatomy and physiology (concerning the nature of jaundice and the function of the liver). The point here is simply that some principles of reason assessment apply only in specialized domains, and require specialized knowledge. Principles of reason assessment can be either subject-neutral or subject-specific. To the extent that a student is a critical thinker, she knows, understands, and knows how to apply both sorts of principles of reason assessment. Critical thinking, consequently, is wrongly construed as either entirely subject-neutral or entirely subject-specific. It is both. Arguments over whether it is one or the other, then, are not particularly enlightening or important.[4] Similar remarks apply to those who urge that critical thinking is thinking which is context-dependent, rather than context-independent: critical thinking is sometimes context-dependent, and sometimes not.[5]

The main point here is simply that critical thinking centrally involves reason assessment, and that a student is a critical thinker only insofar as she is a competent assessor of the power and convicting force of reasons. To be so competent, she must have an intellectual and functional mastery of a large and disparate variety of principles of reason assessment.

The Critical Spirit

Suppose that a student is able to assess reasons competently. Is she then a critical thinker? No. Competent reason assessment is a necessary, but not a sufficient, condition of critical thinking. To be a critical thinker one must not only be a competent assessor of reasons; one must also possess a *critical spirit*.

The ability to assess reasons is not sufficient for critical thinking, for it is easy to imagine people who are quite competent at reason assessment, but who fail to exercise that competence. The case of the brilliant professor who gets fooled by the used car salesperson is one stereotype of such a person; a sophist is another; a politician who uses her skills of reasoning to favor her own ends or to protect her basic principles from critical assessment is still another. In all these cases, the person in question fails to utilize her critical abilities in ways which fairly treat the subject matter at hand.

The critical thinker, in contrast, is one who not only has highly developed skills of reason assessment, but is also *disposed* to utilize them in a non-self-interested way. She has a tendency, and a willingness, to demand reasons and evidence for judgments and actions under consideration; she has a disposition to question even – perhaps especially – her own most fundamental beliefs and attitudes. She has certain habits of mind, and a certain sort of *character*: namely, one which takes as central the demand, and quest, for reasons, and which manifests a desire to conform belief, judgment and action to the results of the fairminded evaluation of reasons. She respects reasons, and lives her life accordingly; her life manifests a love of reason.

A person who does not have the dispositions, habits of mind and character traits constitutive of the critical spirit does not qualify as a critical thinker, however adept at reason assessment she might be. Similarly, a person with the critical spirit, but without the ability to assess reasons, also fails to be a critical thinker. Both components of critical thinking – the reason assessment component, and the critical spirit component – are necessary for critical thinking; they are only jointly sufficient. So understood, the ideal of critical thinking is the ideal of a certain sort of *person* as much as a certain sort of thinking.[6]

Critical Thinking as an Educational Ideal

To take critical thinking as a fundamental educational ideal is to place reasons, and rationality, at the center of our educational conceptions and endeavors. In striving to foster critical thinking, we are striving to foster both skills of reason assessment and the critical spirit; insofar, we are striving to bring about a certain sort of person, with certain sorts of dispositions and character traits, as well as a certain sort of education. This befits a philosophical characterization of a fundamental educational ideal, since education fundamentally involves the persons we strive to educate, and our best hopes for those persons. It involves, that is to say, our ideals of the educated person.[7]

But the ideal sketched thus far is not yet entirely clear. I have argued that the critical thinker is one who is appropriately moved by reasons, and have spelled out this conception in terms of the dual components of abilities of reason assessment, and critical spirit. We must ask next how each of these components relates to the characterization of critical thinking in terms of being "appropriately moved by reasons." Doing so will force the recognition of an ambiguity concerning that phrase. Treatment of this ambiguity will force the drawing of a distinction which will further clarify the reasons conception of critical thinking.

Two Dimensions of Being "Appropriately Moved By Reasons"

What is it to be "appropriately moved by reasons"? There are, I think, two different aspects of being so moved, which can be isolated and identified by emphasizing each of the first two words of that phrase in turn.

To be *appropriately* moved by reasons is to have one's beliefs, judgments and actions conform to the degree of support afforded them by reasons. In the context of our earlier examples, I am appropriately moved by reasons if I do not believe (2) on the basis of (1); if I judge (4) to be somewhat likely on the basis of (3); and if I confidently act consistently with (5) on the basis of (3). In each of these cases, I am *appropriately* moved because my belief, judgment and action is shaped and controlled by the power of the (putative) reasons in question to warrant the relevant beliefs, judgments and actions. In contrast, if I believe (2) on the basis of (1), and thus do not recognize that (1) begs the question (or recognize it but do not care), I would be *in*appropriately moved by reasons, in that my belief does not conform to or adequately reflect the force of the reasons offered in support of that belief.[8] The general point concerning appropriateness is this: reasons stand in certain evidential or probative relation-ships to the beliefs, judgments and actions for which they are reasons; reasons have *probative* or *evidential force*. To be *appropriately* moved by reasons is to believe, judge and act in accordance with the probative force possessed by one's reasons. Here the fundamental task of the critical thinker is to assess accurately the probative force of reasons. What one is assessing, when one is assessing reasons, is the probative force of those reasons. This is the role of the reason assessment component of critical thinking.

This component is not sufficient for critical thinking, however, because (as we have seen) I may realize that (1) fails to support (2) but believe it anyway; I may realize that (3) strongly supports (5), believe (3), yet fail to act as if (5) were true. In such cases my powers of reason assessment are functioning properly, but I fail to conform my belief, judgment and action to the probative force of the reasons I have adequately assessed. Here I fail to be appropriately *moved* by reasons. To be appropriately so moved, I must *be moved* appropri-ately: I must not only recognize the probative force of reasons; I must also recognize the *normative impact* of reasons. That is, I must actually conform my beliefs, actions and judgments to the strength of relevant reasons. The critical spirit can and should be seen as that component of critical thinking which sees to it that one is *affected* and *influenced* appropriately by the probative force of reasons. One recognizes and is open to the normative impact of reasons insofar as one is disposed to conform belief, judgment and action to the probative force of reasons, and insofar as one has a character such that one typically is, and seeks to be, appropriately moved by them.

There are, then, two dimensions of being "appropriately moved by rea-sons." One must be *appropriately* moved by reasons; and one must be appro-priately *moved* by reasons. These two dimensions are captured by distinguishing between the *probative force* and the *normative impact* of rea-sons.[9] Reasons have both probative force and normative impact; the critical thinker is appropriately moved by reasons insofar as she recognizes, and conforms to, both aspects of reasons. Both aspects of reasons are crucial to being appropriately moved by them.

Justifying the Ideal

There is more to say about the justification of critical thinking as an educational ideal than I can say here.[10] But there are two points worth noting.

First, there is a strong and obvious *pragmatic* justification for regarding critical thinking as an educational ideal. Students who are critical thinkers are in a much better position to defend themselves from the hoards of unscrupulous advertisers, ideologs, and other manipulators of their beliefs which students continually face, than students who are not. Students who are critical thinkers stand to gain more from their courses than students who are not. The self-sufficiency resulting from critical thinking can plausibly be expected to enhance the pursuit and enjoyment of respectable and satisfying careers (and lives). In general, there are powerful pragmatic reasons for regarding critical thinking as an educational ideal: the results of an'education informed by the ideal can reasonably be thought to be quite salutary. When one takes into account the current, seemingly endless, "crisis" in education in the United States and elsewhere (on which more below), it is difficult to conceive of a redirection of education with more potential for desirable practical effects than a redirection driven by the ideal of critical thinking.

Second, there is a powerful *moral* justification for regarding critical thinking as a fundamental educational ideal. For critical thinking is the only educational ideal which takes as central the fostering of autonomy and independent judgment which are basic to treating students with respect. Insofar as treating students with respect involves respecting their independent judgment and autonomy, any educational ideal which treats students with respect will centrally involve the ideal of critical thinking. Morally acceptable educational efforts must strive to empower students to direct, ever more competently, their beliefs, actions, and lives; critical thinking is the relevant agent of empowerment, which as such has important moral dimensions. Indeed, education for critical thinking is morally required, for it is the only sort of education which treats students with respect, and which takes such respect as central. Critical thinking is an educational ideal which rejects indoctrination and which places education on a firm moral footing; as such, the ideal enjoys a powerful moral justification.[11]

Critical Thinking and the Language of Inquiry

Earlier we considered the generality of critical thinking; we recognized then that some principles of reason assessment are not general but are subject- or context-specific. Nevertheless, there is an important sense in which critical thinking is general and subject-neutral (in addition to the point that some principles of reason assessment are). I shall try to articulate that sense in terms of a "language of inquiry."

Inquiry is not univocal. We inquire into many different matters, in many different ways. Inquiry concerning the precise determination of the charge of an electron is conducted in quite a different way from that concerning the large-scale geometry of the universe; inquiry concerning the etiology of AIDS involves techniques (e.g. of observation) and theories (e.g. of virology) quite different from inquiry concerning the values of cultures very different from our own. Similar remarks apply to inquiry concerning the virtues of Presidential candidates and the defects of cars that won't start. All of these cases are cases of inquiry; all of them utilize very different techniques. Understood in terms of *techniques* of inquiry, there is no common *method* of inquiry.[12]

Nevertheless, there are some aspects of inquiry which are constant across different types of inquiry. For example, in all the scientific examples just mentioned, observations – whether made with the naked eye, telescopes, electron microscopes, or glasses – are integral ingredients of each of the several inquiries. Moreover, these observations play similar roles in these various inquiries: for instance, we make observations to test hypotheses concerning the geometry of space-time, the structure of the HIV virus, the charge of an electron, the meaning of a foreign cultural practice, the car's failure to start, and the desirability of a political candidate. In all these cases, observations provide reasons for thinking that our hypotheses and theories are true, acceptable, worthy of belief, false, not worth further investigation, or not worth believing. Other aspects of the activity of inquiry, e.g. hypothesizing, theorizing, inferring, imagining, and testing, also provide reasons for conclusions concerning the objects of inquiry. In all these sorts of inquiries, then, there is a common structure – one that defines the effort to inquire responsibly and effectively into the matter at hand – and a common language as well. The common language is just the language of critical thinking, or, more simply, the language of reasons.

The language of inquiry, I am claiming, just is the "language of reasons." It is the totality of our linguistic apparatus relevant to the conducting of responsible inquiry and the establishment of warrantable and warranted hypotheses. Specific linguistic conventions might be adopted by investigators in disparate areas of inquiry, just as different domains of inquiry may differ with respect to relevant principles of inquiry and assessment. For example, a physicist might say that she "sees" neutrinos in a way in which non-specialists cannot[13]; a mathematician, a biologist, and a non-scientist might mean different things when each claims to have "proved" something; members of different schools of literary theory may disagree over whether an author's intentions count as "evidence" concerning the meaning of a work. Similarly, "empathy" may be part of the language of inquiry of the cultural anthropologist but not of the particle physicist; "intention" may be part of the language of inquiry of the historian but not of the molecular biologist; "cell" may be part of the language of inquiry of the biologist but not of the psychologist or cosmologist. With respect to these and similar considerations, we can speak of different languages (and principles) of inquiry operating in different disciplines and inquiry situations.

Nevertheless, inquiry can and should be conceived as fundamentally the same activity across contexts: namely, the activity of investigating matters relevant to responsible belief, judgment and action. Inquiry is in this basic way univocal. It involves the creation[14] and critical examination of reasons and their power to warrant hypotheses; and it results, ideally, in belief, judgment and action which conform to the results of such critical examination. The language of inquiry is similarly univocal. Just as there can be a univocal scientific method which stands alongside and makes sense of diverse techniques of scientific investigation,[15] so too there can be a univocal language of inquiry, which stands alongside and makes sense of diverse "languages" and principles which function in diverse disciplines and areas of inquiry. The univocal language of inquiry is the language of critical thinking – the language of reasons – which empowers us to comprehend diverse disciplinary activity as inquiry in specialized disciplinary settings, to make sense of the fruits of discipline-bound inquiry, to extend the results of such inquiry beyond the bounds of its narrow disciplinary home, and to evaluate critically those results in a broader extra-disciplinary context. All this is possible only because there is a language of inquiry, and a conception of inquiry which makes sense of that language, which extends far beyond the "languages" of inquiry utilized in the disparate disciplinary arenas in which specialized inquiry takes place. The task for investigators of the many "languages of inquiry" is just to relate those "languages" to the language of reasons.[16]

Reasons and Science Education

If the account of critical thinking offered thus far is correct, then it should tell us something about education and its proper pursuit in standard curriculum areas. I believe it does. In this section I apply the reasons conception of critical thinking to science education, in order to illustrate the application to curriculum more generally.[17]

Taking critical thinking as a fundamental educational ideal has fundamental ramifications for science education and for our conception of the science curriculum. Science education, in this light, involves primarily the ability of science students to evaluate, appreciate the force of, and be moved by reasons in science. *Reasons in science* is on this view the key to science education.

To regard reasons as a key component of science education is to reject the view of science education that Schwab derides as a "rhetoric of conclusions"; it is also to reject the related view of science education, inspired by Kuhn, as one which aims at indoctrinating students into the reigning paradigm of the day.[18] It is rather to envision science education as aiming at providing students with an understanding of the reasons we have for favoring one theory over another; for conducting this experiment rather than that; for constructing it this way rather than in some other way; for interpreting results in one way rather than another; and so on. This sort of education calls for the active consideration and comparison of alternative, rival theories and hypotheses. It also calls for sustained, explicit attention to the methodology of scientific inquiry as a means of establishing the rational warrant of alternative claims and hypotheses. A *critical* science education aims at fostering in students an understanding of the strengths and weaknesses of alternative hypotheses and methods of investigation; that is, an understanding of the reasons which ground our evaluations of those alternatives. A science student who has such understanding has an understanding of the criteria and principles which determine the character and strength of putative reasons in science. Such a student has a grasp of the way in which theoretical calculation, experimental design, and experimental result provide us with reasons for preferring one theory or hypothesis to another; she has as well an understanding of the principles of reason assessment, utilized in science, which ground the assessment of such reasons.

In order to have this sort of understanding, she must have some understanding of the epistemology/philosophy of science, and a critical science education should include explicit and sustained attention to philosophical and methodological considerations which underlie scientific practice. Otherwise our student will have at best only a shallow understanding of why some particular experimental result strongly favors one theory, why another result only weakly favors a rival, or why another result fails to support some other rival at all. Philosophy of science consists in large part in the study of the warranting force of reasons in science – issues concerning methodology, experimental design, confirmation, induction, falsification, the logic of science, explanation, progress, and the rationality of science all touch in more or less direct ways on the power of reasons to warrant scientific hypotheses. A critical science education aims at empowering students to understand the rational status of scientific hypotheses and theories by providing an understanding of the principles and considerations which ground our assessment of those hypotheses and theories. An awareness of philosophical controversies concerning such considerations – for example, concerning the nature of explanation and the relevance of explanatory power to the rational evaluation of theory, or concerning the problem of induction and the confirmationist/falsificationist controversy over the ability of evidence positively to support theories – can only enhance the ability of students to understand the nature and warranting force of reasons in science. Thus the philosophy of science should be an integral part of the science curriculum, just as epistemology should be an integral part of the critical thinking curriculum more generally.[19]

A critical science education, then, rejects the Kuhnian suggestion that we should distort the history of science to hide major theoretical controversies and differences in conceptualization of scientific domains and of problems in need of investigation; rejects the idea that the aim of science education is the production of students who believe the theories we tell them are "correct"; and rejects a science education which results in students who are blind to their own theoretical commitments. A critical science education, on the contrary, emphasizes the active consideration of alternative theories and hypotheses; the critical evaluation of those alternatives; and the philosophical considerations which underlie such evaluation. In all of this, the quest for an understanding of the nature and role of reasons in science is central.

In this respect, moreover, the language of inquiry in science is simply the language of reasons applied to various specialized scientific domains of research. In so far, my suggestions concerning science education extend naturally to other curriculum areas. The focus on reasons in history is central to critical history education; the focus on reasons in literature is central to critical literature education; and so on. In all curriculum areas, an education which fosters critical thinking in those areas emphasizes the nature and role of reasons, the active consideration of alternative theoretical and critical perspectives, and the philosophical issues and concerns, studied by the philosophy-of[20] the relevant discipline, which inform our understanding of the principles governing the evaluation of reasons in those areas. I hope, then, that my remarks concerning science education can be generalized to other curriculum areas. While there are surely differences between such areas – what counts as a reason in literature may well differ from what counts as a reason in biology, and the language with which such reasons are discussed and understood may differ equally as much – the language of inquiry and the quest for reasons is nevertheless central to inquiry, and to education, throughout the curriculum.

The Place of Reasons in Education

I conclude with a plea for the recognition of rationality, and its educational cognate, critical thinking, as a fundamental educational ideal; and for the recognition of the central role which philosophical theorizing concerning education should play in our conception and understanding of educational affairs.

One of the basic problems with education, and its scholarship, is the "fad" phenomenon: the rapid adoption and rejection of new, global educational panaceas. This is a phenomenon with which we are all only too familiar. A major explanation of this phenomenon is the failure of education to be informed by any enduring, underlying philosophical perspective. I should of course be delighted if the view I have argued for here came to constitute that enduring perspective. But wouldn't I be fooling myself if I thought that any philosophical view – even my own – will endure? Aren't there philosophical as well as educational fads?

Perhaps there are. Moreover, there is no question that critical thinking is in many respects a new idea, and that the contemporary critical thinking "movement" bears many of the marks of an educational fad. Nevertheless – to hark back to my introduction – I think that critical thinking is best regarded as an educational ideal which is both new *and* tried and true.

Critical thinking is undoubtedly in many respects a new educational idea. It is recognized and thought of as a "movement'" – the Critical Thinking Movement – and has been the subject of many national and international conferences, several new journals and newsletters, and a host of newly designed curricular materials; it has given rise, in turn, to an army of experts and authorities on the theory and practice of critical thinking; and grand promises for the virtues and benefits of making critical thinking central to our educational endeavors have been made. In all this critical thinking looks very much like another education fad and putative panacea. If it were just another fad, moreover, then I think we would have good inductive evidence concerning its power and potential for transforming and radically improving education. This evidence would not be in its favor.

However, critical thinking is not simply new. It is also an educational ideal with impressive philosophical credentials. Throughout the history of Western philosophy, major philosophers of education have articulated, endorsed and defended educational visions to which critical thinking has been central. Socrates is perhaps the clearest example of a philosopher who urged that education and society strive to imbue in all students and persons, to the greatest extent possible, the skills, dispositions and character traits constitutive of critical thinking. Plato similarly venerated critical thinking and rationality, although he was a bit less sanguine concerning the degree to which the ideal could be successfully realized. Aristotle too championed rationality, both in theory and in practice, and uttered remarkably modern-sounding ideas concerning education's duty to develop character traits we now associate with the critical thinker. The great philosophers of the Middle Ages, no less than those of Antiquity, similarly championed an education aimed at the fostering and development of rationality, believing it to be requisite for a full realization of Christian faith. Locke, Hume, Kant, Rousseau, Mill, and other great figures of the Modern and Enlightenment periods also venerated rationality and praised it as an educational aim, the realization of which would enable humans to achieve their full potential as rational beings. More recently, Bertrand Russell extolled and defended the virtues of an education in service of the ideal of critical thinking[21] and John Dewey developed a highly refined philosophy of education which placed rationality, reasons, and critical thinking at its centre.[22] More recently still, R.S. Peters and his British associates endorsed a version of the ideal of critical thinking, and placed reasons and rationality at the heart of their educational philosophy; and the preeminent contemporary philosopher of education Israel Scheffler conceives of critical thinking as being "of the first importance in the conception and organization of educational activities."[23] In short, from Socrates to the present day, philosophers of education have by and large championed rationality and critical thinking as fundamental educational desiderata. Critical thinking is thus an ideal which is both new *and* tried and true.

Of course, critical thinking's being tried and true among philosophers is quite different from its being tried and true for having been tested in the crucible of educational practice. It has not been so tested. This failure to ground educational practice in enduring philosophical thought is one main reason for the sorry state of contemporary education, and for the ubiquity of the fad phenomenon. Indeed, the depressingly enduring "crisis" in education seems to be mainly a function of education's failure to ground itself on appropriate ideals: its failure to treat students with respect, and to see what is involved in so treating them; its failure to foster, and to strive to foster, rationality, independent judgment, and critical thinking. Not only has education in the main failed to foster these traits, it has failed to recognize them as traits it ought to foster. This recognition is basic to education for critical thinking; it is also basic to the revitalization of contemporary education. Consequently, this failure is also a reason for being excited about the way in which critical thinking is new. Perhaps, as a faddish educational movement, critical thinking will have its chance to inform educational practice. If so, then all of us will have the chance to see what philosophers of education have seen and said for so long.

Notes

[1]This essay is a modestly revised version of an essay entitled "The Role of Reasons in (Science) Education" which was presented as the 1988 Robert Jackson Memorial Lecture at the School of Education, Dalhousie University, Halifax, Nova Scotia and subsequently published in William Hare (ed.), *Reason in Teaching and Education* (Halifax: Dalhousie University School of Education, 1989, 5-21).

[2]Some of what follows draws upon my *Educating Reason: Rationality, Critical Thinking, and Education* (London: Routledge, 1988). I refer the reader to this source for a more systematic treatment of critical thinking, its relationship to rationality, its

status as an educational ideal, and its ramifications for educational policy and practice and for the curriculum.

[3]I am assuming here that (3) is itself justified; if it is not, then of course it fails to support either (4) or (5).

[4]The main protagonists here are John McPeck (subject-specific) and Robert Ennis (subject-neutral). I discuss the debate between them in more detail in *Educating Reason*. For a more recent treatment, see my "The Generalizability of Critical Thinking," *Educational Philosophy and Theory*, 23, 1, 1991: 18-30.

[5]Here I am thinking mainly of Matthew Lipman, who emphasizes in his account of critical thinking its context-dependency. See, for example, Lipman, "The Concept of Critical Thinking," *Teaching Thinking and Problem Solving*, 10, 3, 1988: 5-7.

[6]This discussion of the critical spirit is far too brief to be adequate. For further amplification, see *Educating Reason*.

[7]Here too my discussion is unduly brief. For further consideration of critical thinking as an educational ideal, see *Educating Reason*.

[8]My belief in this case fails to be "proportional to the evidence," or, more accurately, fails to be proportional to an adequate evaluation of the evidence. The general position I am sketching is *evidentialist*; I regret that space forbids consideration of the many epistemological niceties concerning the desirability of conforming belief to the evidence and those concerning the "ethics of belief." For a recent, sophisticated statement of evidentialism, see Richard Feldman and Earl Conee, "Evidentialism," *Philosophical Studies* 48, 1985: 15-34.

[9]I first drew this distinction in "Teaching, Reasoning, and Dostoyevsky's *The Brothers Karamazov*," in Philip Jackson and Sophie Haroutunian-Gordon (eds.), *From Socrates to Software: The Teacher as Text and the Text as Teacher* (Chicago: National Society for the Study of Education, 1989), 115-134.

[10]Once again I must beg the reader's indulgence, and refer her to *Educating Reason*, chapter 3, for a more sustained discussion.

[11]See *Educating Reason*, chapters 3 and 5 for further discussion.

[12]The distinction between methods of inquiry versus techniques of inquiry is drawn, in connection with the rationality of science, in my "What is the Question Concerning the Rationality of Science?" *Philosophy of Science*, 52, 4, 1985: 517-537.

[13]See Dudley Shapere, "The Concept of Observation in Science and Philosophy," *Philosophy of Science*, 49, 4, 1982: 485-525.

[14]Thus it would be a mistake to sharply distinguish creative and critical thinking. See, here Sharon Bailin's excellent *Achieving Extraordinary Ends: An Essay on Creativity* (Dordrecht: Martinus Nijhoff, 1988).

[15]As I argue in "What is the Question Concerning the Rationality of Science?"

[16]And to epistemology, i.e., to the general philosophical study of the power and convicting force of reasons. Here the close relationship between critical thinking and epistemology should be apparent. I develop this theme in "Epistemology, Critical Thinking, and Critical Thinking Pedagogy," *Argumentation*, 3, 1989: 127-140.

[17]In this section I borrow from *Educating Reason*, chapter 6, which discusses in detail the differences between "critical" and "uncritical" science education; and from "The Rationality of Science, Critical Thinking, and Science Education," *Synthese*, 80, 1, 1989: 9-41.

[18]The relevant texts here are Joseph J. Schwab, *The Teaching of Science as Enquiry* (Cambridge MA: Harvard University Press, 1962); and Thomas S. Kuhn, *The Structure of Scientific Revolutions* (Chicago, University of Chicago Press, 1970). For discussion of both, see *Educating Reason*, chapter 6.

[19]See "Epistemology, Critical Thinking, and Critical Thinking Pedagogy."

[20]See Israel Scheffler, "Philosophies-of and the Curriculum" in J. F. Doyle (ed.), *Educational Judgments* (London, Routledge & Kegan Paul, 1973), 209-218.

[21]This somewhat unusual interpretation of Russell's philosophy of education is, I think, conclusively secured by William Hare. See his "Russell's Contribution to Philosophy of Education," *Russell*, 7, 1, 1987: 25-41.

[22]Although Dewey's understanding of these notions, and the epistemology underlying them, differs markedly from my own. For brief comment, see my remarks on Dewey in *Educating Reason*.

[23]I. Scheffler, *Reason and Teaching* (London, Routledge & Kegan Paul, 1973), 1.

Part Three

Controversy in the Classroom

Even when students have the benefit of an education in which the ideals of critical teaching are taken seriously, there will inevitably be very many occasions when they will have no choice but to rely on the advice or pronouncements of experts. There will be no serious possibility of deciding the issue for themselves in such cases; they simply lack the knowledge and/or skills necessary to arrive at satisfactory conclusions independently. We all, in fact, have numerous beliefs which we cannot ourselves verify or support; we may, indeed, have little or no idea how these beliefs are to be defended or what counts in their favor. The result is that we must defer to someone else whose expertise is greater than our own; and our claim to know the truth in question rests on the trust we place in someone thought to be an expert. Philosophers now describe this situation as epistemic dependence, and one implication may be that we are not as self-sufficient with respect to knowledge as we may think, nor as autonomous as our education may have led us to believe.

The tradition of progressive education in the twentieth century has placed a good deal of emphasis on the recognition and discussion of controversial issues in the classroom. Russell wanted teachers to promote vehement and impassioned debate on all sides of every question. Dewey was anxious to promote reflective thinking and judgment in schools so as to avoid producing a passive body of citizens who would be managed and exploited. An emphasis on controversy seems appropriate, even essential, if we think that indoctrination and the mere acquisition of unexamined information are to be avoided, but the problems with respect to expertise suggested above may give us pause. Russell, for example, observed that where the experts are not agreed – where, that is, the matter is controversial – no opinion can be regarded as certain by a non-expert. We may wonder, then, about the wisdom of encouraging students to try to formulate their own views about such issues. What, in short, is the educational value of discussing controversial issues? How can relatively inexperienced students make progress on questions which have baffled the experts?

Further questions are immediately suggested. If controversial issues are discussed in the classroom, what role is the teacher to play? Is the teacher allowed, encouraged, perhaps even required, to reveal, and defend, his or her own position on the matter in question, or should the teacher remain neutral insofar as that is possible? Are there some views which a teacher is precluded from showing sympathy towards, inside or outside the classroom, because such support would be incompatible with the teacher's position as role model for the students and with the school's commitment to the fundamental principle of respect for all students? If students, like everyone else, need to trust experts and authorities, and are encouraged to trust their teachers, how can they learn to do so wisely and cautiously?

These and other questions are taken up in the readings in this section. Robert Dearden presents a helpful characterization of what makes a matter controversial, as well as examples of types of cases where the problems of resolution become increasingly complex. A partial answer to the doubt about including controversial issues in the curriculum raised earlier is Dearden's argument that not to do so would be to misrepresent the subjects in the curriculum with respect to both their present status and their historical development. Dearden also argues that teacher neutrality with respect to controversial issues is a technique, not an absolute principle, but Mary Warnock goes much further than this in claiming that teachers will simply fail in their duty if they do not abandon neutrality and tell the students plainly where they personally believe the evidence points. In a review of cases ranging from empirical issues to moral questions, she argues that a teacher needs to demonstrate how conclusions are drawn from evidence, and maintains that a teacher cannot sit on the fence forever.

The Keegstra case, in which a teacher systematically spread anti-semitic propaganda in his classroom over a period of years, raises the issue of freedom of speech and opinion versus other rights, including the right to an education free from indoctrination. Supporters of Keegstra claimed that the ideal of open-mindedness, often appealed to by progressive educators in justifying the inclusion of controversial issues, should offer him protection. Opponents replied that there were good reasons for removing Keegstra from the classroom and that the appeal to open-mindedness rests on confusion. More problematic still is the case of Malcolm Ross, discussed by Sheva Medjuck, who did not put forward his anti-semitic views in his classes but did openly publish them under his own name and appeared on television to defend them. Did this notoriety create a "poisoned" environment which adversely affected the educational rights and opportunities of students? Even if this were the case, should teachers nevertheless have the same freedom of expression in their personal lives which other members of the community enjoy?

Finally, all of these discussions raise questions about the teacher/student relationship. If a teacher is free to bring controversial issues into the classroom, free to maintain an independent point of view, and free to support various causes in private life, how do we ensure that the trust we expect students to place in their teachers is not abused?

Further Readings

Bruce Carrington and Barry Troyna (eds.), *Children and Controversial Issues.* London: Falmer, 1988.

John Dewey, "Social Purposes in Education," reprinted in Jo Ann Boydston (ed.), *John Dewey: The Middle Works 1889-1924.* Carbondale: Southern Illinois University Press, 1983, 158-69.

Peter Gardner, "Neutrality in Education," in Robert E. Goodin and Andrew Reeve (eds.), *Liberal Neutrality.* New York: Routledge, 1989, 106-29.

John Hardwick, "Epistemic Dependence," *Journal of Philosophy*, 82, 7, 1985: 335-49.

William Hare, "Controversial Issues and the Teacher," in William Hare, *Controversies in Teaching.* London, Ont.: Althouse Press, 1985, ch. 11.

Michael E. Manley-Casimir and Stuart M. Piddocke, "Teachers in a Goldfish Bowl: A Case of 'Misconduct'," *Education and Law Journal*, 3, 1990-91: 115-48.

Dorothy Nelkin, "Controversies and the Authority of Science," in H. Tristram Engelhardt Jr. and Arthur L. Caplan (eds.), *Scientific Controversies.* Cambridge: Cambridge University Press, 1987, ch. 10.

Allen T. Pearson, "Teaching and Rationality: The Case of Jim Keegstra," *Journal of Educational Thought*, 20, 1, 1986: 1-7.

Bertrand Russell, "Education for Democracy," *Addresses and Proceedings of the National Education Association*, 77, 1939: 527-34.

Bertrand Russell, *Sceptical Essays.* London: Unwin, 1977, ch. 1. (Originally published, 1928.)

Robert Stradling, "The Teaching of Controversial Issues: An Evaluation," *Educational Review*, 36, 2, 1984: 121-29.

9

Controversial Issues and the Curriculum

R.F. Dearden

If by "Logical Positivism" is meant that particular kind of hard-headedness presented by A.J. Ayer in his philosophical classic *Language, Truth and Logic,* then it seems to be very much in decline in academic philosophy. But it often happens that a philosophical position is a critical elaboration of an attitude or outlook which is abundantly present in a less examined way at the level of commonsense, or for that matter in non-philosophical educational theorizing. For example, much that is of a positivist spirit is to be found in behaviorism and its offspring, such as the behavioral objectives movement and certain calls for more objective styles of assessment and more generally in strong attachment to the observable and quantifiable as our sole guiding light.

If a curriculum were to be based on the principles of Logical Positivism, whether knowingly or unknowingly, it would presumably have to avoid those subject areas designated by Ayer as "nonsense." The nature of "nonsense" here was determined by what is excluded from a classification of significant propositions into two broad categories: those which are analytic and *a priori* and those which are synthetic and empirical. That is very roughly to say that significant propositions must either be known from a consideration of the meanings of terms (perhaps mathematics and certain aspects of language) or else known by reference to sense-experience (for example, science and geography). Any other seemingly propositional area would be designated as "nonsense" (I pass over the possible confusion between meaning and truth). Thus "nonsense" would embrace much that in the normal school curriculum is included under such subject headings as moral or social education, political education, religious education and literature and the arts. Such studies should largely disappear if the curriculum were henceforth to concern itself solely with knowledge, positivistically defined, as opposed to what would be seen as the non-cognitive social conditioning of attitudes or the mere expression of emotions.

Such an approach to deciding the content of the curriculum would necessarily exclude all reference to *controversial* matters, and many people who have given thought to the curriculum as a whole would feel that this brisk and brusque dismissal of the controversial on the grounds that it was not "knowledge" was unwarranted. I want to argue in this essay that their intuitive reluctance would be right: the controversial is not simply an epistemological disaster area into which the responsible curriculum constructor should not care to go.

Accordingly, I propose to examine more closely the notion of the controversial and then to see what implications that examination might have for the curriculum. This is, of course, not the same thing as to examine Logical Positivism itself. A project of such large scope is not my intention. I shall here confine myself to a consideration of one consequence of its application to the design of curricula.

An immediate difficulty that has to be faced is that what is meant by "controversial" may itself be a matter of controversy. For example, it is evident that some writers have adopted a behavioral criterion of the controversial. Charles Bailey writes: "that an issue is controversial is, of course, a matter of social fact. That is, an issue is controversial if numbers of people are observed to disagree about statements and assertions made in connection with the issue."[1] But is it really so obvious that this behavioral criterion is the most appropriate one to adopt? I shall argue that the adoption of such a criterion has at least two unfortunate consequences.

In the first place, much of the disagreement which socially occurs reflects either simple ignorance or else mere undisciplined assertiveness. Children will dispute endlessly about the capital cities of countries, spellings of words, authors of books and explanations of well-understood natural phenomena, yet in each case there exists a clear decision-procedure and typically there is also a publicly known and available answer. These matters are not controversial at all. The answers are definitely known. What is controversial cannot, therefore, be a simple "matter of social fact."

In the second place, Bailey's criterion could give undeserved encouragement to relativism (quite contrary to his own declared sympathies, it must be said). If all that is needed is for a number of people to assert a counter-opinion for the matter to become controversial, regardless of that counter-assertion's ungroundedness, inconsistency, invalidity or mere expressiveness of a vested interest, then even the shape of the Earth becomes at once controversial. Some say, and many more in the past have said, that its shape is flat. That is a matter of social fact. But what have such social facts got to do with the shape of the Earth? This planet goes imperturbably on its way regardless of our utterances, and its shape can be known by anyone concerned seriously to find out. The behavioral criterion of the controversial therefore encourages the thought that what is true should be collapsed into what some group regards as true, with epidemic relativism and a sociological carnival as the result.

What I suggest, by contrast, is an *epistemic* criterion of the controversial. Such a criterion might be formulated somewhat as follows: a matter is controversial if contrary views can be held on it without those views being contrary to reason. By "reason" here is not meant something timeless and unhistorical but the body of public knowledge, criteria of truth, critical standards and verification procedures which at any given time has been so far developed. It follows that what at one time is controversial may later be definitely settled, as with many opinions about the nature of the surface of the Moon and the character of the side that faces away from the Earth. At one time these were matters of legitimate dispute in a way which at least some of them no longer are.

By way of further illustration, several possible kinds of controversial issue may be distinguished. First, there are those cases where we simply have insufficient evidence to settle the matter, though in principle there is no reason why it should not be settled as more or better evidence becomes available. Thus at a particular juncture the government of the day may create mortgage controls in order to slow down the rise in house prices. Will the measure have the desired effect? That is controversial; some evidence both for and against its likely effectiveness is available.

A second type of case is where consideration-making criteria are agreed but the weight to be given to them is not. Thus all will agree that in considering whether the Vale of Belvoir should have its underground coal resources exploited both environmental and economic criteria are relevant. But presumably local residents and the National Coal Board weight these consideration-making criteria rather differently. The matter is controversial, and probably more intractably so than in the first type of case.

A third and still more intractable case may be found where there is no agreement even on the criteria as to what will count. In considering the admissibility of torture to obtain information from prisoners, some will assume a consequentialist criterion and so pick out resultant benefit and harm as what should settle the matter. Others will take a more intrinsicalist view and argue that torture by its very nature, and quite apart from its consequences, has a certain inherent moral character. To take another case, in the assessing of essays the disputes which arise between markers may well be of this third type, as when accuracy is prized by one and imaginative expression by another (disputes about assessment may also be of types one or two, of course).

There is still a fourth possible case. This is where not just individual criteria but whole frameworks of understanding are different. Suppose that a person feels somewhat depressed, as many of us from time-to-time are apt to do. Should that depression be regarded from a medical perspective as something calling for treatment, perhaps the prescription of some pills, or should it be regarded from an ethical perspective as something calling for a display of patience, fortitude, courage or endurance? If that seems to be an unreal contrast, try reading Illich's critique of the medical profession, especially the American medical profession.[2] To take an educational case, consider the differences of possible approach that might be adopted towards pupil behavior that is perceived as undesirable. Should we look at it most appropriately as in need of re-shaping by the techniques of behavior modification; or as in need of investigation in terms of psycho-analytic causes; or as in need of interpreting along the lines of a Marxist social analysis making reference to alienation and class dominance; or more simply as expressive of an unsuitable choice of curricular material or staff attitudes along the lines that Rutter[3] has investigated – or just as perverse? The matter is controversial. A final example of this fourth type of controversy would be the controversy between the religious believer and non-believer over the correct description of a great many things in the world.

We now have before us both a suggested epistemic criterion of the controversial ("contrary views can be held without those views being contrary to reason") and an illustrative range of types of controversial issue. But before proceeding to draw some educational implications, I would like to make certain general comments on the type of subject matter that may be controversial. For it seems often to be assumed, and not least by those of positivist sympathies with whom we began, that it is especially matters of *value* which are controversial. Lawrence Stenhouse was apparently of this opinion when he wrote "by a controversial issue we mean one which divides students, parents and teachers because it involves an element of value-judgment which prevents the issue being settled by evidence and experiment."[4] Stenhouse's difficulty is at least epistemological and not just social, but there is a strong hint of positivist assumptions here.

But this confinement of the controversial to matters of value is a misconception. Many empirically factual matters can also be controversial, so that having to do with values is by no means a necessary condition. Why did the dinosaurs die out? How is one to explain what look like water-courses on Mars? These are matters of scientific controversy. Even mathematics is not exempt. Is every even number the sum of two primes? Can n be any whole number greater than 2 in the equation $x^n + y^n = z^n$? These are controversial mathematical issues.

Having to do with values is not even a sufficient condition for being controversial, let alone a necessary condition. There are value-judgments which are entirely uncontroversial. Consider for example the entirely uncontroversial aesthetic value-judgment that Turner was a vastly superior painter to myself (and probably yourself too). Consider the moral value-judgment that it is not only wrong but viciously so when someone amuses himself or herself by stubbing out burning cigarettes on a baby entrusted to his or her care (I draw my example from life).

What can be said about the predilection for citing value matters as examples of the controversial is probably this. The justification of value-judgments is, at least at certain points, importantly different from the grounding of scientific or mathematical assertions. You could not ultimately settle the moral character of baby-burning by appeal solely to scientific (and still less to mathematical) reasoning. And the ways in which value-judgments are different may make it more likely that they will prove controversial. But this is not to say either that all, or that only, value-judgments are controversial. And let us also note that even the most tightly controlled of scientific enquiries is itself shot through with values. Why has the inquirer chosen that problem? What of the social consequences of the discovery he or she is about to make and the resources used in making it? Does not the very process of inquiry itself embody important virtues constitutive of what we might call the "ethics of belief" (you ought not to rush to conclusions, you ought to be patient with difficulties, do justice to objections, submit your work to criticism, etc. etc.)? The Logical Positivist himself or herself is presumably prescribing to us what he or she regards, however misconceivedly, as a proper sense of responsibility about our epistemic claims. If values are dirty, his or her own hands are far from clean.

By way of final general comment on the type of subject matter that may be controversial, let us note that being controversial is no reason to cease from trying to settle a matter. I suggested earlier that all kinds of historical contingencies affect what at any given time is properly to be regarded as controversial. A matter which is in principle capable of definite settlement will only come to be definitely settled if we do not cease from trying to settle it. And where value-judgments are concerned, as Nordenbo[5] observes, to regard them as being controversial at least assumes a cognitive theory of ethics. What is controversial is precisely the truth, correctness or rightness of some view, which presupposes that at least it makes sense to search for these things even if we do not attain them. Without that presupposition, there is nothing controversial but just different personal preferences, susceptible of explanation perhaps, but not appropriately open to calls for further justification or the citing of evidence.

Is it educationally desirable that controversial issues should be included in the curriculum? One implication of the previous argument is that this question cannot be answered in terms of a division between controversial and uncontroversial *subjects,* since all subjects have both controversial and uncontroversial areas in them. The simple positivist division between science and mathematics, for example, and social, moral, political, religious and aesthetic values is not just simple but simplistic. The division between the controversial and the uncontroversial cuts right across such a subject division, though no doubt the extent of what is definitely settled as against what is more open to the holding of contrary views will vary in different subjects.

Granted that much, the question may still be raised whether the controversial in each subject should, provided that its level of difficulty or presupposed maturity are appropriate, be tackled as part of the curriculum. There are at least two good reasons why it should be tackled. The first reason is given by Lawrence Stenhouse. In spite of Stenhouse's well-known attachment to the principle of "procedural neutrality" he certainly was not neutral towards the inclusion of controversial issues. Where these concern matters of "widespread and enduring significance" he thinks that an education which ignored them would be seriously inadequate. And I agree with him. If, for example, the relationships between men and women, or the principles according to which benefits and burdens are distributed in a society, or family relationships, or attitudes towards work, or the proper uses to be made of our knowledge, or how we live, are never given any attention in the course of our education, then matters of very great importance will have been neglected and opportunities for developing a better informed, more sensitive, more discriminating and in general more adequate understanding of these matters will have been missed, perhaps even in some cases irrevocably. But much to do with these matters is indeed controversial.

The second reason for including the controversial is not unrelated to the first. It is just that to teach a subject in a way that makes no reference to the controversial parts of it is to misrepresent it. This misrepresentation may arise simply through giving the impression that a subject is a monolithic block of certain knowledge which requires only that we turn to the appropriate authority in order for any problem concerning it to be solved. In this way the truth-criteria, critical standards and verification procedures appropriate to the subject may never themselves be mentioned. If, however, controversial matters are raised, then immediately there is an open invitation explicitly to consider how they might be settled.

But this is still not enough. Ignoring the controversial further misrepresents the subject in its nature as a historically developed line of enquiry. The slightest acquaintance with this historical dimension would reveal that progress has been very far from smooth and automatic. The history of science, for example, is littered with the wreckage of successfully contested theories. At the cutting-edge of any subject, much, if not everything, will be controversial and if that cutting-edge is at present too remote from anything that could be grasped by pupils at school, this is not so if we look to the past of the subject. Even something so uncontroversial now as the function of the heart and the circulation of the blood was at first hotly contested. And it is not an idle luxury to appreciate this. It is essential to an adequate grasp of the nature of human inquiry, of its dependence on imaginative ideas, of the place of criticism in it, of its advancement sometimes by fruitful wrong ideas rather than by pedestrian right ones, and of its tools and standards.

How should the controversial be tackled? Stenhouse's answer was in terms of "procedural neutrality." According to this principle, which has undergone modifications and restatements, the teacher should not indicate his or her own preferred solution or loyalty. On that he or she should preserve a silence (though much besides the mouth may speak). Indeed, he or she should "protect divergence," or encourage a full range of diverse views. But his or her role is not to be otherwise passive. On the contrary, the teacher should seek "improved understanding" by a process of feeding into the discussion or inquiry "rich, diverse and balanced evidence." Reactions to these procedural proposals have varied from incomprehension, through doubt as to their desirability, to denial of their possibility.

It is in fact quite possible to be epistemically neutral on some matters, for example acupuncture. This may seem not to be so if we are faced with the dilemma that, regarding any particular candidate for belief, we must either believe it or not believe it, from which the conclusion is drawn that we cannot be neutral. However, "not believing" is not necessarily disbelieving. We may have no view about it at all, or never have considered it. Smith must either believe in acupuncture or not believe in it. If we suppose him not to believe in it, this does not necessarily mean he disbelieves in acupuncture: he may be either completely ignorant of this medical practice, or he may be aware of its existence but have formed no view on it at all. Therefore epistemic neutrality on some matters is quite possible.

But is such neutrality possible for a *teacher* of the matter in question? One cannot teach without framing intentions about what is to be learnt and about how it is to be learnt. And it will not be possible to frame such intentions without some definite, even if provisional, view on the epistemic status of what is taught. Does the teacher intend it to be realized that the view is definitely true or false, correct or mistaken, right or wrong – or controversial? Whatever the answer here, including the answer that the view is to be seen as controversial, there is a definite epistemic commitment. It is as much an epistemic commitment to regard the existence of God as controversial as it is to regard it as known to be either true or false. Furthermore, in general the teacher is, or if he or she is not then he or she ought to be, better able than his or her pupils to assess the various views and claims that are made in his or her curriculum area. Where the teacher's judgment is that a matter is both controversial and important enough to teach, then a realization on the part of the pupils of that controversiality will be precisely one of his or her teaching objectives. And the teaching procedures which he or she should adopt will follow from that.

Much that was puzzling in Stenhouse's approach can now be made clearer, or perhaps corrected. "Improved understanding" will, amongst other things no doubt, imply an appreciation of the controversial nature of the matter in hand, which may of course involve moving the pupil away from inadequately based certainties. "Protecting divergence" may be the appropriate way of disclosing this controversiality, but merely ignorant alternatives or mere undisciplined assertiveness imply a behavioral and not an epistemic criterion of the controversial. And the teacher may confront such massive prejudice that *he* or *she* is the only source of possible "divergence" – in which case one can scarcely retain "procedural neutrality." Again, what "evidence" should he or she supply, when should it be introduced, with what force or insistence, how often should it be recalled and when is it "balanced"? No progress can be made in answering such necessary questions until the epistemic objective is determined: seeing the matter as true, or as false, or perhaps as controversial.

If this is right, then it is to pitch camp in the wrong place to insist on "procedural neutrality" as a principle. It is just a technique, not a principle, and one which is sometimes useful and sometimes not. There are many other techniques of teaching the controversial: stating both sides of the question, getting committed and even enthusiastic one-sided statements which are contextually understood to be one-sided, putting the missing side oneself, practising role-reversal (for example stating the opposite to one's own view oneself), debates, simulation games, framing alternative hypotheses, and so on.

Granted that the context is an educational one, and not one in which indoctrination is sought, then the corresponding dangers are fairly clear: covertly biased presentation, catechetical questioning seeking to establish a contentious orthodoxy, systematic institutional reinforcement of just one view, and the like. The usual examples illustrative of these dangers are religious, as when the Plowden Report (paragraph 572) asserted that pupils "should not be confused by being taught to doubt before faith is established." But we might equally turn to politics for examples. A 1978 national college-entrance examination in China contained the following obviously catechetical questions: "Why must countries having a dictatorship of the proletariat practise democracy towards the people and impose dictatorship on the enemy? Criticize the Gang of Four's counter-revolutionary crimes of reversing the relations between the enemy and ourselves and imposing a fascist dictatorship on the people."[6] But although this illiberal way of treating what are really controversial issues is most obviously to be found in such areas as the religious and the political, it may exist wherever a matter is epistemically controversial, for instance in science, geography, history, or for that matter in educational theory. Consider the often naive faith exhibited by those who preface their claims by saying, with innocent confidence, "research shows." This, too, can be a result of teaching.

A final perplexity deserves mention, I have assumed throughout this discussion that there will be a concurrence of judgment, at least amongst serious inquirers if not amongst the ignorant or merely assertive, as to what *is* controversial. But suppose that that assumption is false. Suppose that there is no agreement as between a biology and a religious education teacher over the evolution of species, the one regarding it as a known historical fact while the other regards it as, if not definitely false, then at least controversial. To take another example, consider the arguments against letting Stenhouse go ahead with the publication of his pack on race relations as a controversial issue. One such argument put forward was that race relations are not a controversial issue for anyone who regards them with moral seriousness.

The point here is that serious and mature people can be in disagreement precisely over what is controversial, in the epistemic sense. One party regards the matter as definitely known while the other regards it as controversial. Can there be a rational solution in such cases? Does it just depend on who is finally in a position to enforce his or her view? Should it, or more pertinently could it, be settled by some such democratic procedure as voting? (See Phillips[7]) Should the step be taken of calling in the "experts" to pronounce, in which case what would be the character of their expertise? Perhaps it is fortunate that concerning much that is controversial, it is at least uncontroversial that it *is* controversial.

Notes

I am grateful to my colleagues Michael Grimmitt, John Hull and Ieuan Lloyd for their comments on this paper.

[1]C. Bailey, "Neutrality and rationality in teaching," in D. Bridges and P. Scrimshaw (eds.), *Values and Authority in Schools* (London: Hodder and Stoughton, 1975), 122.

[2]I. Illich, *Limits to Medicine* (Harmondsworth: Penguin, 1977).

[3]M. Rutter, et. al., *Fifteen Thousand Hours* (London: Open Books, 1979).

[4]Schools Council/Nuffield Foundation, *The Humanities Project* (London: Heinermann, 1970), 6.

[5]S.E. Nordenbo, "Pluralism, Relativism and the Neutral Teacher," *Proceedings of the Philosophy of Education Society,* 12 (1978), 131.

[6]See "Testing Times for the Chinese" in *Times Higher Educational Supplement,* 14 December 1979, 373, 5.

[7]D.Z. Phillips, "Another Outbreak of Misology," *Education for Teaching,* 95, Autumn 1974.

10

The Neutral Teacher

Mary Warnock

Those who advocate neutrality in teachers do so, in my experience, with great passion. There appear to be two major grounds for their advocacy, which are not, however, totally distinct from each other. The first ground is the desire to avoid turning teaching into indoctrination. The second is the desire that pupils may learn whatever they do learn by discovering through experiment, trial and error and genuine argument; that they may have the pleasure of coming independently to their own conclusions, with the teacher simply as chairperson of their meetings.

I want briefly to consider the indoctrination argument first, but this will not take long, since it will be clear already how this argument shades off into the second. It is worth considering the *word* "indoctrination," however, since it is rather a vogue word just at the moment. Indoctrination means the imposing upon a captive child the body of doctrines held by the teacher (or supposed to be held. It would obviously be possible for a freethinking teacher to impose Christian doctrine on a child, but we need not consider this case.) The essence of the situation is that what the teacher says is true is to be accepted by the child uncritically. The bad feature of indoctrination therefore (and the word is obviously pejorative) lies precisely in the docile and uncritical state of mind which it produces in the pupil. The concept of indoctrination certainly has some use; but there are great difficulties in marking off its limits exactly. For instance, if the teacher is a charismatic person it may well be that the pupils are disinclined to doubt what he or she says, even in areas where doubt is perfectly reasonable. In the opposite case, whatever the teacher says may seem dubious or at least unmemorable to the pupils. Again, it is not clear whether the word "indoctrinate" means "to induce uncritical belief deliberately" or not. If I am an absolutely convinced believer in the single authorship of the *Iliad* and the *Odyssey,* such that I have never even raised the question whether Homer was one author or several, then I may teach my class that the *Iliad* and the *Odyssey* were written by one Greek whose name was Homer, and they may go through the rest of their lives believing this, especially if they do not develop any particular interest in Greek poetry. It may become simply part of the seldom-examined furniture of their minds. Have they then been indoctrinated? I certainly did not *mean* to indoctrinate them. I simply meant to tell them what I took to be the truth. I did not even know that it was controversial. But, it may be asked, does anyone ever set out deliberately to indoctrinate another? Do we not always attempt simply to teach them the truth? Perhaps sometimes, in cases where there is a received body of dogma which hangs together, and belief in which is thought to be particularly desirable in its effects, a teacher may say, like the Jesuits, I will catch them young, and ensure that they accept it all, lock stock and barrel. But when you come to think of it this is a pretty rare phenomenon. For most teachers the question whether or not to indoctrinate in this narrow sense, hardly ever arises. Apart, then, from "indoctrination" in the narrow sense, the word seems mostly to be used of other people, when we ourselves disapprove either of the content of their teaching, or of the methods. As such it is perhaps not a very useful word to analyse further.

Let us move on, therefore, to consider the second ground for holding that a teacher should be neutral. This is the desire that pupils should learn by discovering things for themselves rather than by being told; and this course of discovery will include among other items the discovery that it is possible to hold different views about a vast number of subjects, between which views they will have to choose. Thus, the neutral teacher will present to the pupils the different views that exist, will put them in the way of evidence or other considerations which might favor the different views, and will then sit back and allow them to make up their own minds. Now it will be obvious at once that this kind of description of the teacher's role applies only to certain kinds of material, if at all. There are some sorts of teaching situations in which the question of the pupils' deciding something for themselves does not really arise, and this even where the material is, in a sense, controversial. Let us suppose, for example, that I am trying to teach someone to do something. In the very simple kind of cases, such as where I may try to teach you to ride a bicycle, there will be very little theoretical content to my teaching; I will merely guide your efforts with advice and physical support. If I am trying to teach you, on the other hand, to drive a car or play the French horn, there may be a good deal of theory involved. But nonetheless my aim in teaching is to get you to be able to do something. And when you can do it reasonably efficiently, then you can perfect your technique by practice, rejecting some of my teaching if you find it better to do so, that is if you find it more efficient. The question of neutrality can hardly be made to bear on such cases at all. A great deal of what one teaches at school is in fact of this kind, disagreeable though it may be for some theorists to accept this. Reading and writing are indeed often spoken of as "skills" and it is acknowledged that in teaching them we are teaching children how to do something. But a great deal of mathematics must also be learned as a matter of skill or technique; and in the case of languages, the aim is also to teach people how to talk, write, or translate. Of course a teacher may get things wrong. He or she may simply teach the pupils to write bad French, or give them a cumbersome or confusing method for solving equations. But this again has virtually nothing to do with whether the teacher is neutral or not. It is a matter of whether one is intelligent and understands the subject matter. I mention these cases only to show that there is a vast area of very important teaching, (though somewhat neglected in the writings of educationalists) which is the teaching of techniques or skills, and where it does not enter our heads to demand neutrality. The question of whether the teacher is neutral or not, again, does not arise.

But obviously, embedded in these technique-subjects there generally lies a core of fact and of theory. I teach someone to read Latin, and teach him or her in doing so *that* Cicero uses the subjunctive in relative clauses to convey this or that nuance. This is taught as a fact, which can be verified by appeal to the texts. And behind this fact lies a theory, or at least a system, which enables me to split up written words (in this case) into sentences, and sentences into clauses, to distinguish nouns from verbs, and to distinguish, within the class of verbs, those which are indicative from those which are subjunctive in mood. And so on. At last we may begin to see some of the difficulties. How are we to distinguish, in what lies behind the taught technique, between fact and theory? Are we to teach the theory as well as the fact? Must we preface all our teaching of Latin syntax (to stick to this example) with the words "This is a subjunctive verb according to our present classification; but of course there could be other classifications"? How much do such provisos actually add to one's understanding? Do we want the pupils to be thinking all the time about alternative geometries, or do we first want them to learn a bit about Euclidean geometry, and then contemplate alternatives? One thing is certain. In teaching such subjects as Latin syntax, a teacher cannot simply act as a chairperson. One's duty is to provide positive information, which must be made intelligible by as many examples as possible. No child can be expected to discover Latin syntax unaided from the ancient texts. In such a case the teacher must actually teach, that is pass on information and understanding which he or she has and the pupils, so far, have not. Whether or not the teacher wishes to preface all the teaching with remarks of the form "things being as they are" or "using the syntactical classification we do," the teacher must at some stage actually assert what is the case. I think that, empirically speaking, it would create endless confusion if he or she always put in the covering clause; and no sensible teacher who actually wanted to get the pupils to learn something would think of doing so.

We have come upon a case, then (and there are very many such), where although it is logically possible to regard the matter in a wholly different light, yet the teacher is justified in teaching certain facts as facts, as an aid to teaching certain skills. The teacher need not continually point out that someone else might deny that what he or she had taught was a fact. It may be suggested by the teacher that there could be a different frame of reference within which things would look different, but to point this out is most of the time irrelevant to one's purpose. A teacher who never pointed this out, who either did not believe it, or had never thought about it one way or another, need not be described as doctrinaire, nor need his or her teaching be described as indoctrinating. A person who accepts some facts as such, and passes on knowledge of them is not failing to be neutral.

However, up till now, we have been dealing with the easy cases. We have looked only at cases where the pupils have little scope either for discovering facts for themselves or making up their own minds between conflicting accounts. But we have only to think of a few more lessons in the school day to come upon subjects where the distinction between what is a fact and what is not is much harder to draw. In the discussion of history and geography (as they used to be called), indeed of the social sciences generally, it is frequently claimed that it is absolutely impossible to distinguish between facts and non-facts, that the notion of a fact is dangerously misleading, and that teachers must not deceive or bully their pupils by telling them things on the assumption that this distinction can be made. I want now to examine this claim a little further.

In the first place, it will be agreed that in the teaching of, for example, history, there has to be considerable selection of material, even if the teacher does not do it, but relies on a text book or syllabus-maker. Selection, notoriously, may be biased or one-sided. Good teachers will do their best to supplement material which they feel is inadequate in this sort of respect; but they would find it very hard radically to change the assumptions of our whole culture about what is worth discussing and what is not. The main historical issues to be examined will remain the same, changing only gradually, for many generations. The teacher cannot aspire to a god-like status as far as selecting material goes. If one chooses, one may preface all one's remarks with the warning that one is looking at the thing from the standpoint of a twentieth-century historian. But this warning, like the general warnings we looked at before, turns out to be empty, because one cannot specify at all exactly what alternatives there may some day be. The teacher *is* after all a twentieth-century historian. That he or she will be teaching from largely preselected material, then is necessarily true, and need not be taken to impair his or her neutrality, nor need it be taken to undermine the whole concept of the fact. But this is not the whole story. In most branches of the social sciences, the main purpose of the teacher is not only to impart information but to give to pupils a sense of evidence, of what does and what does not count as an argument, so that they may if they wish go on with the subject by themselves. It is in this area that the demand for neutrality is likely to become insistent. A teacher must present evidence fairly; he or she must not conceal evidence, nor exaggerate that which is favorable to one side or the other. The pupils must weigh the evidence and decide on the truth. Is the teacher thus put, whether he or she likes it or not, into the chair? Is being a chairperson enough? Let us take a concrete example. Suppose a class to be discussing the history of Mary Queen of Scots. They have arrived at the stage of the murder of Darnley. The question arises, was Mary or was she not implicated in this murder? Now one thing is certain. Pupils in an ordinary school class cannot examine any fresh evidence on this point. They cannot even read the secondary sources in detail, still less can they go back to contemporary sources. They must use evidence which is merely described to them, rather than presented in detail. The teacher must tell them what the sources are, and must tell them, for example, that Buchanan's history was specifically designed to incriminate Mary, that it contains inconsistencies, and cannot be taken as true or unbiased. The teacher must help the pupils to reconstruct the probable course of events, relying on his or her own knowledge of the period, and common sense and experience of how people in general behave. But in helping the pupils, is the teacher not to tell them what he or she thinks is the most likely account? Of course in a case like this no one cares very much one way or the other, and no one is likely to attack the teacher for non-neutrality even if the teacher does say what he or she thinks.

But there is a point in choosing such an example since the principles governing the teacher's behavior in this case are general, and apply equally to cases in which the passions are likely to be involved. I would argue that unless the teacher comes out into the open, and says in what direction the evidence points, he or she will have failed in his or her duty as a teacher. For what the pupils have to learn is not only, in an abstract way, what counts as evidence, but how people draw conclusions from evidence. The whole notion of evidence independent of any probable conclusion is meaningless. Of course there may be cases where the teacher thinks the evidence is genuinely inconclusive, and in this case must say that there is really no ground for coming down on one side or the other. But such cases are rare. If all evidence were inconclusive, then the concept of evidence itself would be, if not empty, at least radically different. Thus the teacher must in teaching pupils to assess evidence fairly, give them actual examples of how the teacher does this himself or herself. The pupils may disagree with the teacher. The more adult they become, and the better their earlier experience of arguments, the more capable they will be of weighing the probabilities differently. But unless they see before them the spectacle of a rational person drawing conclusions rationally, they will never learn what rational probabilities are. Obviously all kinds of factors personal to the teacher come in here. If one is dynamic and likeable one's views may tend to be uncritically accepted. If one is despised, they may be uncritically opposed. But all the same to see that the teacher is committed to a view which he or she thinks rationally follows from the evidence is of tremendous value in itself, whether or not his pupils follow him or her. The teacher must be a *leader* in argument if he or she is to teach argument. And a leader cannot sit on the fence for ever.

So far I have been treating only of facts, albeit selected and dubious facts. In this area I hope I have suggested that uncommitted neutrality in the teacher, in so far as it is possible, is not desirable. I want now to consider whether this conclusion has any bearing on the real question, the problem that all the fuss is about, namely the question whether or not a teacher should be neutral when the subject of the class is a matter of values. I do not wish to embark on the problem of distinguishing facts from values. It is sometimes argued that as there is no such thing as a pure fact, no proper distinction can be drawn between fact and value. If so, then perhaps we could take a short way with the subject and say that what has been said about facts ought to be said about values since they cannot be distinguished. But this would not be convincing. I would rather assume that we can all of us give examples of what, in non-philosophical moments, we should be prepared to call statements of fact. An example would be that Mary Queen of Scots knew that Darnley was to be murdered on February 9th, 1567, or that she did not know. (The fact that many people would be inclined to condemn her for conniving at the murder of her husband, however unsatisfactory, is neither here nor there. The factual question is, did she know about it or did she not?) We can, I shall assume, also all of us produce instances of obviously evaluative statements, such as that the publication of pornography ought to be severely restricted by law. It is to the second kind of statement, and the arguments which may take place in class about them that I want now to turn.

Now it is a truism that matters of fact may be relevant to the drawing of evaluative conclusions, though they may not entail these conclusions. That being so (and especially since relevance is one of the main lessons one has to teach), it follows that all the duties a teacher may have with respect to evidence in the historical examples already considered will be equally incumbent upon him or her in the evaluative case. And of course many of the historical cases may also be evaluative. But the collection and presentation of evidence is likely to be fraught with difficulties in the evaluative cases. Notoriously, for example, it is hard to discover what the effect of pornography is upon its willing consumers, even if an agreed starting definition of pornography can be arrived at. It is perhaps still harder to discover its effects upon those who have to consume it whether they like it or not. All evidence of the form "people in general do or suffer x" is extraordinarily hard to collect or present fairly. Still worse is evidence of the form "people suffer harm if x is done to them." For it is not only the scope of the generalization which causes difficulties, but the conceptual content as well. What is to count as harm? Such difficulties as these must be faced by the teacher who is trying to present the material on which the pupils are to base their judgment of whether or not pornography ought to be radically further restricted by law. But the teacher must be neither daunted nor deflected by this. One must plough one's way on as best one can, making it absolutely clear what one is doing, where one is assuming something that cannot be proven, and what one is preparing them to do. The material must be used, as far as possible, as *grounds* upon which to found a judgment. But now what happens? Does the teacher jib at forming a judgement, and simply demand that his or her pupils make one? Or does he or she state, as I have maintained that one should in the relatively "pure" historical case, his or her own view? Once again, I have no doubt whatever that one should state one's own view, and thus demonstrate to the pupils the whole process of basing a judgment on an interpretation of the facts. Insofar as the argument we are supposing is just an argument, the very same considerations apply to it as applied to the argument about Mary Queen of Scots. A pupil cannot understand the relevance of factual considerations to conclusions, without experience of the conclusion's being actually drawn. But in the evaluative case there are other and more important considerations as well.

First, as will be obvious from a consideration of the foregoing example, the facts cannot be absolutely determined. Interpretation is going to enter into the presentation of the grounds right from the start. It is therefore virtually impossible to separate a conclusion from its grounds. The conclusion, as it were, enters into the presentation of the grounds. But even if such separation were possible in practice, other objections would remain. There is a psychological objection to the spectacle of someone's remaining neutral in a highly charged dispute about a subject which is supposed to affect everyone and therefore be everyone's concern. The neutral person cannot but seem uninterested, and however much one claims to be *putting* aside one's own beliefs, in order to act the part of neutral chairperson, this does not prevent the teacher seeming either alarmingly remote, or positively scornful or patronizing, if he or she will not join in the dispute. There is a kind of nightmare in which one is in danger or pain or in some state of emotional tension of a painful kind and all the time on the sidelines, there is a perfectly impassive observer, taking no steps to help or comfort, or even to acknowledge the existence of a crisis. It is the nightmare of the knitters at the guillotine, or of the absolutely rational parent observing a child's tantrum and letting the child simply go on screaming. Something of this nightmarish sense is conveyed to pupils whose teacher will not take part in a debate, or state his or her own moral view.

It may be argued that this is a neurotic, or at any rate an exaggerated, reaction. Any such disagreeable effects are far outweighed by the desirability of getting pupils to see both sides of any question so as to ensure that they judge, when they do, rationally and without prejudice. Since a teacher has, it is argued, no right to impose his or her own prejudices on the pupils, he or she had better not voice them. One cannot expect the pupils to eliminate prejudice from their minds if one is seen to be guilty of prejudice oneself. So runs the argument for neutrality. The weakness of the argument lies, self-evidently, in the word "prejudice." I wish to distinguish between a prejudice and a moral belief, and thus to conclude that if a teacher states clearly his or her own moral belief, he or she is not displaying prejudice. The teacher has not *pre*judged anything. In the case supposed, he or she has examined and assessed the significance of what facts it has been possible to assemble, and then made a moral judgment of what ought to occur.

Very well, it may be said, let the moral belief be expressed, provided that it is shown how it was arrived at, and the teacher is careful to say that it is simply *his or her opinion*. Let the teacher by no means seek to impose this opinion on the pupils. If one cannot keep one's mouth shut, or if one feels that one must state one's own conclusion in order to demonstrate the drawing of a conclusion, let it at least be clearly shown that one realizes that other opinions are just as good (or, as people prefer to say, as valid).

But alas, this is impossible in the nature of the case. And here we have come upon the real nature of evaluative judgments. It is strictly impossible at one and the same time to say "this is wrong" and "but you need not think so." Although we all know perfectly well that values are relative to our society and our culture (or even to our little bit of society or culture) yet it is impossible to assert this truth *and* in the same breath seriously to assert a value judgment. We are inevitably and for ever divided in our minds. Either we make no value judgments, and are content to stand outside the making of them, or, if we do make them, we must for the time being put on one side our anthropological spectacles through which we survey the conflicting opinions of the human race. Moreover, if we have come to our moral judgment by the route of serious thought and a consideration of the evidence as fair as we can make it, then we cannot think that an opposite judgment follows equally "validly" from this same evidence. If we have concluded that something is wrong, we *must* think that everyone ought to hold it wrong, even though we know that they do not, and that we must put up with this. Now this feature of evaluative judgments is something that at some time or other pupils must learn to recognize, and, if possible, understand; and they can start to understand it from the expression of genuine moral convictions by their teacher. They will learn that someone who sincerely holds a moral conviction does not and cannot feel that any other conviction is *just* as good. That is the nature of the case. Moral relativism may be a fact; but it is not a fact that we feel while we are forming moral judgments. If we really believed that any moral view was as good and worthy to be adopted as any other, then we would of course make no moral judgments at all. And the same is true of all other, non-moral, evaluations. We cannot evaluate, and accept another evaluation at the same time as equally sound. Moral views, then, are not prejudices; but they are also totally distinct from matters of opinion.

One may, of course, raise the question what is the point of getting people at school to discuss such topics as whether or not the legislation about pornography should be changed. Part of the point, as has been suggested already, is to teach them to judge fairly on the evidence, and to understand the arguments both for and against the proposition. But part of the point is also actually to get them to think about right and wrong, good and evil, to think, that is to say, about morals. If this is accepted as part of their education, then they must not be deprived of the spectacle of a teacher who holds, and clearly expresses, moral views. There is nothing but benefit in the contemplation of a man or woman of principle. A person without moral views is after all a monster, and it is hard for pupils, especially if they are quite young, to realize that the neutral teacher is only play-acting. Moreover, if they do realize this, they resent it. Practically speaking, one of the things one learns from teaching children is that play-acting is despicable. The first rule of teaching is sincerity, even if one's sincerity is dotty or eccentric. A person ought to have and to express moral beliefs, and this entails that as a teacher one cannot remain neutral. For holding a moral belief is in some respects like having a vision. It is in a sense, an imaginative vision of how things ought to be though they are not. Expressing a moral belief is thus attempting to share a vision or way of looking, and this cannot be done without in some sense attempting to get your interlocutor to see things as you do, if only for the time. Pupils may discover, in the course of discussion, what they themselves think, what moral views they hold. But they cannot do this without exercising their imagination to see *in* the material under discussion a moral issue.

They must see it as a starting point from which they may envisage a world in which such things do not happen, or do happen freely. The teacher must help them to exercise their imagination; it is indeed the teacher's only serious function; and thus the teacher must help them to see the material as morally significant. This one can do only by demonstrating that it appears so to oneself. If a teacher, by the attractiveness of his or her personality, causes the pupils for the most part to share his or her vision, aesthetic or moral or of whatever other sort, the passage of time will remedy this, if remedy is needed. To have been conscious at some stage of one's life how someone else, a grown up, actually saw the world is far from harmful, even if later the viewpoint is totally abandoned. I conclude therefore that in the sphere of the evaluative, as of the factual, the teacher has a positive obligation, if he or she is to teach well, to be non-neutral; and that this is necessary because of the nature of moral, and other evaluative judgment.

It will be noted that in the foregoing argument I have seemed to assume that the teacher is older than the pupil, more knowledgeable and more rational, and also possessed of more experience, common sense and imagination. I make this assumption knowingly. I realize that there are teachers who are in all these respects (except generally that of age) the inferior of their pupils. Nevertheless the teacher's essential role is to be in all these respects the pupil's superior, and this is the role one must try to fill, necessarily. It is the role which creates the teaching situation, with all its intrinsic authority, and it is this *role*, not any particular occupier of it, which has been the subject of discussion. In such a role, I have maintained, the teacher will fail if he or she attempts to remain neutral.

facts & evidence
evaluation → conclusion
teacher as sincere
neutrality = monster
            nightmare
charisma!?!
validity of others' opinions

11

Propaganda in the Classroom: The Keegstra Case

William Hare

Memories are short, and soon a reference to Jim Keegstra, or an allusion to the Keegstra affair, will no doubt call for an explanatory footnote.[1] But in 1983-5, at the height of media attention in Canada, it seemed that an eponymous synonym for bigotry was about to enter the language. The Keegstra affair came almost overnight[2] to be seen as a paradigm case of indoctrination. There was general revulsion as the truth emerged, but we should follow Socrates in demanding more than a clear example. This was a case of miseducation, and we must be on guard against a number of potential misinterpretations. The idea of open-minded education excludes the possibility of viewing Keegstra as an "honest heretic" championing unpopular ideas in a free market.[3]

The General Background

Jim Keegstra believes in an international Jewish conspiracy to establish a world government, and regards the infamous *Protocols of the Learned Elders of Zion* as authentic. The fact that every reputable historian thinks this document a hoax is further proof for him that the conspiracy is alive and well. Keegstra's belief was central in his interpretation of historical events, and permeated his teaching throughout the year. In dealing with the Second World War, Keegstra taught that Zionists invented the Holocaust to attract supporters for their cause. When challenged by the authorities, Keegstra did not deny what he had been teaching, but sought to show that it was correct. His views were not smuggled in the course of dealing with other issues. The Jewish conspiracy thesis *dominated* Keegstra's lessons and he remains eager to defend it. His willingness springs from a profound conviction that he possesses a truth which must be communicated to others who have been duped:

Keegstra's perverse historical views were such, and presented in such a way, that his teaching displayed and fostered anti-Semitic attitudes. When students made disparaging remarks about Jews in their essays, Keegstra added marginal comments to reinforce these ideas. The conspiracy allegation, combined with other dreadful fictions about Jews, led students to write about Jews as thugs, rapists and assassins. Essays often argued that it was necessary to rid the world of dangerous Jews.

Disclosures of these teaching practices shocked Canadian society, and prompted the Province of Alberta to set up a Committee on Tolerance and Understanding in June 1983 which presented its final report in December 1984. The chairperson of the Committee remarked optimistically that "shocking revelations can become the catalyst from which flow a myriad of positive responses."[4] If teachers are not to shun controversy, however, a number of confused responses to the case need to be considered.

Villains are sometimes portrayed as martyrs. One hears mutterings about the value of open-mindedness, and the suggestion that Keegstra championed free inquiry. Many close to the scene were confused about the application of fundamental principles. Most Canadians now think that justice was done in dismissing Keegstra from the teaching profession, but since a revisionist thesis might be advanced, we need a clear grasp of the reasons which warranted termination of his contract and expulsion from the profession.

Buttons proclaiming "Freedom of Speech" were very much in evidence at the various judicial proceedings which began in 1984. Keegstra's lawyer, Douglas Christie, reportedly declared the case would be "the greatest test of freedom of speech this country has ever seen."[5] The Alberta Teachers' Association representative assigned to assist Keegstra answer the various charges brought by the Board, also insisted Keegstra's freedom of speech in the classroom was being curtailed.[6] Canadian civil libertarians denounced the prosecution of Keegstra as censorship, though some agreed that he had abused his position as a teacher and was rightly dismissed.[7]

Some of Keegstra's former students continue to believe he was silenced because the authorities were not committed to open inquiry. One student is quoted as saying that "perhaps people are scared he's stumbled onto the truth, and they don't want to know about it." The winner of the school's highest graduating award remained a loyal supporter of Keegstra *and* his ideas: "I'm trying so hard to be open-minded and they're close-minded."[8] Keegstra insisted he had presented an alternative point of view to make his students think,[9] and claimed that he advised his students that the position he defended "was only a theory,"[10] and not widely accepted.

The charge of bias came up frequently. One commentator, however, in reviewing the allegation that the students were not offered well-articulated alternatives, adds the qualification that "the problem of biased teaching will arise with every teacher."[11] A student is quoted as saying he had abandoned the idea of a career in teaching because he might slip up, say something inappropriate and land in jail.[12] The idea lurking behind both of these reactions is that bias is inevitable.

Keegstra was widely regarded, by students, colleagues, and the Alberta Teachers' Association as a good teacher. The principal at the time of Keegstra's dismissal testified that Keegstra did "a very thorough job" of classroom preparation, and that he had never heard Keegstra "call down another group except maybe Communists or Zionists."[13] A former principal commented that Keegstra's first qualification as a teacher was his "command of discipline."[14] Keegstra's classroom management skills have earned near universal praise. The Superintendent who pursued the case against Keegstra said that the issue was not Keegstra's competence as a teacher or his ability to teach the subject matter.[15]

There is enough confusion in these various reactions to warrant a careful examination of the assumptions which they reveal. We shall see that some who have shed light on this affair have also added to the confusion. Furthermore, there are ideas in circulation, advanced by philosophers who may never have heard of this case, which come to grief in the light of this sorry episode.

An Honest Heretic?

A liberal in the tradition of John Stuart Mill will, I think, experience some tension in considering this case:

> If all mankind minus one were of one opinion, mankind would be no more justified in silencing that one person than he, if he had the power, would be justified in silencing mankind.[16]

Yet, effectively, Keegstra *was* silenced, since the revocation of his teaching license removed a necessary condition of his employment. Where, in the words of Justice Holmes, is that "free trade in ideas" which ought to characterize education? Have we abandoned the idea that "the best test of truth is the power of the thought to get itself accepted in the competition of the market"?

In some ways, moreover, Keegstra does resemble the honest heretic rather than the furtive conspirator. Sidney Hook's classic distinction revealed differences showing why the heretic must be tolerated and the conspirator suppressed. The liberal, Hook wrote, "stands ready to defend the honest heretic no matter what his views against any attempt to curb him."[17] Like the heretic, Keegstra did not shrink from publicity. In the words of one commentator, "furtiveness is alien to him."[18] Keegstra, as far as we know, was in the service of no organized movement, though he joined the Canadian League of Rights and obtained much of his material from this group. There is every reason to agree that Keegstra sees himself as a solitary soldier.[19] The telltale signs of conspiracy are not to be found and not because the tracks have been covered.

Although no conspirator, however, Keegstra is only in part an honest heretic. Concerning the frank admission of the *content* of his views, Keegstra *is* the honest, forthright individual generally portrayed.[20] Keegstra did not conceal what he had been teaching when cross-examined at the Board of Reference inquiry, and his claim to have been teaching the required curriculum was not a lie but a mistaken belief. When we consider Keegstra's *methodology*, however, the ascription of honesty becomes suspect. Keegstra did alert his students to the fact that his theories were not widely shared and may even have advised them of the importance of examining different points of view.[21] But the evidence overwhelmingly suggests that his practice violated these principles.

First, Justice McFadyen established that *none* of the sources to which Keegstra directed his students contained a different point of view on the theory of history he propounded.[22] It is inconceivable that Keegstra was unaware of any such. Second, when students ventured to draw on sources other than those Keegstra approved, either their work was not assessed at all or assessed adversely.[23] Keegstra believes that sources critical of his position have been censored to conceal the truth, but he owed his students an honest account of alternative views in terms which defenders might accept as full and fair.[24] Third, Keegstra *encouraged* sweeping generalizations by his students by making comments calculated to confirm or support such views.[25] This makes a mockery of Keegstra's claim to be fostering the ability to discriminate between alternatives.[26]

Keegstra fails to qualify as an honest heretic in the classroom and forfeits the protection otherwise due. Appeal to the notion of a marketplace of ideas collapses because Keegstra's classes were systematically biased to inculcate at every opportunity the Jewish conspiracy theory. The notes, topics, readings, written comments, attitudes, and a grading system which rewarded agreement, were part of a strategy intended to convince students that a certain view of history was true. The decisive point is that the ground was cut from under the feet of any opposition by making the theory *immune* to counter-evidence. Potential counter-evidence was taken as *further* evidence of the conspiracy portrayed as controlling the *sources* of evidence, namely textbooks, the media and so on. Conspiracies can occur, of course, and it is doctrinaire to dismiss such claims *a priori*. But we need evidence that one exists, and refutation must be possible in principle. In frustrating the falsification challenge,[27] Keegstra revealed the disingenuous character of his teaching.

These criticisms are consistent with support for that strong tradition in philosophy of education which encourages students to become involved in the critical examination of controversy. Passmore has pointed out the limitations of teaching for critical thinking when criticism is reserved for "those who do not fully adhere to the accepted beliefs."[28] Russell advocated "the most vehement and terrific argumentation on all sides of every question,"[29] and maintained that there must be no requirement that teachers express only majority opinions. Strong enthusiasms, Russell said, are perfectly appropriate.[30] In protecting his own, one-sided view from criticism, however, Keegstra subverted the critical approach to teaching.

Unfortunately, some commentators have not questioned the plausibility of the marketplace defence used by Keegstra supporters. Consider the following suggestions:

The School is Not a Marketplace of Ideas

Keegstra did not, however, attempt to foster a marketplace of ideas and it is misguided to suggest, as some have done, that this case shows the inappropriateness of the marketplace ideal in public schooling:

> The elementary and high-school systems are not viewed by civil libertarians as part of the public forum we seek to protect from censorship. We doubt it makes sense to apply a notion such as "censorship" when we judge the professional wisdom of what is chosen for the attention of not yet fully-fledged minds.[31]

The common assumption, exemplified here, is that academic freedom has application only in the university context.[32] But if an open forum for discussion is appropriate at *any* level, then progressively there must be an anticipation of the practice during earlier stages of education. A rigid division between different levels is arbitrary. The "not yet fully-fledged minds" include 18-year-old adults in grade XII, or equivalent, who will be university students within three months. We might label the error here the fallacy of the magic transition. Finally, there is no reason to conclude that the concept of censorship does not apply in the school context. When books are removed from the library and words deleted from textbooks to accommodate complaints, censorship certainly exists.

Teaching is not Preaching

Anthony Blair distinguishes two uses of argument to illustrate what he sees as the defect in Keegstra's approach.[33] He distinguishes between (a) argument used to *convince* and (b) argument used to *inquire*, and Keegstra emerges as having attempted to convert the students to his position rather than as having shown them how to employ argument to test ideas. Keegstra's use of argument to convince, Blair claims, is very different from the attempt to foster open-mindedness.

First, however, notice the either/or nature of Blair's suggestion. The implication is that the teacher must opt for the second use of argument, i.e., to inquire, since argument used to convince "will often be perceived by those untutored in its deployment as an instrument of coercion."[34] Certainly, teachers who take a stand on some question and attempt to convince their students must *also* teach the use of argument as a tool of inquiry if the students are to have the wherewithal to assess the teacher's position critically. But the use of argument to convince is not in itself a violation of educational principles. What matters is how the argument is *conducted*. Keegstra's approach was a travesty of the Socratic ideal of following the argument where it leads, and for this he stands condemned. The obvious danger in Blair's diagnosis is that we are close to embracing teacher neutrality as an absolute principle.

Second, open-mindedness does not require neutrality. Blair glosses open-mindedness as "withholding judgment until one has thoroughly canvassed alternatives and seriously considered points of view other than one's own."[35] Though popular, this is inadequate as a general account. What matters is how one's convictions are held.[36] Here the central question is whether or not they are regarded as revisable in the light of emerging evidence and fresh argument. Keegstra is no champion of open-mindedness not because he held, and defended, certain convictions, but because these were *not* revisable; they had been granted immunity. Teaching is not preaching, but this is consistent with teachers employing argument in the attempt to convince.

Keegstra's student who claims to be open-minded is typical of those John Dewey criticized,[37] who naively think open-mindedness is indicated by merely adopting, or flirting with, unconventional ideas. Ironically, this student has been *prevented* from rationally reviewing his beliefs by coming to think all contrary evidence is untrustworthy. Moreover, the student has been discouraged from developing the capacity to recognize that his position comes with a spurious guarantee of its own certainty.

Despite endless debate over the analysis of indoctrination, it is reassuring that the parent responsible for initiating the complaint that eventually led to decisive action against Keegstra closed her letter to the Superintendent with the words: "As our children are being sent to school for education, not indoctrination, I appeal to you to dismiss Mr. Keegstra from teaching those classes in which our children will be enrolled."[38] This is the apposite distinction because the students were adopting beliefs in such a way that rational criticisms were defused. Many professionals were not able to articulate or even recognize the distinction in question. Some students did *eventually* start to question what they had come to believe following certain extraordinary steps including, for some, a trip to Dachau. (Even these measures were not uniformly successful.) The crucial point is not that the students' beliefs could *never* be dislodged, but that a *pattern* of thinking had emerged inimical to evidence and argument.[39]

Allen Pearson fears that certain presuppositions in the teaching context helped bring about the undesirable consequence of closed-minded allegiance to irrational beliefs.[40] The logic of the teaching situation, he argues, is that any teacher must be considered rational otherwise there would be no point attending to him or her: "One cannot be a learner if one does not accept that the teacher is acting rationally."[41] Teachers like Keegstra, Pearson adds, have difficulty with cynical or very sceptical students, but these are hardly desirable traits.

Pearson's pessimism is, I think, premature. Cynicism and scepticism are *not* the only defences against an irrational teacher. Inexplicably, Pearson fails to mention *critical reflection*. If schools developed critical ability in students, and discouraged deferential acceptance, learners would not be so vulnerable. There is an unavoidable criticism here of the teachers who taught these students before Keegstra. Few philosophers have noted that students need to be trained to resist indoctrination.[42] Keegstra's skill shows how important such an ability is, for Keegstra was unable to recognize his own teaching as indoctrination. The psychology of the classroom is often such that uncritical acquiescence results,[43] but there is no *logical* barrier to success as Pearson implies. One can learn from teachers even if one fails to agree with their ideas, or suspects that the ideas presented are spurious. One can *understand* what the beliefs are and why some people hold them, and resolve to assess their merits. Typically, we presume that the teacher believes what he or she is saying, but we need not, and must not, assume that the claims are true. Pearson overlooks provisional agreement where we accept "for the sake of argument" but reserve the right to subject the beliefs in question to later critical examination. If these attitudes sound sophisticated, the Keegstra case nevertheless indicates their necessity. We expect we can learn something valuable from our teachers, but expectations are not always fulfilled.

The Principle of Tolerance

The Province of Alberta moved soon after the Keegstra revelations to establish a Committee on Tolerance and Understanding. Its interim report maintained that a basic aim of education is to instil in children an appreciation of our democratic traditions, characterized by an attitude of tolerance, understanding and respect for others, *no matter what their origins or values may be.*[44] The final report, however, omitted these concluding words. It likely occurred to someone that the deleted statement made no sense in the light of the circumstances which gave rise to the Committee's work. Were tolerance required no matter what a person's values, then Keegstra's intolerance would itself have to be tolerated.

Certainly some took that quixotic course. The Alberta Teachers' Association representative who defended Keegstra at the early hearings said he could accept different points of view being a fairly tolerant person. He maintained that Keegstra had advanced a different point of view as was his right.[45] This comment exemplifies the confusion mentioned earlier that leads some to see Keegstra as a champion of free inquiry silenced by an intolerant society.[46] Keegstra's right to *mention* and *discuss* alternative points of view and interpretations had never been challenged by the School Board, though it had given directions about balance. In his first letter to Keegstra, Superintendent David wrote he had not intended to muzzle Keegstra's academic freedom nor to limit his intellectual integrity. Controversial interpretations were not to be suppressed but all positions were to be presented in as unbiased a way as possible.[47] Appealing uncritically to the principle of tolerance, the Alberta Teachers' Association in effect extended tolerance to indoctrination.

The wording on bias avoids the naive position that a bias-free presentation is possible without suggesting that the amount and nature of bias is quite beyond our control. The problem of biased teaching may arise with every teacher, but not in the same way nor to the same degree. Although teachers can slip into bias, tolerance here is appropriate when teachers display a willingness to review their performances and the judgments of others critically. Keegstra sincerely believed his own position was correct, but he could and should have been aware that he was not presenting other views impartially. If we tolerate the systematic distortion of issues in teaching, we cannot claim to have a serious concern for our students' education.

The Keegstra case is useful in philosophy of education as a touchstone for testing philosophical generalizations.[48] If we have confidence in a particular judgment, we can ask how a certain general principle fares when viewed in the light of that judgment. Mary Warnock argues that a teacher is not invariably required to remain neutral on controversial issues.[49] It would be a pity if confusion resulting from the Keegstra case gave undeserved support to the neutral teacher movement. Russell saw clearly that a teacher could display strong enthusiasms but there remained an obligation to give an impartial account of what really happened. Mary Warnock, however, exaggerates the benefits of non-neutrality risking undue teacher influence on students. She maintains there is only benefit in the contemplation of someone who has principles: "The first rule of teaching is sincerity, even if one's sincerity is dotty or eccentric."[50] Concerning the danger of winning over students too easily, she assures us that time will remedy this, if remedy is needed. Mary Warnock was not commenting on Keegstra, but how do her comments stand up in the light of this case?

A number of points should be made. First, it is clear we cannot say that Keegstra has no principles. He does not have, as Mackie once put it, a new principle for every case.[51] Keegstra has his own principles and will not abandon them for convenience or advantage. But although we may admire his courage and sincerity, it is not true that there is *nothing but benefit* in contemplating his actions. His principles are flawed from an educational perspective. Keegstra's concern for truth, which he often stressed, amounted to an all-consuming desire that his students believe what he accepted as true. In Russell's language, the will to believe overshadowed the wish to find out.[52] This desire was not tempered by a concern to help students weigh evidence and formulate independent judgments. The clearest evidence of Keegstra's position and his blind attachment to it is his lack of concern over the appalling ignorance and illiteracy displayed in student essays.[53]

Second, in characterizing perverse sincerity as eccentric or dotty, Mary Warnock has overlooked more serious harms. We smile at eccentricity or dottiness, but these friendly descriptions hardly capture Keegstra's mind-set. Having students think of Jews as "gutter rats" cannot be airily dismissed as eccentricity. When a student writes that we must get rid of every Jew in existence, we have gone beyond the dotty. The case shows a failure of imagination on Mary Warnock's part with respect to the forms perversity can take. Furthermore, this case makes one less sanguine about time effecting a remedy. Bercuson and Wertheimer fear that Keegstra's students may become the bearers of medieval myths in the future.[54] Interviews with some students two years after Keegstra's dismissal provide little basis for sharing Mary Warnock's confidence, yet much more than the mere passage of time was at work in this case.[55] Mary Warnock had not envisaged a case where the beliefs acquired immunised one against counter-evidence, so that the passage of time would make no difference or even make matters worse.

We should be reluctant to embrace the level of tolerance suggested by Mary Warnock's comment. Should we even tolerate the *inclusion* of ideas such as the Jewish conspiracy theory? Many will find the theory offensive and it is widely regarded as totally implausible. There is, however, a powerful tradition in philosophy of education which supports the inclusion of controversial material and open discussion of related issues. But it is doubtful that the Jewish conspiracy theory properly counts as a controversial historical thesis. Reputable historians do not seriously debate it. A few dispute the opinion held by experts but have not succeeded in making the matter controversial. From the perspective of historical research, the theory is a non-starter.

Should it also be ignored in teaching? Surely, the school might give the theory unwitting support by deeming it worthy of mention. Its exclusion, however, might fuel the suspicion that the theory has some credibility, a suspicion actually voiced by some students.[56] If suppression of such a view could be effectively carried out in society as a whole, this danger would disappear, but that is not a realistic possibility quite apart from considerations of moral acceptability. Given this dilemma, a compromise might be proposed, namely to ignore the theory unless it is brought up by a student. This strategy, however, presupposes that students genuinely feel comfortable raising issues, otherwise they might be privately nursing their suspicions. We need to remember here that students raise few questions of any kind in class.[57]

The traditional response to the dilemma invokes the ideal that truth should emerge in open discussion. There is no need to exclude the theory since its absurdity can be demonstrated. We can explain that it is included not because it is important, interesting or plausible, but simply because students may encounter it. Recently, however, Schauer has cast doubt on the so-called argument from truth:

> The argument from truth is very much a child of the Enlightenment, and of the optimistic view of the rationality and perfectibility of humanity it embodied. . . . People are not nearly so rational as the Enlightenment assumed, and without this assumption the empirical support for the argument from truth evaporates.[58]

Schauer reminds us that truth has no inherent ability to gain general acceptance. The argument from truth leads to the dubious assumption that the search for truth is the supreme value.

It is not evident, however, that these points carry weight in the context of education. In tolerating open discussion of reprehensible views, the assumption is not that students are thoroughly rational. Rather, one of the central aims of education is to *further* their development as rational agents. To curtail discussion in schools because people are not always rational would deprive students of the very practice that might lead to the development of rational abilities. If it is true now that people are not particularly good at distinguishing truth from falsity, it is especially important for schools to look for ways in which this ability can be developed. Particular considerations might outweigh the importance of open discussion of certain issues at certain times, but present abilities are not the determining factor. Schauer says that we must take the public as it is, but in the context of education our sights must be on what the students *can be*. The study of bad arguments is an important part of learning to argue effectively. Prior practice in this area would have served Keegstra's students well.

If we tolerate the discussion of such a theory, should we also tolerate the teacher indicating support for it? Keegstra's own approach was obviously unacceptable, and we might note Russell's point that when the experts agree, the opposite opinion cannot be regarded as certain. This alone would condemn Keegstra's teaching as profoundly misleading.[59] What, however, of the teacher who avoids that error, presents all views fully and fairly, but reveals a personal inclination to accept a theory universally discredited and offensive.

Let us distinguish this case from two others. Consider, first, the fact that various groups find aspects of the school curriculum offensive. An example might be a reference to atrocities carried out in the past. Here, it is vital to ask if the atrocities are indeed part of the historical record. If so, we would distort historical inquiry were we to allow our preferences to dictate what enters our history books or lessons. There is a positive obligation to be faithful to the discipline and report what happened. There is also a moral obligation to try to ensure that such facts do not lead to prejudice against those associated with the country in question.

Consider, secondly, the debate over creation science. This position is utterly discredited, but it is not in itself morally offensive whatever one may think of the tactics sometimes employed in its defence. One simply reveals naivete in subscribing to such views. If a teacher reveals sympathy for creation science, appeal to eccentricity will suffice to justify tolerance if the teacher at the same time manages to present orthodox science as it would be presented by a teacher who personally regarded it as serious.

The Jewish conspiracy theory, however, is both discredited and offensive. A teacher who reveals that he or she accepts it necessarily alienates all those students, not only Jews, who take offence at others being falsely accused of general wickedness. In ordinary life, we can usually avoid those who utter offensive remarks, but reasonable avoidability does not exist at school.[60] Students are obliged to attend and not normally permitted to choose which section of a course they will take, and therefore which teacher they will have, when multiple sections are available.[61] I conclude that in such cases the expression of the teacher's private sympathies should not be permitted.

Concluding Comment

Recall that Keegstra was widely hailed as a "good teacher." This suggests the dispiriting conclusion that this appraisal has lost its essential meaning. The judgment was based on the fact that Keegstra maintained discipline, and was totally unrelated to any consideration of the knowledge, skills and attitudes being learned by his students. Possibly this case will lead us to think out more carefully what a good teacher does. In doing this, we will be stimulated, I think, by an observation from Russell that might have applied to this very case:

> Love of power is the chief danger of the educator, as of the politician; the man who can be trusted in education must care for his pupils on their own account, not merely as potential soldiers in an army of propagandists for a cause.[62]

Notes

[1]It might read as follows. James Keegstra (b. 1934) taught in the province of Alberta from 1961 to 1983. Having qualified as an auto mechanic in 1957, he enrolled as a part-time student at what is now the University of Calgary, pursuing a B.Ed. program with a concentration in industrial arts. Before graduating in 1967, he taught industrial arts and other subjects, finally securing a permanent position at Eckville High School, Eckville, in 1968. He gradually came to teach classes in history and social studies, and it was his teaching here and his failure to conform to the prescribed curriculum which led to his dismissal from the school, effective January 1983. This decision was upheld by Justice Elizabeth McFadyen in a Board of Reference ruling in April 1983. In October 1983, the Alberta Minister of Education revoked Keegstra's teaching license, and he was expelled from the Alberta Teachers' Association. In July 1985, Keegstra was convicted under section 281.2 of the Canadian Criminal Code of wilfully promoting hatred against the Jews, a charge arising directly from his classroom activities, and fined $5000. In June 1988, the conviction was overturned by the Alberta Court of Appeal on the grounds that the law in question violates the Canadian Charter of Rights and Freedoms. The Crown's appeal was heard in the Supreme Court of Canada in December 1989, and in December 1990 the Supreme Court of Canada ruled in a 4-3 judgment that the hate-promotion statute is constitutional. The case was sent back to the Alberta Court of Appeal where the original conviction was overturned in 1991 on a technicality. In July 1992 following a new trial on the same charge, Keegstra was again found guilty and fined $3000.00. In September 1994, the Alberta Court of Appeal struck down the conviction in a 2-1 decision, the majority holding that he had not been given a fair trial. In a unanimous 9-0 ruling in February 1996, the Supreme Court of Canada restored the conviction on the charge of promoting hatred, and reaffirmed its 1990 ruling that the hate law is constitutionally valid.

[2]Much of the credit for bringing the case to national attention must go to the documentary "Lessons in Hate" shown on the CBC's *The Journal*, May 2, 1983.

[3]The best general introduction to the case is: David Bercuson and Douglas Wertheimer, *A Trust Betrayed: The Keegstra Affair* (Toronto: Doubleday Canada, 1985).

[4]Committee on Tolerance and Understanding, *Final Report* Edmonton, Alberta, 1984. Headed by Ron Ghitter, the committee came to be known as the Ghitter Committee.

[5]*MacLean's* June 25, 1984: 29.

[6]See D. Bercuson and D. Wertheimer, *A Trust Betrayed*, 106.

[7]See John Dixon, "The Politics of opinion," *The Canadian Forum* 66, April 1986: 7-10.

[8]For the reactions of the students, see Robert Mason Lee, "Keegstra's children," *Saturday Night*, May 1985: 38-46.

[9]See D. Bercuson and D. Wertheimer, *A Trust Betrayed*, 112.

[10]This phrase is used in the report of the Board of Reference, presumably echoing Keegstra's testimony. See footnote 1 above.

[11]Christopher Podmore, "Our Freedoms of Expression: Reflections on the Zundel and Keegstra Affairs," *Humanist in Canada*, 18, 4, 1985-6: 16-17.

[12]See Steve Mertl and John Ward, *Keegstra: The Issues, The Trial, The Consequences* (Saskatoon: Western Producer Prairie Books, 1985), 133.

[13]Cited in Arthur M. Schwartz, "Teaching Hatred: the Politics and Morality of Canada's Keegstra Affair," *Canadian and International Education*, 15, 2, 1986: 5-28. Apparently, abuse is acceptable if the targets are limited.

[14]See Schwartz, "Teaching Hatred," 13.

[15]Letter from Robert K. David to James Keegstra, March 9, 1982. Document 3 in the appendix to D. Bercuson and D. Wertheimer, *A Trust Betrayed*.

[16]John Stuart Mill, *On Liberty* (Harmondsworth: Penguin Books, 1977), chapter 2.

17.Sidney Hook, "Heresy, Yes -- Conspiracy, No," in Harry K. Girvetz (ed.), *Contemporary Moral Issues* (Belmont: Wadsworth), 1963, 62-71. An extract from a book by Sidney Hook with the same title.

[18]Kasper Mazurek, "Indictment of a Profession: The Continuing Failure of Professional Accountability," *Teacher Education*, 32, 1988: 58.

[19]D. Bercuson and D. Wertheimer, *A Trust Betrayed*, 15.

[20]K. Mazurek, "Indictment of a Profession," 58.

[21]D. Bercuson and D. Wertheimer, *A Trust Betrayed*, 50.

[22]Appeal to Board of Reference, 1983, p. 19 of transcript.

[23]D. Bercuson and D. Wertheimer, *A Trust Betrayed*, 61.

[24]See Alan Montefiore (ed.), *Neutrality and Impartiality: The University and Political Commitment* (London: Cambridge University Press, 1975), 18.

[25]R.M. Lee, "Keegstra's children," 38.

[26]Letter from Keegstra to Superintendent David, March 18, 1982. See document 4 in the appendix to Bercuson and Wertheimer, *A Trust Betrayed*.

[27]Antony Flew, *Thinking About Thinking* (Glasgow: Fontana/Collins, 1975), 55.

[28]John Passmore, "On teaching to be critical," in R. S. Peters (ed.), *The Concept of Education* (London: Routledge and Kegan Paul, 1967), 197.

[29]Bertrand Russell, "Education for Democracy," *Addresses and Proceedings of the National Education Association*, 77, (2-6 July), 1939, 529.

[30]Bertrand Russell and Dora Russell, *Prospects of Industrial Civilization* (New York: Century, 1923), 255.

[31]John Dixon, "The Politics of Opinion," 7. At the time the article was published, John Dixon was President of the British Columbia Civil Liberties Association.

[32]See, for example, Anthony O'Hear, "Academic Freedom and the University," *Journal of Philosophy of Education*, 22, 1, 1988: 13-21. This point does not imply that academic freedom and freedom of speech are equivalent notions.

[33]J. Anthony Blair, "The Keegstra Affair: A Test Case for Critical Thinking," *History and Social Science Teacher* 21, 3, 1986: 158-164.

[34]Ibid., 161-162.

[35]Ibid., 162.

[36]See my *Open-mindedness and Education* (Montreal, Que.: McGill-Queens University Press, 1979); and my *In Defence of Open-mindedness* (Montreal, PQ: McGill-Queen's University Press, 1985).

[37]A good example is in John Dewey, *Democracy and Education* (New York: Macmillan, 1966), 175.

[38]Letter from Susan Maddox to R. K. David, October 11, 1982. Document 6 in the appendix to D. Bercuson and D. Wertheimer, *A Trust Betrayed.*

[39]The testimony of the teacher who had the unwelcome task of succeeding Keegstra at Eckville High and of counteracting his efforts is clear. See *The Globe and Mail* April 11, 1985: 1-2.

[40]Allen T. Pearson, "Teaching and Rationality: The Case of Jim Keegstra," *Journal of Educational Thought*, 20, 1, 1986: 1-7.

[41]Ibid., 5.

[42]An exception is Noam Chomsky. See his "Toward a Humanistic Conception of Education," in Walter Feinberg and Henry Rosemount, Jr. (eds.), *Work, Technology, and Education* (Urbana: University of Illinois Press, 1975), 204-20.

[43]See Jim MacKenzie, "Authority," *Journal of Philosophy of Education*, 22, 1, 1988: 57-65.

[44]A portion of the interim report was published in *Canadian School Executive*, 4, 2, 1984: 34. Emphasis mine.

[45]See D. Bercuson and D. Wertheimer, *A Trust Betrayed*, 117.

[46]Unfortunately, Bercuson and Wertheimer inadvertently add to the confusion. In making it clear that Harrison, the ATA's representative, had *not* defended Keegstra's right to teach the Jewish conspiracy theory as a *fact* of history, they add (as a criticism of the short clip of a longer interview with Harrison shown on CBC television) the comment that the public perception was that Harrison had defended "Keegstra's right to teach his students about a Jewish conspiracy." But, of course, Harrison *had* defended this, and the School Board had never challenged it. The wording blurs the very distinction needed between teaching as a fact and teaching about a claim. See *A Trust Betrayed*, 117-118.

[47]Letter from R. K. David to Keegstra, December 18, 1981. See Document 1 in the appendix to D. Bercuson and D. Wertheimer, *A Trust Betrayed.*

[48]Compare Joel Feinberg, *Social Philosophy* (Englewood Cliffs, NJ: Prentice-Hall, 1973).

[49]Mary Warnock, "The neutral teacher," reprinted in this collection.

[50]Ibid.

[51]John L. Mackie, *Ethics: Inventing Right and Wrong* (Harmondsworth: Penguin Books, 1977), 156.

[52] See Bertrand Russell, "Free Thought and Official Propaganda," in Russell, *The Will To Doubt* (New York: Philosophical Library, 1958), 23.

[53] One such essay is reproduced as document 11 in D. Bercuson and D. Wertheimer, *A Trust Betrayed*.

[54] D. Bercuson and D. Wertheimer, *A Trust Betrayed*, 187.

[55] See R.M. Lee, "Keegstra's Children."

[56] See earlier footnote 8.

[57] See James T. Dillon, "The Remedial Status of Student Questioning," *Journal of Curriculum Studies*, 20, 3, 1988: 197-210.

[58] Frederick Schauer, *Free Speech: A Philosophical Enquiry* (Cambridge: Cambridge University Press, 1982, 26.

[59] Bertrand Russell, "On the Value of Scepticism," in Russell, *The Will to Doubt*, 39.

[60] See Joel Feinberg, *Social Philosophy*, 44.

[61] This practice, incidentally, reveals the near universal assumption that a student in school may not evaluate his or her teachers, an assumption which clearly increases the difficulty any student would face in challenging someone like Keegstra.

[62] Bertrand Russell, *Power: A New Social Analysis* (London: George Allen and Unwin, 1938), 304.

- need for equal presentation
- options not truths
- unconventional ideals — what is their place
- voicing opinion
- open minded not empty. or narrow.

12

Re-examining the Meaning of Freedom of Expression: The Case of Malcolm Ross

Sheva Medjuck

Introduction

The Human Rights Inquiry in New Brunswick investigating the complaint of business person and parent David Attis against the Moncton School Board,[1] the employer of Malcolm Ross (hereafter referred to as the Ross case), provides yet another context for analyzing a whole series of complex issues important not only in terms of Canadian jurisprudence, but also in terms of our fundamental definitions of Canadian society. There is a wide range of serious ethical and legal questions raised by Ross and similar cases, for example, the role of the teacher, the meaning of academic freedom, the nature of education, and the issue of responsibility for educational equality to name just a few. The most controversial debate, however, centres around the issue of freedom of expression.

Although the complaint by David Attis was launched against the Moncton School Board and not against Malcolm Ross, this did not deter counsels from arguing their cases to some degree based on Malcolm Ross's right to freedom of expression as defined in Section 2(b) of the Canadian Charter.[2] While the arguments presented at the New Brunswick Human Rights Inquiry, the Judicial Review, the Court of Appeal for New Brunswick and the Supreme Court of Canada represented numerous points in law, the issue of freedom of expression remained highly salient throughout the case. Defining the parameters of freedom of expression has potentially enormous impact on our conception of Canadian society. There are important differences in the manner in which the Ross case was heard compared to other similar high profile cases – the Ross case under Human Rights provisions, the Zundel case under false news legislation in the Criminal code and the Keegstra case under anti-hate legislation in the Criminal Code – and thus there are differing legislative consequences.[3] Nevertheless, there are important similarities in terms of their societal consequences. It is these broader societal consequences that I wish to address.

Particulary, I suggest that those who argue for virtually limitless freedom of speech have misinterpreted both the moral and legal intent of freedom of expression guarantees. Before these issues are discussed, it is necessary first to provide a brief background to the Ross case.

The Events Leading up to the Human Rights Inquiry

In September 1988 a Human Rights Board of Inquiry was appointed in the Province of New Brunswick in order to investigate the complaint of David Attis, a Jewish parent in Moncton, New Brunswick against the Board of School Trustees, District 15. David Attis's complaint, in brief, concerned the School Board's failure to take appropriate action against school teacher, Malcolm Ross, who, it was alleged, made racist, discriminatory, and bigoted statements both to his students and in published statements and writings. By its failure to take appropriate action against Malcolm Ross, the complainant alleged that the School Board condoned an anti-Jewish role model and breached section 5(1) of the Human Rights Act of New Brunswick.

While the complaint against Ross was filed in September 1988, concerns about the writings of Malcolm Ross significantly predate this date. By 1978, as a consequence of numerous controversial letters by Malcolm Ross to the editor of various New Brunswick newspapers, as well as the publication of the book *Web of Deceit,* Julius Israeli had requested, in letters to the Director of School district 15 and the principal of Magnetic Hill School, that Ross be dismissed because of these writings. In June, 1978, Noel Kinsella, then Chairman of the Human Rights Commission, wrote to the School Board expressing concern over Ross's writings and requesting that his classroom performance be supervised. The School Board at this time maintained the position that what a school teacher did on his own time should not be brought before the Board. The Department of Justice of New Brunswick rejected Julius Israeli's request to prosecute Ross for his book *Web of Deceit* because it felt that there was insufficient evidence, in the opinion of the crown prosecutor, to sustain a prosecution. In 1983 and 1984 Malcolm Ross published two additional works, *The Real Holocaust* and *The Battle for Truth: Christianity v. Judeo-Christianity.* As a consequence of a complaint by Julius Israeli, the Moncton Police in 1985 asked the Department of Justice to investigate if these books were hate literature. However, in 1986 the Minister of Justice, David Clark, refused to take Malcolm Ross to court over the books arguing that the materials were presently unavailable; that there was no evidence that Ross had any intention to publish or distribute materials in the future; and that the public awareness of the material at that present time seemed minimal.

Although there were several meetings with Malcolm Ross and the School Board during this period, an important turning point in this case was an "interview" Ross conducted with himself in October 1986 in the newspaper, the *Miramichi Leader.* This interview indicated that Ross was continuing to preach his Jewish conspiracy theory, that his books were easily obtained, and furthermore that he planned to keep writing. After a meeting with Ross over this article, the School Board established a monitoring system for Malcolm Ross's classes. The School Board in a letter to Malcolm Ross expressed its concern over articles in the media and inquiries that had been made to the School Board by the Departments of Justice and Education about Malcolm Ross. This action by the School Board, however, failed to quell the growing controversy over the writings of Malcolm Ross.

Finally, in January 1987, shortly after the CBC program, *Sunday Morning,* aired a broadcast regarding Malcolm Ross's writings, the School Board decided to appoint a Review Committee. A little less than one month later, the School Board exonerated Malcolm Ross. The Committee argued that there was no evidence that Ross was teaching his private beliefs in the classroom. It was further noted that Ross's classes were supervised three times a week by the school and twice a month by the district. The Committee concluded that the publicity surrounding the case had no negative effect on the human relations within the present school or between the school and the community (defined only as the community immediately around Magnetic Hill School where Ross taught). This report was accepted by the Board with only one dissenting vote, that of Audrey Lampert. The Board, however, refused to release this report wanting to "finally lay to rest" the Malcolm Ross issue. Audrey Lampert, the sole dissenter to the report, failed to get a seconder to her motion that District 15 School Board "publicly express its repugnance of all forms of racism and its vehement opposition to hate mongering by any individual.".

A second attempt in April 1987 to convince the Attorney General of New Brunswick, David Clark, to lay charges against Malcolm Ross was not successful. The Attorney General felt, after reviewing RCMP reports, that there was "no reasonable prospect of conviction based on the evidence." A subsequent election, with the Liberals sweeping New Brunswick, and the appointment of James Lockyer as the Attorney General, did not change this position. James Lockyer argued that federal law made it impossible for him to win a conviction against Ross.

The publication of Malcolm Ross's fourth book, *Spectre of Power,* in 1988, once again stirred up controversy. The New Brunswick Department of Justice reviewed this book. The Minister of Education, Shirley Dysart, claimed that School Board 15 had the power to discipline an employee when his actions call the school system into disrepute and expressed confidence that the Board would review the situation and act responsibly. However, she stated that "It's not in my position to say I want to fire him. I will act on any decision the school board makes." The next day, Premier McKenna commented: "I'm not happy with his [Ross] presence in the classroom – I find it unconscionable. Whether or not it's being taught in a classroom does not minimize the seriousness. He is a publicly paid employee enunciating beliefs totally contrary to what is being taught in the educational system."

Although it did not wish to reopen the Malcolm Ross case, the School Board did establish a four member committee which, in fact, concluded that the activities of Malcolm Ross were "inhibiting the employer's ability to effectively manage and direct the educational process." Further "the board of school trustees strongly disapproves of his continued publication of materials expressing controversial views and reprimands him for such activities." The School Board advised Ross that any further publication or engaging in any public forum or discussion of his views or in relation to his publications, now or in the future, would result in more severe disciplinary action by the Board – including dismissal. This decision, referred to as the "gag" order, was unsuccessfully grieved by Ross.

In April of 1988 a formal complaint by David Attis was made to the Human Right Commission against District 15 School Board. In undertaking its investigation, the Human Rights Commission was denied by the School Board access to Malcolm Ross's records, and to the copy of the 1987 Review Committee Report. Failing to resolve the complaint, the Board of Inquiry was established, but did not begin its hearings until December 1990 owing to a long series of legal challenges.

While these legal challenges were being heard, the School Board established new guidelines for teachers intending to ensure students of a positive and safe learning environment which taught respect for individuals' rights and freedoms and providing disciplinary action against any employee who hindered the provision of school services (Policy 5006). In September 1989, the School Board lifted the gag order against Ross, removed the letter of reprimand from his file, and asked Ross to abide by this new Policy 5006. Two months later, Malcolm Ross appeared on Cable television in Moncton espousing his views. The School Board issued a written reprimand to Ross concerning the remarks he made on this television program, indicating that his remarks were contrary to Policy 5006. A letter to Malcolm Ross indicated that the School Board is "sincerely requesting that you refrain from publicly assailing another religious belief – the Jewish religion – when proclaiming your faith."

The Legal Process

The Human Rights Board of Inquiry investigating the complaint of David Attis heard eight days of testimony in December 1990 and a further 14 days of testimony in April 1991, rendering its decision in August 1991. David Attis alleged that the School Board violated Section 5(1) of the Human Rights Act by discriminating against him and his children in the provision of accommodation, services or facilities on the basis of religion and ancestry. Attis argued that the School Board, by its own statements and its failure to take action against the statements of Malcolm Ross,

> has condoned his views, has thus provided a racist and anti-Jewish role model for its students, has fostered a climate where students feel more at ease expressing anti-Jewish views, . . . thus depriving Jewish and other minority students of equal opportunity within the educational system . . .[4]

It is important to note that the Board of Inquiry had considerable latitude. Board Chairperson, Brian Bruce ruled that the District 15 School Board, in fact, had discriminated against the Complainant contrary to Subsection 5(1) of the Act, not only directly by its own actions, but also indirectly through the actions of its employee, Malcolm Ross. The findings of the Board of Inquiry indicate that: there are numerous references in the writings of Malcolm Ross which are discriminatory against persons of the Jewish faith; the public statements and writings of Malcolm Ross have created a poisoned environment within School District 15 which interfered with the educational services provided to the Complainant and his children; and the reluctance of the School Board to take disciplinary action prior to 1988 can be seen as creating the effect that the School Board was in fact supporting and condoning the views of Malcolm Ross.

The Board of Inquiry imposed several remedies. While these remedies involve pro-active direction to the Department of Education with respect to provincial action, it is the remedies directed at the School Board which were most contentious. These included: placing Malcolm Ross on immediate leave of absence without pay for a period of eighteen months; appointing him to a non-teaching position if, within that period one became available for which he was qualified; and terminating his employment at the end of the eighteen month leave of absence if a non-teaching position were not found. Finally, Bruce ordered that the School Board terminate Malcolm Ross' employment immediately if, at any time during the leave of absence or during his employment in a non-teaching position, he continued his publication or wrote for the purpose of publication anything that mentions a Jewish or Zionist conspiracy or attacks followers of the Jewish religion.[5] Subsequent to this decision, a Judicial Review, upheld the dismissal of Malcolm Ross from a teaching position, but removed Clause 2(d), the prohibition on his writings as well as those remedies directed at the Department of Education.[6] Ross appealed to the Court of Appeal for New Brunswick which in December 1993 allowed Ross's appeal on a 2-1 split decision, quashing both the gag order and his removal from the classroom.[7]

In September 1994 leave to appeal was granted by the Supreme Court of Canada and in October 1995 the case was argued. Three appeals by the New Brunswick Human Rights Commission, the Canadian Jewish Congress, and David Attis were heard. Interestingly David Attis appealed only the quashing of the removal of Ross from the classroom and did not appeal the gag order. The Human Rights Commission appealed to the Supreme Court the entire decision of the New Brunswick Court of Appeal. On April 3, 1996, over eight years after the complaint was initially laid against Ross by parent David Attis, the Supreme Court of Canada reversed the 1993 decision by the New Brunswick Court of Appeal. In their unanimous decision, written by Justice Gerald La Forest, all nine justices ruled that Malcolm Ross would not be allowed back into his New Brunswick classroom. The Supreme Court argued that Jewish children would perceive "a poisonous educational environment" because of Ross's writings and beliefs. The court ruled that it was irrelevant that Ross kept his anti-Jewish views outside the classroom, arguing that "young children are especially vulnerable to the messages conveyed by their teachers. They are less likely to make an intellectual distinction between comments a teacher makes in the school and those the teacher makes outside the school."[8] With respect to freedom of expression, the Court argued that "to give protection to views that attack and condemn the views, beliefs and practices of others is to undermine the principle that all views deserve equal protection, and muzzles the voice of truth."[9]

There are two important issues raised by the Ross Inquiry. The first concerns the appropriate conduct for a teacher both within and outside the classroom, and the second, and by far more contentious issue, has to do with the right of any individual to express his or her views no matter how unacceptable these views may be. While the former, the appropriate conduct for a teacher, at first glance is clearly the easier of the two, the initial quashing by the New Brunswick Court of Appeal of the ruling to remove Malcolm Ross from the classroom (although subsequently reversed by the Supreme Court of Canada), suggests that even this issue has important dissenters. It is instructive to note, however, that with respect to a teacher's conduct both within and outside the classroom even civil libertarians acknowledge "that certain expressions outside the classroom could render teachers unworthy recipients of trust for teaching, guidance, and evaluation."[10] With respect to the second issue, which centres around the definition of freedom of expression, the failure of the Attorneys-General of New Brunswick to prosecute Malcolm Ross under the anti-hate provisions of the Criminal Code, the reversal of the Judicial Review on the banning of Ross's publications, the decision of the New Brunswick Court of Appeal to uphold this reversal, all suggest that the Canadian justice system continues to grapple with the balance between principles guaranteeing equality to all and principles guaranteeing freedom of expression.

The Arguments Concerning Freedom of Expression

Opposition to controls on freedom of expression centres around a number of key issues. While these issues are integrally intertwined, for analytic purposes it is useful to consider each in turn.

The Preservation of Democracy

At its most basic, it is argued that legislation which prohibits speech behavior violates our basic rights of freedom of expression. Freedom of expression is argued in terms of the guarantees in the Charter. For proponents of its centrality, freedom of expression is referred to as "the lifeblood of the democratic system" and "the vehicle through which the quest for truth may be pursued."[11]

As an abstract principle, there are few who would deny that freedom of expression is a central tenet of democratic society. However, while at first glance freedom of expression should not contradict the right to equal treatment of everyone, recent events in Canada suggest that this is, indeed, the case. When most Canadians conceive of the idea of democracy, they conceive of both individual freedom *and* of equality. Too broad a definition of freedom of expression, in fact, may contradict one of the basic tenets of Canadian society and guaranteed in the Charter (Section 15 (1)):

> Every individual is equal before and under the law and has the right to the equal protection and equal benefit of the law without discrimination and, in particular, without discrimination based on race, national or ethnic origin, colour, religion, sex, age or mental or physical disability.[12]

This principle of equality is so central that its inclusion in the Charter was seen as essential by many minority groups and by women. It seems difficult to understand how those who argue for freedom of expression, even the right to vilify or defame, can frame these arguments in terms of democratic principles, without recognizing that this distorted definition of "democracy," creates a society which denies to members of the groups so vilified basic rights of equality. Is this not essentially contrary to the Canadian notion of democracy?

It is not only individual equality that is guaranteed in the Charter, however, but also the equality of ethnic and racial groups. Canadian society so prides itself on the promotion of multiculturalism, that we have entrenched this in Section 27 of the Charter: "This Charter shall be interpreted in a manner consistent with the preservation and enhancement of the multicultural heritage of Canadians."[13]

While freedom of expression is one of the rights that is protected in the Canadian Charter, it is clear that the rights so guaranteed are not absolute but are subject "only to such reasonable limits prescribed by law as can be demonstrably justified in a free and democratic society."[14] Given the struggles of Canadians to include sections 15(1) and 27 in the Charter, it is clear that these principles are regarded as fundamental to the Canadian definition of equality and as such are reasonable limits on freedom of expression prescribed by law as can be demonstrably justified in a free and democratic society. Hate propaganda as found in the writings of Malcolm Ross cannot hide behind Charter rights. Indeed, the argument can be made that the Charter prohibits such virulent hate. As J. Quigley of the Alberta Court of Queen's Bench wrote on the pre-trial application of James Keegstra to have section 319(2) of the Criminal Code declared unconstitutional:

> The willful promotion of hatred under circumstances which fall within [s. 319(2)] of the Criminal Code – negates or limits the rights and freedoms of such target groups, and in particular denies them the right to the equal protection and benefit of the law without discrimination. Hate propaganda in its promotion of racist ideas, denies the inherent equality of all persons, and as such is antithetical to the Canadian concept of democracy.[15]

Allowing Malcolm Ross's virulent hate propaganda to be published and distributed unchecked condones blatant discrimination against Jews, and violates the integrity of our multicultural and multiracial society. "Freedom becomes a fetish where bitter unfreedoms are inflicted upon innocent and vulnerable others."[16]

The Search for Truth

Unbridled free expression is argued in terms of its necessity for the advancement of knowledge and the discovery of truth.[17] It is through the "marketplace of ideas" that new truths can be developed.

While there is some validity in this argument, to argue that hate propaganda is an essential part of the exploration of ideas would, I suggest, elevate it to a position with which most Canadians would have grave reservations. To define the right of those who espouse hate propaganda in terms of the discovery of "truth" seems antithetical to our quest for truth and "strikes more and more deeply at the personal and social values we cherish and hold fundamental to the society."[18] How can truth be advanced when those who speak seek to vilify and defame others? As Chief Justice Brian Dickson wrote in the Keegstra judgment (December 13, 1990):

> There is very little chance that statements intended to promote hatred against an identifiable group are true, or that their vision will lead to a better world. To portray such statements as crucial to the truth and the betterment of the political and social milieu is therefore misguided.[19]

Can we define the pursuit of truth in terms that strike at our fundamental beliefs in equality? Can we sacrifice our moral commitment to create in Canadian society a society in which all individuals enjoy equality? To defend the writings of Malcolm Ross as the pursuit of truth, pollutes this noble ideal, and corrodes its foundation, causing one of our central pillars of justice, truth, to crumble.

The Camel's Nose in the Tent

This argument, known as the slippery slope or the problem of drawing the line, suggests that it is impossible to draw a line that would not infringe on the kind of speech that we want to protect. It is closely related to the search for truth argument in that presumably the speech we wish to protect is necessary to advance ideas and to promote discourse. Since this argument is a central tenet of those who oppose anti-hate legislation it should not be taken lightly. Nevertheless, this argument is usually wrapped in language that goes far beyond the issue of line drawing and needs to be disentangled from the more general line drawing argument.

The guarantees of freedom of expression for hatemongers is regarded as essential for the good of society as a whole. Thus, even speech which vilifies and degrades must be tolerated in order to assure that speech which promotes the good of society is not excluded. Therefore, the issue is not just the problem of drawing lines but rather that the protection of speech, even hate speech, is regarded as a fundamental part of our society. The *abuse* of the right of freedom of expression is not seen as distinct from the right itself, and so the protection of the former is regarded as necessary for a free and democratic society. However, as Bollinger argues:

> . . . one can intuit some sense that the protection of this speech contains some deeper significance for us than that of incapacity to draw lines. There is the suggestion that we should be proud of this result, not just accepting of life's imperfections or even just glad that acceptance protects us.[20]

Separating the line drawing argument from the language in which it is couched, allows us to recognize that this is a recurrent concern in our justice system. In a democratic society a degree of uncertainty in the processes of justice is inevitable. Indeed, if there were not uncertainty then the entire judicial process as developed in Canada could be substantially streamlined. We accept, and in fact, encourage judicial interpretation of our laws. The only way to eliminate line drawing as an issue is avoidance altogether. It is certain that those who suggest that legislation against hatemongers should not exist because of their concern for line-drawing, would not extend this line-drawing argument to all Criminal and Civil law as this would make it impossible to develop a democratic legal system.

> The choice we face is not between a legal system without the uncertainty of language and one with it. The problem we face is not how much uncertainty a given legal rule will introduce into our law but also when we will choose to live with that uncertainty and when we will not.[21]

Those who oppose restrictions on speech argue that the issue of line-drawing is far more critical when considering freedom of expression because it is such a dominant principle of Canadian democracy. With specific reference to the anti-hate legislation, this position argues that it is impossible to articulate a prohibition which is precise enough to curb racist propaganda without

> ... catching in the same net a lot of other material that it would be clearly unconscionable for a democratic society to suppress. How does a blunt instrument like the criminal law distinguish between destructive hatred and constructive tension?[22]

In order to buttress this argument, examples of cases in which the anti-hate law was used erroneously are given. Perhaps the most common example was the conviction of Buzzanga and Durocher, two French-Canadian nationalists, who had distributed anti-French material in order to create pro-French sympathy. Their conviction was reversed on appeal by the Ontario Court of Appeal.[23] Similarly, a number of questionable investigations based on the anti-hate legislation none of which resulted in charges being laid are cited.[24]

It is important to stress that the Buzzanga and Durocher conviction was overturned and that all the questionable investigations referred to by Borovoy, in fact, did not result in any charges being laid. In virtually all cases, with this one exception, therefore, one would have to conclude that little or no harm, was done to the principle of freedom of speech. One must ask the question whether this one conviction was a consequence of the anti-hate legislation itself or of gross misunderstanding on the part of the prosecutors. The fact that the conviction was subsequently reversed gives weight to the latter interpretation. We cannot throw out every law in which charges were inappropriately brought against an individual. While recognizing that *misuse* of anti-hate legislation potentially threatens one of the basic principles of a democratic society, freedom of expression, the risks seem grossly overstated.

It is ironic that while civil libertarians express concern that anti-hate legislation casts too broad a net, at the same time, Attorneys-General of various provinces are unwilling to lay charges under the anti-hate legislation. The reluctance of the Attorney-General of Alberta to lay charges against James Keegstra and the refusal of two Attorneys-General in New Brunswick on several occasions to lay charges against Malcolm Ross, suggests that the fear that the effect of the law may be too broad is empirically unjustified. In fact, many critics of the legislation note how difficult it is to lay charges not only because of the numerous defenses in the law and the need to prove "willfulness" but also because, unlike most other legislation, charges must be brought by the Attorney-General. This latter safeguard, while cumbersome and frustrating, ensures that trivial or inappropriate charges will not be made.

The Question of Harm

The argument against restrictions on speech suggests that the harm done by words is not in any way similar to the harm done by deeds and that we should work for the elimination of *acts* of discrimination. This argument displays both an insensitivity to the tremendous hurt that words can inflict on individuals, as well as the harmful consequences to society as a whole. The harm, therefore, is not just to the specific target group, but also to the society generally by the creation and dissemination of discriminatory attitudes and practices. As Irwin Cotler notes:

> This exercise, then, in the debasement and degradation of the human person – and the target group of which he or she is a member is prejudicial to the very dignity and self-worth of the individual person, the very self-government and democratic process that is the very rationale and justification for freedom of expression itself: and that is why I say that there is no inherent contradiction in freedom from certain forms of expression on the one hand and the freedom of expression itself on the other.[25]

Hateful speech which vilifies its victims has many harms. It can affect the self-esteem of the victim. Its threat creates fear among members of the target groups. It can persuade others to believe this vilification and hence think less of the victims. These effects interact as we view ourselves through the eyes of others. The harm, however, goes beyond the personal level to the societal level. Our response (or nonresponse) to hate propaganda serves to create a definition of who we are as a society. As Eugene Kaellis argues:

Ignoring the Holocaust or attempting to trivialize it doesn't affect its victims. They can never be brought back and their world has died with them. It does, however, degrade us by diminishing our sensitivity to evil or the potential for evil in all of us, stealing our opportunity for growth, and reducing the promise, not of our perfection, but our perfectibility. In that case we are numbered among the victims.[26]

Those who oppose regulations against hate propaganda argue that the harm is restricted because there are few advocates of hate propaganda and, hence the risks of anti-hate legislation are incurred "in order to nail a minuscule group of pathetic peripheral creeps whose constituencies could not fill a telephone booth."[27] The response to hatemongering, according to civil libertarian Alan Borovoy, should be limited to raising

> . . . political hell whenever racist utterances emanate from people of authority or social standing. As for the more peripheral racists, I think our response should generally be indirect. We should continue to strengthen our laws against racially discriminatory behavior – in jobs, housing, public accommodations, etc.[28]

Unfortunately there are many examples that indicate that racist speech is not the sole purview of a few of society's outcasts. It is reported, in fact, that Canada ranks second in the production of anti-semitic propaganda (after West Germany). Stanley Barrett and Philip Rosen provide us with ample evidence of the extent of racial groups and activities in Canada.[29]

The objective of hatemongers is to eliminate those they so vilify from the society. Since they are prohibited by law from acts of genocide, they focus their attack on attempts to make these individuals so socially repugnant that they will be social outcasts. While the limits of their influence is an empirical question, there is no doubt that these statements not only harm the target group, but also attack our sense of justice. Maxwell Cohen in his report on hate propaganda in Canada stated that the "potential psychological and social damage of hate propaganda, both to a desensitized majority and sensitive minority target groups is incalculable."[30]

Will the criminal prosecution of hatemongers eliminate the harm? No one is so naive as to suggest that prosecuting racist activity will eradicate racism, but it will clarify who we are as a society and what we value – a society that regards equality for all as fundamental and is willing to protect all its citizens against the harm of hate. Anti-hate legislation will not heal centuries of ethnocentric white-Anglo-Saxon bias (However, it not only protects individuals and individual groups but also defines who and what we are and articulates our concept of justice and moral integrity.) "What is at stake is inherent human dignity, wherein, if all our citizens are not accorded the treatment of equals, the centre falls apart."[31] If we allow these values to be compromised by our tolerance of hate propaganda, then we undermine the basic norms which have defined Canadian society. To use the cloak of freedom to deny the rights of others and to destroy their dignity, is an abuse of freedom and must be understood not only as contrary to the Charter but also contrary to the requirements of a just and democratic society. As a society if we allow hate propaganda to continue unchecked we are greatly diminished.

The Problem of State Control

This argument claims that we should not grant to State officials a greater level of rationality and intelligence than we allow ourselves as citizens.[32] With respect to restricting hate propaganda, this position contends that the State will use its own biases and prejudices in defining what is hate and what is not, and that State officials are no more rational nor honest than the run-of-the-mill citizen in a democracy. There is probably no one that would argue that State officials are necessarily any more honest or rational than the citizenry. Nevertheless, it is not the State, acting alone, that has made the commitment to equality of the individual and of ethnic and racial groups but the citizens themselves. As Bollinger effectively argues:

> But if the people themselves, acting after full and open discussion, decide *in accordance with democratic procedures* that some speech will no longer be tolerated then it is not "the government" that is depriving "us," the citizens, of our freedom to choose, but *we* as citizens deciding what the rules of conduct within the community will be.[33]

Conclusions

It is imperative to recognize that the opposition to the position for virtually unlimited freedom of expression stems from our deep concern over the serious consequences of racial intolerance. To argue that speech that promotes racial hatred should be curtailed by law is not to stand in the way of freedom, but to work toward the elimination of all forms of racism in Canadian society. Speech, as abused by hatemongers is a weapon of intolerance. Allowing this intolerance to go unchecked is to strike at the very heart of a free and democratic society:

> Freedom of expression is based on, and expresses, the principle of tolerance. If we value freedom of expression we cannot attach very much, if any, value to the promotion of intolerance. Intolerance, and particularly hatred, are ideas which cannot stand on an equal footing with the other competitors in the marketplace.[34]

It is erroneous to believe that our belief in freedom of speech collides with our belief in ethnic and racial dignity.[35] This imagery suggests that these values are antithetical to each other while, in fact, they serve to complement each other, each helping to define the boundaries of the other. We do not abandon one when we assert the centrality of the other. Both are important in our definition of democracy. Our commitment to both individual and ethnic and racial equality, our recognition of the real harm that hatemongering inflicts, the need to provide individuals and groups freedom *from* expression, and our vision of a multicultural and multiracial Canada, makes it imperative that we eliminate this form of racism. If we are committed to equality for all our citizens then the prosecution of hatemongers is not only constitutionally justified but ethically necessary. The so-called individual "rights" of hatemongers must not take precedence over the collective rights of groups to equality. Defending the speech of Malcolm Ross must in no way be seen as ennobling us, but rather must be recognized as antithetical to our commitment to a multicultural society and debasing and denigrating to the principles of equality for all that we as Canadians have defined as essential in our quest for justice.[36]

Notes

[1]Attis v. Board of Education of District 15, (1991), 15 C.H.R.R. D/339, (*sub nom.* Attis v. Board of Education No. 15) 121 n.b.r. (2D) 1, 304 a.p.r. 1 (Board of Inquiry). This reference is to the original Human Rights Board of Inquiry.

[2]Canadian Charter of Rights and Freedoms, 1982.

[3]Regina v. Zundel 58 O.R. (2d) 129, 35 D.L.R. (4th) 338 (C.A.), 1987; and Regina v. Keegstra, Supreme Court of Canada, December 13, 1990.

[4]Attis' letter is reprinted in the Report of the Human Rights Board of Inquiry.

[5]See Attis v. Board of Education of District 15.

[6]Ross v. Moncton Board of School Trustees, District No. 15 (1991), 86 D.L.R. (4th) 749, 121 N.B.R. (2d) 361, 304 A.P.R. 361. This reference is to the Judicial Review.

[7]Ross v. New Brunswick School District No. 15 (1993) 16 C.H.R.R. D/250 (Q.B.), 19 C.H.R.R. D/173, 110 D.L.R. (4th) 241, 142, N.B.R. (2d) 1, 364 A.P.R. 1 (C.A.). This reference is to the New Brunswick Court of Appeal.

[8]Supreme Court of Canada, April 3. 1996: 47.

[9]Ibid., 52.

[10]Allan Borovoy, *Globe and Mail*, March 30, 1989.

[11]A. Borovoy, "Freedom of Expression: Some Recurring Impediments," in R.S. Abella and M. L. Rothman (eds.), *Justice Beyond Orwell* (Montreal: Les Editions Yvan Blais Inc., 1985), 125.

[12]See Canadian Charter of Rights and Freedoms.

[13]Ibid.

[14]Ibid., section 1.

[15]J, Quigley, *R. v. Keegstra*, C.C.C. (3d), 1984: 268.

[16]P. D. Lawlor, *Group Defamation*, Submissions to the Attorney General of Ontario, March 1984: 4.

[17]See John Stuart Mill, *On Liberty* (New York: Liberal Arts Press, 1956).

[18]Lee C. Bollinger, *The Tolerant Society* (Oxford: Clarendon Press, 1986), 9.

[19]Regina v. Keegstra, Supreme Court of Canada, December 13, 1990.

[20]L. C. Bollinger, *The Tolerant Society*, 35.

[21]Ibid., 36-37.

[22]Allan Borovoy, *When Freedoms Collide* (Toronto: Lester & Orpen Dennys, 1988), 42.

[23]Regina v. Buzzanga and Durocher, 49 C.C.C. (2d) 369 (Ont. C.A.), September 1979.

[24]A. Borovoy, *When Freedoms Collide*, 42-43.

[25]Irwin Cotler, "Hate Literature," in R. S. Abella and M. L. Rothman (eds.), *Justice Beyond Orwell*, 121.

[26]Eugene Kaellis, *The Moncton Times-Transcript*, October 29, 1988.

[27]A. Borovoy, "Freedom of Expression: Some Recurring Impediments," in R. S. Abella and M. L. Rothman (eds.), *Justice Beyond Orwell*, 142.

[28]Ibid., 144.

[29]One can identify at least two waves of racist activities in Canada since the 1960s. In the mid 1960s anti-Jewish and anti-Black hate propaganda was widespread in Canada, especially in Quebec and Ontario. Neo-Nazi and white supremacist groups from the United States were active in Canada. Since the mid-1970s there has been a second wave of racist groups. These include the Edmund Burke Society, Nationalist Party of Canada, the Western Guard, the Ku Klux Klan and Aryan Nations groups. Hate propaganda in Canada is in the form of leaflets and pamphlets, video cassettes, computer hook-ups and telephone calls, as well as historical revisionist writings. See S. Barrett, *Is God a Racist? The Right Wing in Canada* (Toronto: University of Toronto Press, 1987); and P. Rosen, *Hate Propaganda* (Ottawa: Research Branch, Library of Parliament, Current Issue Review, revised ed. 12 April 1991, 85-6E), for a detailed account of these developments.

[30]Maxwell Cohen, *Report to the Minister of Justice of the Special Committee on Hate Propaganda in Canada* (Ottawa: Queen's Printer, 1966), 9.

[31]P. D. Lawlor, *Group Defamation*, 1984, 1.

[32]T. Heinrichs, "Free Speech and the Zundel Trial," *Queen's Quarterly*, 95, 4, 1988: 837-854.

[33]L. C. Bollinger, *The Tolerant Society*, 50.

[34]A. Fish, "Hate Promotion and Freedom of Expression: Truth and Consequences," *Canadian Journal of Law and Jurisprudence*, 2, 2, 1989: 111-137.

[35]A. Borovoy, *When Freedoms Collide*, 1988, 3.

[36]This is a revised version of an earlier article "Rehinking Canadian Justice: Hate Must Not Define Democracy," *UNB Law Journal*, 41, 1992: 285-294.

- rights
- conduct out side of class
-

Part Four

Conceptions of Education

There may be ready agreement that justice requires that everyone be treated equally except where relevant reasons exist for inequality; but this exception will almost certainly give rise to very different conceptions of a just distribution or a just society. It would be naive to expect that there will be general agreement about what are relevant reasons in particular contexts because, quite apart from disagreement over what is to count as a true description of the actual context in question, different ideals, principles and values will be invoked in the course of justifying or denying the exception. Everyone may seek justice but what this requires is understood in very different ways. Similarly, it would be surprising indeed if people did not hold rival conceptions of education. At a very general level, it may be agreed that education is concerned with learning that which is considered valuable; but beyond this definitional point lies great controversy which ultimately involves our views on what constitutes a good person and a worthwhile life.

Herbert Spencer's famous question, "What knowledge is of most worth?" has been answered in many different ways by people whose conceptions of education differ even though they would agree that worthwhile knowledge is the cornerstone of a sound curriculum. Spencer, for example, tried to make the case for science against those who defended traditional, classical learning. Others have attempted to break away from a debate defined in terms of one area of knowledge versus another, and have proposed a view of education which emphasizes an introduction to the various forms or modes of inquiry. Dewey, as was noted in the Introduction to Part Two, supported an emphasis on developing critical judgment as to what really constitutes knowledge at all. Some believe that Spencer's very formulation in terms of knowledge already builds in a certain distortion. Harry Broudy, for example, argues that general education should "furnish a repertoire of images and concepts *with* which we think, imagine and feel." All of these views reflect different conceptions of the purpose and value of education.

The above is a mere illustration of the way in which the same question can take people in very diferent directions, and these directions reveal their underlying conceptions of education. This collection as a whole itself illustrates the theme of a plurality of conceptions, since every chapter in the book, implicitly or explicitly, invokes a conception of education, some overlapping, some conflicting. This is because whatever position one takes – on such questions and issues as the right of students to form their own views, the importance of standards in schooling, the need to try to fuse theory and practice, the ideals considered central in the activity of teaching, or the implications of multiculturalism, – is shaped and influenced by the views one holds about the values, attitudes, and beliefs we wish to see fostered in children, and about the kind of society in which we wish to live.

Paulo Freire, for example, has a vision of teachers who can share their ideals with students without imposing them, who know how to challenge students to have their own dreams and define their own choices. Freire is sceptical of allegedly neutral conceptions of education because he fears that "neutrality" will come to mean support for whatever ideology happens to be dominant. His conception of education as liberation is intimately connected with his ideals of teaching, and with his analysis of reading as interpretation. The notion of nurturing dreams recurs in Maxine Greene's discussion, with her emphasis on keeping choices, possibilities and questions open. Certainly it is important for teachers to formulate a conception of education to provide general guidance, but Greene wants to remind us that horizons shift and perspectives alter, and thus we are forever remaking our aims as we take decisions in particular contexts. Consequently, individual choice, and the responsibility which comes with such freedom, is central to her conception of education.

Richard Rorty's essay shows clearly how people who all claim allegiance to such values as truth and freedom can hold conceptions of education which are very far apart on the political spectrum. Rorty himself favors a view of education which sees it as comprising two distinct processes, socialization and individuation. With such a distinction in mind, Rorty sugests that the function of pre-college education is socialization; that is, familiarizing the young with what is presently *held* to be true, the conventional wisdom. It is against this picture of reality, this image of the past, that students at college will be encouraged to rebel in order to reshape themselves in a process of individuation. Teachers at college would seek to provoke students into a realization of the stark contrast between professed ideals and actual experience in their own society, and in this way ensure that the endless critical conversation is kept alive.

Jane Roland Martin provokes the reader into realizing that a conception of education which has long been viewed as the ideal is, in fact, problematic. We are startled to realize that a certain educational "success story" may be, in many ways, a narrative of loss. Martin's target is that familar conception of liberal education which emphasizes knowledge, understanding, reflection, reason and truth; and she maintains that it is a conception which ignores, or spurns, many other important values and traits, such as emotional response, passionate feeling, cooperation, compassion, and intimacy. She suggests that the dichotomy which is revealed has its source in the fact that certain traits have been genderized. Related ideas are apparent in Nel Noddings' discussion, which presents a conception of education in which moral education is central, but the view of moral education in question is based on an ethics of care rather than an ethics of duty and principle. Noddings believes that a conception of education rooted in care and human relationships will have profound implication for every aspect of schooling, from curriculum content to methods of evaluation, from the size of schools to the goals of instruction.

Further Readings

Arno Bellack, "What Knowledge is of Most Worth?" *High School Journal*, 48, 1965: 318-332.

Harry S. Broudy, "What Knowledge is of Most Worth?" *Educational Leadership*, May 1982: 574-578.

Eamonn Callan, "Finding a Common Voice," *Educational Theory*, 42, 4, 1992: 429-441.

W. B. Gallie, "Essentially Contested Concepts," *Proceedings of the Aristotelian Society*, 1955-6: 167-198.

Paul Hirst, "Liberal Education," in Lee C. Deighton (ed.), *The Encyclpoaedia of Education*. New York: Macmillan and Free Press, 1971, Vol 5: 505-509.

John White, "The Aims of Education," in Noel Entwistle (ed.), *Handbook of Educational Ideas and Practices*. London: Routledge, 1990, 23-32.

13

Reading the World and Reading the Word:
An Interview with Paulo Freire

Teaching and Educating

Language Arts: Paulo, you are known for your work in what people call liberation education – education to help learners overcome oppression and achieve various kinds of freedom – and the special role which dialogue and literacy play in that process. The teacher's role in this experience is key. Would you describe what being a teacher means to you?[1]

Paulo Freire: I love being a teacher. To me, being a teacher does *not* mean being a missionary, or having received a certain command from heaven. Rather a teacher is a professional, one who must constantly seek to improve and to develop certain qualities or virtues, which are not received but must be created. The capacity to renew ourselves everyday is very important. It prevents us from falling into what I call "bureaucratization of mind." I am a teacher.

Language Arts: What are some of these virtues or qualities you see as important for the professional teacher?

Paulo Freire: Virtues are qualities which you re-create through action and through practice, qualities which make us consistent and coherent concerning our dreams – a consistency which teachers try to achieve within what they are doing.

Humility is an important virtue for a teacher, the quality of recognizing – without any kind of suffering – our limits of knowledge concerning what we can and cannot do through education. Humility accepts the need we have to learn and relearn again and again, the humility to know *with* those whom we help to know. You must be humble because you don't have any reason not to be humble. But being humble does not mean that you accept being humiliated. Humility implies understanding the pain of others, the feelings of others. We should respect the expectations that students have and the knowledge students have. Our tendency as teachers is to start from the point at which we are and not from the point at which the students are. The teacher has to be *free* to say to students "You convinced me." Dialogue is not an empty instructional tactic, but a natural part of the process of knowing.

Another important virtue for the teacher is patience and its opposite, impatience. We teachers must learn how to make a life together with our students who may be different from us. This kind of learning implies patience and impatience. We must always be impatient about achieving our dream and helping students achieve theirs. Yet if we and our students push too hard and too fast for our dreams, we may destroy them. Thus, we must be patiently impatient.

Tolerance is another virtue which is very important. It involves both humility and patience. Tolerance means learning how to confront the antagonist. For instance, a classroom of students is not a social class as such, but is made up of individual students who bring to class with them various social class backgrounds. As a teacher my relationship with them is not a class relationship. My values may be different from the students', but I cannot for that reason take them as my enemies. I must be tolerant.

The story is told about Chairman Mao's niece complaining to him about "Viva Chiang Kai-Shek!" found scrawled on a blackboard at her university. In response to Mao's questions, she told him there were only about two reactionaries among the five thousand students at her university that would have written it. Mao replied that it was too bad there were only two, that it would be better for the Communist side if there were more reactionaries around. He pointed out that people had the right to say what they thought, but that the Communist side also had the right to try to convince them they are wrong.

All these virtues connect. For instance being tolerant implies respect, and being tolerant implies assuming the naivety of the student. A teacher must accept the naivety of the student for practical reasons. You cannot overcome a student's naivety by decree. We must start at the point where the students are. If we start from the point where we are, we must make connections with the position in which the students are. In order for students to go beyond their naivety, it is necessary for them to grasp their naivety into their own hands and then they will try to make the important leap, but they will leap with you. Assuming the naivety of the students doesn't mean becoming naive or staying at the naive level of the students. To assume the naivety of the student is to understand the naivety and not to refuse it dogmatically, but to say yes to the naivety and mediate to challenge the naive student, so they can go beyond their naive understanding of reality.

The final virtue, if possible, is the ability to love students, in spite of everything. I don't mean a kind of soft or sweet love, but on the contrary a very affirmative love, a love which accepts, a love for students which pushes us to go beyond, which makes us more and more responsible for our task.

Language Arts: You have often used the phrase "teacher learner" in reference to the teacher in the classroom. In a teaching situation how do you see the teacher as a learner?

Paulo Freire: I consider it an important quality or virtue to understand the impossible separation of teaching and learning. Teachers should be conscious every day that they are coming to school to learn and not just to teach. This way we are not just teachers but teacher learners. It is really impossible to teach without learning as well as learning without teaching. We cannot separate one from the other; we create a violence when we try. Over a period of time we no longer perceive it as violence when we continually separate teaching from learning. Then we conclude that the teacher teaches and the student learns. That unfortunately is when students are convinced that they come to school to be taught and that being taught often means transference of knowledge.

Knowing the concept of an object implies apprehending the object. I first apprehend the object, in apprehending the object I know it, and because I know it, I then memorize it. Apprehending precedes memorization. Learning does not exist without knowing. Teaching for me then is challenging the students to know, to apprehend the object.

As teachers, we learn from the process of teaching and we learn with the students for whom we make possible the conditions to learn. We also learn from the process that the students are also teaching us.

Language Arts: What is your vision of education? What do you hope education would do for the growth of young children?

Paulo Freire: For me education is simultaneously an act of knowing, a political act, and an artistic event. Thus, I no longer speak about a political dimension of education. I no longer speak about a knowing dimension of education. As well, I don't speak about education through art. On the contrary I say education *is* politics, art, and knowing. Education is a certain theory of knowledge put into practice every day, but it is clothed in a certain aesthetic dress. Our very preoccupation with helping kids shape themselves as beings is an artistic aspect of education. While being a teacher demands that we be simultaneously a politician, an epistemologist, and an artist, I recognize that it is not easy to be these three things together.

Thus, to the extent that we are responsible, we must become prepared, competent, capable. We should not frustrate those students who come to us hoping for answers to their expectations, to their doubts, to their desire to know. We must have some knowledge, of course, about our subject, but we must also know how to help them to know. This dimension of *how* is also an artistic one and not just a methodological one.

Many issues and questions arise from this understanding of the act of education. For example, it suggests that we teachers should be constantly asking questions of ourselves and of our students, to create a spirit in which we are certain by not being certain of our certainties. To the extent that we are not quite sure about our certainties, we begin to "walk toward" certainties.

Another example is that education has politicity, the quality of being political. As well, politics has educability, the quality of being educational. Political events are educational and vice versa. Because education *is* politicity, it is never neutral. When we try to be neutral, like Pilate, we support the dominant ideology. Not being neutral, education must be either liberating or domesticating. (Yet I also recognize that we probably never experience it as purely one or the other but rather a mixture of both.) Thus, we have to recognize ourselves as politicians. It does not mean that we have the right to *impose* on students our political choice. But we do have the duty not to hide our choice. Students have the right to know what our political dream is. They are then free to accept it, reject it, or modify it. Our task is not to impose our dreams on them, but to challenge them to have their own dreams, to define their choices, not just to uncritically assume them.

Many teachers unfortunately have been destroyed by the dominant ideology of a society and they tend to impose that way of seeing the world and behaving on kids. They usually view it as "saving" kids, as a missionary would. This tendency stems from a superiority complex. When we fall into this way of thinking, we are touching kids with surgical masks and gloves. The dominant ideology, which serves the interests of the socially powerful, makes the world opaque to us. We often believe the ideological words that are told to us – and which we repeat – rather than believing what we're living. The only way to escape that ideological trap, to unveil reality, is to create a counter-ideology to help us break the dominant ideology. This is accomplished by reflecting critically on our concrete experiences, to consider the raison d'etre of the facts we reflect on. Teachers must be able to play with children, to dream with them. They must wet their bodies in the waters of children's culture first. Then they will see how to teach reading and writing.

Once teachers see the contradiction between their words and their actions, they have two choices. They can become shrewdly clear and aware of their need to be reactionary, or they can accept a critical position to engage in action to transform reality. I call it "making Easter" every day, to die as the dominator and be born again as the dominated, fighting to overcome oppression.

The Role of Language and Reading

Language Arts: How does language, especially reading, fit in with your vision of education? How can it help develop critical consciousness to know our dreams in order to be free and move toward those dreams?

Paulo Freire: If we think of education as an act of knowing, then reading has to do with knowing. The act of reading cannot be explained as merely reading words since every act of reading words implies a previous reading of the world and a subsequent rereading of the world. There is a permanent movement back and forth between "reading" reality and reading words – the spoken word too is our reading of the world. We can go further, however, and say that reading the word is not only preceded by reading the world, but also by a certain form of writing it or rewriting it. In other words, of transforming it by means of conscious practical action. For me, this dynamic movement is central to literacy.

Thus, we see how reading is a matter of studying reality that is alive, reality that we are living inside of, reality as history being made and also making us. We can also see how it is impossible to read texts without reading the context of the text, without establishing the relationship between the discourse and the reality which shapes the discourse. This emphasizes, I believe, the responsibility which reading a text implies. We must try to read the context of a text and also relate it to the context in which we are reading the text. And so reading is not so simple. Reading mediates knowing and is also knowing, because language is knowledge and not just mediation of knowledge.

Perhaps I can illustrate by referring to the title of a book written by my daughter, Madalena. She teaches young children in Brazil and helps them learn to read and write, but above all she helps them know the world. Her book describes her work with the children and the nature of their learning. It is entitled *The Passion to Know the World*, not *How to Teach Kids to Read and Write*. No matter the level or the age of the students we teach, from preschool to graduate school, reading critically is absolutely important and fundamental. Reading always involves critical perception, interpretation, and "rewriting" what is read. Its task is to unveil what is hidden in the text. I always say to the students with whom I work, "Reading is not walking on the words; it's grasping the soul of them."

Language Arts: It seems that when children come to school, they already know how to "read" in the sense that they already know how to come to know the world, how to transform it. Yet as we try to work within an uncritical, reproductive education system, it seems that can get in the way and that reading can become "walking on words" – an empty, technical process. How do we prevent that from happening? How is Madalena with the kids; how does she fan the flames of their passion to know the world?

Paulo Freire: Reading words, and writing them, must come from the dynamic movement of reading the world. The question is how to create a fluid continuity between on the one hand reading the world, of speaking about experience, of talking freely with spontaneity and on the other hand the moment of writing and then learning how to read, so that the words which become the starting point for learning to read and write come from the kids' ideas and not from the teacher's reading book.

In the last analysis, the kids should come full of spontaneity – with their feelings, with their questions, with their creativity, with their risk to create, getting their own words "into their own hands" in order to do beautiful things with them. The basis for critical reading in young children is their curiosity.

Once again, teaching kids to read and write should be an artistic event. Instead, many teachers transform these experiences into a technical event, into something without emotions, without invention, without creativity – but with *repetition*. Many teachers work bureaucratically when they should work artistically. Teaching kids how to read words in the world is something which cannot really be put inside of a program. Normally, kids live imaginatively vis-a-vis reality, but they can feel guilty if they read this way within a technical, bureaucratic reading program and eventually can give up their imaginative, critical reading for a behavioristic process.

Reading is more than a technical event for me. It's something that takes my conscious body into action. I must be the subject, with the teacher, of my act of reading and writing and not a mere object of the teaching of how to read and write. I must know! I must get into my hands the process of reading and writing.

Madalena introduces the kids, without any kind of violence, to a serious understanding of the world, of the dimensions of their reality by talking with them, by bringing into the class a text or articles from the newspapers, by reading for them and to them, inviting parents to come and talk about their experiences in life, encouraging the kids to bring in texts, objects, and experiences, constantly putting in print generative words from the kids which express their expectations. The kids begin to reflect on their own language, getting the language "into their hands." Little by little they learn to read and write critically. And this can be done without turning them into arrogant academics.

The teacher must be one with young children – by being curious with them – without being one of them, since children need adults. They need to know that we know more than they do, but also that we are *knowing*. One of

Madalena's pupils was shocked one day to learn that Madalena did not know a certain thing, but saw in the next few days how she went about learning it. Such an experience has ideological dimensions for schooling and learning. By making the teacher vulnerable, it demystifies her and makes her more lovable. This demystification of adults is the only way for kids to grow up.

The basic question in school is how not to separate reading the word and reading the world, reading the text and reading the context.

Language Arts: It seems that we've come full circle in this conversation. As I look back, I'm afraid I was dichotomizing as I listened to you by focusing at one time on what the teacher does and at another time on what the child does. Actually it seems to be all one question – and one answer. It seems that the kind of reader and writer we want young children to be, we have to be. We have to know it – and teach it – by living it.

Paulo Freire: Yes, that's right!

Language Arts: If teachers have a passion to know the world, if they are curious and wondering, it seems that reading and writing will be treated that way in the classroom, indeed, could be treated in no other way.

Paulo Freire: Yes, I agree. For example, it would have been impossible for Madalena to have done what she did if she had a bureaucratic understanding of reading and education. (I mention Madalena only because we talked about her book. There are many teachers in Brazil who do similar things.) If a teacher has a bureaucraticized understanding of education, of reality, of existence, then necessarily that teacher's understanding of reading will also be a bureaucratized one. The challenge for teachers is to re-know for themselves the objects the kids are trying to learn, to find meanings in them hidden to them before. If they don't there is the danger that they may uncritically transmit their knowledge to students. Whether or not a child reads critically depends on whom the child reads with and for.

Let's say that a teacher has me in a course and encounters a new way of thinking – about existence, about education, about reality. If the teacher does not have enough time to reshape his or her understandings, if she or he accepts my ideas just intellectually but not emotionally, not politically, not existentially, what can happen is that she or he returns to working with kids and transforms all the dynamism I suggested for reading the world and reading words into a formula. Once again, the teacher will turn reading into a bureaucracy and maybe will become frustrated because she or he cannot do it the way they thought and will say that Paulo Freire is absolutely mistaken. Rather the teacher was not able to die as a bureaucratized mind in order to be born again as an open mind, a creative mind.

In knowing as teachers, we must have a humble conviction. When we are too convinced, we often can't accept change. Of course we need to be convinced, but with humility, always waiting to overcome our "convincement." If you are not convinced in a humble way, not only of the principles but also of the concrete experience, you risk transforming these ideas into a bandage and they will not work.

Language Arts: Thank you very much. Is there any final comment you'd like to add?

Paulo Freire: I just want to thank the readers for reading this conversation. I also ask them not just to accept what we said, but to think critically of what we said.

Notes

[1]This is an interview which Paulo Freire gave to the journal *Language Arts* in 1985.

14

Teacher as Stranger

Maxine Greene

And must not an animal be a lover of learning who determines what is or is not friendly to him by the test of knowledge and ignorance?

Most assuredly.

And is not the love of learning the love of wisdom, which is philosophy?

They are the same, he replied.

And may we not say confidently of man also, that he who is likely to be gentle to his friends and acquaintances, must by nature be a lover of wisdom and knowledge?

That we may safely affirm.

Then he who is to be a really good and noble guardian of the State will require to unite in himself philosophy and spirit and swiftness and strength?

Undoubtedly.

Then we have found the desired natures; and now that we have found them, how are they to be reared and educated?

Plato:*The Re-
public*

The University! So he had passed beyond the challenge of the sentries who had stood as guardians of his boyhood and had sought to keep him among them that he might be subject to them and serve their ends. Pride after satisfaction uplifted him like long slow waves. The end he had been born to serve yet did not see had led him to escape by an unseen path: and now it beckoned to him once more and a new adventure was about to be opened to him.

James Joyce: *A Portrait of the Artist as a Young Man*

To take a stranger's vantage point on everyday reality is to look inquiringly and wonderingly on the world in which one lives. It is like returning home from a long stay in some other place. The homecomer notices details and patterns in his or her environment one never saw before. One finds that one has to think about local rituals and customs to make sense of them once more. For a time he or she feels quite separate from the person who is wholly at home in the ingroup and takes the familiar world for granted. Such a person, writes Alfred

Schutz, ordinarily "accepts the ready-made standardized scheme of the cultural pattern handed down to him by ancestors, teachers, and authorities as an unquestioned and unquestionable guide in all the situations which normally occur within the social world.[1] The homecomer may have been such a person. Now, looking through new eyes, one cannot take the cultural pattern for granted. It may seem arbitrary or incoherent or deficient in some way. To make it meaningful again, he or she must interpret and reorder what one sees in the light of one's changed experience. One must consciously engage in inquiry.

When thinking-as-usual becomes untenable for anyone, the individual is bound to experience a crisis of consciousness. The formerly unquestioned has become questionable; the submerged has become visible. One may become like Meursault in Albert Camus' *The Stranger,* when he looks at his own murder trial and sees an ingroup ritual:

> Just then I noticed that almost all the people in the courtroom were greeting each other, exchanging remarks and forming groups – behaving, in fact, as in a club where the company of others of one's own tastes and standing makes one feel at ease. That, no doubt, explained the odd impression I had of being *de trop* here, a sort of gate-crasher.[2]

Or one may come to resemble Hester Prynne, in Nathaniel Hawthorne's *The Scarlet Letter.* Ostracized for having committed adultery, Hester is forced to live at the edge of the wilderness, on the outskirts of the Puritan community. Because she has "a mind of native courage and activity," her "estranged point of view" enables her to look critically at institutions once taken for granted, to criticize all "with hardly more reverence than the Indian would feel for the clerical band, the judicial robe, the pillory, the gallows, the fireside, or the church."[3] Both Meursault and Hester are strangers in the sense that they do not share the conventional vision. Camus describes an entirely honest man who will not pretend to share the cultural pieties; Hawthorne describes a woman who is "emancipated." Both see more than their less conscious fellow citizens could possibly see. Both are ready to wonder and question; and it is in wonder and questioning that learning begins.

We do not ask that the teacher perceive his or her existence as absurd; nor do we demand that he or she estrange himself or herself from the community. We simply suggest that he or she struggle against unthinking submergence in the social reality that prevails. If one wishes to present oneself as a person actively engaged in critical thinking and authentic choosing, one cannot accept any "ready-made standardized scheme" at face value. One cannot even take for granted the value of intelligence, rationality, or education. Why, after all, *should* a human being act intelligently or rationally? How *does* a teacher justify the educational policies he or she is assigned to carry out within his or her school? If the teacher does not pose such questions to himself or herself, he or she cannot expect the students to pose the kinds of questions about experience which will involve them in self-aware inquiry.

Maurice Merleau-Ponty attributes the feeling of certainty that rules out questioning to the ancient notion that each human being carries within him a *homunculus,* or "little man," who can "see" what is real and true. This *homunculus* represents what is best in the human being; and, unlike the person involved with the natural world and other people, the phantom creature inside always knows the Ideal. Merleau-Ponty writes:

> The "little man within man" is only the phantom of our successful expressive operations; and the admirable man is not this phantom but the man who – installed in his fragile body, in a language which has already done so much speaking, and in a reeling history – gathers himself together and begins to see, to understand, and to signify. There is no longer anything decorous or decorative about today's humanism. It no longer loves man in opposition to his body, mind in opposition to its language, values in opposition to facts. It no longer speaks of man and mind except in a sober way, with modesty: mind and man never are; they show through the movement by which the body becomes gesture, language an oeuvre, and coexistence truth.[4]

The teacher is frequently addressed as if he or she had no life of his or her own, no body, and no inwardness. Lecturers seem to presuppose a "man within man" when they describe a good teacher as infinitely controlled and accommodating, technically efficient, impervious to moods. They are likely to define him or her by the role he or she is *expected* to play in a classroom, with all his or her loose ends gathered up and all his or her doubts resolved. The numerous realities in which one exists as a living person are overlooked. One's personal biography is overlooked; so are the many ways in which one expresses one's private self in language, the horizons one perceives, the perspectives through which one looks on the world.

Our concern throughout has been to make that person visible to himself or herself. If the teacher agrees to submerge himself or herself into the system, if he or she consents to being defined by others' views of what he or she is supposed to be, he or she gives up his or her freedom "to see, to understand, and to signify" for himself or herself. If one is immersed and impermeable, one can hardly stir others to define themselves as individuals. If, on the other hand, one is willing to take the view of the homecomer and create a new perspective on what one has habitually considered real, one's teaching may become the project of a person vitally open to one's students and the world. Then one will be in a position to define oneself as "admirable" in Merleau-Ponty's sense. One will be continuously engaged in interpreting a reality forever new; one will feel more alive than one ever has before.

Seeking the communicative gesture and the expressive word, such a teacher will try consciously to move among and reflect together with his or her students. Coexisting with them, opening up perspectival possibilities along with them, the teacher and the students may journey toward some important truths as the days go on. "Sometimes one starts to dream," Merleau-Ponty writes, "about what culture, literary life, and teaching could be if all those who participate, having for once rejected idols, would give themselves up to the happiness of reflecting together."[5] The teacher in the United States, facing the adversity of one's historic moment, facing violence and inequities and irrationality, may believe the dream to be impossible. Yet, at some level of his or her consciousness, he or she may insist on just this kind of happiness. In Albert Camus' *The Plague,* the doctor says he thinks it is *right* to refuse to be balked of happiness. Later, when the plague has reached its peak and he is exhausted by the hopeless battle against it, he still can smile at a young journalist who wants to break the quarantine and escape from the town; in fact, he tells the journalist to hurry "because I, too, would like to do my bit for happiness." There are no good arguments against such a desire. The teacher who feels he or she too is fighting plague can still nurture the dream.

In this discussion, we shall have the dream in mind as we talk of possibility and moral choosing and the arts. There will be no closure for us; there cannot be. The questions implicit remain open: the questions having to do with defining *education,* determining educational purposes, achieving democracy. Customarily, books on educational philosophy conclude with talk of the democratic character, summon up visions of a "good society," or explain the relationships between world understanding and effective public schools. There is always a tendency to drive toward completion, to finish the design, to stand back and look at an articulated whole. Recognizing that each reader must strive toward such completion for himself or herself, we choose to conclude in the mood expressed by Nick Henry in Ernest Hemingway's *A Farewell to Arms*:

> I was always embarrassed by the words sacred, glorious and sacrifice and the expression in vain. We had heard them, sometimes standing in the rain almost out of earshot, so that only the shouted words came through, and had read them, on proclamations that were slapped up by billposters over other proclamations, now for a long time, and I had seen nothing sacred, and the things that were glorious had no glory and the sacrifices were like the stockyards at Chicago if nothing was done with the meat except to bury it. There were many words that you could not stand to hear.[6]

Of course, the teacher's experience is not identical with that of a soldier in a retreat; but most teachers know the meaning of the slogans and pieties they hear on loudspeaker systems and the proclamations they read on bulletin boards, reminders of the glorious purposes pursued by the institution. What teacher has seen anything sacred in the corridors? Do the things called "glorious" have glory? Charles Silberman quotes a high school principal, who says: "Maybe the public may think the schools are democratic. They are democratic as far as the rights of the individual, but as far as the operation, they are not democratic. In order to get efficiency in a school system, there has to be a clear pattern of operation, behavior, rules and regulation. Then there's not time for a group of people to sit down and thrash out a variety of ideas and to come up with a quick, clear-cut and efficient policy.'"[7] Writing about a singing lesson in an American school, Jules Henry describes how the student must substitute the teacher's criteria for his own: "He must learn that the proper way to sing is tunelessly and not the way *he* hears music; that the proper way to paint is the way the teacher says, not the way he sees it; that the proper attitude is not pleasure but competitive horror at the success of his classmates, and so on."[8]

Names and concrete nouns are not the only words that ought to be used in talk about education. But if the teacher can think what he or she is doing in the concrete situations of his or her life, he or she must be aware of the conventions currently used to organize reality. One must be conscious that the "fictions" used in sense making (in the schools as well as outside the schools) are mental constructs, human-made schemata, deserving only "conditional assent."[9] This point is particularly important in a time like the present, an era distinctive for the walls of images and words constantly being erected between us and actuality. We need only recall the bombardment of media images that replace the "reality" they purport to represent, that make "the 11 o'clock News" out of wartime atrocities, protest demonstrations, prison riots, political pronouncements, accidents, deformities, deaths. We need only recall the proliferating euphemisms, "waste the enemy," "protective reaction," "correctional facility," "national security," "behavioral engineering," "off the pig," "power to the people," and the rest. It has become all too easy to distance and distort what is experienced with language of that kind. It has become all too easy to cope with social relationships through the taking on and the assigning of roles.

The teacher is continually being asked (at least obliquely) to write a pious and authoritative role for himself or herself and submissive or savage or special roles for the young people he or she teaches. One has to make a deliberate effort to realize that no role can fully encompass a personality, just as no slogan or abstraction or popular phrase can do justice to a human situation. Unless he or she is careful, the teacher may tend to oversimplify by means of language, to smooth over the rough places, to live by self-serving myths. For this reason, we are unwilling to conclude by spelling out overarching purposes or slapping still another proclamation on the schoolroom wall.

It makes little difference if the proclamation calls for the defense of the nation or personal liberation, citizenship or spontaneity. Once we spell out aims in general, we are in danger of "embarrassing" ourselves. Moreover, the teacher's feeling of responsibility may well be eroded by an implicit demand that he or she be the agent of an externally defined purpose, which he or she can only understand as a slogan or still another expression of prevailing piety. We would emphasize once more the need for self-consciousness and clarity on the part of the individual, the need to frame conditional orders. His or her aims, therefore, can only be specific ones, identified in concrete situations with respect to concrete tasks and subject matters, where structures and relevancies are not always clear. They must be pursued as lacks are perceived and actions undertaken. Because persons differ, achievements vary, horizons shift, perspectives alter, one's aims can never be twice the same.

It must be clear by now that, no matter how carefully one deliberates, how artfully one develops alternative modes of instruction, the teacher is forever involved in constituting meanings. This act of forming applies to perspectives on the teaching act, on education viewed as intentional undertaking and as social enterprise. It applies to the perspectives through which persons are seen, knowledge structures apprehended, ethical problems resolved. Also it applies to questions touching on dissent, reform, and the transformation of cultural institutions; it applies to the methods chosen for responding to the inhumanities of the time. The teacher can not assert that the schools should or should not "dare to change the social order." The teacher must choose the part he or she will play in such an effort. He or she must even choose how to conceive the "social order": as an oppressive, impersonal system, as a series of fluid human communities, as "the best of all possible worlds."

At a time of major tensions among groups and moral systems, no educator is in a position to impose designs for harmonizing clashing interests. In his or her school, for example, the teacher may *propose* resolutions when racial groups are fighting with each other; one may, in time of dire emergency, suppress conflict by force. But it appears to be immoral, at this time, to decide *for* any individual or group what is fair, decent, or humane. Expertise no longer possesses transfer value for other people's private, immediately apprehended experiences, for predicaments that must be phenomenologically understood. The educational task, in the moral domain as well as in others, is to find out how to enable individuals to choose intelligently and authentically for themselves. It involves learning how to equip them with the conceptual tools, the self-respect, and the opportunities to choose – in specific circumstances – how to do what they consider right.

This may be a troubling solution for the teacher who is committed to certain values, causes, or patterns of social change. As citizen or layperson, one has the right (and perhaps the obligation) to work for the reforms in which one professes to believe. If one does not act on one's beliefs, in fact, one may be said to be in "bad faith," expected to feel "shame." If one has no commitments, if one remains uninvolved, one may not be the engaged, wide-awake teacher young people appear to need. But this causes an inevitable conflict once one commits oneself to arousing students to create their own values and seek their own resolutions. Impartial in some areas (when dealing with students as individuals or in their groups), one cannot be impartial or neutral on, say, the Vietnamese War, racial discrimination, drug addiction, or the many injustices that plague American life. Some philosophers attach so much importance to cool rationality that they would advise the teacher to sublimate his or her political and social enthusiasms when working at school. The teacher has enough to do, they would say, to initiate young people into such activities as "science, poetry, and engineering and possibly a variety of games and pastimes. Most of these are intimately connected not only with occupations and professions but also with possible vocations and ideals of life."[10] Other philosophers would recommend the temperate use of intelligence in cooperative attempts to solve such problems. Still others would draw attention to crisis and adversity. They would insist that political and social commitments permeate an individual's life and that the teacher defines himself or herself as much by the ends he or she pursues outside the school as by the values he or she creates within. Conceivably, the activist teacher can struggle for peace and justice for the same reasons he or she tries to liberate the young to choose for themselves. The teacher knows, as well and as clearly as the analytic philosopher (although on different grounds), that it is morally indefensible to indoctrinate or to tell students categorically that only one mode of action is "right." He or she may feel, as Jean Paul Sartre has said, that "in choosing myself, I choose man;"[11] but one's sense of the universality, even the absoluteness of one's choice does not justify one's willing against others' freedom. And this is precisely what one would be doing if one tried to use one's position to impose one's own beliefs.

To lecture against smoking marijuana is obviously questionable; and to proscribe, on moral grounds, use of heroin is futile. What of the student who refuses to attend school regularly because he or she thinks (as, indeed, his or her teacher might) that the compulsory school manipulates and imprisons, that he or she learns far more outside? What of the controversies over sex education? What of the books (such as Piri Thomas' *Down These Mean Streets* or George Jackson's *Soledad Brother*) some charge with being pornographic, subversive, or "inciting to violence?" What, more traditionally, of education for truth telling, decency, cooperativeness, playing fair?

We cannot presume that the teacher functions in an ordered world or a spacious society, where each person's duties in the various departments of his or her life are clearly set forth. Nor can we take for granted that fundamental agreements lie below the surfaces on a morality viewed as "an instrument of society as a whole for the guidance of individuals and smaller groups."[12] The assumption may be true in the few homogeneous small towns left in America; but it is not likely to be generally true. We have talked about the disintegrating norms throughout the culture, about the loss of trust, about the defiance of codes and the sometimes shocking acceptance of lawbreaking. Much has been written recently about so-called "new crimes": "trashing," pointless vandalism, shoplifting for sport. Gresham Sykes uses divorce as an example, because divorce was once considered shameful and now has little stigma attached to it. He goes on to say that "there are a number of areas of behavior labelled criminal by the law, for which this same sort of 'slipping out from morality' may be occurring for a number of people. The use of drugs, particularly in the case of marijuana, may often be of this order; similarly, certain kinds of sexual behavior, such as premarital sexual relations, seem to be losing a good deal of their moral resonance. The question of whether to engage in such behavior becomes very pragmatic; the question is whether one will be caught."[13]

Complicated problems confront any teacher who attempts "moral education." If one believes, as the positivist philosophers do, that only principles can be taught, along with the nature of good reasons, one still must determine which principles can be made meaningful to the contemporary young. One must determine what sorts of actions have "moral resonance," which do not and which should not. If one considers that guidelines are impossible to define any longer, if one is more concerned with the way people respond to appeals from "conscience" and the way they create themselves as norm-regarding beings, one will still find oneself in tension as one watches individuals do violent and careless things. And indeed, no matter what one's philosophical approach, the teacher cannot help recognize that human beings are always being demeaned and maltreated, that students are capable of hatred and bigotries, that it is difficult for anyone *not* to falsify himself or herself. Whether one tries consistently to remain "calm and cool" in the knowledge "that the way of life one prefers, all things considered, includes the moral way of life,"[14] whether one chooses to live "in unsatisfied indignation" because "too high a price is asked for harmony,"[15] one will find oneself entangled in the problematic, haunted by open questions. In one's capacity as teacher one is expected to know the answers, to have prescriptions at hand which tell the young how they ought to live. Unable to tolerate major personal uncertainties when he or she is engaged in teaching, the teacher is likely to tell himself or herself that he or she does indeed have it all worked out, that he or she *knows*. Camus once wrote: "There is not one human being who, above a certain elementary level of consciousness, does not exhaust himself in trying to find formulae or attitudes which will give his existence the unity it lacks . . . It is therefore justifiable to say that man has an idea of a better world than this. But better does not mean different, it means unified."[16] This desire for unity or meaning may be the source of impulse to reach out and to learn; but it can be extremely disquieting, especially for the self-conscious teacher. He or she can only engage in the movement we have spoken of, at the side of his or her students, making efforts to constitute meanings – caring intensely about the kind of thinking going on and the choices being made. As aware of one's students' incompleteness as one must be of one's own, the teacher can only strain to encounter his or her students without objectifying them; he or she can only act to help them, as autonomous beings, to choose.

Let us take, as an example, the predicament of a teacher confronted with a Peace Moratorium, a day on which students stay away from classes in symbolic protest against a war. Like many other such situations, this gesture may provide occasion for a considerable amount of moral education if the teacher makes no arbitrary decisions and if the students are free to decide what they think is right to do. Let us suppose the teacher has been much involved with peace campaigns, has belonged to various peace organizations, and has participated in marches and demonstrations. Let us also suppose the teacher is deeply convinced that atrocities are being committed in the current war and that they present a moral issue of consequence for every American. The teacher may believe a wide-spread indifference partly accounts for the massacres that have taken place, the torture, the indiscriminate bombings, and the rest. He or she may be convinced the Moratorium will have positive results, so positive that they will erase the negative effects of violent protests carried on in the past. As the teacher sees it, then, there is every reason for saying the Moratorium is worth supporting. The teacher is eager, in fact, for the students to turn out in a body to demonstrate their support.

The teacher has, however, other convictions too. The particular lessons he or she has been teaching are important. He or she does not believe learning sequences ought to be whimsically or foolishly interrupted and thinks that classroom activity, because it brings him or her in contact with the students, contributes measurably to their education. A lost day, as he or she sees it, might mean a setback for some of the pupils, missed learning opportunities for others; and, obviously observing the Moratorium means losing the day in that sense. The teacher realizes, in addition, that observing it might suggest to the less motivated that there are more worthwhile things to do than studying; to others it might seem an excuse for time off to observe minor holidays, to celebrate World Series victories, and so on. Taking all this into account, the teacher still

202 Conceptions of Education

believes it is more worthwhile to support the peace action than to do nothing at all.

Some would say that, in coming to this conclusion, the teacher should anticipate the consequences (moral and pedagogical) of each course. Others would stress that one must be clear about one's own priority system. Still others would talk about the extremity of the war situation and the need, if only in the interests of decency, for each person to rebel. We have been describing a fairly deliberate and rational teacher, who is preoccupied with acting justly in and outside of school. He or she might well set up as a first principle the idea of justice: human beings ought to be treated with a proper concern for their interests; that they ought never to be discriminated against unless there are relevant grounds for treating them differently (as infant children, criminals, and mentally ill people are treated differently). Thinking of the war and the men, women, and children suffering because of it, the teacher can reasonably say that it is unjust for them to be deprived not only of the right to live in peace but of opportunities for education, economic security, and the kinds of fulfilment Americans take for granted. It makes good sense to present this idea to the students as well as to explain why commitment to such a principle makes relevant their idea that the war should be ended, that people should do whatever is in their power to see that this end is brought about.

The same principle of justice, however, may require that the teacher provide each member in the class with the freedom to deliberate on what ought to be done in this instance: whether they should support the Moratorium. If the teacher does not permit this kind of deliberation, he or she will be interfering with their freedom; and such interference would also be unjust. Personally involved with the Moratorium as the teacher is, he or she can still recognize that as a teacher one's primary obligation is to teach students the principle of justice in the hope that they will be able to make future decisions, holding that principle clearly in mind. "Morality," writes R.M. Hare, "retains its vigor when ordinary people have learnt afresh to decide for themselves what principles to live by, and more especially what principles to teach their children."[17] The children, too, have to learn afresh as they make decisions of principle. Neither teacher nor parent can feel assured that the young will act as their elders would have done or even as their elders recommend. The point is that the young understand certain principles, make clear the reasons for their decisions, and revise their norms intelligently in response to the contingencies of the world. For the person of rational passion this ought to be enough. He or she wants the young to know, above all, what they are doing and why, wants them to be able to explain in understandable language, and wants them to make sense.

When they do understand and make sense, the teacher we have been describing can say he or she has been successful as a moral educator in one specific situation. To demonstrate that success, the teacher can ask people to listen to the talk proceeding in the classroom, to the way the students go about deliberating on the matter of the Moratorium. Perhaps they will decide not to support it; and they may make their decision cooperatively, slowly, rationally, paying attention to consequences and to the logic of what they are saying. The teacher can only feel gratified because they have achieved a type of mastery new to them. Of course, they could always have decided, with equivalent deliberateness, to support the Moratorium. Or, without much thought, they could have decided to march out of the classroom to join the action because it was so highly publicized, because their friends and their teacher were so much involved. In the latter case, the good teacher (activist or not) would have to feel he or she had failed.

A kind of heroism is demanded of the principled teacher eager to initiate students into principled decision making and a rational way of life. *What* they decide is always in question. There are no guarantees that they will be "good" or humane people. The teacher must acknowledge that one can only deal justly with individuals one hopes will learn how to learn. When faced with issues more personally consequential than a Peace Moratorium or when dealing with elementary school children, the teacher may focus on the formation of good habits or the cultivation of the dispositions required for reflective conduct. But here too there are no certainties, even if one resorts to traditional "habit training" or the use of punishments and rewards. We might consider the problem of drugs, for instance – clearly a far more complex question than whether existing laws should be obeyed. Peter Marin has written sympathetically about young people in search of a supportive community life, who "turn to drugs for all the things they cannot find without them." He describes the ways in which the drug cultures answer young people's needs for communities protected from adults, adult ambitions, and what the young see as adult hypocrisy. "They can walk the streets high or sit stoned in class and still be *inside* it (meaning, their own community) – among adults but momentarily free of them, a world *within* which one is at home."[18] Marin recommends a kind of loving detachment, dealing with these young people as if they composed a friendly neighborhood tribe. Whether he is right or wrong in a pragmatic sense, the detachment he recommends may enable the teacher at least to help them articulate the criteria governing their choices of life-style. Refusing to blame them, simply taking them to talk about how and why they live as they do, the teacher may be in a position to make them aware of their principles, which have often turned out to be much akin to "Christian" principles. Even though he or she may not convince them to give up marijuana, for example, the teacher may help them see the "moral resonance" of the decisions they are making day by day. Marin, of course, has marijuana in mind when he speaks so empathetically about the "stoned"; and he knows, as most teachers do, that far more serious issues are raised by the "hard" and dangerous drugs. When confronted with proselytizing addicts, the teacher can do little; nor can one be persuasive with youth who boast experiences of "expanding consciousness" they know the teacher cannot share. Trying, sometimes in the face of chaos, to suggest alternative ways of getting through life, one can point to consequences and dangers, even as one gives reluctant credence to the delights that are claimed. The least productive road here, as in other moral domains, is the path of tyranny and suppression. Even here many teachers will opt for the values of justice, which (in Lawrence Kohlberg's words) "prohibit the imposition of beliefs of one group upon another."[19] But this does not mean the teacher will give licence to the self-destructive; nor does it mean that he or she will do nothing to change their habits or their style. One might even call in legal authorities and still feel that one was, in Kohlberg's sense, "just." One is a teacher; and, in the case we have been discussing, a teacher with a poor commitment to rationality. The teacher's obligation, as he or she perceives it, is primarily to induce young people to decide in principled fashion what they *conceive* (not merely "feel" or "intuit") to be worthwhile.

How would a teacher with a more existential orientation handle the problems of moral education? There are many different problems, not all revolving around the matter of principles and guidelines. Obviously, one would put great stress on one's own and one's students' freedom and on the need to make choices within frequently "extreme" situations. One would take seriously what the analytically inclined teacher is prone to ignore: the moods the teacher and the student are bound to experience – anguish, boredom, guilt. For him or her these are anything but pathological states. They are appropriate responses to the contemporary universe with its injustice and impersonality, its underlying "absurdity." Furthermore, they create the affective and subjective context in which choices are made and values defined; doing so, they make unthinkable the predominantly cool, calculative approach to moral life. This does not mean that human beings are determined by their passions, because they can choose whether to give in to them. Nor does it mean that mere impulse or feeling governs moral choice. Sartre talks about "creating the man we want to be." Every act we perform creates an image of a human as we *think* he or she ought to be. "To choose to be this or that is to affirm at the same time the value of what we choose, because we can never choose evil. We always choose the good, and nothing can be good for us without being good for all."[20] Our responsibility, then, is immense, especially when we consider that (for the existentialist) there are no predefined values, no moral principles which determine in advance what is good. Alone and condemned to freedom, the individual *must* choose. One experiences anxiety or anguish because one cannot even be sure that the person one chooses oneself to be at one moment is the same as the one he or she will be at a later time. A student, for example, choosing to be a chemist, investing all energies in what he or she has determined to be valuable, cannot know that the "essence" he or she has fashioned for himself or herself will be the same the following year; yet, in the interim, the student will have chosen *not* to do a great many things that might have been relevant to what he or she eventually decided to become. Anguish is the way freedom reveals itself. It is the expression of the nagging desire for completion – without any guarantee that the completion sought will be valuable when it is achieved. Boredom is the way the threat of nothingness and indifference reveal themselves to consciousness. Choices are made in the face of a "profound boredom" many times, "drifting" (as Martin Heidegger says) "hither and thither in the abysses of existence like a mute fog," drawing all things together in "a queer kind of indifference."[21] What, after all, does it matter? What is the point? These questions, too, are functions of the dreadful freedom in which the individual decides; and the existential teacher would have to take this notion seriously into account. Then there is the matter of guilt, so frequently suppressed or ignored. Guilt may be the expression of a feeling that the individual is not acting on his or her possibilities, not shaping his or her future; and yet here too the teacher can never be sure. The existential teacher would not try to assuage such feelings or to evade them. He or she would consciously stimulate the disquietude they entail, and would provoke to responsible action persons absolutely free to choose themselves.

Given the problem of a Peace Moratorium, such a teacher could not will against the students' freedom or enforce his or her commitments on them. The teacher would, however, emphasize the evasions that led to refusals to act. Simply to sit back and condemn a war one recognizes to be unjust and evil is to be guilty of bad faith, especially if there is the possibility of action. For this reason, the German who detested Nazism and still did nothing to demonstrate his or her opposition is called so ironically a "good German," someone who took no responsibility, who lived his or her life in bad faith. Therefore, more explicitly than the analytically inclined teacher, the existential educator would underline the inescapability of responsibility. Each person is "the author" of the situation in which *one* gives meaning to one's world, but through action, through one's project, not by well-meaning thought. If a student declared his or her opposition to a war but was not inclined to do anything about it or be actively concerned about what was being done in his or her name, he or she could be charged with evasion and irresponsibility, even though no one would *tell* him or her what to do.

Notes

[1]Alfred Schutz, "The Stranger," *Studies in Social Theory,* Collected Papers II (The Hague: Martinus Nijhoff, 1964), 95.

[2]Albert Camus, *The Stranger* (New York: Vintage Books, 1954), 104.

[3]Nathaniel Hawthorne, *The Scarlet Letter,* in Malcolm Cowley (ed.), *The Portable Hawthorne* (New York: Viking Press, 1955), 425.

[4]Maurice Merleau-Ponty, "Man and Adversity," in *Signes,* tr. Richard C. McCleary (Evanston, Ill.: Northwestern University Press, 1965), 240.

[5]Ibid., 242.

[6]Ernest Hemingway, *A Farewell to Arms* (London: Jonathan Cape, 1952), 186.

[7]Charles E. Silberman, *Crisis in the Classroom* (New York: Random House, 1970), 126-127.

[8]Jules Henry, *Culture Against Man* (New York: Random House, 1963), 291.

[9]Frank Kermode, *The Sense of an Ending* (New York: Oxford University Press, 1967), 39.

[10]Richard S. Peters, "Concrete Principles and the Rational Passions," in *Moral Education: Five Lectures* by James M. Gustafson, Richard S. Peters, Lawrence Kohlberg, Bruno Bettelheim and Kenneth Keniston (Cambridge, Mass.: Harvard University Press, 1970), 39.

[11]Jean-Paul Sartre, *Existentialism,* tr. Bernard Frechtman (New York: Philosophical Library, 1947), 21.

[12]William K. Frankena, *Ethics* (Englewood Cliffs, N.J.: Prentice-Hall, 1963), 5-6.

[13]Gresham M. Sykes, "New Crimes for Old," *The American Scholar,* autumn 1971, 598.

[14]William K. Frankena, *Ethics,* 98.

[15]Fyodor Dostoevsky, *The Brothers Karamazov,* tr. Constance Garnett (New York: The Modern Library, 1945), 291.

[16]Albert Camus, *The Rebel,* tr. Anthony Bower (New York: Alfred A. Knopf, 1954), 231.

[17]Richard M. Hare, *The Language of Morals* (New York: Oxford University Press, 1964), 73.

[18]Peter Marin and Allan Y. Cohen, *Understanding Drug Use* (New York: Harper & Row, Publishers, 1971), 15.

[19]Lawrence Kohlberg, "Education for Justice: A Modern Statement of the Platonic View," in *Moral Education,* 70.

[20]Jean-Paul Sartre, *Existentialism,* 20.

[21]Martin Heidegger, "What is Metaphysics?" in *Existence and* Being, tr. R.F.C. Hull and Alan Crick (Chicago: Henry Regnery Company, 1965), 334.

15

Education without Dogma:
Truth, Freedom, and Our Universities

Richard Rorty

When people on the political right talk about education, they immediately start talking about the truth. Typically, they enumerate what they take to be familiar and self-evident truths and regret that these are no longer being inculcated in the young. When people on the political left talk about education, they talk first about freedom. The left typically views the old familiar truths cherished by the right as a crust of convention that needs to be broken through, vestiges of old-fashioned modes of thought from which the new generation should be freed.

When this opposition between truth and freedom becomes explicit, both sides wax philosophical and produce theories about the nature of truth and freedom. The right usually offers a theory according to which, if you have truth, freedom will follow automatically. Human beings, says this theory, have within them a truth-tracking faculty called "reason," an instrument capable of uncovering the intrinsic nature of things. Once such obstacles as the passions or sin are overcome, the natural light of reason will guide us to the truth. Deep within our souls there is a spark that the right sort of education can fan into flame. Once the soul is afire with love of truth, freedom will follow – for freedom consists in realizing one's *true* self; that is, in the actualization of one's capacity to be rational. So, the right concludes, only the truth can make us free.

This Platonic picture of education as the awakening of the true self can easily be adapted to the needs of the left. The left dismisses Platonic asceticism and exalts Socratic social criticism. It identifies the obstacles to freedom that education must overcome, not with the passions or with sin, but with convention and prejudice. What the right calls "overcoming the passions," the left calls "stifling healthy animal instincts." What the right thinks of as the triumph of reason, the left describes as the triumph of acculturation – acculturation engineered by the powers that be. What the right describes as civilizing the young, the left describes as alienating them from their true selves. In the tradition of Rousseau, Marx, Nietzsche, and Foucault, the left pictures society as depriving the young of their freedom and of their essential humanity so that they may function as frictionless cogs in a vast, inhuman socioeconomic machine. So, for the left, the proper function of education is to make the young realize that they should not consent to this alienating process of socialization. On the leftist's inverted version of Plato, if you take care of freedom – especially political and economic freedom – truth will take care of itself. For truth is what will be believed once the alienating and repressive forces of society are removed.

On both the original, rightist, and the inverted, leftist account of the matter, there is a natural connection between truth and freedom. Both argue for this connection on the basis of distinctions between nature and convention and between what is essentially human and what is inhuman. Both accept the identification of truth and freedom with the essentially human. The difference between them is simply over the question: Is the present socio-economic setup in accordance, more or less, with nature? Is it, on the whole, a realization of human potentialities or rather a way of frustrating those potentialities? Will acculturation to the norms of our society produce freedom or alienation?

On abstract philosophical topics, therefore, the right and the left are largely in agreement. The interesting differences between right and left about education are concretely political. Conservatives think that the present setup is, if not exactly good, at least better than any alternative suggested by the radical left. They think that at least some of the traditional slogans of our society, some pieces of its conventional wisdom, are the deliverance of "reason." That is why they think education should concentrate on resurrecting and reestablishing what they call "fundamental truths which are now neglected or despised." Radicals, in contrast, share Frank Lentricchia's view that the society in which we live is "mainly unreasonable." So they regard the conservative's "fundamental truths" as what Foucault calls "the discourse of power." They think that continuing to inculcate the conventional wisdom amounts to betraying the students.

In the liberal democracies of recent times, the tension between these two attitudes has been resolved by a fairly simple, fairly satisfactory, compromise. The right has pretty much kept control of primary and secondary education and the left has gradually gotten control of nonvocational higher education. In America, our system of local school boards means that pre-college teachers cannot, in the classroom, move very far from the local consensus. By contrast, the success of the American Association of University Professors (AAUP) in enforcing academic freedom means that many college teachers set their own agendas. So education up to the age of eighteen or nineteen is mostly a matter of socialization – of getting the students to take over the moral and political common sense of the society as it is. It is obviously not only that, since sympathetic high-school teachers often assist curious or troubled students by showing them where to find alternatives to this common sense. But these exceptions cannot be made the rule. For any society has a right to expect that, whatever else happens in the course of adolescence, the schools will inculcate most of what is generally believed.

Around the age of eighteen or nineteen, however, American students whose parents are affluent enough to send them to reasonably good colleges find themselves in the hands of teachers well to the left of the teachers they met in high school. These teachers do their best to nudge each successive college generation a little more to the left, to make them a little more conscious of the cruelty built into our institutions, of the need for reform, of the need to be sceptical about the current consensus. Obviously this is not all that happens in college, since a lot of college is, explicitly or implicitly, vocational training. But our hope that colleges will be more than vocational schools is largely a hope that they will encourage such Socratic scepticism. We hope that the students can be distracted from their struggle to get into a high-paying profession, and that the professors will not *simply* try to reproduce themselves by preparing the students to enter graduate study in their own disciplines.

This means that most of the skirmishing about education between left and right occurs on the borders between secondary and higher education. Even ardent radicals, for all their talk of "education for freedom," secretly hope that the elementary schools will teach the kids to wait their turn in line, not to shoot up in the johns, to obey the cop on the corner, and to spell, punctuate, multiply, and divide. They do not really want the high schools to produce, every year, a graduating class of amateur Zarathustras. Conversely, only the most resentful and blinkered conservatives want to ensure that colleges hire only teachers who will endorse the status quo. Things get difficult when one tries to figure out where socialization should stop and criticism start.

This difficulty is aggravated by the fact that both conservatives and radicals have trouble realizing that education is not a continuous process from age five to age twenty-two. Both tend to ignore the fact that the word "education" covers two entirely distinct, and equally necessary, processes – socialization and individuation. They both fall into the trap of thinking that a single set of ideas will work for both high school and college education. That is why both have had trouble noticing the differences between Allan Bloom's *The Closing of the American Mind* and E.D. Hirsch's *Cultural Literacy*.[1] The cultural left in America sees Bloom and Hirsch as examples of a single assault on freedom, twin symptoms of a fatuous Reaganite complacency. Conservatives, on the other hand, overlook the difference between Bloom's Straussian doubts about democracy and Hirsch's Deweyan hopes for a better educated democratic electorate: They think of both books as urging us to educate for truth, and to worry less about freedom.

Let me now put some of my own cards on the table. I think Hirsch is largely right about the high schools and Bloom largely wrong about the colleges. I think that conservatives are wrong in thinking that we have either a truth-tracking faculty called "reason" or a true self that education brings to consciousness. I think that the radicals are right in saying that if you take care of political, economic, cultural, and academic freedom, then truth will take care of itself. But I think the radicals are wrong in believing that there is a true self that will emerge once the repressive influence of society is removed. There is no such thing as human nature, in the deep sense in which Plato and Strauss use this term. Nor is there such a thing as alienation from one's essential humanity due to societal repression, in the deep sense made familiar by Rousseau and the Marxists. There is only the shaping of an animal into a human being by a process of socialization, followed (with luck) by the self-individualization and self-creation of that human being through his or her own later revolt against that very process. Hirsch is dead right in saying that we Americans no longer give our children a secondary education that enables them to function as citizens of a democracy. Bloom is dead wrong in thinking that the point of higher education is to help students grasp the "natural" superiority of those who lead "the theoretical life." The point of nonvocational higher education is, instead, to help students realize that they can reshape themselves – that they can rework the self-image foisted on them by their past, the self-image that makes them competent citizens, into a new self-image, one that they themselves have helped to create.

I take myself, in holding these opinions, to be a fairly faithful follower of John Dewey. Dewey's great contribution to the theory of education was to help us get rid of the idea that education is a matter of either inducing or educing truth. Primary and secondary education will always be a matter of familiarizing the young with what their elders take to be true, whether it is true or not. It is not, and never will be, the function of lower-level education to challenge the prevailing consensus about what is true. Socialization has to come before individuation, and education for freedom cannot begin before some constraints have been imposed. But, for quite different reasons, nonvocational higher education is also not a matter of inculcating or educing truth. It is, instead, a matter of inciting doubt and stimulating imagination, thereby challenging the prevailing consensus. If pre-college education produces literate citizens and college education produces self-creating individuals, then questions about whether students are being taught the truth can safely be neglected.

Dewey put a new twist on the idea that if you take care of freedom, truth will take care of itself. For both the original Platonism of the right and the inverted Platonism of the left, that claim means that if you free the true self from various constraints it will automatically see truth. Dewey showed us how to drop the notion of "the true self" and how to drop the distinction between nature and convention. He taught us to call "true" whatever belief results from a free and open encounter of opinions, without asking whether this result agrees with something beyond that encounter. For Dewey, the sort of freedom that guarantees truth is not freedom from the passions or sin. Nor is it freedom from tradition or from what Foucault called "power." It is simply sociopolitical freedom, the sort of freedom found in bourgeois democracies. Instead of justifying democratic freedoms by reference to an account of human nature and the nature of reason, Dewey takes the desire to preserve and expand such freedoms as a starting point – something we need not look behind. Instead of saying that free and open encounters track truth by permitting a mythical faculty called "reason" to function unfettered, he says simply that we have no better criterion of truth than "what results from such encounters."

This account of truth – the account that has recently been revived by Jurgen Habermas – amounts to putting aside the notion that truth is correspondence to reality. More generally, it puts aside the idea that inquiry aims at accurately representing what lies outside the human mind (whether this be conceived as the will of God, or the layout of Plato's realm of ideas, or the arrangement of atoms in the void). It thereby gets rid of the idea that sociopolitical institutions need to be "based" on some such outside foundation.

For Dewey, as for Habermas, what takes the place of the urge to represent reality accurately is the urge to come to free agreement with our fellow human beings – to be full participating members of a free community of inquiry. Dewey offered neither the conservative's philosophical justification of democracy by reference to eternal values nor the radical's justification by reference to decreasing alienation. He did not try to justify democracy at all. He saw democracy not as founded upon the nature of human beings or reason or reality, but as a promising experiment engaged in by a particular herd of a particular species of animal – our species and our herd. He asks us to put our faith in ourselves – in the utopian hope characteristic of a democratic community – rather than asking for reassurance or backup from outside.

This notion of a species of animals gradually taking control of its own evolution by changing its environmental conditions leads Dewey to say, in good Darwinian language, that "growth itself is the moral end" and that to "protect, sustain and direct growth is the chief *ideal* of education." Dewey's conservative critics denounced him for fuzziness, for not giving us a criterion of growth. But Dewey rightly saw that any such criterion would cut the future down to the size of the present. Asking for such a criterion is like asking a dinosaur to specify what would make for a good mammal or asking a fourth-century Athenian to propose forms of life for the citizens of a twentieth-century industrial democracy.

Instead of criteria, Deweyans offer inspiring narratives and fuzzy utopias. Dewey had stories to tell about our progress from Plato to Bacon to the Mills, from religion to rationalism to experimentalism, from tyranny to feudalism to democracy. In their later stages, his stories merged with Emerson's and Whitman's descriptions of the democratic vistas – with their vision of America as the place where human beings will become unimaginably wonderful, different, and free. For Dewey, Emerson's talent for criterionless hope was the essence of his value to his country. In 1903 Dewey wrote: "[T]he coming century may well make evident what is just now dawning, that Emerson is not only a philosopher, but that he is the Philosopher of Democracy." Dewey's point was that Emerson did not offer truth, but simply hope. Hope – the ability to believe that the future will be unspecifiably different from, and unspecifiably freer than, the past – is the condition of growth. That sort of hope was all that Dewey himself offered us, and by offering it he became our century's Philosopher of Democracy.

Let me now turn to the topic of how a Deweyan conceives of the relation between pre-college and college education, between the need for socialization and the need to remove the barriers that socialization inevitably imposes. There is a standard caricature of Dewey's views that says Dewey thought that kids should learn to multiply or to obey the cop on the corner only if they have democratically chosen that lesson for the day, or only if this particular learning experience happens to meet their currently felt needs. This sort of nondirective nonsense was not what Dewey had in mind. It is true, as Hirsch says, that Dewey "too hastily rejected 'the piling up of information.'" But I doubt that it ever occurred to Dewey that a day would come when students could graduate from an American high school not knowing who came first: Plato or Shakespeare, Napoleon or Lincoln, Frederick Douglass or Martin Luther King, Jr. Dewey too hastily assumed that nothing would ever stop the schools from piling on the information and that the only problem was to get them to do other things as well.

Dewey was wrong about this. But he could not have foreseen the educationist establishment with which Hirsch is currently battling. He could not have foreseen that the United States would decide to pay its pre-college teachers a fifth of what it pays its doctors. Nor did he foresee that an increasingly greedy and heartless American middle class would let the quality of education a child receives become proportional to the assessed value of the parents' real estate. Finally, he did not foresee that most children would spend thirty hours a week watching televised fantasies, nor that the cynicism of those who produce these fantasies would carry over into our children's vocabularies of moral deliberation.

But Dewey's failures of prescience do not count against his account of truth and freedom. Nor should they prevent us from accepting his notion of the socialization American children should receive. For Dewey, this socialization consisted in acquiring an image of themselves as heirs to a tradition of increasing liberty and rising hope. Updating Dewey a bit, we can think of him as wanting the children to come to think of themselves as proud and loyal citizens of a country that, slowly and painfully, threw off a foreign yoke, freed its slaves, enfranchised its women, restrained its robber barons and licensed its trade unions, liberalized its religious practices and broadened its religious and moral tolerance, and built colleges in which 50 percent of its population could enroll – a country that numbered Jefferson, Thoreau, Susan B. Anthony, Eugene Debs, Woodrow Wilson, Walter Reuther, FDR, Rosa Parks, and James Baldwin among its citizens. Dewey wanted the inculcation of this narrative of freedom and hope to be the core of the socializing process.

As Hirsch quite rightly says, that narrative will not be intelligible unless a lot of information gets piled up in the children's heads. Radical critics of Hirsch's books have assumed that he wants education to be a matter of memorizing lists rather than reading interesting books, but this does not follow from what Hirsch says. All that follows is that the students be examined on their familiarity with the people, things, and events mentioned in those books. Hirsch's radical critics would sound more plausible if they offered some concrete suggestions about how to get such a narrative inculcated without setting examinations tailored to lists like Hirsch's, or if they had some suggestions about how eighteen-year-olds who find *Newsweek* over their heads are to choose between political candidates.

Let us suppose, for a moment, that Hirsch's dreams come true. Suppose we succeed not only in inculcating such a narrative of national hope in most of our students but in setting it in the larger context of a narrative of world history and literature, all this against the background of the world-picture offered by the natural scientists. Suppose, that is, that after pouring money into precollege education, firing the curriculum experts, abolishing the licensing requirements, building brand-new, magnificently equipped schools in the inner cities, and instituting Hirsch-like school-leaving examinations, it proves possible to make most American nineteen-year-olds as culturally literate as Dewey and Hirsch have dreamed they might be. What, in such a utopia, would be the educational function of American colleges? What would policymakers in higher education worry about?

I think all that they would then need to worry about would be finding teachers who were not exclusively concerned with preparing people to be graduate students in their various specialities and then making sure that these teachers get a chance to give whatever courses they feel like giving. They would still need to worry about making sure that higher education was not purely vocational – not simply a matter of fulfilling prerequisites for professional schools or reproducing current disciplinary matrices. They would not, however, have to worry about the integrity of the curriculum or about the challenge of connecting learning – any more than administrators in French and German universities worry about such things. That sort of worry would be left to secondary-school administrators. If Hirsch's dreams ever come true, then the colleges will be free to get on with their proper business. That business is to offer a blend of specialized vocational training and provocation to self-creation.

The socially most important provocations will be offered by teachers who make vivid and concrete the failure of the country of which we remain loyal citizens to live up to its own ideals – the failure of America to be what it knows it ought to become. This is the traditional function of the reformist liberal left, as opposed to the revolutionary radical left. In recent decades, it has been the main function of American college teachers in the humanities and social sciences. Carrying out this function, however, cannot be made a matter of explicit institutional policy. For, if it is being done right, it is too complicated, controversial, and tendentious to be the subject of agreement in a faculty meeting. Nor is it the sort of thing that can be easily explained to the governmental authorities or the trustees who supply the cash. It is a matter that has to be left up to individual college teachers to do or not do as they think fit, as their sense of responsibility to their students and their society inspires them. To say that, whatever their other faults, American colleges and universities remain bastions of academic freedom, is to say that the typical administrator would not dream of trying to interfere with a teacher's attempt to carry out such responsibilities.

In short, if the high schools were doing the job that lots of money and determination might make them able to do, the colleges would not have to worry about Great Books, or general education, or overcrowding fragmentation. The faculty could just teach whatever seemed good to them to teach, and the administrators could get along nicely without much knowledge of what was being taught. They could rest content with making sure that teachers who want to teach a course that had never been taught before, or assign materials that had never been assigned before, or otherwise break out of the disciplinary matrix that some academic department has been perpetuating are free to do so – as well as trying to ensure that teachers who might want to do such things get appointed to the faculty.

But, in the real world, the nineteen-year-olds arrive at the doors of the colleges not knowing a lot of the words on Hisrch's list. They still have to be taught a lot of memorizable conventional wisdom of the sort that gets dinned into heads of their coevals in other countries. So the colleges have to serve as finishing schools, and the administrators sometimes have to dragoon the faculty into helping with this task. As things unfortunately – and with luck only temporarily – are, the colleges have to finish the job of socialization. Worse yet, they have to do this when the students are already too old and too restless to put up with such a process. It would be well for the colleges to remind us that nineteen is an age when young people should have finished absorbing the best that has been thought and said and should have started becoming suspicious of it. It would also be well for them to remind us that the remedial work that society currently forces college faculties to undertake – the kind of work that Great Books curricula are typically invented in order to carry out – is just an extra chore, analogous to the custodial functions forced upon the high-school teachers. Such courses may, of course, be immensely valuable to students – as they were to Allan Bloom and me when we took them at the University of Chicago forty years ago. Nevertheless, carrying out such remedial tasks is not the social function of colleges and universities.

We Deweyans think that the social function of American colleges is to help the students see that the national narrative around which their socialization has centered is an open-ended one. It is to tempt the students to make themselves into people who can stand to their own pasts as Emerson and Anthony, Debs and Baldwin, stood to *their* pasts. This is done by helping the students realize that, despite the progress that the present has made over the past, the good has once again become the enemy of the better. With a bit of help, the students will start noticing everything that is paltry and mean and unfree in their surroundings. With luck, the best of them will succeed in altering the conventional wisdom, so that the next generation is socialized in a somewhat different way than they themselves were socialized. To hope that this way will only be somewhat different is to hope that the society will remain reformist and democratic, rather than being convulsed by revolution. To hope that it will nevertheless be perceptibly different is to remind oneself that growth is indeed the only end that democratic higher education can serve and also to remind oneself that the direction of growth is unpredictable.

This is why we Deweyans think that, although Hirsch is right in asking "What should they know when they come out of high school?" and "What remedial work remains, things being as they are, for the colleges to do?" the

What should we know how to do?

question "What should they learn in college?" had better go unasked. Such questions suggest that college faculties are instrumentalities that can be ordered to a purpose. The temptation to suggest this comes over administrators occasionally, as does the feeling that higher education is too important to be left to the professors. From an administrative point of view, the professors often seem self-indulgent and self-obsessed. They look like loose cannons, people whose habit of setting their own agendas needs to be curbed. But administrators sometimes forget that college students badly need to find themselves in a place in which people are not ordered to a purpose, in which loose cannons are free to roll about. The only point of having real live professors around instead of just computer terminals, videotapes, and mimeoed lecture notes is that students need to have freedom enacted before their eyes by actual human beings. That is why tenure and academic freedom are more than just trade union demands. Teachers setting their own agendas – putting their individual, lovingly prepared specialities on display in the curricular cafeteria, without regard to any larger end, much less any institutional plan – is what nonvocational higher education is all about.

Such enactments of freedom are the principal occasions of the erotic relationships between teacher and student that Socrates and Allan Bloom celebrate and that Plato unfortunately tried to capture in a theory of human nature and of the liberal arts curriculum. But love is notoriously untheorizable. Such erotic relationships are occasions of growth, and their occurrence and their development are as unpredictable as growth itself. Yet nothing important happens in nonvocational higher education without them. Most of these relationships are with the dead teachers who wrote the books the students are assigned, but some will be with the live teachers who are giving the lectures. In either case, the sparks that leap back and forth between teacher and students, connecting them in a relationship that has little to do with socialization but much to do with self-creation, are the principal means by which the institutions of a liberal society get changed. Unless some such relationships are formed, the students will never realize what democratic institutions are good for: namely, making possible the invention of new forms of human freedom, taking liberties never taken before.

I shall end by returning to the conservative-radical contrast with which I began. I have been trying to separate both the conservative's insistence on community and the radical's insistence on individuality from philosophical theories about human nature and about the foundations of democratic society. Platonism and Nietzche's inversion of Platonism seem to me equally unfruitful in thinking about education. As an alternative, I have offered Dewey's exaltation of democracy for its own sake and of growth for its own sake – an exaltation as fruitful as it is fuzzy.

This fuzziness annoys the conservatives because it does not provide enough sense of direction and enough constraints. The same fuzziness annoys the radicals because it provides neither enough fuel for resentment nor enough hope for sudden, revolutionary change. But the fuzziness that Dewey shared with Emerson is emblematic of what Wallace Stevens and Harold Bloom call "the American Sublime." That Sublime still lifts up the hearts of some fraction of each generation of college students. Whatever we may decide to do by way of connecting learning, we should do nothing that would make such exaltation less likely.

Notes

[1]Allan D. Bloom, *The Closing of the American Mind: How Higher Education has Failed Democracy and Impoverished the Souls of Today's Students* (New York: Simon and Schuster, 1987), and E.D. Hirsch, *Cultural Literacy: What Every American Needs to Know* (Boston: Houghton Mifflin, 1987).

16

Becoming Educated:
A Journey of Alienation or Integration?

Jane Roland Martin

In his educational autobiography *Hunger of Memory*[1], Richard Rodriguez tells of growing up in Sacramento, California, the third of four children in a Spanish-speaking family. Upon entering first grade he could understand perhaps fifty English words. Within the year his teachers convinced his parents to speak only English at home and Rodriguez soon became fluent in the language. By the time he graduated from elementary school with citations galore and entered high school, he had read hundreds of books. He went on to attend Stanford University and, twenty years after his parents' decision to abandon their native tongue, he sat in the British Museum writing a Ph.D dissertation in English literature.

Rodriguez learned to speak English and went on to acquire a liberal education. History, literature, science, mathematics, philosophy: these he studied and made his own. Rodriguez's story is of the cultural assimilation of a Mexican-American, but it is more than this, for by no means do all assimilated Americans conform to our image of a well-educated person. Rodriguez does because, to use the terms the philosopher R.S. Peters[2] employs in his analysis of the concept of the educated man, he did not simply acquire knowledge and skill. He acquired conceptual schemes to raise his knowledge beyond the level of a collection of disjointed facts and to enable him to understand the "reason why" of things. Moreover, the knowledge he acquired is not "inert": it characterizes the way he looks at the world and it involves the kind of commitment to the standards of evidence and canons of proof of the various disciplines that come from "getting on the inside of a form of thought and awareness."[3]

Quite a success story, yet *Hunger of Memory* is notable primarily as a narrative of loss. In becoming an educated person, Rodriguez loses his fluency in Spanish, but that is the least of it. As soon as English becomes the language of the Rodriguez family, the special feeling of closeness at home is diminished. Furthermore, as his days are increasingly devoted to understanding the meaning of words, it becomes difficult for Rodriguez to hear intimate family voices. When it is Spanish-speaking, his home is a noisy, playful, warm, emotionally charged environment; with the advent of English the atmosphere becomes quiet

219

and restrained. There is no acrimony. The family remains loving, but the experience of "feeling individualized" by family members is now rare, and occasions for intimacy are infrequent.

Rodriguez tells a story of alienation: from his parents, for whom he soon has no names; from the Spanish language, in which he loses his childhood fluency; from his Mexican roots, in which he shows no interest; from his own feelings and emotions, which all but disappear as he learns to control them; from his body itself, as he discovers when he takes a construction job after his senior year in college.

John Dewey spent his life trying to combat the tendency of educators to divorce mind from body and reason from emotion. Rodriguez's educational autobiography documents these divorces, and another one Dewey deplores, that of self from other. Above all, *Hunger of Memory* depicts a journey from intimacy to isolation. Close ties with family members are dissolved as public anonymity replaces private attention. Rodriguez becomes a spectator in his own home as noise gives way to silence and connection to distance. School, says Rodriguez, bade him trust "lonely" reason primarily. And there is enough time and "silence," he adds, "to think about ideas (big ideas)."[4]

What is the significance of this narrative of loss? Not every American has Rodriguez's good fortune of being born into a loving home filled with the warm sounds of intimacy, yet the separation and distance he ultimately experienced are not unique to him. On the contrary, they represent the natural end point of the educational journey Rodriguez took.

Dewey repeatedly pointed out that the distinction educators draw between liberal and vocational education represents a separation of mind from body, head from hand, thought from action. Since we define an educated person as one who has had and has profited from a liberal education, these splits are built into our ideal of the educated person. Since most definitions of excellence in education derive from that ideal, these splits are built into them as well. A split between reason and emotion is built into our definitions of excellence too, for we take the aim of a liberal education to be the development not of mind as a whole, but of rational mind. We define this in terms of the acquisition of knowledge and understanding, construed narrowly.[5] It is not surprising that Rodriguez acquires habits of quiet reflection rather than noisy activity, reasoned deliberation rather than spontaneous reaction, dispassionate inquiry rather than emotional response, abstract analytic theorizing rather than concrete storytelling. These are integral to the ideal of the educated person that has come down to us from Plato.

Upon completion of his educational journey, Rodriguez bears a remarkable resemblance to the guardians of the Just State that Plato constructs in the

Republic. Those worthies are to acquire through their education a wide range of theoretical knowledge, highly developed powers of reasoning, and the qualities of objectivity and emotional distance. To be sure, not one of Plato's guardians will be the "disembodied mind" Rodriguez becomes, for Plato believed that a strong mind requires a strong body. But Plato designed for his guardians an education of heads, not hands. (Presumably the artisans of the Just State would serve as their hands.) Moreover, considering the passions to be unruly and untrustworthy, Plato held up for the guardians an ideal of self-discipline and self-government in which reason keeps feeling and emotion under tight control. As a consequence, although he wanted the guardians of the Just State to be so connected to one another that they would feel each other's pains and pleasures, the educational ideal he developed emphasizes "inner" harmony at the expense of "outward" connecton. If his guardians do not begin their lives in intimacy, as Rodriguez did, their education, like his, is intended to confirm in them a sense of self in isolation from others.

Do the separations bequeathed to us by Plato matter? The great irony of the liberal education that comes down to us from Plato and still today as the mark of an educated person is that it is neither tolerant nor generous.[6] As Richard Rodriguez discovered, there is no place in it for education of the body, and since most action involves bodily movements, this means there is little room in it for education of action. Nor is there room for education of other-regarding feelings and emotions. The liberally-educated person will be provided with knowledge about others, but will not be taught to care about their welfare nor to act kindly toward them. That person will be given some understanding of society, but will not be taught to feel its injustices or even to be concerned over its fate. The liberally-educated person will be an ivory tower person – one who can reason but who has no desire to solve real problems in the real world – or else a technical person who likes to solve real problems but does not care about the solutions' consequences for real people and for the earth itself.

The case of Rodriguez illuminates several unhappy aspects of our Platonic heritage, while concealing another. No one who has seen Frederick Wiseman's film "High School" can forget the woman who reads to the assembled students a letter she has received from a pupil now in Vietnam. But for a few teachers who cared, she tells her audience, Bob Walters, a sub-average student academically, "might have been a nobody." Instead, while awaiting a plane that is to drop him behind the DMZ, he has written to her to say that he has made the school the beneficiary of his life insurance policy. "I am a little jittery right now," she reads. She is not to worry about him, however, because "I am only a body doing a job." Measuring his worth as a human being by his provision for the school, she overlooks the fact that Bob Walters was not merely participating in a war of dubious morality but was taking pride in being an automaton.

"High School" was made in 1968, but Bob Walters' words were echoed many times over by eighteen- and nineteen-year-old Marine recruits in the days immediately following the Grenada invasion. Readers of *Hunger of Memory* will not be surprised. The underside of a liberal education devoted to the development of "disembodied minds" is a vocational education the business of which is the production of "mindless bodies." In Plato's Just State, where, because of their rational powers, the specially educated few will rule the many, a young man's image of himself as "only a body doing a job" is the desired one. That the educational theory and practice of a democracy derives from Plato's explicitly undemocratic philosophical vision is disturbing. We are not supposed to have two classes of people, those who think and those who do not. We are not supposed to have two kinds of people, those who rule and those who obey.

The Council for Basic Education has long recommended, and some people concerned with excellence in education now suggest, that a liberal education at least through high school be extended to all. For the sake of argument, let us suppose this program can be carried out without making more acute the inequities it is meant to ease. We would then presumably have a world in which no one thinks of himself or herself as simply a body doing a job. We would, however, have a world filled with unconnected, uncaring, emotionally impoverished people. Even if it were egalitarian, it would be a sorry place in which to live. Nor would the world be better if somehow we combined Rodriguez's liberal education with a vocational one. For assuming it to be peopled by individuals who joined head and hand, reason would still be divorced from feeling and emotion, and each individual cut off from others.

The world we live in is just such a place. It is a world of child abuse and family violence,[7] a world in which one out of every four women will be raped at some time in her life.[8] Our world is on the brink of nuclear and/or ecological disaster. Efforts to overcome these problems, as well as the related ones of poverty and economic scarcity, flounder today under the direction of people who try hard to be rational, objective, autonomous agents, but, like Plato's guardians, do not know how to sustain human relationships or respond directly to human needs. Indeed, they do not even see the value of trying to do so. Of course, it is a mistake to suppose that education alone can solve this world's problems. Yet if there is to be hope of the continuation of life on earth, let alone a good life for all, as educators we must strive to do more than join mind and body, head and hand, thought and action.

Redefining Education

For Rodriguez, the English language is a metaphor. In the literal sense of the term he had to learn English to become an educated American, yet, in his narrative the learning of English represents the acquisition not so much of a new natural language as of new ways of thinking, acting, and being that he associates with the public world. Rodriguez makes it clear that the transition from Spanish to English represented for him the transition almost every child in our society makes from the "private world" of home to the "public world" of business, politics, and culture. He realizes that Spanish is not intrinsically a private language and English a public one, although his own experiences make it seem this way. He knows that the larger significance of his story lies in the fact that education inducts one into new activities and processes.

In my research on the place of women in educational thought[9] I have invoked a distinction between the productive and the reproductive processes of society and have argued that both historians of educational thought and contemporary philosophers of education define the educational realm in relation to society's productive processes only. Briefly, the reproductive processes include not simply the biological reproduction of the species, but the rearing of children to maturity and the related activities of keeping house, managing a household, and serving the needs and purposes of family members. In turn, the productive processes include political, social, and cultural activities as well as economic ones. This distinction is related to the one Rodriguez repeatedly draws between public and private worlds, for in our society reproductive processes are for the most part carried on in the private world of the home and domesticity, and productive processes in the public world of politics and work. Rodriguez's autobiography reveals that the definition of education as preparation solely for carrying on the productive processes of society is not a figment of the academic imagination.

Needless to say, the liberal education Rodriguez received did not fit him to carry on all productive processes of society. Aiming at the development of rational mind, his liberal education prepared him to be a consumer and creator of ideas, not an auto mechanic nor a factory worker. A vocational education, had he received one, would have prepared him to work with his hands and use procedures designed by others. They are very different kinds of education, yet both are designed to fit students to carry on productive, not reproductive, societal processes.

Why do I stress the connection between the definition of education and the productive processes of society? *Hunger of Memory* contains a wonderful

non-rational
home
spanish

rational
public
english

account of Rodriguez's grandmother telling him stories of her life. He is moved by the sounds she makes and by the message of intimacy her person transmits. The words themselves are not important to him, for he perceives the private world in which she moves – the world of childrearing and homemaking – to be one of feeling and emotion, intimacy and connection, and hence a realm of the nonrational. In contrast, he sees the public world – the world of productive processes for which his education fit him – as the realm of the rational. Feeling and emotion have no place in it, and neither do intimacy and connection. Instead, analysis, critical thinking, and self-sufficiency are the dominant values.

Rodriguez's assumption that feeling and emotion, intimacy and connection are naturally related to the home and society's reproductive processes and that these qualities are irrelevant to carrying on the productive processes is commonly accepted. But then, it is to be expected that their development is ignored by education in general and by liberal education in particular. Since education is supposed to equip people for carrying on productive societal processes, from a practical standpoint would it not be foolhardy for liberal *or* vocational studies to foster these traits?

Only in light of the fact that education turns its back on the reproductive processes of society and the private world of the home can Rodriguez's story of alienation be understood. His alienation from his body will re-occur so long as we equate being an educated person with having a liberal education. His journey of isolation and divorce from his emotions will be repeated so long as we define education exclusively in relation to the productive processes of society. But the assumption of inevitability underlying *Hunger of Memory* is mistaken. Education need not separate mind from body and thought from action, for it need not draw a sharp line between liberal and vocational education. More to the point, it need not separate reason from emotion and self from other. The reproductive processes *can* be brought into the educational realm thereby overriding the theoretical and practical grounds for ignoring feeling and emotion, intimacy and connection.

If we define education in relation to *both* kinds of societal processes and act upon our redefinition, future generations will not have to experience Rodriguez's pain. He never questions the fundamental dichotomies upon which his education rests. We must question them so that we can effect the reconciliation of reason and emotion, self and other, that Dewey sought. There are, moreover, two overwhelming reasons for favoring such a redefinition, both of which take us beyond Dewey.

All of us – male and female – participate in the reproductive processes of society. In the past, many have thought that education for carrying them on was not necessary: these processes were assumed to be the responsibility of women and it was supposed that by instinct a woman would automatically acquire the traits or qualities associated with them. The contemporary statistics on child abuse are enough by themselves to put to rest the doctrine of maternal instinct. Furthermore, both sexes have responsibility for making the reproductive processes of society work well. Family living and childrearing are not today, if they ever were, solely in the hands of women. Nor should they be. Thus, both sexes need to learn to carry on the reproductive processes of society just as in the 1980s both sexes needed to learn to carry on the productive ones.

The reproductive processes are of central importance to society, yet it would be a terrible mistake to suppose that the traits and qualities traditionally associated with these processes have no relevance beyond them. Jonathan Schell has said, "The nuclear peril makes all of us, whether we happen to have children of our own or not, the parents of all future generations" and that the will we must have to save the human species is a form of love resembling "the generative love of parents."[10] He is speaking of what Nancy Chodorow calls nurturing capacities[11] and Carol Gilligan calls an "ethics of care."[12] Schell is right. The fate of the earth depends on all of us possessing these qualities. Thus, although these qualities are associated in our minds with the reproductive processes of society, they have the broadest moral, social, and political significance. Care, concern, connectedness, nurturance are as important for carrying on society's economic, political, and social processes as its reproductive ones. If education is to help us acquire them, it must be redefined.

The Workings of Gender

It is no accident that in *Hunger of Memory* the person who embodies nurturing capacities and an ethics of care is a woman – Rodriguez's grandmother. The two kinds of societal processes are gender-related and so are the traits our culture associates with them. According to our cultural stereotypes, males are objective, analytical, rational, interested in ideas and things. They have no interpersonal orientation; they are not nurturant nor supportive, empathetic nor sensitive. Women, on the other hand, possess the traits men lack.[13]

Education is also gender-related. Our definition of its function makes it so. For if education is viewed as preparation for carrying on processes historically associated with males, it will inculcate traits the culture considers masculine. If the concept of education is tied by definition to the productive processes of society, our ideal of the educated person will coincide with the cultural stereotype of a male human being, and our definitions of excellence in education will embody "masculine" traits.

Of course, it is possible for members of one sex to acquire personal traits or qualities our cultural stereotypes attribute to the other. Thus, females can and do acquire traits incorporated in our educational ideal. However, it must be understood that these traits are *genderized*; that is, they are appraised differentially when they are possessed by males and females.[14] For example, whereas a male will be admired for his rational powers, a woman who is analytical and critical will be derided or shunned or will be told that she thinks like a man. Even if this latter is intended as a compliment, since we take masculinity and femininity to lie at opposite ends of a single continuum, she will thereby be judged as lacking in femininity and, as a consequence, be judged abnormal or unnatural. Elizabeth Janeway has said, and I am afraid she is right, that "unnatural" and "abnormal" are the equivalent for our age of what "damned" meant to our ancestors.[15]

Because his hands were soft, Rodriguez worried that his education was making him effeminate.[16] Imagine his anxieties on that score if he had been educated in those supposedly feminine virtues of caring and concern and had been taught to sustain intimate relationships and value connection. To be sure, had his education fostered these qualities, Rodriguez would not have had to travel a road from intimacy to isolation. I do not mean to suggest that there would have been no alienation at all; his is a complex case involving class, ethnicity, and color. But an education in which reason was joined to feeling and emotion and self to other would have yielded a very different life story. Had his education fostered these qualities, however, Rodriguez would have experienced another kind of hardship.

The pain Rodriguez suffers is a consequence of the loss of intimacy and the stunting of emotional growth that are themselves consequences of education. Now it is possible that Rodriguez's experience is more representative of males than of females. But if it be the case that females tend to maintain emotional growth and intimate connections better than males do, one thing is certain: educated girls are penalized for what Rodriguez considers his *gains*. If they become analytic, objective thinkers, and autonomous agents, they are judged less feminine than they should be. Thus, for them the essential myth of childhood is every bit as painful as it was for Rodriguez, for they are alienated from their own identity as females.

When education is defined so as to give the reproductive processes of society their due, and the virtues of nurturance and care associated with those processes are fostered in both males and females, educated men can expect to suffer for possessing traits genderized in favor of females as educated women now do for possessing traits genderized in favor of males. This is not to say that males will be placed in the double bind educated females find themselves in now, for males will acquire traits genderized in their own favor as well as ones genderized in favor of females, whereas the traits educated females must acquire today are *all* genderized in favor of males. On the other hand, since traits genderized in favor of females are considered lesser virtues, if virtues at all,[17] and the societal processes with which they are associated are throught to be relatively unimportant, males will be placed in the position of having to acquire traits both they and their society consider inferior.

One of the most important findings of contemporary scholarship is that our culture embraces a hierarchy of values, that places the productive processes of society and their associated traits above society's reproductive processes and the associated traits of care and nurturance. There is nothing new about this. We are the inheritors of a tradition of Western thought according to which the functions, tasks, and traits associated with females are deemed less valuable than those associated with males. In view of these findings, the difficulties facing those of us who would transform Rodriguez's educational journey from one of alienation to one of the integration of reason and emotion, of self and other, become apparent.

It is important to understand the magnitude of the changes to be wrought by an education that takes the integration of reason and emotion, self and other, seriously. Granted, when girls today embark on Rodriguez's journey they acquire traits genderized in favor of the "opposite" sex; but if on account of trait genderization they experience hardships Rodriguez did not, they can at least console themselves that their newly acquired traits, along with the societal processes to which the traits are attached, are considered valuable. Were we to attempt to change the nature of our educational ideal without also changing our value hierarchy, boys and men would have no such consolation. Without this consolation, however, we can be quite sure that the change we desire would not come to pass.

Toward an Integrated Curriculum

Just as the value structure I have been describing is reflected in our ideal of the educated person, so too it is reflected in the curriculum such a person is supposed to study. A large body of scholarship documents the extent to which the academic fields constituting the subjects of the liberal curriculum exclude women's lives, works, and experiences from their subject matter or else distort them by projecting the cultural stereotype of a female onto the evidence.[18] History, philosophy, politics; art and music; the social and behavioral sciences; even the biological and physical sciences give pride of place to male experience and achievements and to the societal processes thought to belong to men.

The research to which I refer reveals the place of women – or rather the absence thereof – in the theories, interpretations, and narratives constituting the disciplines of knowledge. Since the subject matter of the liberal curriculum is drawn from these disciplines, that curriculum gives pride of place to male experience and achievements and to the societal processes associated with men. In so doing, it is the bearer of bad news about women and the reproductive processes of society. Can it be doubted that when the works of women are excluded from the subject matter of the fields into which they are being initiated, students of both sexes will come to believe, or else will have their existing belief reinforced, that males are superior and females are inferior human beings? Can it be doubted that when in the course of this initiation the lives and experiences of women are scarcely mentioned, males and females will come to believe, or else believe more strongly than ever, that the ways in which women have lived and the things women have done throughout history have no value?

At campuses across North America projects are underway to incorporate the growing body of new scholarship on women into the liberal curriculum. Such efforts must be undertaken at all levels of schooling, not simply because women comprise one half the world's population, but because the exclusion of women from the subject matter of the "curriculum proper" constitutes a hidden curriculum in the validation of one gender, its associated tasks, traits, and functions, and the denigration of the other. Supporting our culture's genderized hierarchy of value even as it reflects it, this hidden curriculum must be raised to consciousness and counteracted.[19] Introduction of the new scholarship on women into the liberal curriculum proper – and for that matter into the vocational curriculum, too – makes this possible, on the one hand because it allows students to understand the workings of gender and, on the other, because it provides them with the opportuniy to appreciate women's traditional tasks, traits, and functions.

In a curriculum encompassing the experience of one sex, not two, questions of gender are automatically eliminated. For the value hierarchy under discussion to be understood, as it must be if it is to be abolished, its genderized roots must be exposed. Furthermore, if intimacy and connection are to be valued as highly as independence and distance, and if emotion and feeling are to be viewed as positive rather than untrustworthy elements of personality, women must no longer be viewed as different and alien – as the Other, to use Simone de Beauvoir's expression.[20]

Thus, we need to incorporate the study of women into curricula so that females – their lives, experiences, works, and attributes – are devalued by neither sex. But simply incorporating the new scholarship on women in the curriculum does not address the alienation and loss Rodriguez describes so well.

To overcome these we must seek not only a transformation of the content of curriculum proper, but an expansion of the educational realm to include the reproductive processes of society and a corresponding redefinition of what it means to become educated.

The expansion of the educational realm I propose does not entail an extension of a skill-oriented home economics education to males. Although it is important for both sexes to learn to cook and sew, I have in mind something different when I say that education must give the reproductive processes of society their due. The traits associated with women as wives and mothers – nurturance, care, compassion, connection, sensitivity to others, a willingness to put aside one's own projects, a desire to build and maintain relationships – need to be incorporated into our ideal. This does not mean that we should fill up the curriculum with courses in the three Cs of caring, concern, and connection. Given a redefinition of education, Compassion 101A need no more be listed in a school's course offerings than Objectivity 101A is now. Just as the productive processes of society have given us the general curricular goals of rationality and individual autonomy, so too, the reproductive processes yield general goals. And just as rationality and autonomy are posited as goals of particular subjects, e.g., science, as well as the curriculum as a whole, so nurturance and connection can be understood as overarching educational goals and also as the goals of particular subjects.

But now a puzzling question arises. Given that the standard subjects of the curriculum derive from the productive processes of society, must we not insert cooking and sewing and perhaps childrearing into the curriculum if we want caring, concern, and connection to be educational objectives? Science, math, history, literature, auto mechanics, refrigeration, typing: these are the subjects of the curriculum now and these derive from productive processes. If for subjects deriving from productive processes we set educational goals the source of which is the reproductive processes of society, do we not distort these subjects beyond recognition? But then, ought we not to opt instead for a divided curriculum with two sets of subjects? One set might be derived from the productive processes of society and foster traits associated with those, with the other set derived from the reproductive processes of society and fostering their associated traits. Is this the only way to do justice to both sets of traits?

If possible, a replication within the curriculum of the split between the productive and reproductive processes of society is to be avoided. So long as education insists on linking nurturing capacities and the three Cs to subjects arising out of the reproductive processes, we will lose sight of their *general* moral, social, and political significance. Moreover, so long as rationality and autonomous judgment are considered to belong exclusively to the productive processes of society, the reproductive ones will continue to be devalued. Thus, unless it is essential to divide up curricular goals according to the classification of a subject as productive or reproductive, we ought not to do so. That it is not essential becomes clear once we give up our stereotypical pictures of the two kinds of societal processes.

Readers of June Goodfield's *An Imagined World*[21] will know that feeling and emotion, intimacy and connection can be an integral part of the processes of scientific discovery.[22] Goodfield recorded the day-to-day activities of Anna, a Portuguese scientist studying lymphocytes in a cancer laboratory in New York. Anna's relationship to her colleagues *and* to the cells she studies provides quite a contrast to the rationalistic, atomistic vision of scientists and scientific discovery most of us have. To be sure, some years ago James Watson made it clear that scientists are human.[23] But Watson portrayed scientific discovery as a race between ambitious, aggressive, highly competitive contestants while Goodfield's Anna calls it "a kind of birth." Fear, urgency, intense joy; loneliness, intimacy, and a desire to share: these are some of the emotions that motivate and shape Anna's thought even as her reasoned analysis and her objective scrutiny of evidence engender passion. Moreover, she is bound closely to her colleagues in the lab by feeling, as well as by scientific need, and she empathizes with the lymphocytes she studies as well as with the sick people she hopes will one day benefit from her work.

If scientific activity can flourish in an atmosphere of cooperation and connection, and important scientific discoveries can take place when passionate feeling motivates and shapes thought, then surely it is not necessary for science education to be directed solely toward rationalistic, atomistic goals. And if nurturance capacities and the three Cs of caring, concern, and connection can become goals of science teaching without that subject being betrayed or abandoned, surely they can become the goals of *any* subject.

By the same token, if rational thought and independent judgment are components of successful childrearing and family living, it is not necessary to design education in subjects deriving from the reproductive processes of society solely around "affective" goals. That they can and should be part and parcel of these activities was argued long ago, and very convincingly, by both Mary Wollstonecraft and Catharine Beecher[24] and is a basic tenet of the home economics profession today.

Thus, just as nurturance and concern can be goals of any subject, rationality and independent judgment can also be. The temptation to institute a sharp separation of goals within an expanded educational realm corresponding to a sharp separation of subjects must, then, be resisted so that the general significance of the very real virtues we associate with women and the reproductive processes of society is understood and these virtues themselves are fostered in everyone.

Conclusion

In becoming educated one does not have to travel Rodriguez's road from intimacy to isolation. His journey of alienation is a function of a definition of education, a particular ideal of the educated person, and a particular definition of excellence – all of which can be rejected. Becoming educated can be a journey of integration, not alienation. The detailed task of restructuring an ideal of the educated person to guide this new journey I leave for another occasion. The general problem to be solved is that of uniting thought and action, reason and emotion, self and other. This was the problem Dewey addressed, but his failure to understand the workings of gender made it impossible for him to solve.

I leave the task of mapping the precise contours of a transformed curriculum for another occasion too. The general problem to be solved here is that of giving the reproductive processes of society – and the females who have traditionally been assigned responsibility for carrying them on – their due. Only then will feeling and emotion, intimacy and connection be perceived as valuable qualities so that a journey of integration is possible.

Loss, pain, isolation: it is a tragedy that these should be the results of becoming educated, the consequences of excellence. An alternative journey to Rodriguez's requires fundamental changes in both educational theory and practice. Since these changes will make it possible to diffuse throughout the population the nurturant capacities and the ethics of care that are absolutely essential to the survival of society itself, indeed, to the survival of life on earth, they should ultimately be welcomed even by those who would claim that the loss, pain, and isolation Rodriguez experienced in becoming educated did him no harm.

Notes

[1] Richard Rodriguez, *Hunger of Memory* (Boston: David R. Godine, 1982).

[2] See R.S. Peters, *Ethics and Education* (London: Allen & Unwin, 1966); and R.S. Peters, "Education and the Educated Man," in R.F. Dearden, P.H. Hirst, and R.S. Peters (eds.). *A Critique of Current Educational Aims* (London: Routledge and Kegan Paul, 1972).

[3] Peters, *Ethics and Education*, 9.

[4] R. Rodriguez, *Hunger of Memory*, 4.

[5] J.R. Martin, "Needed: A New Paradigm for Liberal Education," in J.F. Soltis (ed.). *Philosophy and Education* (Chicago: University of Chicago Press, 1981), 37-59.

[6]Ibid.

[7]W. Breines and L. Gordon, "The New Scholarship on Family Violence," *Signs*, 8, 3, 1983: 493-507.

[8]A.G. Johnson, "On the Prevalence of Rape in the United States," *Signs*, 6, 1, 1980: 136-146; and B. Lott, M.E. Reilly and D.R. Howard, "Sexual Assault and Harassment: A Campus Community Case Study," *Signs* 8, 2, 1982: 296-319.

[9]J.R. Martin, "Excluding Women from the Educational Realm," *Harvard Educational Review*, 52, 2, 1982: 133-148; and J.R. Martin, *Reclaiming a Conversation: The Ideal of the Educated Woman* (New Haven: Yale University Press, 1985).

[10]Jonathan Schell, *The Fate of the Earth* (New York: Avon, 1982), 175.

[11]Nancy Chodorow, *The Reproduction of Mothering* (Berkeley: University of California Press, 1978).

[12]Carol Gilligan, *In a Different Voice* (Cambridge: Harvard University Press, 1982).

[13]A.G. Kaplan and J . Bean, (eds.). *Beyond Sex-Role Stereotypes* (Boston: Little, Brown, 1976); also A.G. Kaplan and M.A. Sedney, *Psychology and Sex Roles* (Boston: Little, Brown, 1980).

[14]E. Beardsley, "Traits and Genderization," in M. Vetterling-Braggin, F.A. Elliston, and J. English (eds.), *Feminism and Philosophy* (Totowa, NJ: Littlefield, 1977), 117-123; and J.R. Martin, "The Ideal of the Educated Person," *Educational Theory* 31, 2, 1981: 97-109; and Martin, *Reclaiming a Conversation.*

[15]Elizabeth Janeway, *Man's World, Woman's Place* (New York: Morrow, 1971), 96.

[16]Quite clearly, Rodriguez's class background is a factor in this judgment. Notice, however, that the form his fear takes relates to gender.

[17]L. Blum, *Friendship, Altruism, and Morality* (London: Routledge and Kegan Paul, 1980).

[18]This scholarship cannot possibly be cited here. For reviews of the literature in the various academic disciplines see past issues of *Signs: Journal of Women in Culture and Society.*

[19]J.R. Martin, "What Should We Do with a Hidden Curriculum When We Find One?," *Curriculum Inquiry*, 6, 2, 1976: 135-151.

[20]Simone de Beauvoir, *The Second Sex* (New York: Bantom, 1961).

[21]June Goodfield, *An Imagined World* (New York: Harper and Row, 1981).

[22]See also E.F. Keller, *A Feeling for the Organism* (San Francisco: W.H. Freeman, 1983).

[23]James D. Watson, *The Double Helix* (New York: New American Library, 1969).

[24]Martin, *Reclaiming a Conversation.*

17

An Ethic of Caring and Its Implications for Instructional Arrangements

Nel Noddings

Until recent years, most Americans seem to have assumed that a funda-mental aim of schooling should be the production of a moral citizenry. It could be argued that, although this assumption is sound and still widely held, the hypocrisy inherent in a blend of Christian doctrine and individualist ideology has created opposition to traditional forms of moral education. What is needed, then, is not a new assumption but a more appropriate conception of morality. An ethic of caring arising out of both ancient notions of agapism and contemporary feminism will be suggested as an alternative approach. After describing caring as a moral perspective, I will discuss the vast changes that such an orientation implies in schooling, and one of these will be explored in some depth. In conclusion, I will suggest ways in which educational research might contribute to this important project.

Morality as an Educational Aim

Morality has been a long-standing interest in schools. Indeed, the detachment of schools from explicitly moral aims is a product of the last few decades. It would have been unthinkable early in this century – even in programs guided by highly technical lists of specific objectives – to ask such a question as, must we educate?[1] We sometimes forget that even Franklin Bobbitt and others who were advocates of the technological or factory model of progressivism were nonetheless interested in the development of moral persons, good citizens, adequate parents, and serene spirits. Bobbitt himself said: "The social point of view herein expressed is sometimes characterized as being utilitarian. It may be so; but not in any narrow or undesirable sense. It demands that training be as wide as life itself. It looks to human activities of one's family duties; one's recreations; one's reading and meditation; and the rest of the things that are done by the complete man or woman."[2]

Yet today it seems innovative – even intrusive – to suggest that the schools should consciously aim at educating people for moral life and that perhaps the best way to accomplish this aim is to conduct the process in a thoroughly moral way. People who should know better continually claim that schools can do only one thing well – the direct teaching of basic skills. In a recent letter that apparently reflects the position espoused in their book,[3] L.H. Gann and Peter Duignan say "Above all, we should avoid the temptation to regard the school as an instrument that can cure all social ills. The school's job is to teach basic academic skills."[4] This statement captures a tiny corner of truth, but it ignores the citadel to which this corner belongs.

An honest appraisal of American traditions of schooling reveals that academic skills have long been thought of as a vehicle for the development of character. This was true in colonial days, it was true throughout the nineteenth century, and it was still true in the first half of the twentieth century. Schools have always been considered as incubators for acceptable citizens, and citizenship has not always been defined in terms of academic achievement scores. The morality stressed by nineteenth- and early twentieth-century schools contained a measure of hypocrisy, to be sure. Drawing on both Christian doctrine and an ideology of individualism, recommendations on moral education emphasized both self-sacrifice and success through determination, ambition, and competition. The influential Character Development League, for example, stated in the opening paragraph of its *Character Lessons*: "Character in its primary principle and groundwork is *self-control* and *self-giving*, and the only practical method of enforcing this upon the habit of children is to keep before them examples of self-control and self-sacrifice."[5] *Character Lessons*, however, is liberally laced with success stories, and, indeed, teachers are urged to credit each child for her or his contributions to a "Golden Deed Book." In the closing paragraphs of his Introduction, Carr suggests, "A small prize for the grade having the best "Golden Deed Book" and another to the pupil of the grade having the most Deeds to his credit, will arouse a discriminating interest."[6] Thus, educators were urged to encourage both Christian charity and American entrepreneurship. In describing a mid-nineteenth-century school's operations, David Tyack and Elizabeth Hansot comment: "These mid-century themes suggest how deeply the absolutist morality of the evangelical movement became interwoven with a work ethic and ideology favoring the development of capitalism. Just as Christianity was inseparable from Americanism, so the entrepreneurial economic values seemed so self-evidently correct as to be taken for granted. *The school* gave everyone a chance to become hard-working, literate, temperate, frugal, a good planner."[7]

The school was not expected to cure social ills; in this Gann and Duignan are correct. Rather, it was expected to teach vigorously the values of a society that thought it was righteous. The spirit was evangelical at every level from home and school to national and international politics, where speakers, writers, and statesmen regularly took the position that the United States had a God-given mission to export its righteous way of life to the rest of the world.[8] However wrong we may now consider this arrogant posture, it is clear that hardly anyone thought that the school's major or only job was to teach academic skills. This we did in the service of moral ends, not as an end in itself.

I am certainly not recommending a return to the self-righteous moralizing of the nineteenth century. On the contrary, I would argue for a strong rejection of this attitude, accompanied by a thorough study of its history and ideology. We cannot overcome a perspective, a worldview, as powerful as this one by ignoring it; we have to explore it both appreciatively and critically. Indeed, I would go so far as to suggest that proponents of "basic skills only" may really want to maintain the earlier attitude of Christian-American supremacy and that avoidance of moral issues and social ills is the only currently feasible way to accomplish this. The apparent consensus of earlier times has been lost. Further, attempts to restore the values of a diminishing majority have not been successful. Too many feisty minorities have found their voices and are beginning to suggest alternatives among moral priorities. In such a climate, the only way left for the weakening group in power is to block discussion entirely and hope that hegemonic structures will press things down into the old containers. The need for moral education is apparent to everyone, but concerns about the form it should take induce paralysis. Thus, I suggest that our forebears were right in establishing the education of a moral people as the primary aim of schooling, but they were often shortsighted and arrogant in their description of what it means to be moral.

Caring as a Moral Orientation in Teaching

Although schools and other institutions have in general withdrawn from the task of moral education (some exceptions will be noted), there is a philosophical revival of interest in practical ethics. Several authors have commented on the arrogance and poverty of philosophical views that conceive of ethics solely as a domain for philosophical analysis.[9] Further, there is increased interest in both ethics of virtue (the modelling or biographical approach advocated in *Character Lessons*)[10] and in ethics of need and love. Joseph Fletcher contrasts the latter with ethics of law and rights. "As seen from the ethical perspective," he notes, "the legalistic or moralistic temper gives the first-order position to rights, whereas the agapistic temper gives the first place *to needs*."[11] A blend of these views that tries to avoid both the elitism in Artistole's ethics of virtue and the dogmatism of Christian agapism is found in the current feminist emphasis on ethics of caring, relation, and response.[12]

As an ethical orientation, caring has often been characterized as feminine because it seems to arise more naturally out of woman's experience than man's.

When this ethical orientation is reflected on and technically elaborated, we find that it is a form of what may be called *relational ethics*.[13] A relational ethics remains tightly tied to experience because all its deliberations focus on the human beings involved in the situation under consideration and their relations to each other. A relation is here construed as any pairing or connection of individuals characterized by some affective awareness in each. It is an encounter or series of encounters in which the involved parties feel something toward each other. Relations may be characterized by love or hate, anger or sorrow, admiration or envy; or, of course, they may reveal mixed affects – one party feeling, say, love and the other revulsion. One who is concerned with behaving ethically strives always to preserve or convert a given relation into a caring relation. This does not mean that all relations must approach that of the prototypical mother-child relation in either intensity or intimacy. On the contrary, an appropriate and particular form of caring must be found in every relation, and the behaviors and feelings that mark the mother-child relation are rarely appropriate for other relations; the characteristics of *all* caring relations can be described only at a rather high level of abstraction.

A relational ethic, an ethic of caring, differs dramatically from traditional ethics. The most important difference for our present purpose is that ethics of caring turn the traditional emphasis on duty upside down. Whereas Kant insisted that only those acts performed out of duty (in conformity to principle) should be labelled moral, an ethic of caring prefers acts done out of love and natural inclination. Acting out of caring, one calls on a sense of duty or special obligation only when love or inclination fails. Ethical agents adopting this perspective do not judge their own acts solely by their conformity to rule or principle, nor do they judge them only by the likely production of pre-assessed non-moral goods such as happiness. While such agents may certainly consider both principles and utilities, their primary concern is the relation itself – not only what happens physically to others involved in the relation and in connected relations but what they may feel and how they may respond to the act under consideration. From a traditional perspective, it seems very odd to include the response of another in a judgment of our own ethical acts. Indeed, some consider the great achievement of Kantian ethics to be its liberation of the individual from the social complexities that characterized earlier ethics. A supremely lonely and heroic ethical agent marks both Kantian ethics and the age of individualism. An ethic of caring returns us to an earlier orientation – one that is directly concerned with the relations in which we all must live.

A relational ethic is rooted in and dependent on natural caring. Instead of striving away from affection and toward behaving always out of duty as Kant has prescribed, one acting from a perspective of caring moves consciously in the other direction; that is, he or she calls on a sense of obligation in order to stimulate natural caring. The superior state – one far more efficient because it energizes the giver as well as the receiver – is one of natural caring. Ethical caring is its servant. Because natural caring is both the source and the terminus of ethical caring, it is reasonable to use the mother-child relation as its proto-type, so long as we keep in mind the caveats mentioned above.

The first member of the relational dyad (the carer or "one caring") responds to the needs, wants, and initiations of the second. *Her* mode of response is characterized by *engrossment* (nonselective attention or total presence to *him*, the other, for the duration of the caring interval) and *displacement of motivation* (her motive energy flows in the direction of the other's needs and projects). She feels with the other and acts in his behalf. The second member (the one cared for) contributes to the relation by recognizing and responding to the caring.[14] In the infant, this response may consist of smiles and wriggles; in the student, it may reveal itself in energetic pursuit of the student's own projects. A mature relationship may, of course, be mutual, and two parties may regularly exchange places in the relation, but the contributions of the one caring (whichever person may hold the position momentarily) remain distinct from those of the cared for. It is clear from this brief description why an ethic of caring is often characterized in terms of responsibility and response.

A view similar in many ways to that of caring may be found in Sara Ruddick's analysis of maternal thinking.[15] A mother, Ruddick says, puts her thinking into the service of three great interests: preserving the life of the child, fostering his growth, and shaping an acceptable child. Similarly, Milton May-eroff describes caring in terms of fostering the growth of another.[16] Thus, it is clear that at least some contemporary theorists recognize the thinking, practice, and skill required in the work traditionally done by women – work that has long been considered something anyone with a warm heart and little intellect could undertake. Caring as a rational moral orientation and maternal thinking with its threefold interests are richly applicable to teaching.

Caring and Instructional Arrangements

Even though the emphasis during this half of the twentieth century has been on intellectual goals – first, on advanced or deep structural knowledge of the disciplines and then, more modestly, on the so-called basics – a few educators and theorists have continued to suggest that schools must pay attention to the moral and social growth of their citizens. Ernest Boyer and his colleagues, for example, recommend that high school students engage in community service as part of their school experience.[17] Theodore Sizer expresses concern about the impersonal relationships that develop between highly specialized teachers and students with whom they have only fleeting and technical contact, for example, in grading, recording attendance, disciplining.[18] Lawrence Kohlberg and his associates concentrate explicitly on the just community that should be both the source and the end of a truly moral education.[19] But none of these concerns has captured either the national interest or that of educators in a way that might bring a mandate for significant change. The current emphasis remains on academic achievement. The influential reports of both the Holmes Group and the Carnegie Task Force, for example, almost entirely ignore the ethical aspects of education.[20] They mention neither the ethical considerations that should enter into teachers' choices of content, methods, and instructional arrangements, nor the basic responsibility of schools to contribute to the moral growth of students.

If we were to explore seriously the ideas suggested by an ethic of caring for education, we might suggest changes in almost every aspect of schooling: the current hierarchical structure of management, the rigid mode of allocating time, the kind of relationships encouraged, the size of schools and classes, the goals of instruction, modes of evaluation, patterns of interaction, and selection of content. Obviously all of those topics cannot be discussed here. I will therefore confine my analysis to the topic of relationships, which I believe is central to a thorough consideration of most of the other topics.

From the perspective of caring, the growth of those cared for is a matter of central importance. Feminists are certainly not the first to point this out. For John Dewey, for example, the centrality of growth implied major changes in the traditional patterns of schooling. In particular, since a major teacher function is to guide students in a well-informed exploration of areas meaningful to them, learning objectives must be mutually constructed by students and teachers.[21] Dewey was unequivocal in his insistence on the mutuality of this task. Teachers have an obligation to support, anticipate, evaluate, and encourage worthwhile activities, and students have a right to pursue projects mutually constructed and approved. It has long been recognized that Dewey's recommendations require teachers who are superbly well educated, people who know the basic fields of study so well that they can spot naive interests that hold promise for rigorous intellectual activity.

There is, however, more than intellectual growth at stake in the teaching enterprise. Teachers, like mothers, want to produce acceptable persons – persons who will support worthy institutions, live compassionately, work productively but not obsessively, care for older and younger generations, be admired, trusted, and respected. To shape such persons, teachers need not only intellectual capabilities but also a fund of knowledge about the particular persons with whom they are working. In particular, if teachers approach their responsibility for moral education from a caring orientation rather than an ethic of principle, they cannot teach moral education as one might teach geometry or European history or English; that is, moral education cannot be formulated into a course of study or set of principles to be learned. Rather, each student must be guided toward an ethical life – or, we might say, an ethical ideal – that is relationally constructed.

The relational construction of an ethical ideal demands significant contributions from the growing ethical agent and also from those in relation with this agent. There is, clearly, a large subjective component of such an ideal; modes of behavior must be evaluated as worthy by the person living them. But there is also a significant objective component, and this is contributed by the careful guidance of a host of persons who enter into relation with the developing agent. The teacher, for example, brings his or her own subjectivity into active play in the relation but also takes responsibility for directing the student's attention to the objective conditions of choice and judgment; both teacher and student are influenced by and influence the subjectivity of other agents. Hence, in a basic and crucial sense, each of us is a rationally defined entity and not a totally autonomous agent. Our goodness and our wickedness are both, at least in part, induced, supported, enhanced, or diminished by the interventions and influence of those with whom we are related.

In every human encounter, there arises the possibility of a caring occasion.[22] If I bump into you on the street, both of us are affected not only by the physical collision but also by what follows it. It matters whether I say, "Oh, dear, I'm so sorry," or "You fool! Can't you watch where you're going?" In every caring occasion, the parties involved must decide how they will respond to each other. Each such occasion involves negotiation of a sort: an initiation, a response, a decision to elaborate or terminate. Clearly, teaching is filled with caring occasions or, quite often, with attempts to avoid such occasions. Attempts to avoid caring occasions by the overuse of lecture without discussion, of impersonal grading in written, quantitative form, of modes of discipline that respond only to the behavior but refuse to encounter the person all risk losing opportunities for moral education and mutual growth.

Moral education, from the perspective of an ethic of caring, involves modelling, dialog, practice, and confirmation. These components are not unique to ethics of caring, of course, but their combination and interpretation are central to this view or moral education.[23] Teachers model caring when they steadfastly encourage responsible self-affirmation in their students.[24] Such teachers are, of course, concerned with their students' academic achievement, but, more importantly, they are interested in the development of fully moral persons. This is not a zero-sum game. There is no reason why excellent mathematics teaching cannot enhance ethical life as well. Because the emphasis in the present discussion is on human relationships, it should be noted that the teacher models not only admirable patterns of intellectual activity but also desirable ways of interacting with people. Such teachers treat students with respect and consideration and encourage them to treat each other in a similar fashion. They use teaching moments as caring occasions.

Dialog is essential in this approach to moral education. True dialog is open; that is, conclusions are not held by one or more of the parties at the outset. The search for enlightenment, or responsible choice, or perspective, or means to problem solution is mutual and marked by appropriate signs of reciprocity. This does not mean that participants in dialog must give up any principles they hold and succumb to relativism. If I firmly believe that an act one of my students has committed is wrong, I do not enter a dialog with him on whether or not the act is wrong. Such a dialog could not be genuine. I can, however, engage him in dialog about the possible justification for our opposing positions, about the likely consequences of such acts to himself and others, about the personal history of my own belief. I can share my reflections with him, and he may exert considerable influence on me by pointing out that I have not suffered the sort of experience that led him to his act. Clearly, time is required for such dialog. Teacher and student must know each other well enough for trust to develop.

The caring teacher also wants students to have practice in caring. This suggests changes beyond the well-intended inclusion of community service in high school graduation requirements. Service, after all, can be rendered in either caring or noncaring ways. In a classroom dedicated to caring, students are encouraged to support each other; opportunities for peer interaction are provided, and the quality of that interaction is as important (to both teacher and students) as the academic outcomes. Small group work may enhance achievement in mathematics, for example, and can also provide caring occasions. The object is to develop a caring community through modelling, dialog, and practice.

Although modelling, dialog, practice, and confirmation are all important, the component I wish to emphasize here is confirmation. In caring or maternal thinking, we often use caring occasions to confirm the cared for. The idea here is to shape an acceptable child by assisting in the construction of his ethical ideal. He has a picture of a good self, and we, too, have such a picture. But as adults we have experience that enables us to envision and appreciate a great host of wonderful selves – people with all sorts of talents, projects, ethical strengths, and weaknesses kept courageously under control. As we come to understand what the child wants to be and what we can honestly approve in him, we know what to encourage. We know how to respond to his acts – both those we approve and those we disapprove. When he does something of which we disapprove, we can often impute a worthy motive for an otherwise unworthy act. Indeed, this is a central aspect of confirmation: "When we attribute the best possible motive consonant with reality to the cared-for, we confirm him; that is, we reveal to him an attainable image of himself that is lovelier than that manifested in his present acts. In an important sense, we embrace him as one with us in devotion to caring. In education, what we reveal to a student about himself as an ethical and intellectual being has the power to nurture the ethical ideal or to destroy it."[25]

Confirmation is of such importance in moral education that we must ask about the settings in which it can effectively take place. Educators often come close to recognizing the significance of confirmation in a simplistic way. We talk about the importance of expectations, for example, and urge teachers to have high expectations for all their students. But, taken as a formula, this is an empty exhortation. If, without knowing a student – what he loves, strives for, fears, hopes – I merely expect him to do uniformly well in everything I present to him, I treat him like an unreflective animal. A high expectation can be a mark of respect, but so can a relatively low one. If a mathematics teacher knows, for example, that one of her students, Rose, is talented in art and wants more than anything to be an artist, the teacher may properly lower her expectations for Rose in math. Indeed, she and Rose may consciously work together to construct a mathematical experience for Rose that will honestly satisfy the institution, take as little of Rose's effort as possible, and preserve the teacher's integrity as a mathematics teacher. Teacher and student may chat about art, and the teacher may learn something. They will surely talk about the requirements of the art schools to which Rose intends to apply – their GPA demands, how much math they require, and the like. Teacher and student become partners in fostering the student's growth. The student accepts responsibility for both completion of the work negotiated and the mutually constructed decision to do just this much mathematics. This is illustrative of responsible self-affirmation. The picture painted here is so vastly different from the one pressed on teachers currently that it seems almost alien. To confirm in this relational fashion, teachers need a setting different from those we place them in today.

To be responsible participants in the construction of ethical ideals, teachers need more time with students than we currently allow them. If we cared deeply about fostering growth and shaping both acceptable and caring people, we could surely find ways to extend contact between teachers and students. There is no good reason why teachers should not stay with one group of students for three years rather than one in the elementary years, and this arrangement can be adapted to high school as well. A mathematics teacher might, for example, take on a group of students when they enter high school and guide them through their entire high school mathematics curriculum. The advantages in such a

242 Conceptions of Education

scheme are obvious and multiple: First, a setting may be established in which moral education is possible – teacher and students can develop a relation that makes confirmation possible. Second, academic and professional benefits may be realized – the teacher may enjoy the stimulation of a variety of mathematical subjects and avoid the deadly boredom of teaching five classes of Algebra I; the teacher may come to understand the whole math curriculum and not just a tiny part of it; the teacher takes on true responsibility for students' mathematical development, in contrast to the narrow accountability of teachers today; the teacher encounters relatively few new students each year and welcomes back many that she already knows well.

Are there disadvantages? Those usually mentioned are artifacts of the present system. Some people ask, for example, what would happen to students who are assigned to poor teachers for three or four years. One answer is that students should not have a demonstrably poor teacher for even one year, but a better answer is to follow out the implications of this fear. My suggestion is that students and teachers stay together by mutual consent and with the approval of parents. Ultimately, really poor teachers would be squeezed out in such a system, and all the fuss and feathers of detailed administrative evaluation would be cut considerably. Supportive and substantial supervision would be required instead, because teachers – now deeply and clearly responsible for a significant chunk of their students' growth – might well seek to foster their own growth and, thus, ensure a steady stream of satisfied clients.

Suggestions like the one above for extended contact – or like Sizer's alternative idea that teachers teach two subjects to 30 students rather than one subject to 60[26] – are not simplistic, nor are they offered as panaceas. They would require imagination, perseverance, changes in training, and diligence to implement, but they can be accomplished. Indeed, these ideas have been used successfully and deserve wider trials. (I myself had this sort of experience in twelve years of teaching in grades 6-12.)

It sometimes seems to feminists and other radical thinkers that this society, including education as an institution, does not really want to solve its problems. There is too much at stake, too much to be lost by those already in positions of power, to risk genuine attempts at solution. What must be maintained, it seems, are the *problems*, and the more complex the better, for then all sorts of experts are required, and, as the problems proliferate (proliferation by definition is especially efficient), still more experts are needed. Helpers come to have an investment in the helping system and their own place in it rather than in the empowerment of their clients.[27]

I have discussed here just one major change that can be rather easily accomplished in establishing settings more conducive to caring and, thus, to moral education. Such a change would induce further changes, for, when we think from this perspective, everything we do in teaching comes under reevaluation. In the fifties, the nation moved toward larger high schools, in part because the influential Conant report persuaded us that only sufficiently large schools could supply the sophisticated academic programs that the nation wanted to make its first priority.[28] Now we might do well to suggest smaller schools that might allow us to embrace older priorities, newly critiqued and defined, and work toward an educational system proudly oriented toward the development of decent, caring, loved, and loving persons.

What Research Can Contribute

If it is not already obvious, let me say explicitly that I think university educators and researchers are part of the problem. Our endless focus on narrow achievement goals, our obsession with sophisticated schemes of evaluation and measurement directed (naturally enough) at things that are relatively easy to measure, our reinforcement of the mad desire to be number one – to compete, to win awards, to acquire more and more of whatever is currently valued – in all these ways we contribute to the proliferation of problems and malaise.

Can researchers play a more constructive role? Consider some possibilities. First, by giving some attention to topics involving affective growth, character, social relations, sharing, and the pursuit of individual projects, researchers can give added legitimacy to educational goals in all these areas. A sign of our neglect is the almost total omission of such topics from the 987 pages of the third *Handbook of Research on Teaching*.[29] Second, researchers can purposefully seek out situations in which educators are trying to establish settings more conducive to moral growth and study these attempts at some length, over a broad range of goals, and with constructive appreciation. That last phrase, "with constructive appreciation," suggests a third way in which researchers might help to solve problems rather than aggravate them. In an article on fidelity, I argued:

> In educational research, fidelity to persons counsels us to choose our problems in such a way that the knowledge gained will promote individual growth and maintain the caring community. It is not clear that we are sufficiently concerned with either criterion at present. William Torbert, for example, has noted that educational research has been oddly uneducational and suggests that one reason for this may be the failure of researchers to engage in collaborative inquiry. There is a pragmatic side to this problem, of course, but from an ethical perspective, the difficulty may be identified as a failure to meet colleagues in genuine mutuality. Researchers have perhaps too often made *persons* (teachers and students) the objects of research. An alternative

is to choose *problems* that interest and concern researchers, students, and teachers.[30]

Here, again, feminists join thinkers like Torbert to endorse modes of research that are directed at the needs rather than the shortcomings and peculiarities of subjects. Dorothy Smith, a sociologist of knowledge, has called for a science *for* women rather than *about* women; "that is," she says, "a sociology which does not transform those it studies into objects but preserves in its analytic procedures the presence of the subject as actor and experience. Subject then is that knower whose grasp of the world may be enlarged by the work of the sociologist."[31]

Similarly, research *for* teaching would concern itself with the needs, views, and actual experience of teachers rather than with the outcomes produced through various instructional procedures. This is not to say that contrasting methods should not be studied, but, when they are studied, researchers should recognize that the commitment of teachers may significantly affect the results obtained through a given method. Research *for* teaching would not treat teachers as interchangeable parts in instructional procedures, but, rather, as professionals capable of making informed choices among proffered alternatives.

Research *for* teaching would address itself to the needs of teachers – much as pharmaceutical research addresses itself to the needs of practicing physicians. This suggests that research and development should become partners in education, as they have in industry. Instead of bemoaning the apparent fact that few teachers use small group methods, for example, researchers could ask teachers what they need to engage in such work comfortably. One answer to this might be materials. Researchers often assume that the answer is training, because this answer better fits their own preparation and research timetables. If materials are needed, however, the partnership of research and development becomes crucial.

Qualitative researchers may suppose that their methods are more compatible with research *for* teaching than the usual quantitative methods. Indeed, Margaret Mead said of fieldwork: "Anthropological research does not have subjects. We work with informants in an atmosphere of trust and mutual respect."[32]

But qualitative researchers, too, can forget that they are part of an educational enterprise that should support a caring community. Qualitative studies that portray teachers as stupid, callous, indifferent, ignorant, or dogmatic do little to improve the conditions of teaching or teachers. I am not arguing that no teachers are stupid, callous, indifferent, and so forth. Rather, I am arguing that teachers so described are sometimes betrayed by the very researchers to whom they have generously given access. What should we do when we come upon gross ignorance or incompetence? One of my colleagues argues strongly that it is our duty to expose incompetence. Would you keep silent if you observed child abuse? he asks. The answer to this is, of course, that we cannot remain silent about child abuse, and it is conceivable that some events we observe as researchers are so dangerous or worrisome that we simply must report them. But at that point, I would say, our research ends. We feel compelled to take up our duties as responsible citizens and to relinquish our quest for knowledge. So long as we seek knowledge in classrooms, we are necessarily dependent on the teachers and students who are there engaged in a constitutively ethical enterprise. To intrude on that, to betray a trust that lets us in, to rupture the possibility of developing a caring community, is to forget that we should be doing research *for* teaching.

Does this mean that we cannot report failures in the classrooms we study? Of course not. But just as we ask teachers to treat the success and failure of students with exquisite sensitivity, we should study teacher success and failure generously and report on it constructively. Teachers may be eager to explore their own failures if their successes are also acknowledged, and if the failures are thoroughly explored to locate the preconditions and lacks responsible for them. Teachers, too, need confirmation.

Conclusion

I have suggested that moral education has long been and should continue to be a primary concern of educational institutions. To approach moral education from the perspective of caring, teachers, teacher-educators, students, and researchers need time to engage in modelling, dialog, practice, and confirmation. This suggests that ways be explored to increase the contact between teachers and students and between researchers and teachers, so that collaborative inquiry may be maintained and so that relationships may develop through which all participants are supported in their quest for better ethical selves.

Notes

[1]Carl Bereiter, *Must We Educate?* (Englewood Cliffs, NJ: Prentice Hall, 1973).

[2]Franklin Bobbitt, *What Do Schools Teach and Might Teach* (Cleveland, OH: Survey Committee of the Cleveland Foundation, 1915), 20.

[3]L. H. Gann and Peter Duignan, *The Hispanics in the United States: A History* (Bolder, CO: Westview, 1986).

[4]L. H. Gann and P. Duignan, "How Should the U.S. Deal with Multicultural Schoolchildren?" *Stanford University Campus Report*, March 4, 1987.

[5]John W. Carr, "Introduction" in James Terry White, *Character Lessons* (New York: Character Development League, 1909).

[6]Ibid.

[7]David Tyack and Elizabeth Hansot, *Managers of Virtue* (New York: Basic, 1982), 28.

[8]See the vivid and well-documented description of this attitude in Daniel C. Maguire, *The Moral Choice* (Garden City, NJ: Doubleday, 1978), 424-429.

[9]Bernard Williams in *Ethics and the Limits of Philosophy* (Cambridge, MA: Harvard University Press, 1985) argues that philosophy plays a limited role in the recreation of ethical life. Alasdair MacIntyre in *After Virtue* (Notre Dame, IN: University of Notre Dame Press, 1984, 2nd. ed.) also argues that morality and ethics belong primarily to the domain of social experience and that philosophy must proceed from there.

[10]See A. MacIntyre, *After Virtue,* 1984.

[11]Joseph Fletcher, "The 'Right' to Live and the 'Right' to Die," in Marvin Kohl (ed.), *Beneficent Euthanasia* (Buffalo, NY: Prometheus, 1975), 45.

[12]Nel Noddings, *Caring: A Feminine Approach to Ethics and Moral Education* (Berkeley, CA: University of California Press, 1984), and Carol Gilligan, *In a Different Voice* (Cambridge, MA: Harvard University Press, 1982).

[13]D. C. Maguire in *The Moral Choice* has also described approaches to relational ethics.

[14]For a fuller analysis of the roles of each, see N. Noddings, *Caring.*

[15]Sara Ruddick, "Maternal Thinking" in Marilyn Pearsall (ed.), *Women and Values* (Belmont, CA: Wadsworth, 1986).

[16]Milton Mayeroff, *On Caring* (New York: Harper and Row, 1971).

[17]Ernest L. Boyer, *High School: A Report on Secondary Education in America* (New York: Harper and Row, 1983).

[18]Theodore R. Sizer, *Horace's Compromise: The Dilemma of the American High School* (Boston, MA: Houghton Mifflin, 1984).

[19]Lawrence Kohlberg, *The Philosophy of Moral Development* (San Francisco, CA: Harper and Row, 1981), and *The Psychology of Moral Development* (San Francisco, CA: Harper and Row, 1984).

[20]*Tomorrow's Teachers: A Report of the Holmes Group* (East Lansing, MI: The Holmes Group, 1986), and *A Nation Prepared: Teachers for the 21st Century* (Report of the Task Force on Teaching as a Profession) (New York: Carnegie Forum on Education and the Economy, 1986).

[21]John Dewey, *Experience and Education* (New York: Collier, 1963).

[22]Jean Watson, *Nursing: Human Science and Human Care* (East Norwalck, CT: Appleton-Century-Crofts, 1985).

[23]N. Noddings, *Caring.*

[24]Paulo Freire in *Pedagogy of the Oppressed* (New York: Herder and Herder, 1970) describes as oppression any situation in which one person hinders another in "his pursuit of self-affirmation as a responsible person."

[25]N. Noddings, *Caring,* 193.

[26]T. Sizer, *Horace's Compromise.*

[27]For a discussion of this unhappy result, see P. Freire, *Pedagogy of the Oppressed*, and Jean-Paul Sartre, *What Is Literature* (New York: Philosophical Library, 1949).

[28]James B. Conant, *The American High School Today* (New York: McGraw-Hill, 1959).

[29]Merlin C. Wittrock (ed.), *Handbook of Research on Teaching* (New York: Macmillan, 1986).

[30]Nel Noddings, "Fidelity in Teaching, Teacher Education, and Research for Teaching," *Harvard Educational Review,* 56, 4, 1986: 496-510. For William Torbert, see "Why Educational Research Has Been So Uneducational: The Case for a New Model of Social Science Based on Collaborative Inquiry," in Peter Reason and John Rowan (eds.). *Human Inquiry* (New York: Wiley, 1981).

[31]Dorothy Smith, "The Experienced World as Problematic: A Feminist Method," Sorokin Lecture No. 12, University of Saskatoon, Saskatoon, 1981, 1.

[32]Margaret Mead, "Research with Human Beings: A Model Derived from Anthropological Practice," *Daedalus*, 98, 1969, 371.

Part Five

Pluralism and Democracy in Education

Although concerns about the nature and worthwhileness of democracy go back at least to 500 BC as, for example, seen in the works of Plato and Aristotle, the application of democracy to education and the connection between democracy and education have only been explored in detail and explicitly in the last two centuries or so. In the Western world, it was John Dewey (1859-1952) who popularized and elaborated on the relationship between democracy and education. Focusing on such a relationship is doubly complex since both education and democracy are deemed to be contested concepts. This complexity raises several thorny questions and issues about, for example, the educational expectations or aims in a democracy; the practical, daily teaching practices in educational contexts; the nature of the curriculum including what to include and exclude; the role of the teacher; and the very nature or structure of schooling itself. The chapters in this section deal with some of these issues.

Notwithstanding the complexities and different perspectives that arise to the issues mentioned above, there are some distinctions and beliefs that one can safely say are commonly held. First, one needs to distinguish between democracy as a form of government and democracy as a way of life. While not arguing against the first meaning of democracy, Dewey reminded us that "democracy is much broader than a special political form, a method of conducting government, of making laws and carrying on governmental administration by means of popular suffrage and elected officers. It is that, of course. But it is something broader and deeper than that." It involves the development of certain attitudes and dispositions which will ideally become part of one's character or being and hence are reflected in one's actions. It also involves the intelligent participation of all those who are mature enough to participate in the development of the values that will guide the practices of society. Unless societies are seen to be static, it follows that the very content of democracy as a way of life needs, to use Dewey's own terms, to be continually "explored afresh" or "reconstructed."

When philosophers of education refer to democracy in relation to education, they normally mean democracy as a way of life. A second common element is that most philosophers of education assume or take for granted, as Bertrand Russell put it, that "democracy is a desirable thing." Yet agreement on this assumption does not guarantee that philosophers of education share a common conception of democracy or that they agree on the educational practices that democracy entails even if they share a common conception or vision. As R.S. Peters noted: "That education should be 'democratic' no one in a democracy would seriously dispute. This would be the equivalent of announcing in the Middle Ages that all education should be Christian. But what such an announcement would commit anyone to is far from clear." The possibility of such a lack of agreement, many argue, is at the core of the democratic spirit. But does this mean that we cannot identify some basic dispositions, attitudes, beliefs and practices that are associated with democracy as a way of life? The authors in this section argue or imply that there are such dispositions, beliefs and practices which include: free discussion and inquiry, reasonableness and rational inquiry, taking differences seriously and ensuring the positive development of such differences, open-mindedness, respect for persons as free, autonomous, and responsible beings.

No one would deny that we live in a pluralist, multicultural society that presumes to be democratic. The major questions that frame this section deal with the nature and purpose of education and schooling in such a society: What kind of education is appropriate *for* and *in* a democracy? To what extent is it educationally possible and plausible to develop the democratic traits in our schools? What kind of values ought to influence education in a democracy? Does 'education for democracy' entail 'democracy in education'? Does the notion of common schooling make sense in a pluralistic and culturally diverse democracy? Or are the notions of common schooling and democracy in opposition or contradictory? Does a liberal democracy call for or imply the development of separate schools? Does diversity really exclude unity? Do multiculturalism and pluralism deny the possibility of a common culture? Does diversity and inclusiveness necessarily entail extreme social constructivism or extreme relativism? Does pluralism really threaten the democratic principles of freedom, equality, and justice?

The authors in this section, while each focussing on a particular aspect of the connections between democracy and education, offer a perspective in relation to these kind of questions. Maxine Greene, who builds on Dewey's conception of "the Great Community," argues for the importance of taking pluralism seriously by bringing to the fore "invisible" and "long-repressed" voices and being open to new educational experiences and curricula entailed by the expression and recognition of such voices. Greene's concern is primarily with openness, variety, inclusion, and dialog since she finds "fixities" and "stereotypes" problematic because they militate against the realization and sustenance of democratic pluralism. Amy Gutmann considers two powerful and competing frameworks as alternatives to a "democratic state of education": a Platonic family state and a liberal state of individuals. Her conclusion is that a democratic theory of education, though more difficult because of the tensions it creates between individual freedom and civic virtue, is, morally and politically, a more suitable alternative since it encourages an open public forum on educational disagreements and takes the threat of repression and discrimination seriously. This implies that we take controversy seriously, and that political and economic institutions have to be more democratic.

How can such a democratic state of education be developed? What form should it take? Such questions are dealt with by Callan and Singh. Callan argues that if schools in a liberal democracy take reasonableness and the principles of reciprocity and equal respect seriously, then the notions of common education (schooling) and separate education (schooling) would not be incompatible. But this entails that public schools have to practice the democratic beliefs associated with cultural diversity and pluralism. Singh, who also takes liberal democratic values as the basis, acknowledges the differences between shared values and values that are particular to ethnic groups. Yet he argues that education in a democracy, which should aim at cultural *development* rather than cultural *maintenance*, would be more able to realize the values of equal recognition of personal worth and dignity in common schools which do not focus exclusively on common values and allow particular values to flourish.

Sharon Bailin focuses on the university context and more specifically on the criticisms of some postmodernists and extreme social constructivists who claim that knowledge promoted by universities is undemocratic since it excludes certain groups. While Bailin agrees that inclusion deserves to be taken more seriously, she finds the postmodernist critique wanting since it denies the centrality of rational inquiry. Such a denial, according to Bailin, is anti-democratic since it undermines the very process of dialoguing and critiquing that democracy calls for.

Taking pluralism and democracy in education seriously is not easy. However, it is clear that it requires that we engage in reasonable, critical and compassionate discussions and inquiry, and sincerely allow such "conversations" to direct our actions rather than the excessive euphoria of slogans and legitimation.

Further Readings

Michael Apple, *Official Knowledge: Democratic Education in a Conservative Age.* New York: Routledge, 1993.

Michael Apple and James A. Beane (eds.), *Democratic Schools.* Alexandra, VA: Association for Supervision and Curriculum Development, 1995.

Democracy and Education: The Magazine for Classroom Teachers (The Institute for Democracy in Education, College of Education, Ohio University, Athens, OH), 45701-2979. E-mail: huntj@ouvaxa.cats.ohiou.edu

Educators for Social Responsibility Journal: Education for Democracy. Available from: 23 Garden Street, Cambridge, MA 02138.

Jesse Goodman, *Elementary Schooling for Critical Democracy.* Albany, NY: State University of New York Press, 1992.

Amy Gutmann, *Democratic Education.* Princeton, NJ: Princeton University Press, 1987.

Clive Harber and Roland Meighan (eds.), *The Democratic Schools: Educational Management and the Practice of Democracy.* Ticknal, Derbyshire, UK: Education Now Publishing Cooperative Ltd., 1989.

Kevin Harris, *Teachers: Constructing the Future.* London: The Falmer Press, 1994.

Robert D. Heslep, *Education in Democracy: Education's Moral Role in the Democratic State.* Ames, Iowa: Iowa State University Press, 1989.

bell hooks, *Teaching to Transgress: Education as the Practice of Freedom.* New York: Routledge, 1994.

A.V. Kelly, *Education and Democracy: Principles and Practices.* London: Paul Chapman Publ. Ltd., 1995.

Ken Osborne, *Teaching for Democratic Citizenship.* Toronto, Ont.: Our Schools/Our Selves Education Foundation, 1991.

Roger Soder (ed.), Democracy, Education, and the Schools. San Francisco: Jossey-Bass Publishers, 1996.

Joel Spring, *Wheels in the Head: Educational Philosophies of Authority, Freedom, and Culture from Socrates to Paulo Freire.* New York: McGraw-Hill Inc., 1994.

George Wood, *Schools that Work: America's Most Innovative Public Education Programs.* New York: Dutton, 1992.

18

The Passions of Pluralism: Multiculturalism and the Expanding Community

Maxine Greene

There have always been newcomers in this country; there have always been strangers. There have always been young persons in our classrooms we did not, could not see or hear. In recent years, however, invisibility has been refused on many sides. Old silences have been shattered; long-repressed voices are making themselves heard. Yes, we are in search of what John Dewey called "the Great Community,"[1] but, at once, we are challenged as never before to confront plurality and multiplicity. Unable to deny or obscure the facts of pluralism, we are asked to choose ourselves with respect to unimaginable diversities. To speak of passions in such a context is not to refer to the strong feelings aroused by what strikes many as a confusion and a cacophony. Rather, it is to have in mind the central sphere for the operation of the passions: "the realm of face-to-face relationships."[2] It seems clear that the more continuous and authentic personal encounters can be, the less likely it will be that categorizing and distancing will take place. People are less likely to be treated instrumentally, to be made "other" by those around them. I want to speak of pluralism and multiculturalism with concrete engagements in mind, actual and imagined: engagements with persons, young persons and older persons, some suffering from exclusion, some from powerlessness, some from poverty, some from ignorance, some from boredom. Also, I want to speak with imagination in mind, and metaphor, and art. Cynthia Ozick writes:

> Through metaphor, the past has the capacity to imagine us, and we it. Through metaphorical concentration, doctors can imagine what it is to be their patients. Those who have no pain can imagine those who suffer. Those at the center can imagine what it is to be outside. The strong can imagine the weak. Illuminated lives can imagine the dark. Poets in their twilight can imagine the borders of stellar fire. We strangers can imagine the familiar hearts of strangers.[3]

Towards a Community of Persons

Passions, then, engagements, and imagining; I want to find a way of speaking of community, an expanding community, taking shape when diverse

253

people, speaking as *who* and not *what* they are, come together in speech and action, as Hannah Arendt puts it, to constitute something in common among themselves. She writes: "Plurality is the condition of human action because we are all the same, that is, human, in such a way that nobody is ever the same as anyone else who ever lived, lives, or will live."[4] For her, those present on a common ground have different locations on that ground; and each one "sees or hears from a different position." An object – a classroom, a neighborhood street, a field of flowers – shows itself differently when encountered by a variety of spectators. The reality of that object (or classroom, or neighborhood, or field of flowers) arises out of the sum total of its appearances. Thinking of those spectators as participants in an ongoing dialog, each one speaking out of a distinct perspective and yet open to those around, I find a kind of paradigm for what I have in mind. I discover another in the work of Henry Louis Gates, Jr., who writes about the fact that "the challenge facing America in the next century will be the shaping, at long last, of a truly common public culture, one responsive to the long-silenced cultures of color."[5] (It is not long, it will be remembered, since the same Professor Gates asked in a *New York Times* article, "Whose canon is it anyway?"[6]) More recently, he has evoked the philosopher Michael Oakeshott and his notion of a conversation with different voices. Education, Gates suggests, might be "an invitation into the art of this conversation in which we learn to recognize the voices, each conditioned by a different perception of the world." Then Gates adds: "Common sense says that you don't bracket out 90 percent of the world's cultural heritage if you really want to learn about the world."[7]

For many, what is common sense for Gates represents an attack on the coherence of what we think of as our heritage, our canon. The notion of different voices conditioned by different perspectives summons up the spectre of relativism; and relativism, according to Clifford Geertz, is the "intellectualist Grande Peur." It makes people uneasy, because it appears to subvert authority; it eats away at what is conceived of as objectively real. "If thought is so much out in the world as this," Geertz asks, as the uneasy might ask, "what is to guarantee its generality, its objectivity, its efficacy, or its truth?"[8] There is irony in Geertz's voice, since he knows and has said: "For our time and forward, the image of a general orientation, perspective, *Weltanschauung*, growing out of humanistic studies (or, for that matter, out of scientific ones) and shaping the direction of the culture is a chimera."[9] He speaks of the "radical variousness of the way we think now" and suggests that the problem of integrating cultural life becomes one of "making it possible for people inhabiting different worlds to have a genuine, and reciprocal, impact upon one another."[10] This is troubling for people seeking assurances, seeking certainties. And yet they, like the rest of us, keep experiencing attacks on what is familiar, what James Clifford calls "the irruption of otherness, the unexpected."[11] It may well be that our ability to tolerate the unexpected relates to our tolerance for multiculturalism, for the very idea of expansion and the notion of plurality.

We are well aware, for all that, that Arthur Schlesinger, Jr., who must be taken seriously, sees a "disuniting of America" in the making if shared commitments shatter, if we lose touch with the democratic idea.[12] Proponents of what is called "civism"[13] are concerned that pluralism threatens the existence of a democratic ethos intended to transcend all differences. The ethos encompasses the principles of freedom, equality, and justice, as well as regard for human rights, and there is fear that the new relativism and particularism will subvert the common faith. And there are those like E.D. Hirsch, Jr., who see the concept of "background knowledge" and the shared content it ensures undermined by "variousness" and the multicultural emphases that distract from the common.[14] What they call "cultural literacy" is undermined as a result, and the national community itself is eroded.[15] At the extreme, of course, are those on the far right who find a conspiracy in challenges to the so-called Eurocentric canon and in what they construct as "politically correct," signifying a new orthodoxy built out of oversensitivity to multicultural concerns.[16] As for the religious fundamentalist right, says Robert Hughes (writing in *The New York Review of Books*), one of the motives driving men like Jesse Helms is to establish themselves as defenders of what they define as the "American way" now (as Hughes puts it) "that their original crusade against the Red Menace has been rendered null and void."[17] Not only do they argue for their construct against the National Endowment for the Arts' grants to avant garde artists; they attack such deviations as multiculturalism. It is important to hold this in mind as we try to work through a conception of pluralism to an affirmation of the struggle to attain the life of "free and enriching communion" John Dewey identified with democracy.[18]

The seer of the life of communion, according to Dewey, was Walt Whitman. Whitman wrote about the many shapes arising in the country in his time, "the shapes of doors giving many exits and entrances" and "shapes of democracy . . . ever projecting other shapes."[19] In "Song of Myself" (in total contradiction to the fundamentalist version of the "American way") he wrote:

> Through me many long dumb voices,
>
> Voices of the interminable generations of prisoners and slaves,
>
> Voices of the diseas'd and despairing and of thieves and dwarfs,
>
> Voices of cycles of preparation and accretion,
>
> And of the threads that connect the stars, and of wombs and of the father-stuff,
>
> And of the rights of them the others are down upon. . . .
>
> Through me forbidden voices. . . .[20]

He was, from all appearances, the seer of a communion arising out of "many shapes," out of multiplicity. There is no suggestion of a melting pot here, nor is there a dread of plurality.

Silence and Invisibility: The Need to Repair

For some of us, just beginning to feel our own stories are worth telling, the reminders of the "long dumb voices," the talk of "the rights of them the others are down upon" cannot but draw attention to the absences and silences that are as much a part of our history as the articulate voices, the shimmering faces, the images of emergence and success. Bartleby, the clerk who "prefers not to" in Herman Melville's story, may suddenly become exemplary.[21] What of those who said no, who found no place, who made no mark? Do they not say something about a society that closed too many doors, that allowed people to be abandoned like "wreckage in the mid-Atlantic"?[22] What of those like Tod Clifton in Ralph Ellison's *Invisible Man*?[23] A former youth leader in the so-called Brotherhood, he ends up selling Sambo dolls in front of the public library. When the police try to dislodge him, he protests; and they kill him. The narrator, watching, wonders:

> Why did he choose to plunge into nothingness, into the void of faceless faces, of soundless voices, lying outside history? . . . All things, it is said, are duly recorded – all things of importance, that is. But not quite; for actually it is only the known, the seen, the heard, and only those events that the recorder regards as important are put down. . . . But the cop would be Clifton's historian, his judge, his witness, his executioner, and I was the only brother in the watching crowd.[24]

The many who ended up "lying outside history" diminished the community, left an empty space on the common ground, left undefined an aspect of reality.

It is true that we cannot know all the absent ones, but they must be present somehow in their absence. Absence, after all, suggests an emptiness, a void to be filled, a wound to be healed, a flaw to be repaired. I think of E. L. Doctorow painting a landscape of denial at the beginning of *Ragtime*, appealing to both wonder and indignation, demanding a kind of repair.[25] He is writing about New Rochelle in 1906, but he is presenting a past that reaches into the present, into *our* present, whether or not we ride trolleys anymore.

> Teddy Roosevelt was President. The population customarily gathered in great numbers either out of doors for parades, public concerts, fish fries, political picnics, social outings, or indoors in meeting halls, vaudeville theatres, operas, ballrooms. There seemed to be no entertainment that did not involve great swarms of people. Trains and steamers and trolleys moved them from one

place to another. That was the style; that was the way people lived. Women were stouter then. They visited the fleet carrying white parasols. Everyone wore white in summer. There was a lot of sexual fainting. There were no Negroes. There were no immigrants.[26]

The story has focally to do with a decent, intelligent Black man named Coalhouse Walker, who is cheated, never acknowledged, never understood, scarcely *seen*, and who begins his own fated strategy of vengeance which ends when promises are broken and he is shot down in cold blood. Why is he unseen? Why were there no Negroes, no immigrants? More than likely because of the condition of the minds of those in power, those in charge. Ellison may explain it when he attributes invisibility to "a peculiar disposition of the eyes of those with whom I come in contact. A matter of the construction of their inner eyes, those eyes with which they look through their physical eyes upon reality."[27] But that disposition must itself have been partly due to the play of power in discourse as well as in social arrangements. We may wonder even now what the assimilation or initiation sought by so many educators signified when there were so many blanked out spaces – "no Negroes . . . no immigrants," oftentimes no full-grown women.

Looking back at the gaps in our own lived experiences, we might think of silences like those Tillie Olsen had in mind when she spoke of literary history "dark with silences," of the "unnatural silences" of women who worked too hard or were too embarrassed to express themselves,[28] of others who did not have the words or had not mastered the proper "ways of knowing."[29] We might ponder the plight of young island women, like Jamaica Kincaid's Lucy from Antigua, forced to be "two-faced" in a post-colonial school: "Outside, I seemed one way, inside I was another; outside false, inside true."[30] For years we knew no more about people like her (who saw "sorrow and bitterness" in the face of daffodils because of the Wordsworth poem she had been forced to learn) than we did about the Barbadians Paule Marshall has described, people living their fragmented lives in Brooklyn.[31] There was little consciousness of what Gloria Anzaldua calls *Borderlands/La Frontera* on which so many Latinos live,[32] or of the Cuban immigrants like the musicians in Oscar Hijuelos's *The Mambo Kings Sing Songs of Love.*[33] Who of us truly wondered about the builders of the railroads, those Maxine Hong Kingston calls "China Men," chopping trees in the Sandalwood and Sierra Nevada Mountains? [34] Who of us could fill the gaps left by such a person as Ah Goong, whose "existence was outlawed by the Chinese Exclusion Acts"? His family, writes Kingston, did not understand his accomplishments as an American ancestor, a holding, homing ancestor of this place. He'd gotten the legal or illegal papers burned in the San Francisco earthquake and fire; he appeared in America in time to be a citizen and to father citizens. He had also been seen carrying a child out of the fire, a child of his

perspective
exclusion under surface
258 *Pluralism and Democracy in Education*

own in spite of the laws against marrying. He had built a railroad out of sweat, why not have an American child out of longing?[35]

Did we pay heed to a person like Michelle Cliff, an Afro-Caribbean woman who felt that speaking in words that were not her own was a form of speechlessness? Or to a child like Pecola Breedlove in Toni Morrison's *The Bluest Eye*, the unloved Black child who wanted to look like Shirley Temple so she could be included in the human reality?[36] Or to a Mary Crow Dog, who finds her own way of saying in the autobiography, *Lakota Woman*?[37] How many of us have been willing to suffer the experiences most recently rendered in Art Spiegelman's two-volume comic book called *Maus*?[38] He tells about his father, the ill-tempered Vladek, a survivor of Auschwitz, and his resentful sharing of his Holocaust memories with his son. Every character in the book is an animal: the Jews, mice; the Germans, cats; the Poles, pigs. It is a reminder, not simply of a particular culture's dissolution. ("Anja's parents, the grandparents, her big sister Tosha, little Bibi, and our Richieu. . . . All what is left, it's the photos."[39]) It is a reminder of the need to recognize that everything is possible, something normal people (including school people) either do not know or do not want to know.

To open up our experience (and, yes, our curricula) to existential possibilities of multiple kinds is to extend and deepen what we think of when we speak of a community. If we break through and even disrupt surface equilibrium and uniformity, this does not mean that particular ethnic or racial traditions ought to replace our own. Toni Morrison writes of pursuing her freedom as a writer in a "genderized, sexualized, wholly racialized world," but this does not keep her from developing a critical project "unencumbered by dreams of subversion or rallying gestures at fortress walls."[40] In her case, the project involves exploring the ways in which what we think of as our Americanness is in many ways a response to an Africanist presence far too long denied. She is not interested in replacing one domination by another; she is interested in showing us what she sees from her own perspective – and, in showing us, enriching our understanding not only of our own culture, but of ourselves. She speaks of themes familiar to us all: "individualism, masculinity, social engagement versus historical isolation; acute and ambiguous moral problematics; the thematics of innocence coupled with an obsession with figurations of death and hell."[41] Then she goes on to query what Americans are alienated from, innocent of, different from. "As for absolute power, over whom is this power held, from whom withheld, to whom distributed? Answers to these questions lie in the potent and egoreinforcing presence of an Africanist population."[42] Even as Americans once defined their moral selves against the wilderness, they began to define their whiteness against what Melville called "the power of blackness;" they understood their achievement of freedom against slavery. Whether we choose to see our history that way or not, she is introducing a vision only she could create, and it offers us alternative vantage points on our world. Indeed, the tension with regard to multiculturalism may be partially due to the suspicion that we have often defined ourselves against some unknown, some darkness, some "otherness" we chose to thrust away, to master, not to understand. In this regard, Morrison says something that seems to me unanswerable: "My project is an effort to avert the critical gaze from the racial object to the racial subject; from the described and imagined to the describers and imaginers; from the serving to the served."[43]

To take this view is not to suggest that curricula should be tailored to the measure of specific cultural groups of young people. Nor is it to suggest, as the Afrocentrists do, that emphasis should be laid on the unique experiences, culture and perspectives of Afro-Americans and their link to African roots. There is no question that what history has overlooked or distorted must be restored – whether it has to do with Afro-Americans, Hispanics, Asians, women, Jews, Native Americans, the Irish, or Poles; but the exclusions and the deformations have not kept artists like Morrison, Ellison, James Baldwin from plunging into and learning from Western literary works, anymore than it has prevented scholars like Gates and Cornel West and Alain Locke from working for more and richer interchanges between Afro-American and Euro-American cultures. Morrison begins her new book with a verse from Eliot and goes on to pay tribute to Homer, Dostoevsky, Faulkner, James, Flaubert, Melville, and Mary Shelley. It is dificult to forget James Baldwin reading Dostoevsky and haunting the public library, to turn attention from West's critiques of Emerson, to ignore Ellison writing about Melville and Hemingway, even as he drew attention to what he called "the Negro stereotype" that was "really an image of the irrational, unorganized forces in American life."[44] We might think of Maya Angelou as well, of her years of self-imposed silence as a child and the reading she did through those years. We might recall Alice Walker engaging with Muriel Rukeyser and Flannery O'Connor, drawing energy from them, even as she went in search of Zora Neale Hurston and Bessie Smith and Sojourner Truth and Gwendolyn Brooks. ("I also loved Ovid and Catullus . . . the poems of E.E. Cummings and William Carlos Williams.")[45] And we are aware that, as time goes on, more and more Afro-American literature and women's literature and Hispanic-American literature are diversifying our experience, changing our ideas of time and life and birth and relationship and memory.

Representation and Ownership

My point has to do with openness and variety as well as with inclusion. It has to do with the avoidance of fixities, of stereotypes, even the stereotypes linked to multiculturalism. To view a person as in some sense "representative" of Asian culture (too frequently grouping together human beings as diverse as Japanese, Koreans, Chinese, and Vietnamese) or Hispanic culture or Afro-American culture is to presume an objective reality called "culture," a homogeneous and fixed presence that *can* be adequately represented by existing subjects. (Do Amy Tan's maternal characters embody the same reality as does Maxine Hong Kingston's "woman warrior"? Does Richard Wright's Bigger Thomas stand for the same thing as Miss Celie stands for in Alice Walker's *The Color Purple*?[46]) We do not know the person in the front row of our classroom, or the one sharing the raft, or the one drinking next to us at the bar by her/his cultural or ethnic affiliation.

Cultural background surely plays a part in shaping identity, but it does not determine identity. It may well create differences that must be honored; it may occasion styles and orientations that must be understood; it may give rise to tastes, values, even prejudices that must be taken into account. It is important to know, for example, without embarrassing or exoticizing her, why Jamaica Kincaid's Antiguan Lucy feels so alienated from a Wordsworth poem, and whether or not (and against what norms) it is necessary to argue her out of her distaste for daffodils. It is important to realize why (as in Bharaka Mukherjee's *Jasmine*[47]) Hindus and Sikhs are so at odds with one another, even in this country, and to seek out ways in which (consulting what we believe to be the Western principle of justice) they can be persuaded to set aside hostility. Or perhaps, striving to sympathize with what they feel, we can communicate our own caring for their well-being in such a fashion as to move them provisionally to reconceive each other's reality. Paulo Freire makes the point that every person ought, on some level, to cherish her or his culture; but he says it should never be absolutized. When it is absolutized, when a person is closed against the new culture surrounding her or him, "you would" Freire says, "even find it hard to learn new things which, placed alongside your personal history, can be meaningful."[48]

There has, however, to be a feeling of ownership of one's personal history. In this culture, because of its brutal and persistent racism, it has been painfully difficult for Afro-American young people to affirm and be proud of what they choose as personal history. Poverty, hopelessness, the disruption of families and communities, the ubiquity of media images, all make it difficult to place new things against a past too often made to appear a past of victimization, shadows, and shame. To make it worse, the mystification that proceeds on all sides gives rise to a meta-narrative of what it means to be respectable and successful in America – a meta-narrative that too often seems to doom minorities to life on the outermost borders, or as Toni Morrison writes in *The Bluest Eye*, "outdoors" where there is no place to go. "Outdoors," she writes, "is the end of something, an irrevocable physical fact, defining and complementing our metaphysical condition. Being a minority in both caste and class, we moved about anyway on the hem of life, struggling to consolidate our weaknesses and hang on, or to creep singly up into the major folds of the garment."[49]

Life Stories and Possibility

It happens that *The Bluest Eye*, because of its use of the first paragraph of the basal reader *Dick and Jane*, dramatizes (as few works do) the coercive and deforming effect of the culture's official story, the meta-narrative of secure suburban family life. As the novel plays itself out, everything that occurs is the obverse of the basal reader's story with its themes of pretty house, loving family, play, laughter, friendship, cat, and dog. The narrator of the main story, Pecola Breedlove's story, is young Claudia – also black and poor, but with a supporting family, a sister, a mother who loves her even as she complains and scolds. A short preface, ostensibly written after Pecola's baby and her rapist father have died, after the seeds would not flower, after Pecola went mad, ends with Claudia saying: "There is really nothing more to say – except why. But since *why* is difficult to handle, one must take refuge in *how*."[50] When very young and then a little older, Claudia tells the story and, in the telling, orders the materials of her own life, her own helplessness, her own longings. She does that in relation to Pecola, whom she could not help, and in relation to the seeds that would not flower and those around her "on the hem of life." She weaves her narrative in such a fashion that she establishes an important connection to the past and (telling about Pecola and her family and her pain) reinterprets her own ethnicity in part through what Michael Fischer calls "the arts of memory." Whatever meaning she can draw from this feeds into an ethic that may be meaningful in the future, an ethic that takes her beyond her own guilt at watching Pecola search the garbage:

> I talk about how I did *not* plant the seeds too deeply, how it was the fault of the earth, the land, of our town. I even think now that the land of the entire country was hostile to marigolds that year.... Certain seeds it will not nurture, certain fruit it will not bear, and when the land kills of its own volition, we acquiesce and say the victim had no right to live. We are wrong, of course, but it doesn't matter. It's too late.[51]

As Charles Taylor and Alasdair MacIntyre have written, we understand our lives in narrative form, as a quest. Taylor writes: "Because we have to determine our place in relation to the good, therefore we cannot be without an orientation to it, and hence must see our life in stories."[52] Clearly, there are different stories connected by the same need to make sense, to make meaning, to find a direction.

To help the Claudias we know, the diverse students we know, articulate their stories is not only to help them pursue the meanings of their lives – to find out *how* things are happening, to keep posing questions about the why. It is to move them to learn the "new things" Freire spoke of, to reach out for the proficiencies and capacities, the craft required to be fully participant in this society, and to do so without losing the consciousness of who they are. That is not all. Stories like the one Claudia tells must break through into what we think of as our tradition or our heritage. They should, with what Cornel West has in mind when he speaks about the importance of acknowledging the "distinctive cultural and political practices of oppressed people" without highlighting their marginality in such a way as to further marginalize them."[53] Not only does he call attention to the resistance of Afro-Americans and that of other long-silenced people. He writes of the need to look at Afro-Americans' multiple contributions to the culture over the generations. We might think of the music, Gospel, jazz, ragtime; we might think of the Black churches; we might summon up the Civil Rights movement and the philosophies, the dreams that informed it; we might ponder – looking back, looking around – the images of courage, the images of survival. West goes on to say:

> Black cultural practices emerge out of a reality they cannot *not* know - the
> ragged edges of the real, of necessity; a reality historically constructed by
> white supremacist practices in North America. . . . These ragged edges – of
> not being able to eat, not to have shelter, not to have health care – all this is
> infused into the strategies and styles of black cultural practices.[54]

Viewed in connection with the idea of multiculturalism, this does not mean that Afro-American culture in all its variousness can be defined mainly in terms of oppression and discrimination. One of the many reasons for opening spaces in which Afro-Americans can tell their own stories is that they, far more than those from other cultures, can explain the ways in which poverty and exclusion have mediated their own sense of the past. It is true that experiences of pain and abandonment have led to a search for roots and, on occasion, for a revision of recorded history. What is crucial is the provision of opportunities for telling all the diverse stories, for interpreting membership as well as ethnicity, for making inescapable the braids of experience woven into the fabric of America's plurality.

In the presence of an increasingly potent Third World, against the sounds of increasingly eloquent postcolonial (and, now, post-totalitarian) voices, we can no longer pretend that the "ragged edges" are an exception. We can no longer talk in terms of seamless totalities under rubrics like "free world," "free market," "equality," or even "democracy." Like the "wreckage in the mid-Atlantic," like the "faceless faces," like the "unnatural silences," the lacks and deprivations have to be made aspects of our plurality as well as of our cultural identity. Publics, after all, take shape in response to unmet needs and broken promises. Human beings are prone to take action in response to the sense of injustice or to the imagination's capacity to look at things as if they could be otherwise. The democratic community, always a community in the making, depends not so much on what has been achieved and funded in the past. It is kept alive: it is energized and radiated by an awareness of future possibility. To develop a vision of such possibility, a vision of what might and ought to be, is very often to be made aware of present deficiencies and present flaws. The seeds did not flower; Pecola and her baby could not be saved. But more and more persons, paying heed, may move beyond acquiescence. They may say, as Claudia does, "We are wrong, of course. . . ." but go on to overcome the "doesn't matter." At that moment, they may reach beyond themselves, choose themselves as who they are, and reach out to the common to repair.

Conclusion

Learning to look through multiple perspectives, young people may be helped to build bridges among themselves; attending to a range of human stories, they may be provoked to heal and to transform. Of course there will be difficulties in affirming plurality and difference and, at once, working to create community. Since the days of De Tocqueville, Americans have wondered how to deal with the conflicts between individualism and the drive to conform. They have wondered how to reconcile the impassioned voices of cultures not yet part of the whole with the requirements of conformity, how not to lose the integrity of those voices in the process, how not to allow the drive to conformity determine what happens at the end. But the community many of us hope for now is not to be identified with conformity. As in Whitman's way of saying, it is a community attentive to difference, open to the idea of plurality. Something life-affirming in diversity must be discovered and rediscovered, as what is held in common becomes always more many-faceted – open and inclusive, drawn to untapped possibility.

No one can predict precisely the common world of possibility, nor can we absolutely justify one kind of community over another. Many of us, however, for all the tensions and disagreements around us, would reaffirm the value of principles like justice and equality and freedom and commitment to human rights since, without these, we cannot even argue for the decency of welcoming. Only if more and more persons incarnate such principles, we might say, and choose to live by them and engage in dialog in accord with them, are we likely to bring about a democratic pluralism and not fly apart in violence and disorder. Unable to provide an objective ground for such hopes and claims, all we can do is speak with others as eloquently and passionately as we can about justice and caring and love and trust. Like Richard Rorty and those he calls pragmatists, we can only articulate our desire for as much intersubjective agreement as possible, "the desire to extend the reference of 'us' as far as we can."[55] But, as we do so, we have to remain aware of the distinctive members of the plurality, appearing before one another with their own perspectives on the common, their own stories entering the culture's story, altering it as it moves through time. We want our classrooms to be just and caring, full of various conceptions of the good. We want them to be articulate, with the dialogue involving as many persons as possible, opening to one another, opening to the world. And we want them to be concerned for one another, as we learn to be concerned for them. We want them to achieve friendships among one another, as each one moves to a heightened sense of craft and wide-awakeness, to a renewed consciousness of worth and possibility.

With voices in mind and the need for visibility, I want to end with a call for human solidarity by Muriel Rukeyser, who – like many of us – wanted to "widen the lens and see standing over the land myths of identity, new signals, processes." And then:

> Carry abroad the urgent need, the scene,
>
> to photograph and to extend the voice,
>
> to speak this meaning.
>
> Voices to speak to us directly. As we move.
>
> As we enrich, growing in larger motion,
>
> this word, this power.[56]

This power, yes, the unexplored power of pluralism, and the wonder of an expanding community.

Notes

[1]John Dewey, *The Public and Its Problems* (Athens, OH: Swallow Press, 1954), 143.

[2]Roberto M. Unger, *Passion: An Essay on Personality* (New York: Free Press, 1984), 107.

[3]Cynthia Ozick, *Metaphor and Memory* (New York: Knopf, 1989), 283.

[4]Hannah Arendt, *The Human Condition* (Chicago: University of Chicago Press, 1958), 57.

[5]Henry Louis Gates Jr., "Goodbye, Columbus? Notes on the Culture of Criticism," *American Literacy History*, 3, 4, 1991: 712.

[6]Henry Louis Gates Jr., "The Master's Pieces: On Canon Formation and the African-American Tradition," in Gates, *Loose Canons* (New York: Oxford University Press, 1992), 17-42.

[7]H.L.Gates, Jr., "Goodbye Columbus?," 712.

[8]Clifford Geertz, *Local Knowledge* (New York: Basic Books, 1983), 153.

[9]Ibid., 161.

[10]Ibid.

[11]Clifford Geertz, *Works and Lives: The Anthropologist as Author* (Stanford, CA: Stanford University Press, 1988), 13.

[12]Arthur Schlesinger Jr., *The Disuniting of America: Reflections on a Multicultural Society* (New York: Norton, 1992).

[13]Richard Pratte, *The Civic Imperative* (New York: Teachers College Press, 1988), 104-107.

[14]E.D.Hirsch, Jr. *Cultural Literacy* (Boston: Houghton Mifflin, 1987).

[15]Ibid.

[16]Dinesh D'Souza, *Illiberal Education: The Politics of Race and Sex on Campus* (New York: Free Press, 1991), 239.

[17]Robert Hughes, "Art, Morality & Mapplethorpe," *The New York Review of Books.*

[18]John Dewey, *Democracy and Education* (New York: Macmillan, 1916).

[19]Walt Whitman, *Leaves of Grass* (New York: Aventine Press, 1931).

[20]Ibid., 53.

[21]Herman Melville, "Bartleby" in H.Melville, *Billy Budd, Sailor and Other Stories* (New York: Bantmam Books, 1986), 95-130.

[22]Ibid., 121.

[23]Ralph Ellison, *Invisible Man* (New York: Signet, 1952).

[24]Ibid., 379.

[25]E.L. Doctorow, *Ragtime* (New York: Random House, 1975).

[26]Ibid., 3-4.

[27]R. Ellison, *Invisible Man*, 7.

[28]Tillie Olson, *Silences* (New York: Delacorte, 1978), 6.

[29]M.F. Belenky, B. Clinchy, N. Goldberger, and J. Tarule, *Women's Ways of Knowing* (New York: Bantam, 1986).

[30]Jamaica Kincaid, *Lucy* (New York: Farar, Straus & Giroux, 1990), 18.

[31]Paule Marshall, *Praisesong for the Widow* (New York: Dutton, 1983).

[32]Gloria Anzaldua, *Borderlands/La Frontera: The New Mestiza* (San Francisco: Spinster/Aunt Lute, 1987).

[33]Oscar Hijuelos, *The Mambo Kings Sing Songs of Love* (New York: Farar Strauss & Giroux, 1989).

[34]Maxine Hong Kingston, *China Men* (New York: Vintage, 1989).

[35]Ibid., 151.

[36]Toni Morrison, *The Bluest Eye* (New York: Pocket Books, 1972).

[37]Mary Crow Dog, *Lakota Woman* (New York: Harper Perenial, 1991).

[38]Art Spiegelman, *Maus II* (New York: Pantheon Books, 1991).

[39]Ibid., 115.

[40]Toni Morrison, *The Bluest Eye*, 4-5.

[41]Ibid.

[42]Ibid., 45.

[43]Ibid.

[44]Ralph Ellison, *Shadow and Act* (New York: Signet, 1964).

[45]Alice Walker, *In Search of Our Mother's Gardens* (Orlando, FL: Harcourt Brace Jovanovich, 1983), 257.

[46]Amy Tan, *The Joy Luck Club* (New York: Putnam, 1989); Maxine Hong Kingston, *The Woman Warrior* (New York: Knopf, 1976); Richard Wright, *Native Son* (New York: Harper and Row, 1969); Alice Walker, *The Color Purple* (New York: Washington Square Press, 1982).

[47]Bharaka Mukherjee, *Jasmine* (New York: Grove Press, 1990).

[48]Paulo Freire and Donald Macedo, *Literacy: Reading the Word and the World* (South Hadley, MA: Bergin & Garvey, 1987), 126.

[49]Toni Morrison, *The Bluest Eye*, 18.

[50]Ibid, 9.

[51]Ibid., 160.

[52]Charles Taylor, *Sources of the Self* (Cambridge, MA: Harvard University Press, 1989), 51.

[53]Cornel West, "Black Culture and Postmodernism," in B. Kruger and P. Martin (eds.). *Remaking History* (Seattle: Bay Press, 1989).

[54]Ibid., 23.

[55]Richard Rorty, "Solidarity or Objectivity," in Rorty, *Objectivity, Relativism, and Truth* (Cambridge, UK: Cambridge University Press, 1991), 23.

[56]Muriel Rukeyser, *The Book of the Dead* (New York: Covici-Friede, 1983), 71.

19

Common Schools for Common Education

Eamonn Callan

Almost a hundred years ago John Dewey announced that the progressive teacher was the "prophet of the true God, and the usherer in of the kingdom of God."[1] The religious language is not to be read at face value. Dewey's divine kingdom was simply a utopian version of democratic society. Progressive teachers in the common school were cast in the roles of prophets and creators of that utopia, and Dewey would provide them with the necessary script for wise prophesy as well as the right pedagogical methods to do their sacred work.

Dewey's faith in schools as the route to democratic salvation seems quaint and foolish as this century draws to a close. We have taught ourselves to expect far less of schools than Dewey hoped for. The common school in particular has come to be widely regarded as an institutional anachronism that is gradually being undermined by educational arrangements more responsive to private preference and cultural diversity. Of course, the erosion of the common school is viewed with alarm in some quarters. One concern is that many policies purporting to respect personal choice, for example, will have a damaging effect on the education of the poor by deflecting resources away from the schools to which they send their children. But typically this argument seems to defend the common school by warning us against policies that might make a bad situation worse. The disdain for the institution among its detractors is almost matched by the disenchantment of its defenders. Both lack the faith that inspired Dewey and the leading educators of his generation.

Our collective loss of faith in the common school is perhaps one of the most significant shifts in educational thought and practice during this century. But I suspect our current attitude may look as wrong to our descendants as Dewey's democratic ardor seems to us. For our current attitude attests to a crude and unambitious understanding of what a common education might be and an insensitivity to the difficulties of supplying the common education worth having without truly common schools. In these respects at least, Dewey's visionary idea of an education for all that ennobles the common school is preferable to our own dour pessimism. This is not to commend the specific content of Dewey's vision; it is merely to say that he posed the right question by asking what suitably rich and inspiring view of a shared educational venture could inform common schooling in a diverse and democratic society. I do not offer here a comprehensive vision of what that venture should be: this essay is not a blueprint for the pedagogical prophets and creators of a new democratic utopia. But I shall argue that an adequate vision of common education for the citizens of a liberal democracy warrants a sober faith in common schools as a potentially powerful instrument of social good, and it should also make us deeply wary of public policies that would undermine them. However, I hope to develop an argument for common schooling that is sensitive to considerations supporting the acceptability, even the desirability, of some kinds of separate schooling.

Education and Schooling

The cardinal distinctions in the argument that follows are between common education and common schooling on the one hand, and separate education and separate schooling on the other. The distinctions matter because rival policies for common or separate schooling are confusedly entangled with competing conceptions of common or separate education.[2]

A conception of common education prescribes a range of educational outcomes – virtues, abilities, different kinds of knowledge – as desirable for all members of the society to which the conception applies. How members might differ on criteria of religion, ethnicity, first language or any other standard that distinguishes them from their fellow citizens is irrelevant to the basic content of common education. A school is common if it welcomes all students of an appropriate age, without regard for these differentiating standards. It must welcome all children not only in the formal sense of forswearing differentiating criteria in its admission criteria; it must also offer a learning environment that is genuinely hospitable to the credal and cultural diversity the society exhibits within limits fixed by the constitutive political morality of that society. Schools that accept diversity formally but not substantively are *de jure* but not *de facto* common schools.

A conception of separate education prescribes a range of educational outcomes as desirable for some particular social group distinguished according to religion, ethnicity, or the like. A school is separate if it welcomes only members of the society who belong to groups that are distinguished in these ways. A *de jure* common school may be a *de facto* separate school if the absence of differentiating criteria in admission requirements coincides with a pedagogy and ethos that is explicitly or implicitly contemptuous of particular groups. Conversely, a *de jure* separate school may grow more like a *de facto* common school as it relaxes doctrinal or other selective criteria of admission and develops a pedagogy and ethos that are no longer uniquely appropriate to the social group for whom that school was originally intended. Something of this sort is what may have happened in some Catholic schools in Canada and the United States in recent decades.[3]

The possible connections between the two categories of educational conceptions and two kinds of schooling are more complex than they might initially seem. To begin with, the success of common education in a diverse society does not necessarily require common schooling. The clearest example of this is easily imagined: a society with an overwhelmingly powerful and pervasive political tradition supporting the ends of common education has no need to make any special institutional provisions to promote them, and so any partiality toward common schooling in state policy would be arbitrary at best and discriminatory at worst. On the other hand, the success of separate education need not require separate schooling in all circumstances. The prospects of success in Catholic separate education were perhaps rather better for the typical Catholic family under Communist rule in Poland than they were for comparably devout families in the seductively secularized societies of western Europe during the same period, despite the ready availability of separate Catholic schools in western Europe and their absence in Communist Poland. Furthermore, it is possible and perhaps often desirable for common schools to become a vehicle of separate education while retaining an overarching commitment to common education. The provision of optional language programs for linguistic minorities, or even specialized religious instruction, are ways in which common schools may attempt to create an educational environment that instantiates *de facto* and not merely *de jure* commonality.

The distinctions I have made help to formulate two claims that should be widely acceptable. First, what is ultimately important is success in whatever common or separate education is worth having, and the institutions of common and separate schooling matter only derivatively as they promote or hinder that success. To think otherwise makes as little sense as supposing that hospitals are good or bad in a way that is independent of their effects on the health of patients. Second, any morally defensible approach to education in a culturally diverse liberal democracy must acknowledge *both* the necessity of some common education and the acceptability of at least certain kinds of separate education for those who would choose them. The necessity of a common education for all follows from the need to secure a sufficiently coherent and decent political culture and the prerequisites of a stable social and economic order. The acceptability of at least some kinds of separate education follows from the need to respect different convictions and cultural affiliations and the divergent educational aspirations that flow from these.

The sharp line I have drawn between education and schooling is not intended to beg the question against those who would insist on a very intimate connection between certain varieties of separate education and separate schooling. Nothing I have said so far rules out the view that a satisfactory separate education of some particular kind cannot be supplied without separate schooling in current social conditions. I consider a possible way of defending that view in the following sections. Yet once we reject the absurd idea that a common education can be completely repudiated, the partisans of separate schooling must do more than talk of what is needed for an adequate separate education; they must also show how a satisfactory common education can be given to children who do not attend common schools. Those who advocate separate schooling are often voluble on the question of why it is necessary for separate education and laconic on the issue of why common schooling is not needed for common education.[4] An interesting way of answering both questions can be constructed, though it is an answer that raises serious difficulties about the alleged dispensability of common schooling.

The Separatist Argument

Suppose we choose an educational end for our children which, so far as it is achieved, brings about a near ubiquitous transformation in how they will live. Suppose further that the end cannot be conscientiously endorsed by many members of the society we inhabit so that it must belong to one conception of separate education among others rather than a vision of common education that all could be reasonably expected to affirm. Religious ends are the most obvious example here, but transformative aims are also embraced when ethnic or racial identity takes on the significance of a unique and all-inclusive world-view, as it does in certain versions of Afrocentric education.[5]

The proposal that our separate educational aim could be effectively accommodated without separate schools, either by providing appropriate curricular options inside common schools or by encouraging separate educational practices outside, should be viewed with some scepticism. A separate educational aim that has a pervasive and transformative effect on how people live cannot be effectively pursued in a school that necessarily aspires to welcome all students, regardless of the ideals of separate education to which they or their parents might subscribe. To be sure, separate educational aims that have a more limited scope, like competence in a particular language or identification with some highly assimilated ethnic group, might find a comfortable place within the ethos of common schools because such aims readily cohere with learning with and from others who do not accept the aims for themselves. That is not so in the case of the kind of educational aim we are considering. The consequences of commitment to the aim must saturate how one studies or teaches literature, how one thinks about the choice of a career or the nature of human intimacy, and virtually any other issue of consequence in a human life. The achievement of such an aim would seem to be threatened in a social setting where one is educated by and with people who do not accept the aim for themselves, however respectful they might be of the convictions of those who do. For the hidden curriculum of the common school must suggest that at least in this environment one can and perhaps should study literature, discuss moral problems and so on, in a way that sets aside commitment to separate educational values which, for their adherents, can *never* be justifiably set aside. The problem is not merely that many participants in the common school cannot themselves exhibit the personal transformation that is desired; they will inevitably be exemplars of ways of living that reject the transformative aim, and to that extent their influence will be anti-educational and not just educationally neutral. The danger this poses will be especially great for the advocate of separate schooling who emphasizes the corruption of those who reject the transformative aim. But even when a benign view is taken of these others, the inability of common schools to accommodate the aim in a way that acknowledges its transformative character may create a pressing need for separate schooling. This completes the first stage of the argument for the provision of separate schools designed for certain kinds of separate educational ends. I call this the separatist argument.

A rough but important distinction can be drawn between radical and moderate versions of the separatist argument. On the radical version, common schooling poses an unacceptable threat to the transformative aim of separate education at any point in the educational process, and therefore all schooling for those who embrace the aim must be separate. Moderate versions of the argument will stress the need for separate schooling during the early stages of the educational process, when the aim has at best a precarious purchase on the child's life. But the need is regarded as decreasingly urgent as the child grows in whatever understanding and commitment the aim entails. Exponents of the argument in its moderate versions will regard common schooling as acceptable at the later stages of the educational process; they may even be persuaded to regard it as desirable on grounds of common education.

Yet as I noted earlier, establishing the need for separate schooling because of the distinctive character of some aim of separate education can be only the first stage of a cogent separatist argument. We also need to be convinced that whatever common education is necessary for us can be adequately served by separate schooling. That task will be more challenging for those who take the radical rather than the moderate separatist tack. The radical will need to show that all the aims of common education can be well served by schooling that remains separate from beginning to end. To assess the separatist argument in either version, we need to know what the appropriate aims of common education are. I shall argue that on one widely assumed conception of common education, the case for even radical separatism looks strong. But that conception fares very badly under critical scrutiny.

Common Education and Social Consensus

The difficulty of reconciling the separatist argument, especially in its radical version, with the requirements of common education is disguised by the widespread assumption that these requirements are minimal and uncontroversial. Common education can doubtless be easily implemented in separate schools once we grant that civic education is reducible to the inculcation of respect for law, and that all other aims derive from a shared concern with economic productivity and competitiveness. To interpret common education in that way is to endorse what I call the "consensual conception" of that concept. For adherents of the consensual conception, the proper content of common education is given by whatever corpus of substantive educational values can be supported by a highly extensive agreement in our society.

Even if empirical research showed that many separate schools were currently ineffective in implementing the consensual conception, the sensible inference would be that they need to be improved in that respect, not that they must be abolished and replaced with common schools. For nothing in the forms of separatist argument and practice that are familiar in our society is seriously at odds with goals like obedience to law, literacy and scientific competence. This is not to deny the notorious friction between religious fundamentalism and scientific orthodoxy on many questions. But that is irrelevant to scientific competence of the sort that is part of the consensual conception in the sense I have specified. In that context, scientific competence is understood as a tool for technological exploitation, and since modern religious fundamentalism has made peace with that narrow use of science, where the separatist argument is used on behalf of fundamentalism it still poses no substantial danger to the pursuit of this particular educational aim. You can be taught that God made the world in six days a few thousand years ago and still grow up to be a model employee in the research division at IBM. Similarly, where literacy is construed expansively to include a command of the imaginative or morally speculative uses of language, serious conflict with some influential conceptions of separate education will certainly occur, but it is a far more austere and technical notion of literacy that belongs to our consensual conception.

Once common schools are dedicated to nothing more than the consensual conception, they will inevitably tend to become unacceptable to the adherents of separate education and uninspiring to those of us who once looked to the common school with fervent social hopes. That is so because consensual common education can embody no more than the lowest common denominator in a society's understanding of what its children should learn, and the more diverse the society is, the lower that common denominator will necessarily become. This means that common schools shackled to the paltry and uncontroversial aims of the consensual conception must offer an education that is at best seriously incomplete and at worst dangerously distorted. It will be seriously incomplete because individual citizens naturally have much more substantial convictions about what is worth teaching and learning than the lowest common denominator can include; it may be dangerously distorted because by excluding all except the lowest common denominator a mistaken view of even that small common ground is apt to become embedded in the hidden curriculum. A conservative Christian, for example, may think that teaching the work-ethic in an institution where work is not publicly interpreted as ministering to the greater glory of God is profoundly misleading, because without that religious context the values of diligence and productivity become contaminated by the rampant greed of secular society.

I have argued that when common education is understood in consensual terms it is easily reconciled with the forms of separate education and separate schooling we are acquainted with. I have also suggested that once common schools see their mission exclusively as the implementation of the consensual conception, they will naturally become an unattractive institution in conditions of cultural diversity. So the separatist argument looks persuasive even in its radical version, and our collective disenchantment with the common schools looks inevitable, once it is assumed that the consensual conception is the best conception of common education.[6] The obvious question now is whether that is true.

Consensus and Equal Respect

The appeal of the consensual conception is easy to understand. Since the creation of state-sponsored schooling on a massive scale in the nineteenth-century, the problem of forging a sufficiently cohesive society in circumstances of diversity has typically been addressed by imposing a conception of common education that expresses the culture and advances the interests of politically dominant groups. The imposition has frequently been a terrible injustice to those outside the same groups, and contemporary discourse about common education is overshadowed by a powerful sense of collective shame regarding the experience of politically marginalized groups in *de jure* common schools.

I suggest that what fuels our sense of collective shame is the thought that justice for a democratic people entails that all citizens are entitled to equal respect. How are we to provide that respect in common schools? An obvious answer is that whatever common education we require must include nothing that any substantial social group would repudiate, including those who have traditionally been disempowered and marginalized. A conception of common education that endorses values unique to some powerful minority, or even confined to a substantial majority of citizens, will be an affront to the dignity of people who think and live otherwise. Therefore, nothing short of the consensual conception can provide the equal respect that all citizens are owed. The resultant common education may indeed be meagre because it must be limited to the lowest common denominator of social commitment, and if the common school is confined to those limits, that will cease to be an appealing institution. Yet all this is perhaps a price we must pay to abide by the principle of equal respect in our interpretation of common education.

The fatal weakness of this argument is its naive reading of the principle of equal respect. A useful way to expose the naivete is by exploring a feature of the consensual conception that some readers may already have found puzzling. I defined the consensual conception in terms of an extensive social consensus on the content of common education. That definition is (deliberately) vague, but it suggests a range of educational aims that have a degree of public support lying somewhere between a bare majority and complete unanimity. Why mark the boundaries of common education between these poles? A bare majority would be unacceptable because enforcing a common education based on that would be flagrantly oppressive toward minorities. Yet complete unanimity would be an impossible requirement because in any large and complex society virtually nothing can be expected to secure that level of agreement. Not everyone is enamored with the goal of ceaseless economic growth upon which contemporary educational discussion is almost obsessively focused, even though the vast majority are. There are also more explicitly sinister departures from unanimity. Respect for religious and racial diversity, even in the weakest and least controversial interpretations of those ambiguous ideals, is rejected by some in our midst. A common education that expresses unanimity is not a feasible social aspiration, and therefore we must settle for something less than that while at the same time eschewing majoritarian tyranny.

Unfortunately, in settling for something less than unanimity, the absurdity of the claim that the consensual conception can be derived from the principle of equal respect becomes starkly exposed. The claim presupposes that equality of respect is violated once common educational aims are imposed by a majority or a powerful elite upon others. But that is precisely the imposition endured by avid racists, for example, whose children are taught respect for racial diversity in the name of consensual common education. From the standpoint of the consensual conception, the only possibly relevant difference between that case and the plight of a native child, for example, whose cultural identity is reviled in the classroom is that native culture *might* belong to a more substantial minority than racist attitudes. But why should the mere size of a minority be a relevant, much less the decisively relevant criterion of when oppression occurs in the imposition of an educational aim? There is no credible answer to that question. The size of a minority whose way of life is unjustly disparaged through the imposition of a particular common educational aim certainly affects the scale of the injustice, but on the prior question of whether injustice has occurred it is entirely irrelevant.

We are perhaps fortunate in having rather more than a bare majority in support of respect for racial diversity. But a consistent advocate of the consensual conception would have to concede that if support for the ideal declined so that substantial minorities embraced overt racism, then it could no longer form part of the consensual conception, and attempts to enforce the ideal through common education would oppress racists. This is a ludicrous implication, and what it really discloses is the contingency of the connection between consensus and equality of respect. A massive consensus on an aim of common education is no guarantee that it expresses equal respect, and by the same token, an aim that is widely and emphatically rejected may express an equality of respect for all citizens that a given society sorely lacks.

As long as we care that citizens are treated with equal respect, the consensual conception of common education cannot be endorsed. That conclusion might seem trivial since the consensual conception has not received serious theoretical defense, and a standard temptation for scholars in education is to confine their critical attention to ideas which have. Yet the consensual conception deserves our scrutiny because it makes explicit a familiar thread of thinking that links together trends in common schooling that have helped to sap our faith in that institution. I have in mind the tendency for teachers and administrators to capitulate to demands for censorship whenever a vocal majority (or minority) objects to what is taught, and the reduction of values education to the promulgation of banalities or, worse still, the policy of suppressing it as far as possible.

Of course, the moral bankruptcy of the consensual conception does not mean that we should be indifferent to whether the best interpretation of common education can win a strong consensus: what it means is that we cannot determine the best conception just by asking what would now secure that consensus. I shall note later on an important connection between equal respect and the effort to create a certain kind of moral consensus in the midst of diversity, but the relevant consensus cannot be complacently identified with the one we happen to have at this moment in history. Current moral agreement is one thing; the moral consensus we would have if we lived together on a basis of equal respect is quite another.

The fact that a thoroughly separate system of schooling should have little difficulty in implementing the consensual conception does nothing to support the radical separatist argument because that conception is utterly inadequate. In the following section, I make some claims about aims that an acceptable common education must include, using the principle of equal respect to defend the claims I make. The separatist argument can then be measured against some of the requirements of a defensible common education.

Rawls and Common Education

The principle of equal respect is our point of departure in answering the question of what a common education should include. Some superficially appealing conceptions of common education cannot be reconciled with any acceptable interpretation of equal respect. That is what we saw in the case of social consensus as a basis of common education. Similarly, reflection may show that certain things must be included in a common education that conforms to the principle of equal respect. I claim that common education must include the aim of reasonableness, understood in a sense that draws on John Rawls' work on the liberal theory of justice.

The necessity of this aim is easily established, even from the standpoint of liberalisms that would diverge from Rawls'. But Rawls is an especially appropriate focus, and not merely because his work has set the agenda in political theory for a generation of scholars. For Rawls' most recent work expounds a liberalism that purports to respect the plurality of values that citizens affirm, and their aspiration to perpetuate those values across generations, in a far more radical way than liberalism has traditionally done.[7] What Rawls calls the "comprehensive liberalism" of Kant or Mill, for example, accommodates diversity only so far as diversity results from the exercise of ideals of autonomy or individuality that are regarded as constitutive of the good life and politically privileged in the institutions of a free society. Rawls' narrowly political liberalism, on the other hand, purports to be as far as possible neutral between comprehensive liberalism and other values that can be found in extant democratic societies. A Rawlsian approach to common education would seem to allow for the legitimacy of approaches to separate education which the ethical liberalisms of Kant or Mill could not countenance.[8] These would be approaches that deny the tenets of comprehensive liberalism while accepting the constraints imposed by liberal political justice. So it is not surprising that when Rawls addresses the question of separate education in families and communities with an ethical orientation at odds with comprehensive liberalism, he is far more sympathetic than many contemporary liberal philosophers are.[9] If we want to find a powerfully argued rationale for common education that both fits the democratic principle of equal respect and completes the second stage of the separatist argument, Rawls' recent work would seem the obvious place to look.[10]

Reasonableness as a virtue of persons involves two related aspects. Acceptance of the principle of reciprocity is the first of these. Reasonable persons are predisposed to propose fair terms of cooperation to others, to heed the proposals others make in the same spirit, to settle differences in mutually acceptable ways, and to abide by agreed terms of cooperation so long as others are prepared to do likewise.[11] Given a context of pluralism, the terms of cooperation that meet the criteria of reciprocity must be settled by arguments that abstract from many of the differences in religious creed, ethnic identity, or ethical conviction that distinguish one reasonable person from another.[12] Political arguments that insist on the superiority of some religious or anti-religious creed, say, cannot instantiate reciprocity where the creed is not shared by some reasonable citizens. This fact about reciprocity under the conditions of pluralism naturally suggests the second condition. Reasonable persons must accept what Rawls calls the "burdens of judgment."

The idea of the burdens of judgment is devised to fulfil two complementary theoretical tasks: it explains the fact that some disagreements about the good and the right among reasonable persons are strictly irreconcilable; it also justifies toleration and mutual accommodation whenever such disagreement threatens to destroy ongoing social cooperation.[13] The core of the idea is the truism that many sources of conflict about the good and the right are not to be ascribed to the vices of unreason, such as closed-mindedness, logical bungling, or ignorance. For example, moral concepts are notoriously subject to hard cases, so that equally reasonable persons will often apply them in divergent ways, irrespective of how open-minded, logically competent, or knowledgeable they might be. Our claims about the right and the good are colored by contingencies of personal history whose effects we cannot completely escape, and therefore different personal histories will tend to yield different judgments, even among persons who are equally reasonable. Similarly, disagreement may stem from the fact that opposing conceptions of the good select from an array of values which do not admit a single reasonable ordering.

Rawls lists several other burdens of judgment, though he does not pretend to be exhaustive.[14] The crucial issue is not the completeness of the list but the practical implications that flow from the general condition of being subject to the burdens of judgment, given a desire to live with others on a basis of reciprocity in a pluralistic society. In that setting, we must acknowledge that many of our fellow citizens subscribe to ethical doctrines at odds with our own without being any less reasonable than we are. Setting the basic terms of social cooperation in a way that imposes the doctrines we favor becomes unconscionable intolerance because it puts the weight of political authority behind values that others reasonably reject. Rawls' notion of public reason – that is, the canons of argument that befit discourse about basic justice among a democratic people – is constructed so as to express and foster the virtue of reasonableness, and his celebrated theory of justice as fairness is now presented as but one way in which public reason might succeed in answering the most fundamental political questions.[15] But there is no need here to pursue the intricacies of Rawls' interpretations of public reason and justice as fairness. Indeed, we may disagree with him on many features of these interpretations and still concur with his stress on the centrality of reasonableness to any adequate understanding of equal respect.[16]

Why is reasonableness central to the practice of equal respect? Suppose we belong to some powerful social group defined by shared religious conviction, and in settling terms of cooperation with outsiders, we seek to make maximum use of our power. Our capacity to dominate means we can insist on arrangements that favor our own values, despite the fact that others reasonably reject these. It follows that we fail to satisfy the Rawlsian conditions of reasonableness. Of course, we might still agree in extending a certain minimal tolerance toward outsiders, and this might even be a morally grounded rather than a merely pragmatic tolerance. We might believe it is wrong, for example, directly to coerce others to conform to the faith we share, but subjecting infidels to discrimination in education, employment, and the like is acceptable to us as a way of expressing our antipathy for their way of life and our determination to contain its evil influence. That example is instructive because it shows that a certain anaemic kind of tolerance can obtain which falls far short of the requirements of equal respect, and what makes it fall short is precisely the absence of the virtue of reasonableness. Although we could plausibly claim that we evince a minimal tolerance in these circumstances, we could not say with any show of reason that we extend to others a respect equal to what we would demand for ourselves. The discriminatory practices we engage in can only be countenanced by flouting the requirements of reciprocity and using our power to extract terms of cooperation that are untenable from any perspective that acknowledges the burdens of judgment. In short, the moral of the story is that no credible conception of the principle of equal respect seems to be available that does not presuppose the virtue of reasonableness, and therefore, a common education that is faithful to the principle must make that virtue one of its necessary ends.

A common education that promotes the virtue of reasonableness entails an aspiration toward consensus, though it is a consensus both more elusive and more morally serious than what we find in the consensual conception of common education. The contrast can be captured through James Fishkin's useful distinction between brute and refined political consensus.[17] Fishkin develops the distinction within the context of philosophical argument about political legitimacy, but the distinction is readily extended to debate about common education. The brute consensus to which the consensual conception defers is merely whatever common values the members of a society can agree on at a particular time, and these may be shaped by processes of socialization and political manipulation that violate the claims of moral reason. A brute consensus on the acceptability of a political regime does not establish its legitimacy because we have no grounds to believe that the processes by which it was formed would produce a legitimate outcome, and for just the same reason, a brute consensus on the content of common education does not establish the desirability of social practices which transmit that content. On the other hand, a political consensus is refined so far as the processes by which it is created and subject to ongoing revision are designed to ensure agreements that deserve our respect, and a common education dedicated to the end of reasonableness is plausibly viewed as one process that is necessary to an adequately refined consensus. For such an education would filter out of political deliberation the many unreasonable views that citizens might be tempted to impose on each other, and among the many equally reasonable views that are possible under the circumstances of pluralism, mutual accommodation and understanding would be fostered. The political consensus toward which a pluralistic society tends when the virtue of reasonableness is broadly and deeply diffused among the citizenry may well be rejected by this or that particular citizen. What is hard to see is how it could reasonably be rejected by any citizen.

Two aspects of a common education that promotes reasonableness need to be stressed. The first of these concerns the processes by which reasonableness might be fostered, and it draws on the familiar Aristotelian thesis that virtues, like skills, are acquired through their exercise.[18] The Aristotelian thesis is that virtues and skills in their most refined forms are the fruit of educational processes in which we exercise them as more primitive habits, becoming ever more adept and discerning as we practise, reflect, and then practise again in light of what the prior practice and reflection have taught us. Now the exercise of reasonableness presupposes a deliberative setting in which citizens with conflicting values and interests can join together to create a morally grounded consensus on how to live together. Reciprocity in the Rawlsian sense can have no application in our lives without that setting. Therefore, the development of reasonableness as a virtue requires that reciprocity be practised in a dialogical context of this kind, and the common school is an obvious way of creating the necessary context. Of course, the context might be simulated with some success in separate schools, although a dialogical setting that really includes students and teachers whose diverse ethical voices represent the pluralism of the larger society would as a rule be preferred. Where a dialogical setting excludes diverse voices, as a separate school must do by welcoming only those who adhere to its separate educational aims, we are compelled to create imaginary interlocutors if we are to "practise" reciprocity, but imaginary interlocutors are a pallid substitute for the real thing.

Second, in learning to be reasonable, human beings will have to learn to accept the burdens of judgment and the implications for reciprocity that these entail. Religious and ethical doctrines do not enter the world with fixed labels enabling us to classify them as reasonable or not. The reasonableness of convictions learnt in the family or elsewhere can only be established on the basis of searching examination that is open to the possibility that received convictions are in fact unreasonable. Moreover, acceptance of the burdens of judgment means that even if my convictions meet the criteria of reasonableness, I must also acknowledge the possibility that many of the opposing beliefs of my compatriots may do so as well, and I must become able to discriminate the ones which do from those which do not. I must come to see how many points of divergence between their political judgments and mine may be hard cases to which the same normative concepts can be reasonably applied in different ways; I must learn how contingencies of personal history may color political judgment in ways that cannot be entirely eliminated by the development of our common capacity to reason; I must learn how the comprehensive religious or ethical ideal I subscribe to selects from the diversity of human goods and organizes these in ways to which there are reasonable alternatives. All these educational tasks require a serious intellectual and imaginative engagement with the plurality of values to which my fellow citizens adhere, and again, there is surely at least a presumptive case for undertaking the tasks in a social environment where the plurality of values is really embodied in the lives of different participants. That is to say, there is at least a presumptive case for common education in common schools.

I have argued that any conception of common education that is faithful to the principle of equal respect must include the aim of reasonableness, and I have suggested that the pursuit of that aim requires a particular kind of deliberative context, as well as a critico-imaginative encounter with the ethical diversity our society currently includes. These educational implications of commitment to the aim of reasonableness create a presumptive case for common schooling. How strong is that presumption?

Reconciling Separate and Common Education

A successful separatist counterargument must defeat the presumptive case for common education. The counterargument needs to be completed in two stages. At the first, the need for separate schooling to achieve some transformative aim of separate education must be established; at the second, the separate schooling characterized at the first stage must be shown to cohere with the requirements of common education. If the requirements must include the promotion of reasonableness, serious difficulties arise for any attempt to complete the radical separatist argument, at least in current circumstances, although the prospects for completing the argument in its moderate version are much better.

The major obstacles to the completion of the radical argument correspond to the two aspects of common education I stressed above. First, how is the particular deliberative context that the development of reciprocity requires to be supplied to children whose schooling is separate from beginning to end? The question would not even interest us in a liberal democratic utopia where powerful institutions for collective deliberation exist outside the boundaries of the school, and everyone can be expected to learn to participate in ways that conduce to reasonableness. But we simply do not inhabit that utopia, and so the question must worry us. A partial simulacrum of the relevant deliberative context might be provided in separate schools where the claims and interests of citizens who reject the separatist orthodoxy can be addressed with some sympathy and open-mindedness. But notice that once the aims of separate education have been liberalised in this way, one premise that is necessary to the radical separatist argument becomes glaringly implausible – that is, the proposal that any departure from separate schooling is an unacceptable threat to the ends of separate education. For the only "threat" that a common schooling dedicated to the aim of reasonableness could pose would be the sympathetic and open-minded exploration of rival convictions, and *ex hypothesi*, the value of that exploration is affirmed in liberalized conceptions of separate education. Alternatively, if the ends of separate education are defined so that their achievement requires a dogmatic and contemptuous rejection of whoever rejects them, then any attempt to create the deliberative context of reciprocity would certainly be antagonistic to those ends. But the same ends could not be acceptable from the perspective of an education that prescribes the virtue of reasonableness, and so the radical separatist argument would founder at the second stage because it could not be reconciled with the exigencies of common education.

A parallel dilemma regarding the burdens of judgment confronts the advocates of radical separatism. Once separate education is interpreted in a way that acknowledges the burdens, it becomes incomprehensible that schooling must be separate from beginning to end for the sake of the liberalized separate education which gives the institution its rationale. On the other hand, the incompatibility of common schooling with varieties of separate education that repudiate the burdens of judgment might be easily established. But precisely because the burdens of judgment are rejected, these forms of separate education must fail to cohere with the requirements of common education.

A retreat to a moderate version of the separatist argument enables exponents of liberalised separate education to escape these dilemmas. For those who subscribe to illiberal ideals of separate education – for example, those who repudiate the virtue of reasonableness – that escape is not available. They will hardly be attracted to the moderate version of the argument to begin with, and even if they were, a separate schooling of even brief duration which works against the necessary ends of common education must fail at the second stage. But it might be objected that the moderate argument is untenable even when it is aligned with separate educational values that have been tempered by liberal social principles. If the ends of separate education are understood in a way that accords with the requirements of common education, why does schooling have to be separate during even its early stages for some future citizens? Of course, there could be nothing inherently objectionable about this kind of separate schooling since it accommodates the demands of common education. But in the absence of a persuasive answer to the question just posed, it must seem that separate schooling protects no vital interest of the students who attend or their parents. Therefore, the grounds for state sponsorship seem weak or non-existent, and the case for restricting access may often be strong since no powerful moral consideration could weigh against reasons of efficiency or the like when these support limitations on access.

To bring out the force of the moderate separatist argument against this line of objection, we need to reflect more deeply on the virtues of practical reason. Reasonableness is only one aspect of competence in practical reason; its companion is practical rationality, which is evinced in the individual's pursuit of her or his own good. Although Rawls insists, rightly in my view, that neither virtue of reason can be derived from the other, there is clearly a sense in which the rational is prior to the reasonable.[19] If I am to be capable of reciprocity and acceptance of the burdens of judgment, I must have a secure understanding of what it is to have a conception of the good and to pursue it rationally; otherwise I cannot understand what is at stake for the good of individuals when they try to settle the terms of cooperation on a fair and reasonable basis. The logical priority of practical rationality does not mean there must be a tidy developmental sequence, with rationality reaching a full ripeness before reasonableness can take hold in our lives. On the contrary, it is much more plausible to imagine a tightly integrated process of psychological development, within which an increasingly complex and discriminating reasonableness draws on an evolving rationality, which is in turn enriched by our developing reasonableness. Reasonableness, as Rawls understands it, is a highly sophisticated virtue, which imposes heavy intellectual and emotional demands on us, and it has obvious origins in simpler dispositional precursors. The mutuality of beneficence a child learns to show and enjoy in a loving family foreshadows the more demanding mutuality that develops later, if all goes well, in somewhat larger-scale associations, and this in turn foreshadows the reciprocity of Rawlsian citizens who attempt to create a fair scheme of cooperation in the midst of radical disagreement about the good.[20] Similarly, acceptance of the burdens of judgment has obvious antecedents in propensities to recognize the fallibility of one's own judgments and to moderate individual demands in response to disagreement. At these more primitive levels as well, the antecedents of a developed reasonableness and rationality are subtly interwoven. For example, the young child who learns to temper claims for parental attention in light of the needs of a new sibling is learning to acknowledge the good of another, and this presupposes a primitive recognition of her own distinct good.

Rawls' rather sparse idea of rationality is expounded without serious attention to the ways in which individuals achieve an initial understanding of their good in a specific cultural setting, where the good is conceived according to a traditional moral vocabulary that fixes the normative content of roles and the social practices they sustain. Although this point is commonly thought to be a fatal objection to the understanding of rationality and the good on which liberal theories like Rawls' are based,[21] I would argue that the point can be easily absorbed into the fabric of such theories. We can acknowledge that initiation into a particular, established view of the good life is indeed the natural starting-point of the development of rationality, and also that whatever kinds of mutual goodwill and cooperation characterize that view are the foundation for the development of reasonableness, without thereby giving up on the cardinal principles of the liberal democratic tradition and the need to transmit them through common education.[22]

The claims I have made about the interdependent development of rationality and reasonableness, and its natural starting-point in received roles and traditions, are the basis for an appealing version of the moderate separatist argument. Separate schooling of limited duration, created for the sake of separate education, may be regarded as one way of creating the developmental antecedents of the mature liberal virtues. From the standpoint of parents who embrace some transformative educational aim for their children, the early years of schooling may be seen as a crucial stage in securing a robust initial understanding of what their way of life means. From the standpoint of the state, the experiences that schooling furnishes may be seen as laying the groundwork for the rationality and reasonableness that characterize the fully virtuous citizen by cultivating the psychological precursors of such virtues; and given the continuity between the values of the family and the ethos of the separate school, it may even be a more solid groundwork than common schools could typically provide.[23] Yet the force of this argument from the state's standpoint depends decisively on its being a *moderate* separatist argument. Because those who might press this argument are willing to accept a schooling system that is common in its culminating years, their separatist demands are easily reconciled with the need for schools to create the deliberative context for full-blown reciprocity at an appropriate developmental stage and to challenge received ideas of the good and the right in the manner required by acceptance of the burdens of judgment. The dilemmas that defeat radical separatism are thus evaded, though at the cost of retreating to a form of separatism much weaker than many extant varieties.

From Principle to Policy

So far I have argued for three closely interlocked normative principles: an acceptable common education for the citizens of a liberal democracy must include the cultivation of reasonableness; that aim creates a presumptive case for common schooling; and the presumptive case can be defeated under certain specified conditions. The argument provides a framework of principle within which many issues of educational policy can be addressed. How are we to make appropriate inferences from the principles I have outlined to the questions of policy upon which they bear? I want to press two claims in response to that question. First, the relevance of the argument for the state regulation and sponsorship of separate schools is uncertain and likely to vary substantially from one social context to another. Second, the argument has implications for the task of transforming *de jure* into *de facto* common schools.

The principles I have outlined might seem to have one striking implication for the regulation of separate schools: all separate schools committed to educational ends at variance with the requirements of reasonableness should be prohibited. But even that seemingly obvious prescription does not immediately follow from my argument. It is one thing to say that a necessary end of common education is the promotion of reasonableness; it is quite another to claim that no children or adolescents should be permitted to attend schools that pursue ends at odds with the requirements of reasonableness. The gap between the two claims is created by a number of considerations. First and most obviously, the political vitality of no society requires that all citizens develop the virtues that inform its distinctive political culture – warrior societies can endure with more than a few cowards in their midst, and liberal democracies can and do thrive with their share of intransigent bigots. Furthermore, one crucial difference between the warrior society and the liberal democratic state lies in the attitudes they foster toward those who fail to evince their constitutive political virtues. For the liberal state is distinctive in requiring a substantial forbearance toward those whose would affirm values in conflict with its ideals, including people who would seek to perpetuate those values across generations. That forbearance can be defended through independent instrumental and non-instrumental moral arguments.

Any extant liberal society will harbor more or less powerful cultural pressures that are pitted against its ideals, and these may be evidenced in controversies about what can permissibly be taught in separate schools regarding race, gender, religion, and the like. Suppose we have compelling grounds to agree that some views that are commonly taught in certain separate schools are in clear conflict with the criteria of reasonableness.[24] If our interest is in securing the eventual triumph of liberal ideals over time, it would not automatically follow that the blunt instrument of coercive law should be used to suppress efforts to teach the offending views. Coercion may exacerbate the political alienation of those who are on the receiving end of suppression, and encourage the continuance of illiberal values that would gradually fade in a more indulgent environment. This instrumental moral argument for a limited forbearance is thus grounded in scepticism about the universal efficacy of political coercion in containing the advocacy of social evils in educational as in other institutions. No doubt scepticism about the universal efficacy of toleration is equally appropriate. My point is merely that any coercive political response to groups who reject the requirements of common education depends in part on difficult predictive judgments about the effects of coercive regulation in particular social circumstances, and since we might expect the effects to vary from one situation to another, coercion cannot be endorsed as a matter of general principle.

The non-instrumental case for a selective forbearance is different and less well understood, and I can only sketch its main outlines here. One of the burdens of judgment which Rawls stresses is the inevitable partiality of anyone's conception of the good, given the vast diversity of human values that are worthy of election.[25] In embracing a life that revolves around teaching, scholarship, and familial intimacy, I choose one honorable way to live at the cost of many other worthwhile possibilities. A common claim about liberal democratic societies is that their distinctive mode of government is neutral between different conceptions of the good, and so unlike theocratic or other illiberal states, the many ways of life citizens practise are free and creative responses to the diversity of goods from which a decent and fulfilling life can be constructed.[26] But this way of trying to capture what is distinctive of liberal politics is suspect, in part because modern liberal societies exert powerful constraints on the lives we lead, making many possibilities decreasingly viable even when they involve no injustice toward others. The thought that not all good lives can be led within the welcoming aegis of liberal society often colors our half-envious or admiring response to some who partially withdraw from it, like certain religious groups, or those whose ancient traditions may be threatened by it, like some aboriginal communities. I think Rawls is right to say that one reason for liberal forbearance in the face of diversity is our acknowledgement of the ethical selectivity and partiality that afflict all our lives. But the same point can be pressed further. Our recognition that some conceptions of the good go against the grain of liberal politics may also support a limited tolerance of ways of life that repudiate the liberal virtues and the educational practices that go with them. This must be a strictly limited tolerance if our commitment to common education is to mean anything at all. Nevertheless, the fact that the ends of common education may be resisted because of a fidelity to goods which liberal societies cannot fully accommodate may moderate the zeal with which we prosecute those ends in dealing with established communities and cultures who reject them.

However, for those of us who maintain a faith in common schools for common education, the crucial practical task is not the policing of separate schools but rather the transformation of *de jure* into *de facto* common schools. So long as our public schools are in the grip of the consensual conception of common education, they do not really welcome the credal and cultural diversity of our society on the only shared basis worth affirming – the basis of equal respect. A schooling system that ignores the deep questions that divide us and stresses instead the increasingly shallow set of substantive values on which almost all of us can currently agree is really contemptuous of who we are because it evades the truth that our identities are deeply implicated in rival answers to ethically divisive questions. A common education for common schools might instead address those questions in a forthright way, while at the same time cultivating a shared reasonableness that would enable us to live together in mutual respect. This may not be the grand project of realizing a democratic "kingdom of God," but it is perhaps the only responsible educational faith we can still endorse.

Notes

[1]John Dewey, "My Pedagogic Creed," in Jo-Ann Boydston (ed.), *The Early Works, Volume 5: Early Essays* (Carbondale, IL: Southern Illinois University Press, 1972), 95.

[2]I use "conception" here in the sense that is central to much of the most important political and legal philosophy produced over the last couple of decades (for example, John Rawls, *A Theory of Justice* (Cambridge, MA: Harvard University Press, 1971); Ronald Dworkin, *Taking Rights Seriously* (Cambridge, MA: Cambridge University Press, 1978) and *Law's Empire* (Cambridge, MA: Harvard University Press, 1986)). Rawls' capsule explanation of the difference between concepts and conceptions is useful: "Roughly, the concept is the meaning of a term, while a particular conception includes as well the principles required to apply it." (*Political Liberalism* (New York: Columbia University Press, 1993), 14n).

[3]See Eamonn Callan, "Religion, Schooling and the Limits of Liberalism," in N. Kach (ed.), *The State and Future of Education: Selected Proceedings of the Alberta Universities Educational Foundations Conference* (Edmonton, AB.: University of Alberta, Faculty of Education, Department of Educational Foundations, 1987), 135-138; Ric Laplante, "The Changing Catholic School in Alberta," in N. Kach (ed.), *The State and Future of Education: Selected Proceedings of the Alberta Universities Educational Foundations Conference*, 110-124.

[4]A notable exception is Brian Crittenden (*Parents, the State and the Right to Educate* (Melbourne: Melbourne University Press, 1988)). Yet I think even Crittenden is insufficiently sensitive to the possibility of radical conflict between the conceptions of religious faith, for example, around which many versions of separate education are constructed and the emphasis on critical reason that public virtue in a liberal democracy requires. This point has been perceptively pursued against Crittenden by Kenneth Strike ("Review Article – Parents, the State and the Right to Educate," *Educational Theory*, 40, 2, 1990: 237-248).

[5]See Molefe Kete Asante, *Afrocentricity* (Buffalo, NY: Amulefi, 1980), and "The Afrocentric Idea of Education," *Journal of Negro Education*, 60, 2, 1991: 170-180.

[6]If the consensual conception were the only or the best one, the case against common schooling would be overwhelming. Mark Holmes's argument against common schooling is based on the assumption that the consensual conception is the only one ("The Place of Religion in Public Education," *Interchange*, 24, 3, 1993: 205-223).

[7]J. Rawls, *Political Liberalism.*

[8]Ibid., 199-200.

[9]Ibid., 200.

[10]I have argued elsewhere ("Political Liberalism and Political Education," *Review of Politics*, 58, 1996: 5-33.) that Rawls does not succeed in distinguishing comprehensive from political liberalism. Nevertheless, his recent work is of great interest partly because it is an attempt to devise a liberalism that is maximally hospitable to ethical diversity.

[11]J. Rawls, *Political Liberalism*, 49-50.

[12]Ibid., 225-226.

[13]Ibid., 54-58.

[14]Ibid., 56-57.

[15]Ibid., xxvii-xxx.

[16]The idea that reasonableness is central to civic virtue in a liberal democracy is shared by writers who do not interpret its requirements quite as Rawls does. Stephen Macedo's account of the liberal virtue of moderation fits this pattern (*Liberal Virtues* (Oxford: Clarendon, 1991), 69-73). So too does the account Amy Gutmann has been developing of the virtues of democratic liberation (Amy Gutmann and Dennis Thompson, "Moral Conflict and Political Consensus," *Ethics*, 101, 1, 1990: 64-88. Amy Gutmann, "The Challenge of Multiculturalism in Political Ethics," *Philosophy and Public Affairs*, 22, 3, 1993: 171-206). For a brilliant essay on public reason that differs sharply from Rawls' in finding a substantial place for religious argument, see Jeremy Waldron, "Religious Considerations in Public Deliberation," *San Diego Law Review*, 30, 4, 1993: 817-848.

[17]James Fishkin, *The Dialogue of Justice* (New Haven, CT: Yale University Press, 1992), 53-67.

[18]Aristotle, *Aristotle's Ethics*, edited by J.L. Ackrill (London: Faber and Faber, 1973), 1103a-b.

[19]J. Rawls, *Political Liberalism*, 52.

[20]J. Rawls, *A Theory of Justice*, 462-479.

[21]Alasdair MacIntyre, *After Virtue* (Notre Dame, IN: Notre Dame University Press, 1981); Michael Sandel, *Liberalism and the Limits of Justice* (Cambridge: Cambridge University Press, 1982).

[22]Will Kymlicka, *Liberalism, Community and Culture* (Oxford: Clarendon, 1989), 47-131.

[23]My argument here converges with Terry McLaughlin's subtle defense of separate schooling within a liberal democratic framework, although he does not make use of my distinction between radical and moderate separatist arguments (Terry McLaughlin, "The Ethics of Separate Schools," in Mal Leicester and Monica Taylor (eds.), *Ethics, Ethnicity and Education* (London: Kogan Page, 1992), 114-136.

[24]It should be noted that such grounds are often elusive. As McLaughlin has noted, it is often difficult to find a sharp line between values that are outside and values inside the liberal democratic tradition ("The Ethics of Separate Schools"). But the practical significance of that point is ambiguous. Our frequent uncertainty about where lines should be drawn means that we should be cautious about claims that coercive intervention is justified. By the same token, it also means we should be equally cautious about claims that forbearance is the justified course. So McLaughlin's premises do not support any general reason for favoring forbearance over coercion.

[25]J. Rawls, *Political Liberalism*, 57.

[26]See Ronald Dworkin "Liberalism," in Stuart Hampshire (ed.), *Public and Private Morality* (Cambridge: Cambridge University Press, 1978), 113-143; Bruce Ackerman, *Social Justice and the Liberal State* (New Haven, CT: Yale University Press, 1980), 139-167.

20

Democratic Education in Difficult Times

Amy Gutmann

These are difficult times because we are difficult people. There are un-doubtedly other, less "personal" reasons that make these difficult times and also other, more "structural" reasons that help explain why we are difficult people, but I want to begin by focusing on the fact that we are – for whatever simple or complicated reasons – difficult people.

When I say we are difficult people, I have something very simple in mind. Most Americans value freedom of speech and also value protection from falsehood, deceit, and defamation. Yet it is impossible to provide complete freedom of speech and still prevent the widespread dissemination of falsehoods, deceits, and defamations. Most Americans value freedom of religion, and also want governments to shape the social environment so that people are predis-posed to believe in "good" religions (or philosophies of life) rather than "bad" ones. Yet a society that grants complete freedom of religion cannot shape an environment resistant to repugnant religions.

Most Americans value living and working where we like, and also value stable, friendly, and familiar places in which to live and work. We value the freedom to choose our sexual partners and rechoose them, and we also place a high value on stable nuclear families. Most Americans want to use their market freedom to secure a standard of living that is staggeringly high by any historical perspective, yet we are also sensitive to the plight of other people's children, which threatens this expectation. Most Americans would like to see our freedoms extended to other people, but we fear that by opening our borders, we decrease the chances of our own (and our children's) educational and econom-ical improvement.

The tension within each set of values – between individual freedom and civic virtue – poses a challenge for educating Americans. It is impossible to educate children to maximize both their freedom and their civic virtue. Yet Americans want both – although some people seem willing to settle for freedom for themselves and civic virtue for others. This formula obviously will not work. Far from obvious, however, is how our educational institutions should come to terms with the tension between individual freedom and civic virtue. Should they try to reconcile these seemingly unreconcilable values? Or give priority to one value over the other? Or find the one, morally best way of coping with each of these tensions? Or should we continue to muddle through much as we have done in the past? Rarely do Americans turn to philosophy for help, except in those rare times when the consequences of muddling through seem unbearable. We then reconcile ourselves to philosophizing; we make a necessity out of a virtue.

While these times are undoubtedly difficult in many ways, philosophy is probably not necessary for getting us through them (and philosophy will certainly not be sufficient). Our nation's political ideals – liberty *and* justice *for all* – remain at risk, but the risks to economically and educationally advantaged Americans are not so great that we have no practical alternative to muddling through. Philosophizing still seems to be a practical luxury. Some of us may be able to withstand the practical risks of politics and education as usual. But, as a society we would do better, both morally and practically, to be more philosophically guided in our educational politics.

By what philosophy should we be guided? The several philosophies that compete for our allegiance suggest radically different ways of dealing with the tensions that make us difficult people. Despite their differences, they all try to *dissolve* the tension between individual freedom and civic virtue in a potent philosophical solution, and thereby avoid the political problems that flow from the tension. Perhaps the most distinctive feature of a democratic theory of education is its simultaneous refusal to dissolve these tensions philosophically and its insistence on finding a principled, rather than simply a pragmatic, way of living with the tensions. Living with the tensions will never be easy, but the alternatives to democratic education that promise to make us easier people are far worse. One of the strongest arguments for democratic education – as for democracy itself – is that the alternatives are worse. So let us consider the two most philosophically potent and politically influential alternatives to a democratic state of education: a Platonic family state and a liberal state of individuals.

The Family State and the Liberal State

One of the greatest treatises on education ever written, Plato's *Republic*, offers a way of dissolving the tensions between individual freedom and civic virtue: Subsume all that is valuable with regard to individual freedom into civic virtue. The means of subsumption is education: Teach children that they cannot realize their own good except by contributing to the social good. Not just any social good will do: Children must be taught the true good, the one that rightly orders their souls, the one consonant with their varying natures. Unless children learn to associate their own good with the social good, a peaceful and prosperous society will be impossible. Unless the social good that they are taught is

who decides the
social good?

consonant with their nature and worthy of their pursuit, they will grow to be unfulfilled and dissatisfied with the society that miseducated them. All education that is not guided by *the* social good and the *truth* in human nature is miseducation. All such societies will degenerate because of internal disharmony.

Peculiarly enough, the Platonic family state provides the philosophical underpinnings of an ongoing American search for "the one best system." The system tries to dissolve the tensions between individual freedom and civic virtue by educating all children to identify their interests with the social good. In practice, the moral costs of dissolving the tension are great: Catholic children were once whipped for refusing to read the ("right") King James version of the Bible; college students today are ridiculed (or dismissed as uneducable) for rereading Plato's *Phaedrus* in the wrong way. (So Allan Bloom asks rhetorically "How does a youngster who sees sublimation where Plato saw divination learn from Plato, let alone think Plato can speak to him?")[1]

Repression of reasonable points of view is half the problem of the family state. The other half is political tyranny in the name of educational enlightenment. In the *Republic*, Socrates tells Glaucon that "it's better for all to be ruled by what is divine and prudent, especially when one has it as his own within himself; but, if not, *set over one from outside*, so that insofar as possible all will be alike and friends, piloted by the same thing."[2] Children must not be set free until the right regime – the "divine and prudent" one – is established within their souls.

Who holds the key to the right regime? Not the Socrates who boasts of being the only Athenian wise enough to know his own ignorance. Socrates imagines that there may be someone wiser even than he, someone who has left the cave, and seen the light, someone who therefore knows the right regime for all souls. To create a family state, that philosopher must return to the cave, become "king," and wipe the social slate clean by exiling "all those in the city who happen to be older than ten: and taking over their children . . . rear them – far away from those dispositions they now have from their parents."[3] This is not a small price to pay for dissolving the tensions with which we now live. Socrates himself recoils from the idea on behalf of his imaginary philosopher king, suggesting that he "won't be willing to mind the political things . . . unless some divine chance coincidentally comes to pass."[4]

This problem with the family state is not a purely practical one – pointing to the impossibility of finding someone wiser than Socrates who could educate well-ordered souls in a poorly ordered society. Even if there were someone wiser than Socrates in our midst, he or she still could not claim the right to order the souls of all citizens. A good life must be one that a person recognizes as such, lived from inside, according to one's own best lights. The neo-Platonic quest for the one best system, which subsumes individual freedom into the social good, denies this insight of individualism. Even if Plato were right about the objectively good life, we would still have to look past the *Republic* for a politically legitimate way of associating individual freedom and civic virtue, through governing.

Radically opposed to the family state is what I call the state of individuals, or the liberal state as it is commonly but misleadingly called. The state of individuals overcomes the tensions between freedom and virtue in a way precisely the opposite of that in the family state: It actively supports only those institutions instrumental to individual freedom of choice. The principled neutrality of the state of individuals aims to maximize the freedom of individuals to pursue their diverse conceptions of the private good. If the Platonic family state strives for the unity of a traditional family, the state of individuals strives for the diversity of a modern shopping mall. To paraphrase John Stuart Mill: All attempts by the state to bias the conclusions of its citizens, including its children, on disputed subjects are evil, as are all unnecessary restrictions on their choices. This is the contemporary liberal credo of neutrality for the sake of opportunity and choice.

Just as the family state provides the philosophical underpinnings for "the one best system," the state of individuals provides philosophical inspiration for "child-centred" education. Of course, proponents of the state of individuals recognize that all educators must limit children's choices, but only for the sake of developing their capacity for rational choice or for the sake of cultural coherence. American schoolchildren are taught English rather than Bengali or Spanish, not by choice but by cultural determination. This culturally determined curriculum, contemporary liberals like Bruce Ackerman tell us, legitimately limits the range of their future choices insofar as such limitation is necessary for cultural coherence. Other limits on children's choices – whether for the sake of moral development or the shaping of democratic character – are unjustified, for these would be based on what Ackerman calls "adult pretensions to moral superiority."[5]

The horticultural imagery so prevalent in Plato – pruning and weeding children's desires, shaping their character – has no place in the state of individuals: "We have no right to look upon future citizens as if we were master gardeners who can tell the difference between a pernicious weed and a beautiful flower."[6] We do have a right, according to Ackerman, perhaps even a duty, to shape the character and bias the choices of children for the sake of cultural coherence. Education in the state of individuals builds on our cultural but not our moral biases. We educate children to be Americans who are free to choose but we do not bias their choices (or shape their character) for the sake of moral goodness. We educate rational shoppers but not good people or virtuous citizens.

Why say that parents and teachers should be free to guide children's choices for the sake of cultural coherence but not for the sake of cultivating good character or choosing a morally good life? After all, sometimes the claim on the part of parents and teachers that they know the difference between morally good and bad, or better and worse, is not a *pretension* to moral superiority, but a reflection of their greater moral understanding. Honesty is better than deceitfulness, industriousness better than sloth, insight better than insensitivity, kindness better than cruelty – and not just because honest, industrious, insightful, and kind people have more freedom of choice. They may have less freedom of choice precisely because they are constrained by these virtues. We nonetheless value these virtues because there is more to a good life and to a good society than freedom; that is one good reason why we are likely to remain difficult people, torn between freedom and other virtues that are not mere means to or byproducts of freedom.

The "neutrality" premise (no authority has a right to act on a belief that one conception of the good life is better than any other) simplifies life for some contemporary liberals, allowing them to defend freedom of choice singlemindedly, but the lameness of the defense is particulary evident in American education. Consumer choice is a reasonable guiding principle for designing a shopping mall, but it is an irresponsible and incomplete principle for designing a high school. Educators must limit students' freedom of choice on some ground; otherwise education simply ceases. Cultural prejudice may seem like the politically safest guide to limiting choice, but it is not a satisfactory substitute for moral principle. Nor is it politically safe: Teaching cultural prejudices is no less politically controversial than teaching moral principles, as recent battles over bilingualism and the content of core curricula indicate.

The family state and the state of individuals offer us the following choice: Either we must educate children so that they are free to choose among the widest range of lives because freedom of choice is the paramount good, or we must educate children so that they will choose *the* life that is best because a rightly ordered soul is the paramount good. Let children define their own identity or define it for them. Give children liberty or give them virtue. This is a morally false choice. Cultivating character and intellect through education constrains children's future choices, but it does not uniquely determine them. There need be nothing illegitimate about such constraints, although some constraints surely are illegitimate. The question we must therefore ask is not whether to maximize freedom or to inculcate virtue, but how to combine freedom with virtue. This creates a new question: which freedoms and what virtues? We must focus not just on the future freedom of children but also the present freedom of parents, not just on the virtues necessary for a good life but also those necessary for a just society.

This reformulation does not resolve but at least it comprehends the problem of associating individual freedom and civic virtue that Americans face today: Citizens of a religiously and ethnically diverse society disagree on the relative value of freedom and virtue; we disagree on the nature of a good life and good character. No political philosophy can authoritatively resolve all our disagreements – not only because no one is smart enough to comprehend a comprehensive good, but because no mortal, no matter how wise, can legitimately impose a good life on people who cannot live that life from the inside. Nor can anyone legitimately impose liberal neutrality on people who value virtue as well as freedom. We stand at a philosophical and political impasse unless we can defend another alternative.

A Democratic Alternative: Public Debate

The alternative I want to defend is democratic in several significant respects. First, it does not tyrannize over common sense, either by subsuming individual freedom into the common social good or by collapsing civic virtue (or social justice) into individual freedom. Second, a democratic theory of education provides principled criticism of all educational authorities (including parents) who tyrannize children in any way, whether by depriving them of an education adequate to citizenship or by repressing reasonable challenges to popular ideas. Third, a democratic theory supports educational institutions that are conducive to democratic deliberation, institutions that make a democratic virtue out of our inevitable disagreements over educational problems. The virtue, too simply stated, is that we can publicly debate educational problems in a way much more likely to increase our understanding of education and each other than if we were to leave the management of schools, as Kant suggested, "to depend entirely upon the judgment of the most enlightened experts."[7] The policies that result from our democratic deliberations will not always be the right ones, but they will be more enlightened – by the values and concerns of the many communities that constitute a democracy – than those that would have been made by unaccountable experts.

This understanding of democratic education is, however, incomplete. The threat of repression and discrimination remains. Democratic processes can be used to destroy democratic education. They can be used to undermine the intellectual foundations of future democratic deliberations by repressing unpopular ways of thinking or excluding some future citizens from an education

Censorship

adequate for participating in democratic politics. A democratic society must not be constrained to legislate what the wisest parent or philosopher wants for his or her child, but it must be constrained not to legislate policies that render democracy repressive or discriminatory. A democratic theory of education recognizes the importance of empowering citizens to make educational policy and also of constraining their choices to a broad range of policies that are nonrepressive and nondiscriminatory, so as to preserve the intellectual and social foundations of democracy. Democracy must be understood not merely (or primarily) as a *process* of majority rule, but rather as an *ideal* of a society whose adults members are, and continue to be, equipped by their education and authorized by political structures to share in ruling. A democratic society must educate all educable children to be capable of participating in collectively shaping their society.

Democracy makes no claim to being an uncontroversial standard. Not all societies or all citizens in our society are committed to democracy (although all, according to this argument, should be). Those who are not committed to democracy are stuck at the impasse I characterized earlier: They assert their commitment to civic virtue or to individual freedom always at the expense of denying the legitimacy of the other value. The practical consequence of this thinking is that basic freedoms are sacrificed to communal virtue or freedom is expanded so far as to forgo the virtues essential to a just society. The legitimating claim of democracy is therefore not that it will be accepted by all citizens (let alone all philosophers) – no political philosophy can sensibly claim such a Panglossian future. Its legitimating claim is one of political morality: A state of democratic education is minimally objectionable insofar as it leaves maximum moral room for citizens deliberately to shape their society, not in their own image, but in an image that they can legitimately identify with their informed, moral choices.

You cannot govern unless you have first been governed. You must govern after you have been governed. These twin maxims, not Platonic but Aristotelian in origin, are at the root of a democratic understanding of both politics and education: being governed and governing in turn, where governing includes the nurturing of children by parents, their formal instruction by professionals, the structuring of public instruction by public officials accountable to citizens, and the shaping of culture by both private and public authorities – constrained or ideally informed by the principles of nonrepression and nondiscrimination.

There are many ways that this democratic understanding (were it more fully elaborated) could make a difference in the way we think about education and practice it. I offer here one small but significant example.

Evolution or Creationism: A Test Case

In October 1986, a federal district court ruled that the public schools of Hawkins County, Tennessee, must exempt the children of a group of fundamentalist Christian parents from basic reading classes. Those classes assigned Holt, Rinehart, & Winston texts, texts that had been unanimously approved by the Hawkins County Board of Education on recommendation of their textbook selection committee. The content of the Holt, Rinehart series offended the religious views of these parents, who had joined together as Citizens Organized for Better Schools (COBS) and unsuccessfully petitioned the school board to have their children taught from unoffensive texts. The parents objected to, among other things: a story depicting a young boy having fun while cooking on grounds that the story "denigrates the differences between the sexes" that the Bible endorses; a story entitled "A Visit to Mars" on grounds that it encourages children to use their imaginations in ways incompatible with fundamentalist faith; a story entitled "Hunchback Madonna," which describes the religious and social practices of an Indian settlement in New Mexico, on grounds that the story teaches Catholicism; and an excerpt from Anne Frank's *Diary of a Young Girl* on grounds that it suggests that nonorthodox belief in God is better than no belief at all. The principal and school board both refused to exempt the children from using the Holt, Rinehart readers. The parents took the Hawkins County Public School District to court.

District Court Judge Thomas Hull found nothing wrong with the Holt, Rinehart series, and said so. Yet he concluded that the children must be exempted from reading the series and therefore from their reading classes because, in his words, plaintiffs (the parents of the children) sincerely believe that the affirmation of these philosophical viewpoints is repulsive to their Christian faith, so repulsive that they must not allow their children to be exposed to the Holt series. This is their religious belief. They have drawn a line, and it is not for us to say that the line they drew was an unreasonable one.[8]

Why is it not for us to say?

Not because the parents of those children should have ultimate authority over their education. If that were the case, it would not be for us (or Judge Hull) to say that they must be educated at all. Yet Judge Hull ruled that the children take standardized tests in reading rather than read standardized texts. If standardized tests are justified, then there must be something that all children should learn independently of what their parents want them to learn.

Not because democratic education is compatible with the fundamentalist view that forbids exposure to knowledge about religions, cultures, and convictions that differ from their own, on grounds that such knowledge corrupts the soul. The parents in this case claimed that their children would be corrupted by exposure to beliefs and values that contradict their own religious views unless it was explained that the other views are incorrect and that their views are the correct ones. Democratic education is surely incompatible with this fundamentalist view of knowledge and morality.

Not because democratic education rests on a conception of the good society that threatens the fundamentalist view of a good life and must defer to fundamentalism for the sake of neutrality. Any defensible political understanding of education depends on some conception of a good society, and every conception worth defending threatens some way of life. It is a sad fact of democracy in the United States that some citizens still hold religious beliefs that reject teaching children the democratic values of mutual respect for reasonable differences of opinion and rational deliberation among differing ways of life. A rejection of democratic values does not, however, constitute a criticism of democracy any more than the rejection by a committed misogynist of the rights of women constitutes a critique of feminism. Both the parents and the misogynists of course have a right to voice their opinions, but in neither case do they have a right to insist that a democratic state teach or sanction their opinions.

Another argument sometimes offered in defense of the claims of fundamentalist parents is that democratic education consists solely of teaching certain facts, not certain values or virtues, to future citizens. This position is superficially similar to John Stuart Mill's conclusion that the state limit its educational authority to public examinations "confined to facts and positive science exclusively."[9] If this is what we should say about public education, it cannot be because knowing facts is more crucial to a good life or good citizenship than being virtuous. Nor can it be because facts are neutral, while values are not. Might it be because citizens can more easily agree on a body of facts than on a set of values or virtues to be taught to all children? Perhaps this argument was soundly prudential when Mill made it, but its premise is surely very shaky today. The political controversies that have raged in recent years over the biases of testing and the claims of creationism against evolution amply demonstrate how controversial the teaching and testing of facts can be. This is no more or less controversial, however, than the teaching (or not teaching) of civic virtue. If it is political controversy that we wish the state above all else to avoid, our only alternative is to advocate repression, in its most thoroughgoing and insidious form.

Neither Discrimination nor Repression

There is no defensible political understanding of education that is not tied
to some conception of a good society, and there is no conception that is not
controversial. Which conception should we therefore defend? Judge Hull
hinted at a conception of liberal neutrality: Secular texts must not be imposed
on fundamentalist children because they are not neutral among all competing
conceptions of the good life. The Holt, Rinehart readers surely are not neutral
between fundamentalist Christianity and secular humanism. Nor, as Judge Hull
recognized, could any readers be neutral between deference to God's will as
literally revealed in the Bible or authoritatively interpreted by a fundamentalist
church, and critical inquiry or mutual respect among persons. Liberal individ-
ualists think of themselves as committed only to the latter set of virtues – critical
inquiry and mutual respect – but the logic of liberal neutrality does not support
their commitment in politics, except as a morally lame expression of personal
opinion. This expression is insufficient to justify any form of public schooling.
The content of public schooling cannot be neutral among competing conceptions of the good life, and if it could, we would not and should not care to support
it.

It is not for us to deny fundamentalist parents the right to draw the wrong
line for their children in their homes and churches. Parental freedom entails this
limited right.[10] It *is* for us to say that parents do not have a right to veto a line
drawn by public schools unless that line is repressive or discriminatory. If
parents, judges, or philosopher-kings are allowed to veto lines drawn by public
schools when those lines are neither repressive nor discriminatory, then democratic institutions are denied their legitimate role in shaping the character of
citizens.

Is democracy not also repressive if it denies the teaching of Christian
fundamentalist convictions within public schools, or, what amounts to the same
thing, if it requires the teaching of views inimical to fundamentalist convictions? This challenge to democratic education rests on a serious misunderstanding: that a policy is repressive simply because it requires publicly funded or
subsidized schools to teach views that are inimical to the sincerely held beliefs
of some parents. Nonrepression requires the prevention of repressive practices,
that is, practices that stifle rational understanding and inquiry. It is a *reductio
ad absurdum* to claim that preventing such prevention itself constitutes repression.

To defend public schools against the charge of repression by fundamentalist parents does not, however, entail defending the status quo in American

public education – far from it. We must criticize schools that fall short of the democratic ideal by, for example, being overly centralized and bureaucratized, and therefore unconducive to the exercise of both democratic deliberation by citizens and democratic professionalism by teachers. (Simply summarized, democratic professionalism authorizes teachers, at the same time that it obligates them, to uphold the principle of nonrepression, for example, by cultivating in future citizens the capacity for critical reflection on their culture. The ideal of democratic professionalism also obligates public officials to create the working conditions that make possible the exercise of democratic professionalism.) These comments can only begin to touch on the problems that plague our schools, judged from the perspective of a democratic ideal of education.

A democratic society cedes to citizens, parents, teachers, and public officials authority over education, but that authority is limited by the very democratic ideal that supports it. Not even an overwhelming majority has the authority to maintain separate schools for blacks, to ban sex education from schools, to teach creationism as science, or to ban politically unpopular books from school libraries. The first two practices are discriminatory, the second two are repressive. The defense of these judgments concerning our educational practices requires interpretation and application of the democratic standards of nonrepression and nondiscrimination. Because the standards are not merely formal, there is no way of mechanically applying them to cases. We cannot, for example, simply ask whether teaching evolution (or creationism) conflicts with some parents' convictions and if it does, conclude that the practice is repressive. The test of nonrepression and nondiscrimination is not popularity among citizens, parents, teachers, or public officials. Repression entails restriction of rational inquiry, not conflict with personal beliefs, however deeply held those beliefs. For every educational practice or institution, we must therefore ask whether the practice or institution in its actual context restricts (or impedes) rational inquiry and therefore is repressive, or whether it excludes some children from educational goods for reasons unrelated to the legitimate social purposes of those goods and therefore is discriminatory.

Some judgments will be relatively easy: Forcing teachers to teach creationism instead of evolution restricts rational inquiry for the sake of furthering sectarian religion and therefore is repressive. Other judgments require more extended argument: Is it repressive to teach evolution but to require equal time for creationism? If equal time for creationism entails teaching that it is as reasonable to believe that the world with all its creatures was created in seven days as it is to believe that it took *much* longer, then the demand for equal time is indirectly repressive: It undermines the secular standards of reasoning that make democratic education possible in this country. If public schools are permitted to teach the reasonableness of creationism, then the same principle will allow them to teach the reasonableness of divine punishment for the sins of non-Christians or any other minority that happens not to control the school curriculum. On the other hand, if teachers may subject creationist ideas to the same standards of reasoning to which other views presented in their classrooms are subjected, then the demand for equal time may be benign – or even conducive to democratic education. Of course, this is not the interpretation of equal time that proponents of creationism have in mind.

Education and Politics

Democratic standards often do not yield either simple or single answers to questions – such as how much money schools should allocate for educating the handicapped, the gifted, and the average student. That democratic standards do not yield simple answers is a necessity, given the complexity of our collective life; that they do not yield single answers is a virtue, which underscores the democratic critique of "the one best system." Democracy is valuable for far more than its capacity to achieve correct outcomes. It is also valuable for enabling societies to govern themselves, rather than to be governed by an intelligence unrelated to their nature. If democratic societies are to be self-governing, they must remain free to make mistakes in educating children, so long as those mistakes do not discriminate against some children or prevent others from governing themselves freely in the future. The promise of a democratic education is to support self-government without sanctioning majority tyranny or sacrificing future self-government.

It is not for me to say whether my theoretical understanding of democratic education fulfils this promise, but I am sure that the practical promise of any decent theory of democratic education is far from fulfilled in the United States today. I believe that the burden of a democratic theory of education is to show how, with the proper will, we could restructure American society to approach the democratic ideal, even if we never realize it entirely. As a democrat, the most I can consistently offer is criticism of our dominant educational ideas and institutions, and constructive suggestions for democratic directions of change. The possibility of constructive change depends on the will of those who wield political and economic power in this country. In a better society, that will would be more democratic.

These are therefore difficult times for democratic education not only because we are difficult people who must find a principled way of accommodating both individual freedom and civic virtue, but also (and as importantly) because our political and economic institutions are so far from being democratic that they discriminate against the very people who would benefit most directly from a more democratic education and therefore would be most likely to support it. Democratic education is unlikely to succeed if these institutions remain significantly undemocratic. We cannot conclude from this that political or economic reform must precede educational reform. Our choices are not so stark, nor so easy. To improve significantly the working conditions, the political opportunities, or the schooling of poor Americans requires political pressure from the poor themselves, yet they are the citizens most likely to have been educated in highly authoritarian schools (and families) and least likely to participate in politics (or to be effective when they do).

To realize democratic education in this country, political and economic institutions must become more democratic. For these institutions to become more democratic, education must be democratized. It would be foolish to focus solely on a single sphere, whether politics, economics, or education: first, because the prospects of success in any sphere are limited, and second, because the spheres are interdependent. Small but significant changes in one often bring small but significant changes in the others.

Democratic education does not simplify our outlook on education, but it reorients it away from conventional goals (such as educating every child for the appropriate occupation or for choice among the widest range of occupations) toward a more political understanding of educational ends. The cultivation of the virtues, knowledge, and skills necessary for democratic deliberation should have primacy over other ends of public education in a democratic society because such political education prepares citizens to share as equals in *consciously* reproducing (not replicating) their own society, rather than being subject to external forces of reproduction beyond their collective control. Conscious social reproduction is the ideal not only of democratic education but of democratic politics as well.

At the level of primary schooling, the primacy of political education supplies a principled argument against tracking, sexist education, racial segregation, and narrowly vocational education. Even when these practices improve the academic achievement of students, they neglect the virtues of citizenship, cultivated by a common education characterized by respect for racial, religious, intellectual, and sexual differences among students. The moral primacy of political education also supports a presumption in favor of more participatory and deliberative over more disciplinary methods of teaching. Even when student participation threatens to produce some degree of disorder within schools, it may be defended on democratic grounds for cultivating political skills and social commitments. Conversely, even when a principal succeeds in bringing order to an unruly student body, as has Joe Clark of Eastside High School in Paterson, New Jersey, he may be criticized on democratic grounds for intimidating students rather than reasoning with them, for not tolerating peaceful dissent among teachers, and for expelling problem students in unprecedented numbers (over a three-year period, more than 1 900 students dropped out of Eastside High, many of them expelled by Clark).

Democratic education aims at the empowerment of free and equal citizens, people who are willing and able to share together in shaping their own society. Democratic education therefore constrains public policies by the principles of nonrepression and nondiscrimination for the sake of securing democratic self-government. Within these constraints, democratic education makes a virtue out of the disagreements that inevitably flow from ethnic, religious, sexual, and intellectual diversity.

Above all, democratic education accepts the fact that we are difficult people. Whereas the Platonic family state denies this fact by subsuming individual freedom into civic virtue and the state of individuals denies it by elevating freedom above virtue, democratic education empowers citizens to make their own decisions on how to combine freedom with virtue. Democratic education thereby authorizes people to direct their individual and collective destinies. Fully recognizing that the aims of democratic education may never be fully realized, difficult people should demand no more of our political and educational institutions, and should settle for no less.

Notes

[1] Allan Bloom, *The Closing of the American Mind* (New York: Simon & Schuster, 1987), 238.

[2] Socrates, *Republic of Plato*, trans. Allan Bloom (New York: Basic Books, 1968), 273 (590D).

[3] Ibid., 220 (541A).

[4] Ibid., 274 (592A).

[5] Bruce Ackerman, *Social Justice in the Liberal State* (New Haven: Yale University Press, 1980), 148.

[6] Ibid., 139.

[7] Immanuel Kant, *Kant on Education*, trans. Annette Churton (Boston: D.C. Heath, 1900), 17.

[8] *Bob Mozert et al. v. Hawkins County Public Schools et al.*, U.S. District Court for the Eastern District of Tennessee, Northeastern Division, No. CIV-2-83-401 (October 24,1986), 12. The United States Court of Appeals (Sixth Circuit) reversed the decision of the district court and remanded with directions to dismiss the complaint (827 F. 2d. 1058 [6th Cir. 1987]).

[9] John Stuart Mill, "On Liberty" in *Utilitarianism, On Liberty, Essays on Bentham* (New York: New American Library, 1962), 241.

[10] The right is limited not by virtue of being weak, but by virtue of leaving room for other educational authorities.

21

Shared Values, Particular Values, and Education for a Multicultural Society

Basil R. Singh

> Equal recognition is not just the appropriate mode for a healthy democratic society. Its refusal can inflict damage on those who are denied it . . . The projection of an inferior or demeaning image on another can actually distort and oppress, to the extent that the image is internalized . . . the withholding of recognition can be a form of oppression.[1]

It is the purpose of this essay to locate the concept of multicultural education within a broader concept of education and more importantly within a liberal democratic value perspective that we all share and which allows for equal recognition of personal worth and personal dignity. The essay thus attempts to shift the debate surrounding multicultural education away from basing it on the existence of multiracial, multicultural groups and their cultures towards a discussion focusing on the liberal democratic value perspective and its consequences for education and human dignity. The essay argues that from a liberal democratic value perspective, one cannot reject or fail to give recognition to the existence of the plurality of value perspectives – many of which may derive from various cultures – without being inconsistent in terms of such a value perspective, which allows for equal recognition.

From a liberal democratic political perspective a person's ethnic identity is not seen as the foundation of equal value. Equal recognition, as argued below, is due to individuals by virtue of their humanity and human potential as rational beings. Thus, the presumption of equal recognition is seen as an underlying moral principle in a liberal democratic state. As a fighting creed, liberalism is underlined by its commitments to freedom, rights, autonomy, rationality, and the dignity of the individual. It is within this latter perspective that the paper attempts to locate multicultural education which is seen in terms of cultural development rather than cultural maintenance.

In most democratic societies today some of the values we all share would include parliamentary democracy, the concept of freedom of speech and assembly, the independence of the judiciary, respect for persons, economic pluralism whereby individuals can advance themselves according to merit, the right to an occupation, the right to advance oneself according to merit and a commitment to learning and speaking the English language as a basic value for all British subjects. Although some of these shared values originate in the heritage of the majority culture, they ultimately become the property of all groups.[2] Such values are acceptable to all minority groups especially when these groups perceive them to be administered in a fair and non-discriminatory manner. In the absence of such discrimination these values could serve as a cementing agent in a plural, multicultural society. Granting all these, then it would seem that cultural pluralism and diverse ethnicity are not necessarily incompatible with the idea of common values mentioned above. The values we all share provide the basis of coexistence whereby various groups live side by side in an atmosphere of tolerance and mutual benefit. This is what liberalism – the underlying principle of democracy – allows.

Liberal Democratic Values and Cultural Pluralism

It is the assumption of this essay that a liberal democratic value which provides a cohesive vision of justice, and freedom of speech and assembly, also provides room for tolerance of significant value differences. Such a democratic value will allow individuals to flourish in a mobile multicultural society and will not underestimate the need of people as members of discrete ethnic, linguistic, and other cultural groups for public recognition. As the underlying value of a democratic state, liberalism does not accept moral absolutes, nor does it accept a fixed hierarchy of values. In accordance with democratic liberalism, no idea of the good life is above criticism. This is not to imply, however, that democratic liberalism leads to directionless relativism where every opinion or view of life is as good as any other. For one thing, and according to Rockefeller,[3] the democratic way conflicts with any idea of, or absolute right, to cultural survival. The democratic way means respect for and openness to all cultures, but it also challenges all cultures to abandon all those values that are inconsistent with the ideals of freedom, equality, and the ongoing cooperative experimental search for truth and well being. It is a creative method of transformation. It facilitates a cross-cultural dialog that transforms human understanding, leading to a "fusion of horizons." It does not allow the preservation of a culture at the expense of individual freedom and equality.[4]

Furthermore, from a "liberal democratic political perspective," a person's ethnic identity is not his or her primary identity and important as respect for diversity is in multicultural democratic societies, ethnic identity is not the foundation of recognition of equal value and the related idea of equal rights. This notion accords well with the notion of human rights declared by the United Nations in 1948. According to this latter notion all people are bearers of human rights, human value, and human dignity, and consequently, all deserve equal respect and equal opportunity for self-realization.[5] Thus, from the perspectives of a liberal democratic state and of human rights, each person has the right to claim equal recognition first and foremost on his or her universal human dignity and human potential as a rational being as well as on the basis of his or her ethnic identity. While our universal identity as human beings is our primary identity, our gender, race or ethnic origin is our particular identity.[6]

Granting what has been said in relation to moral absolutes, fixed hierarchy of values and cultural survival, then it will follow that in a liberal democratic, pluralist society, we would be more concerned about cultural development rather than with cultural maintenance. Cultural development would mean that no culture would be allowed to become fossilized within its core boundary, nor should be seen as a static phenomenon, since, as Smolicz[7] argues, a tradition must be continually reshaped and revalued if it is to meet the changing situation of the group and if it is to survive as a tradition in a changing technological world.

The question we are then faced with is: if a culture is to change and adapt to changing circumstances in order to survive, how is it to do so? How is its core value (to be discussed below), which is integral to the preservation of a culture, to be preserved? In the midst of competing views of the good life, is it through its language, religion, customs or way of life? And what is to be preserved if the identity of a cultural group is to be preserved? These are some of the fundamental questions that teachers, educators, and community leaders must face if they are to prepare students for a multicultural, multiracial, democratic, liberal society.

On Culture

It is not the intention of this essay to engage in a deep analysis of the concept of culture and its relationship to youth culture, but to provide a preliminary sketch of the concept of culture which is directly relevant to the main issues of the essay, namely shared values and particular values as related to the majority and minority groups within this society. However, the essay acknowledges that the group to which an individual belongs – whether these be sub-groups, minority or majority groups – bears an influence on the speed and direction of social behavior and social change. How much the individual is influenced by the group will, according to R. Boudon and F. Bourricaud, depend on the "quality of the relationship between members, the intensity of fusion which is established between themselves or, on the contrary, the distance that separates them, the duration and continuity or discontinuity of their contacts . . ."[8]

Culture in its broadest definition, refers to that part of the total repertoire of human action (and its products) which is socially, as opposed to genetically transmitted.[9] This complex whole, according to E.B. Taylor, "includes knowledge, beliefs, art, morals, law, custom and any other capabilities and habits acquired by man (sic) as a member of society."[10]

Similarly in their well known extensive survey and critical review of the relevant literature on culture, A.L. Kroeber and C. Kluckhohn defined culture as:

> ...patterns, explicit and implicit, of and for behavior acquired and transmitted by symbols, constituting the distinctive achievement of human groups, including their embodiments in artifacts; the essential core of culture consists of traditional (i.e. historically derived and selected) ideas and especially their attached values; culture systems may, on the one hand, be considered as products of action, on the other as conditioning elements of further action.[11]

For Kroeber and Kluckhohn, culture cannot be reduced merely to human behavior. For "part of culture consists in norms for, or standards of, behavior ... part consists in ideologies justifying or rationalizing certain selected ways of behavior."[12]

Others such as R. Firth see culture as a "way of life." According to Firth, "if society is taken to be an aggregate of social relations, then culture is the content of those relations ... Culture emphasises the component of accumulated resources, immaterial as well as material, which people inherit, employ, transmute, add to, and transmit."[13] In this sense culture could be seen as learned ways of thinking, feeling and acting which are transmitted from person to person and from one generation to the next. It would certainly consist of language, "concepts," "models" which people have in their minds for organizing and interpreting their experiences and the world.

As a distinctive "way of life," culture "determines" the ideas of normality and deviance which are relative to particular cultures. Indeed, the essential core of a culture consists of traditional ideas and especially their attached values.[14] Thus culture could be understood as the fundamental value system of a society.[15] It is within this value system that the socialization of individuals takes place. To say this is not to imply that culture is a "unitary" phenomenon. For except perhaps in the case of the most simple societies, the totalistic or holistic conception with which all the members of a society would concur in a single culture, that is, in a common value system, represents an extreme over-simplification.[16] For according to Boudon and Bourricaud socialization must be seen both as a process of interiorization and as a process of adaptation to changing and varying situations. This process is characterised by impositions, compromises and self-interests. Thus, "values and attitudes interiorised by the individual must thus be seen as parameters rather than as determinants of action."[17]

Subculture

Subculture could be seen as a system of values, attitudes, modes of behavior, and lifestyles of a social group which is distinct from, but related to, the dominant culture of a society. In most societies there is a great diversity of such subcultures. It is not often possible to determine the causes of such subcultures. Although the concept does imply the existence of an identifiable dominant culture, the fragmentation of contemporary culture makes the identification of such a common or dominant culture problematic.[18]

Youth Culture

While youth culture can be discussed as a general phenomenon, there is obviously a range of different specific youth cultures, differentiated by gender, class or ethnicity that adopt different styles. Some of these youth cultures may have their own rules of behavior which may run counter to the rules of behavior of the dominant group.[19] As a consequence, youth culture may be treated as deviant and may be seen as expressing an opposition to the dominant culture. Thus because youth culture is usually organized around leisure, lifestyles and around a peer-group with their own tastes in clothes and music, for example, youth culture will not form part of the discussion of this essay on shared and particular values relating to majority and minority ethnic groups. Of course youth culture is not a uniform culture but is divided by gender and ethnicity, as well as by class and education and by a myriad of competing cultural styles.[20]

On Core Values and Cultural Preservation

According to Smolicz, "whenever people feel that there is a direct link between their identity as a group and what they regard as the most crucial and distinguishing element of their culture, the element concerned becomes a core value for the group."[21] Every culture according to Smolicz has certain core elements which represent its heartland and act as identifying values for its members. While for most cultures this core value is represented by the native or mother tongue, in other cultures, at least at the present time, the core element is primarily located in religion (as in the Jewish, Irish, or Malay groups), family network (Italian), or clan or race (Chinese). Language, of course, plays a part in the existence of core values of many cultures. Perhaps, because of the various elements comprising the core of a culture, one should speak of many core values rather than a single value alone. Whatever the core elements of a culture, one thing is clear and that is that no culture and hence no core value can be assumed to be static, as we argued above. A tradition must be continually re-shaped and revalued to meet the changing situation of the group, if it is to survive as a tradition in the modern world.

Language as a Core Element in the Literary Culture of an Ethnic Group

Language is a means by which ethnic minorities identify themselves. As H. Giles and Saint-Jacques put it, "Language is not merely a medium of communication . . . but a unifying factor of a particular culture and often a prerequisite for its survival . . . No other factor is as powerful as language in maintaining by itself the genuine and lasting distinctiveness of an ethnic group."[22] Thus, the claim of the essay is, that in the case of a language-centred culture, the elimination of the native tongue through its gradual reduction to a non-literary domestic form leaves the gate open to the disintegration of the culture to an ethnic residue. Smolicz maintains that a loss of literacy in a minority language, for instance, may follow an absence of intellectual vitality that is necessary for the maintenance and development of the core elements of a culture. Thus, according to Smolicz, even a strongly supported ethnic home may not be sufficient to ensure the transmission of an ethnic literary heritage. In order to preserve the core elements of such heritage we may have to teach them at schools and colleges. Introducing such core elements of a culture in educational institutions would provide students with the opportunity to make use of more than one culture in their everyday lives, be it language, social manners, culture – literature or art. The languages and cultures available for study at the secondary level, for instance, should be seen as societal languages and cultures which have living individuals in the community and often in the classroom.[23]

Equal Recognition and Identity

Identity, as Charles Taylor sees it, designates something like a person's understanding of who they are, of their fundamental defining characteristics as human beings. Taylor argues that: "Our identity is partly shaped by recognition or its absence, often by misrecognition of others, and so a person or a group of people can suffer real damage, real distortion, if the people or society around them mirror back to them a confining or demeaning or contemptible picture of themselves. Nonrecognition or misrecognition can inflict harm, can be a form of oppression, imprisoning someone in a false, distorted and reduced mode of being."[24] If withholding of recognition and more importantly, if withholding the presumption of equal worth of all cultures, is tantamount to a denial of equality and if important consequences flow from people's identity from the absence of recognition, then a case can be made for insisting on the universalization of the presumption as a logical extension of the notion of dignity. Just as all must have equal civil rights and equal voting rights regardless of race or culture, so all should enjoy the presumption that their traditional culture has value. This, according to Taylor, is in accordance with the norm of equal dignity.[25]

A Democratic Society, Collective Goals and Individual Rights

According to Taylor, a society with strong collective goals can be liberal, provided it is also capable of respecting diversity, especially when dealing with those who do not share its common goals, and provided it can offer adequate safeguards for fundamental rights. There will undoubtedly be tensions and difficulties in pursuing these rights or objectives together, but such a pursuit is not impossible and the problems are not in principle greater than those encountered by any liberal society that has to combine, for example, liberty and equality, or prosperity and justice.[26] Consequently, a liberal democratic society may sometimes have to weigh the importance of certain forms of uniform treatment for all individuals within the liberal political framework against the importance of cultural survival and perhaps opt sometimes in favor of the latter. This is not to assume, however, that the society or the state acting on behalf of society, makes a once-and-for-all choice, but that it adopts policies that fit the circumstances. The question will still remain, of course, when does the state choose this way or that way? What circumstances would allow the state to come down on one side rather than another? These are difficult questions to answer, and they are well beyond the scope of this essay. However, one thing seems clear, and that is that the state cannot with justification, within a liberal democratic framework, ban one culture or religion for the preservation of another. It cannot use one culture or religion as a means to the end of preserving another if it abides by the principle of equal recognition and equal dignity referred to above. The presumption of equal recognition is seen here as an underlying moral principle in a liberal democratic state. Within such a state all cultures will be respected and ethnic identities will not be repressed. All ethnic groups will be encouraged to develop their cultural traditions within the liberal democratic ideals of freedom, equality of opportunity, justice before the law, etc. Over a period of time, one may expect to see major cultural transformations for the good of all. All cultures, as we have argued above, can undergo significant intellectual, social, moral, and religious changes, while maintaining continuity with the past.[27]

There is a great deal of fear and resistance, especially among conservative members in most liberal democratic societies to support of any kind of multicultural education or elements of ethnic minority cultures. But such fear is rather groundless. For there is no evidence to show, and certainly recent events around the world have not shown, that elimination or attempts to eliminate ethnic core values will guarantee greater social harmony, greater identification with the society, nor greater equality in the evaluation of minority groups. Smolicz argues that the fading significance of ethnic cultures merely serves to stimulate social discontent that could have implications for the functioning of the whole society. A lack of recognition of ethnic cultures by the state and by educational institutions could serve as a justification for discriminating against those cultures and the individuals who share those cultures.

In spite of the need for equal recognition of all cultures, greater stress must be placed on the development of an ethnic culture, rather than simply on its maintenance, which means that an ethnic culture would not become fossilized within its core boundary. Nevertheless, as Smolicz warns us, "[e]thnic cultures must change in order to survive, but the change must be at their own pace . . ."[28] Cultures in a minority setting, according to Smolicz, are often more conservative than in their homeland, since their members are so preoccupied with the importance of preservation, that any radical alteration may be interpreted as a prelude to assimilation. Such a model stresses both the preservation of ethnic cultures and their adjustment to the overarching values of society as a whole.[29]

On Multiculturalism as an Overarching Value

Multiculturalism can itself become and serve as an overarching value. However, without the acceptance of cultural diversity as a shared value by the majority group, and by society as a whole, there can be no multicultural society. Instead, the way is left open for the pitfalls of assimilation or separation.

As an overarching principle multiculturalism would not be concerned merely or essentially with cultural maintenance. For cultures decay and hence it is not sufficient for a culture to survive in its original form to satisfy the dual aspects of multiculturalism, namely universal primary identity and particular identity. A culture could be seen as a living organism which interacts with other organisms and with its environment. In this process of interaction, it changes and causes other organisms to change. Thus no culture must be sealed off from others, but must be open to allow adaptation and development to take place.

Choosing From Available Cultural Options

As long as ethnic cultural variation continues to exist, individuals will be able to draw upon more than one cultural model in the construction of their personal cultural worlds. In this way the cultural and social life of the country will be enriched, as individuals can choose from a number of cultural options. Cultural co-existence could produce a dual system of values. In other forms of interaction some "blend" or in-between position may be achieved in personal lifestyles as individuals draw upon family traditions and extended networks of primary relations on the one hand, and on the Anglo-Saxon ideal of individualism, self-reliance, independence, and personal autonomy on the other.[30]

So in a pluralist, liberal democratic society children should be allowed to make an informed choice between alternative activities and ways of life. This would demand that they be introduced to a range of possibilities. A public education or common schooling seems to offer the best possibility that a range of competing conceptions of the good life will be offered to all children. If a child's interest could best be served by introducing the child to a range of possibilities of the good life, if the child needs to be introduced and to become aware of the diversity of beliefs and lifestyles that exist in the world and to develop a capacity to make rational informed choices between alternatives[31] then the fundamental questions are: what kind of (education) curriculum should the child be exposed to and what principles should guide the construction of such a curriculum? The *International Covenant on Civil And Political Rights* offers some, but not sufficient, guide to these questions.[32] Article 27 acknowledges the right to the development of one's culture. This includes the right to an equal education, the right to participate in the cultural life of the society, and the right of minorities to enjoy their own culture, to profess and practice their own religion or to use their own language. We should note, from the outset, the provision of the various documents offers a guarantee of the multicultural development of every child and freedom from discrimination on the basis of the child's culture. The right to multicultural development can be distinguished from the right to freedom from discrimination in that it focuses on cultural and linguistic retention, preservation or development in a pluralistic framework rather than on some of the more negative consequences of interaction between cultural groups.

In recent years, multicultural education in many parts of the world has taken on an additional central focus on the elimination of prejudice and discrimination.[33] Its other main focus has been to influence public opinion by promoting awareness and acceptance of diversity.

A right to education as recommended by the United Nations Charters could be seen as a right to multicultural education, which in this context means a positive promotion of the benefits of the multicultural ways of living with its tenets of sharing, inter-cultural understanding, and equal access to the opportunity structure of society. The presumption behind these and other recommendations is that the best interest of the (normal) child could be served by attending a common school and exposure to a multicultural curriculum. Some see this as an absolute requirement if the child is to be given the choice to choose from competing views of the good life.

B. Parekh supports this view and points out that if children never get beyond the framework of their own culture and beliefs (even if these are shared by the majority in their country) they are unlikely to develop lively enquiring minds, imagination or a critical faculty.[34] A monocultural diet is likely to breed "arrogance and insensitivity" among children from the majority culture and "profound self-alienation" and a distorted self-concept among minority children.[35] Multicultural education, according to Parekh, is "an education in freedom – freedom from inherited biases and narrow feelings and sentiments, as well as freedom to explore other cultures and perspectives and make choices in full awareness of the available and practical alternatives."[36]

Education For All

So it would seem from what has been said above that the major question facing educators today is: in the midst of conflicting values perspectives of the various groups in a pluralist society, how are the contents of this multicultural curriculum to be selected to ensure justice for all? How is the process of constructing such a curriculum to be guided and what framework should it adopt? In Britain, *The Swann Report,* appropriately entitled "Education for All," offers some useful guidelines as to what curriculum developers should take into account when embarking on such a task.[37] In the section on "Pluralism in The Nature of Society," *The Swann Report* begins:

> We consider that a multi-racial society such as ours would in fact function most effectively and harmoniously on the basis of pluralism which enables, expects and encourages members of all ethnic groups, both minority and majority, to participate fully in shaping the society as a whole within the framework of commonly accepted values, practices and procedures whilst also allowing, and where necessary, assisting the ethnic minority communities in maintaining their distinct ethnic identities within this common framework.[38]

By a common framework the Report means accepted values, practices, and procedures which transcend, but are compatible with, the separate cultural groupings that make up a pluralist society. The aim is to create "unity in diversity," or a "socially cohesive" but "culturally diverse" society.[39] Parekh, in recognizing the right of a society to preserve its cherished values and essential aspects of its culture, argues, in relation to British society, that it " . . . like any other society, has a certain definite conception of the good life to which its members subscribe and which influences the way they live . . . it is entitled to insist that everyone of its members, immigrant as well as native must conform to . . . those basic minimal values . . . that it regards as constitutive of its conception of the good life."[40]

So, according to Parekh, the curriculum developer must take account of the "basic minimum values" that a society regards as constitutive of its conception of the good life. Perhaps inclusive in this minimum would be a commitment to democracy, freedom of speech and of assembly, respect for persons and individual autonomy. Within these acceptable minimum values, *The Swann Report* recommends that in a pluralist society there should be freedom for the members of minority groups to maintain their distinctive cultures and lifestyles, since assimilation unjustly seeks to deny fundamental freedoms of individuals to differ in areas "where no single way can be justifiably be presented as universally appropriate,"[41] but this freedom is subject to two major constraints: first, priority must be given to taking on "the shared values of the wider pluralist society" (for without these there would be the danger that the society would fragment along ethnic lines) and this would "seriously threaten the stability and cohesion of society as a whole"[42]; and secondly, the group's authority and control over the individual is constrained by the requirement of "free choice for individuals."

The Task of Education

Following from what has been said above, it would seem that one of the tasks of education is to build bridges, with the aim of strengthening and developing the overarching values, without at the same time obliterating the intrinsic cultural features of either the majority or the minorities. Hence the overarching framework has to develop in harmony with the core values of all ethnic groups.[43]

Some general aims of education arising from such concerns will include learning to think rigorously and creatively, to develop a rational and open mind about the educational value of various cultural contributions to the curriculum. Similarly we must understand ourselves, others, our history, our environment, our community, our language, and our political system. These have always been goals whose justification and value have not been disputed.[44] However, controversy does arise when it comes to selecting curriculum content. If we can agree as to the quality of mind and character we ought to develop, then we may be in a position to ask what content or teaching methods would be most appropriate for achieving the agreed objectives. There will still be dispute about the most appropriate content or about the best method, but we would have gone a long way in narrowing down our focus.

In the field of literature, for instance, some works by writers such as Shakespeare may transcend cultural boundaries and his works may be important in defining and shaping our literary and dramatic traditions. Consequently, in the case of Shakespeare there may not be a question of choosing, for including Shakespeare in the curriculum seems to make good educational sense. But as Wolf points out, there are other reasons for including other works of literature drawn from writers of the other sex, or other races or cultures.[45] In addition to the intellectual and aesthetic reasons for including the works of a particular writer in the curriculum, there is a need for a conscientious recognition of cultural diversity, for justice and respect for others. It may be that while present day women writers may strike a deeper cord with women students, writers from ethnic minority backgrounds may appeal more to the deeper emotions and sensitivity of ethnic minority students.

Including Other Cultures in the Curriculum

There is nothing wrong in having an interest in one's culture or history or in the culture and history of one's friends or relatives. For according to Wolf, having a special communal interest in one's own communal culture and one's own communal history is part of what keeps the communal culture alive, part of what creates, reforms, and sustains that culture. However, since our communities are composed of people of many cultures, a curriculum that is committed to the study of a community's culture, must recognize the existence of the many cultures that characterize that community. Our curriculum would, therefore, reflect a multiculture. In the context of a multicultural, multiracial society, in failing to respect the existence or the importance of the distinctive histories, arts, and traditions of ethnic minorities, we fail to respect them as equals, whose interests and values have equal standing in our community.[46]

The curriculum should include, therefore, books expressing and illustrating traditions and legends to which (ethnic minority) children are more closely tied and books in which the characters look and speak more like them and their parents and grandparents themselves. Having these books and reading them, we may come to recognize ourselves as a multicultural community and so recognize and respect the members of that community in all our diversity.

The presumption that all cultures are of equal worth is by no means unproblematic and according to C. Taylor "involves something like an act of faith."[47] Taylor adds that as a presumption, the claim is that all human cultures that have animated whole societies over some considerable stretch of time have something to say to all human beings. But for Taylor "every culture can go through phases of decadence."[48]

Conclusion

This essay recognizes two types of identity. The first is the individual primary or universal identity which is due to the individual by virtue of his or her humanity and the second is the individual particular identity belonging to the individual by virtue of his or her gender, race, or ethnicity. Our main social and educational concern therefore, should be to synthesize these two identities in the lives of all individuals. How this is to be done is still unclear at the present time. Perhaps the search for a common framework that spans various cultural values would help us to find a method by which we could synthesise these two identities in the lives of every student.

Although this essay rejects the notion of moral absolutes, it does not support a directionless relativism. It sees liberalism "as a fighting creed"[49] underlined by certain commitments to freedom, rights, autonomy, rationality, and the dignity of the individual. I have argued that there is a close relationship between democratic liberal values and equal recognition of persons and that in certain circumstances, a denial of equal recognition could constitute a form of oppression especially when such a denial leads to the demeaning of ethnic cultural identity. Moreover the very survival of these groups may well depend on the survival of the core elements of their culture. In some cases the core element may be language or religion, while in others it may be the family or their way of life.

Although the essay recognizes the need for cultural survival, its main emphasis is upon cultural development, individual freedom, dignity and identity. The notion of cultural development we are assuming here is antithetical to cultural fossilization. Cultural development implies cultural adaptation to changing circumstances. Cultural adaptation is important for cultural survival especially in the modern technological world.

In a language-centred (core element of a) culture, efforts should be made, especially at the educational institutional level, to preserve the language element of the core of the culture of an ethnic group. Since the literary heritage of a culture cannot be preserved by the home alone, it is imperative that educational institutions take on this task. To do this attention must be given to multicultural education as outlined above.

This essay argues that retention of certain elements and development of ethnic cultures are generally perfectly compatible with the existence and acceptance of shared values for the whole society. Granting that there are shared values, it is important that these values are accepted as belonging to all groups who should regard them as their common cultural inheritance.[50] It is also vital that these values be transmitted through schools and colleges and that they continue to be shared and activated by all groups and individuals.

Our main educational concerns, therefore, are seen as transmitting shared values as well as with transmitting the core values of all groups within the social matrix that is dynamic and is consequently capable of change.[51] Smolicz calls this type of transmission of core values of groups a viable and developing pluralism, which according to him would remain a sterile notion unless it is seen to permeate the lives of individuals from all groups in society.

In a liberal democratic pluralist state conflicts of values will arise between values relating to universal primary identity and those relating to particularistic cultural identity and sometimes, depending on the circumstances, the state may have to come down on one side or the other. Within such a state, there will also be competing views of the good life, and the state should therefore create conditions whereby individuals are free to choose from the available options. In a pluralist democratic society there will always be tensions between the public interest, the interests of groups and the interests of individuals. When these interests conflict, I contend that the rights and the development of the rational autonomy of the individual should take precedence over the interests of particular groups. Thus, the conditions the state creates should be influenced by considerations relating to the best interest of the individual growing up within a pluralistic liberal democratic state with its commitment to freedom, justice, fairness, and the development of the rational autonomy of the individual, for example the child. Although there is no general consensus about the best interest of the child, most liberals would want to say that at least one thing, the development of personal and moral autonomy, is in the general interest of all children.[52] This judgment is based on the claim that children have a right to certain "primary goods," among which would be an education designed to give them a knowledge of competing conceptions of the good life and to develop their capacity to choose freely and rationally between them.[53] Primary goods are goods which rational people want whatever else they may want such as rights and liberties, opportunities and powers, and self-respect.

In saying that the state would have to make choices in favor of the individual, one is not implying that such choices would be easy. For where there is a conflict of values, there is no overarching, universally acceptable principle, no single argument, experiment, or body of evidence available that would satisfy everyone.

Nevertheless, there are certain "basic minimum values" that in a democratic state could be regarded as constitutive of the "good life." Inclusive in this minimum would be a commitment to democracy, freedom of speech, and of assembly, respect for persons, and individual autonomy. Within this minimum there would be freedom for members of minority groups, for instance, to maintain their distinctive cultures and lifestyles. The essay argues that a common school would be more likely to offer a range of options available to students than a separate school based on, for example, religion or culture. In this sense a common school – a school where children from all sexes, races, or cultures can attend – would be more likely to meet the best interest of students growing up in a multicultural, multiracial, liberal democratic society. In order to meet this requirement, the curriculum of the school has to reflect the culture of that society. However, how elements from the various cultures should be put together to provide a coherent worthwhile education remains problematic at the present time. Perhaps if a common framework could be worked out as *The Swann Report* envisages, then we may be in a position to integrate shared values with particular values. This essay draws attention to some of the discussions relating towards finding a common framework for a multicultural curriculum. Such a curriculum would perhaps, among other things, allow freedom of choice in relation to, for example, literary texts and works of art. Such a framework would perhaps take account of the concept of education for the community – a community made up of many ethnic groups with their own histories, arts, religions, and traditions.

In the search for a common framework which in essence would be a balance between the overarching framework (the shareable and particular values discussed above), one has to accept the fact, as Smolicz points out, that since cultures differ in their core values, the compatibility between cultures will also vary and that some cultures will interact more readily than others. Moreover, some cultures will interact more readily with the shareable political and economic values, than others will do. However, while such variations increase the dimension and complexity of pluralism within a democratic society, they do not undermine its foundation or threaten the stability of the state, since, as we argued above, the differences concerned can be encompassed within the existing and still developing overarching framework of values.[54]

Notes

[1]Charles Taylor, *Multiculturalism and the 'Politics of Recognition'* (Princeton, NJ: Princeton University Press, 1992), 36.

[2]J. Smolicz, "Cultural Pluralism and Educational Policy: In Search of Stable Multiculturalism," *Australian Journal of Education*, 25, 2, 1981: 132.

[3]S.C. Rockefeller, "Comment on Charles Taylor's Paper," in *Multiculturalism and the 'Politics of Recognition.'*

[4]Ibid., 92-93.

[5]Ibid.

[6]Ibid., 88.

[7]J. Smolicz, "Cultural Pluralism and Educational Policy."

[8]R. Boudon and F. Bourricaud, *A Critical Dictionary of Sociology*, trans. by P. Hamilton (London: Routledge, 1982), 186.

[9]G.D. Mitchell, *A New Dictionary of Social Science* (New York: Aldine Publ., 1968).

[10]E.B. Taylor, *Primitive Culture: Researches into the Development of Mythology, Philosophy, Religion, Art and Custom*, 2 vols. (Gloucester, MA: Smith, 1958), vol. 1, 1.

[11]A.L. Kroeber and C. Kluckhohn, *Culture: A Critical Review of Concepts and Definitions* (Cambridge, MA: Harvard University Press, 1951), 181.

[12]Ibid., 189.

[13]R. Firth, *Elements of Social Organization* (London: Watts, 1951), 27.

[14]G.A. Theodorson and A.G. Theodorson. *A Modern Dictionary of Sociology* (New York: Thomas Y. Cromwell, 1969).

[15]R. Boudon and F. Bourricaud, *A Critical Dictionary of Sociology*.

[16]Ibid.

[17]Ibid., 97.

[18]N. Abercrombie, S. Hill, and B.S. Turner, *The Penguin Dictionary of Sociology* (Harmondsworth: Penguin Books, 1984), 245-246.

[19]Ibid.

[20]D. Jary and J. Jary, *Collin's Dictionary of Sociology* (London: Harper Collins, 1991).

[21]J. Smolicz, "Cultural Pluralism and Educational Policy," 76-77.

[22]H. Giles and B. St. Jacques (eds.), *Language and Ethnic Relations* (London: Pergamon Press, 1979), ix.

[23]J. Smolicz, "Shared Values and Cultural Diversity: Education for Multiculturalism," *PIVOT*, 7, 2, 1980, 51.

[24]C. Taylor, *Multiculturalism and the 'Politics of Recognition,'* 25.

[25]Ibid., 68.

[26]Ibid., 60.

[27]S.C. Rockefeller, "Comment on Charles Taylor's Paper," 89.

[28]J. Smolicz, "Multiculturalism and an Overarching Framework of Values: Some Educational Responses for Ethnically Plural Societies," *European Journal of Education*, 19, 1, 1984: 17.

[29]Ibid.

[30]Ibid., 13.

[31]M. Halstead, *Education, Justice and Cultural Diversity – An Examination of the Honeyford Affair 1984-85* (Lewes: Falmer Press, 1988), 225.

[32]*United Nations International Covenant on Civil and Political Rights,* 1966.

[33]R. Samuda et al., *Multiculturalism in Canada* (Toronto: Allyn and Bacon, 1984).

[34]B. Parekh, "The Gifts of Diversity," *Times Educational Supplement*, March 29, 1985: 22-23.

[35]Ibid.

[36]Ibid.

[37]*The Swann Report, Education for All* (London: HMSO, 1985).

[38]Ibid., 5.

[39]Richard Pring, "Education for a Pluralist Society" in M. Leicester and M. Taylor (eds.), *Ethics, Ethnicity and Education* (London: Kogan Page, 1992), 20.

[40]B. Parekh, *Colour, Culture and Consciousness* (London: Allen and Unwin, 1974), 229-230.

[41]*The Swann Report,* 4.

[42]Ibid., 7.

[43]J. Smolicz, "Multiculturalism and an Overarching Framework of Values," 18.

[44]S. Wolf, "Comment on Charles Taylor's Paper," *Multiculturalism and the 'Politics of Recognition,'* 84-85.

[45]Ibid.

[46]Ibid., 81.

[47]C. Taylor, *Multiculturalism and the 'Politics of Recognition,'* 66.

[48]Ibid., 66.

[49]Ibid.

[50]J. Smolicz, "Shared Values and Cultural Diversity: Education for Multiculturalism," 49-50.

[51]J. Smolicz, "Cultural Pluralism and Educational Policy," 121.

[52]Brian S. Crittenden, "Autonomy as an Aim in Education" in K.A. Strike and K. Egan (eds.), *Ethics and Educational Policy* (London: Routledge and Kegan Paul, 1978).

[53]David Bridges, "Non-Paternalistic Arguments in Support of Parents' Rights," *Journal of Philosophy of Education*, 18, 1, 1984: 56.

[54]J. Smolicz, "Multiculturalism and an Overarching Framework of Values," 17.

22

Culture, Democracy, and the University

Sharon Bailin

The calls for democracy within the university are perhaps as strong now as they were in the past, but the form of the demands has altered to some extent. It is not so much towards the governance of the institution that the demand is directed, but rather towards what is transpiring within its classrooms. Thus we have the challenge, emanating from quarters as diverse as critical theory, feminism, and postmodernism, that the bodies of knowledge promulgated by the university are undemocratic, representing a hegemony of Western, middle-class, male culture which excludes some groups, for example, women, minorities, the working class. As a consequence, there is a call for the inclusion of more voices in the curriculum, particularly the voices of those marginalized by the traditional curriculum. It is not only the canons of the particular disciplines which have come under attack, however, but also their standards and methods of inquiry, and indeed the whole notion of rational inquiry itself. It is these criticisms, particularly the last one, that I wish to investigate. I shall attempt to do this by exploring the nature of rational inquiry and its relationship to cultural traditions and to democracy.

The Critique

The works that constitute the syllabus of study for courses at universities tend to be justified in terms of being the culminating products of our cultural traditions. They are thought to represent the current state of knowledge in the sciences and the "best that has been thought and said" in the arts and humanities, those products which have withstood the test of time and the critical scrutiny of expert communities according to their methods and criteria of assessment. Recent critics have begun to question the universality and inclusivity of these cultural traditions, however. They claim that the knowledge that is purveyed in educational institutions has been created largely by and for white, middle-class, European males. These critics question the notion that culture is the exclusive preserve of this group and argue for the inclusion of the cultural attainments of groups whose works have been omitted from the canon, for example women, blacks, aboriginal peoples. The central issue regarding curriculum choice changes, then, from the question of the grounds for selection to the question of

321

whose knowledge is selected and who is authorized to do the selecting. The central issue becomes one of legitimation rather than one of justification. And the argument is made that, on democratic grounds, the works included should be representative of the diversity of groups within society.

This sort of critique often extends beyond a criticism of the canon, however, to include a criticism of the very methods, standards, and criteria of the disciplines themselves. Such methods and criteria are thought to be culturally determined and culturally bound. They enshrine the ways of knowing of one particular group as the only ways of knowing, and exclude the ways of knowing of groups lacking in power. The question of what knowledge is authorized is thus seen to rest on the question of who has power to legitimize their methods as the methods of inquiry, and particular methods of inquiry are seen to have no justification other than that they are the methods adhered to by a particular group.

So, for example, literary critics of a deconstruction orientation claim that there are neither privileged texts nor privileged readings of texts; there are only particular literary communities which set standards of interpretation having no other basis than that they set them.[1] As another example, some feminist critics argue that male bias in science goes beyond the absence of female scientists, female subjects, and issues of concern to females to the very methods of scientific inquiry. They claim that objectivity, disinterestedness, and impartiality are prominent features of male rather than female experience and they argue for a form of science in which subjectivity and engagement would be the ideals guiding inquiry.[2] And the argument is made in aesthetics that the criteria according to which aesthetic worth is determined merely reflect the subjective values and preferences of the dominant groups in society. Thus Nodelman claims that a focus on beauty "suppresses the way in which texts often give status to the values and prejudices of whites, males and Europeans as normal and correct," that "talking about the 'beauty' of literature is just a sneaky way of dismissing the politics in it" and that "calling Shakespeare 'beautiful' is merely an unscrupulous way of reinforcing a particular faction's power by denying that it is factional."[3]

All these criticisms rest, ultimately, on a more fundamental critique of rationality itself and the entire enterprise of rational inquiry. Drawing on sources as diverse as Kuhn, Rorty, Derrida, and Foucault, this postmodern view challenges meta-narratives, epistemological foundationalism, claims to certainty, truth, and progress, and notions of universal reason. All of these are seen as part of the Enlightenment project, a project which is seen to have failed. Rather, truth and reason itself are seen as historically situated and historically relative. What is considered true or rational varies over time according to which groups have the power to legitimate their particular discourses, methods, and truths. Cherryholmes summarizes the point thus: "if truth is discursive and discourses are historically situated, then truth cannot be spoken in the absence of power and each historical arrangement of power has its own truth."[4]

Problems with the Critique

This sort of critique is based on a particular view about the nature of knowledge, namely that knowledge is a social construction. A good statement of this position is given by Fish:

> The conclusion . . . is that all objects are made and not found, and that they are made by the interpretive strategies we set in motion. This does not, however, commit me to subjectivity because the means of which they are made are social and conventional.[5]

Knowledge, then, is seen as purely a construction of the particular groups within societies who share discourse practices and interpretive strategies which determine what will count as knowledge and how this will be established.

There are several problems with this social construction view, however. Perhaps the most devastating problem is that it is self-refuting. The view holds that all knowledge is simply a construction of particular groups and that there are no criteria for judging among the knowledge claims of different groups. Thus, according to the social construction view of knowledge, there could be no reason for assessing the social construction view of knowledge as superior to any alternative view regarding the nature of knowledge, for example the empiricist view. If the proponents of this view really believe it, then they must believe that there are no grounds for so believing and it is difficult to see how it can then be recommended as the "correct" view about the nature of knowledge, a view that others ought to accept and to act upon. This problem is particularly troubling in that the view is accompanied by a series of more particular claims, for example that some groups have been excluded from the activities of knowledge production and legitimation, that this is a bad thing, that we ought to act to remedy this situation, and even that we would be justified in using coercion to attain these ends.[6] These claims ostensibly describe states of affairs, make value judgments regarding these states of affairs, and recommend actions. Yet how can such claims be made and recommended to others if their proponents do not believe that they truly describe the world, that the value judgments are justified, and that the actions are warranted?

The argument which I am proposing here is certainly not a new one. It is a version of an argument refuting relativism which has been rehearsed frequently at least since Plato. Yet I am continually struck by the fact that the proponents of relativistic views seem not to be struck by the devastating force of this argument.

Aside from the problem of self-refutation, there are other difficulties with this view as well. It begins with the observation that there are social influences on what counts as knowledge, but makes an unwarranted leap from there to the conclusion that knowledge is completely determined by social forces. The fact that people's interests may well at times play a role in the process of inquiry does not mean that this is a necessary condition, nor that their inquiry is totally determined by such interests. Moreover, there is a further leap from the insight that knowledge has a constructive dimension to the unwarranted conclusion that knowledge is entirely constructed. It is true, I would argue, that knowledge is constructed by human minds and that we do not simply read off reality in some straightforward way. Our language and our conceptual schemes do affect how we see the world. There is an irreducible element of human mental creativity to our knowledge. This does not imply, however, that knowledge is simply a construction and that we are free to construct in any way we choose. There are constraints on what can plausibly be constructed. We must attend to the results of our experiments in science, the documentary evidence in history, the textual evidence in literary criticism, the coherence of our argument in philosophy. And some constructions will turn out to be better verified, better justified, more reasonable, more compatible with experience than will others.

At this point the social constructionists will doubtless object that this claim begs the question in that the manner in which documentary or textual evidence is attended to or coherence construed will be determined by the particular conceptual framework and discourse practices of the group in question. The problem with this move is that it misrepresents the nature of conceptual frameworks and the disciplinary inquiry which arises from them. Disciplines are not static, monolithic, and self-contained bodies of information and procedures but are, rather, overlapping, open-ended, dynamic, and plural. There are live questions, ongoing debates, and areas of controversy within every discipline and these furnish the arena for evolution and change.[7] Moreover, the principles and procedures of the disciplines represent attempts to embody rationality and to promote rational inquiry, and the prime characteristic of rational inquiry is that it is self-correcting. To quote Lipman: "The most characteristic feature of inquiry . . . is that it aims to discover its own weakness and rectify what is at fault with its own procedures."[8] Thus the critical modes of inquiry provide for the possibility of evolution of the tradition itself in the light of new evidence and arguments and problems and limitations discovered during the course of disciplinary inquiry, but also in the light of insights and criticisms from other traditions and frameworks. Knowledge is always partial, it is true, but rational inquiry, rather than revelling in its partiality, attempts to become less partial by engaging in dialogue and debate. It attempts to develop theories which account for problems and anomalies, which take into account insights in other views, which assess and synthesize in order to arrive at what seems to be the best justified view.

Rational inquiry spawns criticism, and criticisms of a tradition inevitably grow out of the traditions which they criticize, appeal to values inherent in these traditions, and presuppose rationality by appealing to reasons. This is certainly true of the sorts of criticisms which are under consideration here. The criticisms which emanate from critical theory can be traced back through Marx to their roots in Hegelian dialectic. Feminist theories are often rooted in either Marxist or liberal philosophy. And the origins of postmodernism are evident in continental philosophy. Moreover, all these criticisms make strong appeals to Western liberal notions such as equality, justice, and tolerance. Giroux, a critical theorist, acknowledges this debt in the following:

> Modernism provides theoretical elements for analyzing both the limits of its own historical tradition and for developing a political standpoint in which the breadth and specificity of democratic struggles can be expanded through the modernist ideals of freedom, justice, and equality.[9]

A similar point is made by Harding with respect to feminist theory:

> However a specifically feminist alternative to Enlightenment projects may develop, it is not clear how it could completely take leave of Enlightenment assumptions and still remain feminist. The critics are right that feminism (also) stands on Enlightenment ground. Most obviously, critics of the feminist epistemologies join those they criticize in believing in the desirability and the possibility of social progress, and that improved theories about ourselves and the world around us will contribute to that progress.[10]

Perhaps the most important point to be noted with respect to the criticisms being examined here is that, while denying the centrality of rationality, they all appeal to reasons, using arguments to attempt to secure their points of view. Indeed, it could not be otherwise, since any attempt to engage in questioning, criticism, and inquiry presupposes rationality and a recognition of the force of reasons.[11] Criticism rests on rationality. If we discard reason we remove the possibility for criticism and we are left only with power as the means for adjudicating disagreement.

Such a move is profoundly anti-democratic. The view that power is the ultimate arbiter would provide the basis for tyranny, not for democracy. Democracy involves the assessment of points of view as the basis for decisions. And this presupposes discussion and debate, and debate presupposes rationality. Democracy does demand the participation of all in the public forum. But it is not simply a matter of giving equal voice to every point of view, but rather of ensuring that all points of view are brought to the table for assessment, and that everyone participates in the assessment. Ironically, even the critics in question are not in favor of giving equal voice to every point of view simply because some group holds that point of view (a position that ought to follow from their own view). They would not, for example, be in favor of giving equal voice to racist or sexist points of view. Implicit in their view are some standards for assessment of views. Relativism is an epistemological position which cannot ground democracy since it provides no means for arguing against intolerant, anti-democratic, or tyrannical points of view. The epistemological position which can best ground democracy is fallibilism, the view that claims can be assessed according to standards of reason and that some views will be better justified than others but that we cannot ever be certain that the currently accepted view is the best. Consequently there is the demand that we listen to all available points of view and that we are always open to new evidence and new arguments.

Conclusion

Where do these deliberations leave us with respect to the criticisms of academic knowledge as non-democratic? First, there is certainly a case for looking carefully at what has been included in and excluded from the canons of the culture and for reclaiming valuable works which have been neglected. It is important to investigate the social influences on what has been considered worthwhile, to see what has been excluded for irrelevant reasons, and to enlarge the canon to be more inclusive. And certainly the methods and principles of the traditions are also open to criticism. It is in the nature of disciplinary inquiry that the methods and principles evolve as well as the bodies of knowledge, and that there can be a number of alternative methodologies within a discipline. (It would be important that students gain some understanding of the evolutionary and plural nature of disciplinary inquiry).

Such evolution and pluralism are not arbitrary, however, but rather arise in response to difficulties and inadequacies in existing methodologies. Thus both the critique of the canon and the methodologies themselves are justifiable so long as they are not arbitrary but appeal to reasons. Indeed such criticism is a necessary part of inquiry. But what cannot coherently be rejected is reason itself. It is presupposed in the entire enterprise of inquiry, critique, and evolution of knowledge. It is what makes criticism possible and is presupposed in any criticisms, even criticisms of rationality itself. And our traditions of knowledge and culture are attempts to embody principles of rationality. Thus a wholesale rejection of rational modes of inquiry and the cultural traditions in which they are embedded cannot be justified in the name of democracy. Indeed, such a rejection would, I would argue, seriously undermine the possibility for democracy.

Notes

[1]See, Stanley E. Fish, *Is There a Text in This Class?* (Cambridge, MA: Harvard University Press, 1989).

[2]See, Sandra Harding, "Feminism, Science and the Anti-Enlightenment Critiques," in L. Nicholson (ed.), *Feminism/Postmodernism* (New York: Routledge, 1990).

[3]P. Nodelman, "Is 'Beauty' in the Eye of the Politically Correct?," *Globe and Mail*, 25 June 1991.

[4]Cleo Cherryholmes, *Power and Criticism* (New York: Teachers College Press, 1988), 34.

[5]S.E. Fish, *Is There a Text in This Class?*, 331-332.

[6]C. Cherryholmes, *Power and Criticism*, 165.

[7]See, Sharon Bailin, *Achieving Extraordinary Ends: An Essay on Creativity* (Norwood, NJ: Ablex, 1992).

[8]Matthew Lipman, *Thinking in Education* (Cambridge, UK: Cambridge University Press, 1991), 121.

[9]Henry Giroux, *Postmodernism, Feminism and Cultural Politics: Redrawing Educational Boundaries* (Albany, NY: State University of New York Press, 1991), 2-3.

[10]S. Harding, "Feminism, Science and the Anti-Enlightenment Critiques," 99.

[11]See Harvey Siegel, *Educating Reason: Rationality, Critical Thinking and Education* (New York: Routledge, 1988).

Part Six

Standards and Rights: Whose Values?

As the readings in Part Five clearly indicated liberal democracies allow for differences to be expressed and discussed. Ideally this should also be reflected in educational institutions. Yet from a practical point of view, one can ask: Is it possible for all views to be expressed? Are all views equally plausible? And if there are qualitative differences between views, then given mundane constraints, such as time limitations, which or whose views should take prominence? And who should determine this: Should it be the parents or guardians, the experts including teachers and administrators? Should the children have a say in these matters?

Notwithstanding the differences replies to these questions may give rise to, in democracies it is usually assumed or taken for granted that although education can be defined in different ways or from different perspectives, there are certain beliefs and practices which are considered to be educational and others which are clearly uneducational. Education, as seen from the selections in Part Four, is normally associated with awareness, understanding, consciousness raising, responsible and informed choice, open-mindedness and critical thinking, wittingness, sensitivity and care, and autonomy. And hence, indoctrination, severe imposition of ideas, beliefs and values, harsh conditioning and extreme training are considered to be inherently uneducational and morally repugnant. Yet this distinction, while conceptually and ethically sound, does not completely free us from difficult questions that educational practices raise: Within the realm of education, which standards and values should direct our curricula and teaching practices? Do we need standards? What is the purpose of standards? Whose standards should direct our practices and why? Given that in reality there are different values, will taking the interests of the students seriously help to fulfil the values the parents wish to instill in their children? Or, will it be the case that the notion of interests militates against that of standards in the sense that it may lead to the position that any standard is acceptable? But should not developing the interests of the students help safeguard the dangers of indoctrination? These are some of the major questions dealt with in this concluding section.

In response to such questions, some today have declared that what is needed is to take standards seriously, or to have higher standards, or to establish common national standards. Once this is done, it is claimed, the other issues will fall in place. In the first essay in this section, Eisner challenges us to take a closer look at the concept of standards and the implications of the application of such a notion. While he agrees that standards may offer us a sense of what we are trying to achieve as well as the value of what we are actually doing, he raises central questions: Dare we go beyond set standards which after all are socially constructed regulatory norms? Does the notion of rigidly following standards stifle creativity and ingenuity? Is it really educationally and democratically desirable to always insist on uniform, common standards? We need to distinguish between standard as a measurement and standard as a value; the two are not identical. In the educational context we cannot avoid the latter sense of standard since education is infused with value issues. And since, as Eisner reminds us, "variability, not uniformity, is the hallmark of the human condition," the questions of whose values becomes more urgent.

In response to the latter question, as seen from the dialog by Clark and Wilson, some believe that the notion of students' interests will resolve the issue. Yet, distinctions between "what interests a student" and "what is in the interest of a student," and "simply following students' interests" and "developing the students' interests" indicate that the issue is more complex. Given the etymological meaning of "interests," namely the Latin "inter" and "esse," one has to take the notion seriously if one is really concerned about the human condition. But does this mean that the interests of students will continuously determine our educational decisions? Do students' interests really represent the thinking of the students? Or are interests, like many other things, socially constructed, and hence represent the interests of a certain group of people? And if the reply to the latter question is in the affirmative, then if the students are not aware of such an influence, will this not amount to a form of indoctrination?

In the third essay of this section Callan takes up the issue of indoctrination by considering the question of the limits of the parents' rights to influence or determine their children's views. While many would agree that parents' rights are not absolute, some have argued, on the basis of self-determination, that parents have the right to indoctrinate their children in matters such as religious beliefs. But is not indoctrination itself a violation of a child's own right to self-determination? Is it possible for parents to influence the development of their children's beliefs without necessarily indoctrinating them? The same kind of questions arise with regard to the role of teachers especially if teachers are viewed to be *in loco parentis*.

How can we avoid the dangers associated with indoctrination? Bellous, in the fourth essay, explores and argues for the need to teach students to "resist." In our culture, the notion of resistance usually has negative connotations. Yet

Bellous, quite convincingly, argues for a positive notion of resistance – one that is *not* grounded in violence but in empowerment, participation, trust, conversation, human agency, authenticity, and voice which involves "the articulation of critical opinion." Of course, contemporary schools may find such articulation irritating. If that is the case, then as citizens of democracies, we are compelled to ask: Whose values and whose rights are really inspiring our schools?

Further Readings

Eamonn Callan, "Faith, Worship, and Reason in Religious Upbringing" in J.P. Portelli and S. Bailin (eds.), *Reason and Values: New Essays in Philosophy of Education.* Calgary, AB: Detselig, 1993, 67-82.

Mark Halstead (ed.), *Parental Choice and Education.* Kogan Page, 1994.

John P. Portelli and Ann Vibert, *Dialoging Standards: The Missing Debate.* Halifax, NS: Dialog Books, 1995.

Geoffrey Scarre (ed.), *Children, Parents and Politics.* Cambridge: Cambridge University Press, 1989.

Ben Spiecker and Roger Straughan (eds.), *Freedom and Indoctrination in Education: International Perspectives.* London: Cassell, 1991.

Elmer Thiessen, *Teaching for Commitment.* Montreal, PQ: McGill-Queens University Press, 1993.

Max Van Manen, *The Tone of Teaching*, Richmond Hill, ON: Scholastic, 1986.

Nigel Wright, *Assessing Radical Education.* Milton Keynes: Open University Press, 1989.

23

Standards for Schools: Help or Hindrance?

Elliot W. Eisner

Efforts to reform schools are not exactly a novel enterprise. Among the concepts central to current educational reform in many countries throughout the world is the concept of standards. Standards are being formulated not only to specify expected levels of student performance, but for teacher performance as well and for the assessment of curriculum content and learning activities. The concept is an attractive one. Who among us, at first blush at least, would claim that schools – or any other institution for that matter – should be without them? Standards imply high expectations, rigor, things of substance. To be without standards is not to know what to expect or how to determine if expectations have been realized – or so it seems.

Yet once we get past the illusions that the concept invites – once we think hard about the meaning of the term – the picture becomes more complex. To begin with, the meaning of the term is not as self-evident as many seem to believe. A standard meal, for example, is a meal that I think we would agree is *quality id.* nothing to rave about – and the same could be said of a standard hotel room or a standard reply to a question. A standard can also be a banner, something that trumpets one's identity and commitment. A standard can represent a value that people have cared enough about to die for. Standards can also refer to units of measure. The National Bureau of Standards employs standards to measure the quality of manufactured products. Electrical appliances, for example, must achieve a certain standard to get the UL seal of approval.

Which conception of standards do we embrace in the reform movement? Surely we do not mean by standards a typical level of performance, since that is what we already have without an iota of intervention. As for standards that represent beliefs or values, we already have mission statements and position papers in abundance, but they do not have the level of specificity that reformers believe is needed for standards to be useful.

The third conception of standards – as units of measure that make it possible to quantify the performance of students, teachers and schools – seems closer to what we have in mind. We live in a culture that admires technology and efficiency and believes in the possibility of objectivity. The idea of measurement provides us with a procedure that is closely associated with such values.

Measurement makes it possible to describe quantity in ways that allow as little space as possible for subjectivity.[1] For example, the objectivity of an objective test is not a function of the way in which the test items were selected, but of the way in which the test is scored. Objective tests can be scored by machine, with no need for judgment.

Standards in education, as we now idealize them, are to have such features. They are to be objective and, whenever possible, measurable. Once a technology of assessment is invented that will objectively quantify the relationship of student performance to a measurable ideal, we will be able to determine without ambiguity the discrepancy between the former and the latter, and thus we will have a meaningful standard.

Those who have been working in education for 20 or so years or who know the history of American education will also know that the vision I have just described is a recapitulation of older ideals. I refer to the curriculum reform movement of the 1960s. It was an important event in the history of American education, but it was not the only significant movement of that period. You will also remember that it was in the 1960s that American educators became infatuated with "behavioral objectives." Everyone was to have them. The idea then, like the notion of standards today, was to define our educational goals operationally in terms that were sufficiently specific to determine without ambiguity whether or not the student had achieved them

The specifics of the procedures, given prominence by Robert Mager's 1962 book, *Preparing Instructional Objectives*, required that student behavior be identified, that the conditions in which it was to be displayed be described, and that a criterion be specified that made it possible to measure the student's behavior in relation to the criterion.[2] For Mager a behavioral objective might be stated as follows: "At the end of the instructional period, when asked to do so, the student will be able to write a 200 word essay with no more than two spelling errors, one error in punctuation, and no errors in grammar."[3]

It all seemed very neat. What people discovered as they tried to implement the idea was that to have behaviorally defined instructional objectives that met the criteria that Mager specified required the construction of *hundreds* of specific objectives. Heaven knows, school districts tried. But it soon became apparent that teachers would be bogged down with such a load. And even so ardent a supporter of behavioral objectives as James Popham eventually realized that teachers would be better off with just a few such objectives.[4] The quest for certainty, which high-level specificity and precision implied, was soon recognized as counterproductive.

Those who know the history of American education will also know that the desire to specify expected outcomes and to prescribe the most efficient means for achieving them was itself the dominant strain of what has come to be called the "efficiency movement" in education.[5] The efficiency movement, which began in 1913 and lasted until the early 1930s, was designed to apply the principles of scientific management to schools. Its progenitor, Frederick Taylor, the inventor of time-and-motion study, was a management consultant hired by industrialists to make their plants more efficient and hence more profitable. By specifying in detail the desired outcomes of a worker's efforts and by eliminating "wasted motion," output would increase, profits would soar, wages would rise, and everyone would benefit.

American school administrators thought that in Taylor's approach to management of industrial plants they had found a surefire method for producing efficient schools. Moreover, Taylor's approach was based on "science." The prescription of expected outcomes, of the manner of performance, and of the content in which competence is to be displayed is a not-too-distant cousin of the teacher performance standards and curriculum content standards that accompany today's discussions of standards for student performance.

School administrators caught up in the efficiency movement gradually learned that the basic conception and the expectations that flowed from it – namely, that one could mechanize and routinize teaching and learning – did not work. Even if it were possible to give teachers scripts for their performance, it was not possible to give students scripts. There was no "one best method," and there was no way to "teacher-proof" instruction.

My point thus far is that what we are seeing in American education today is a well-intentioned but conceptually shallow effort to improve our schools. My point thus far is to make it plain that the current effort in which we are enmeshed is no novelty; we have been here before. My point thus far is to suggest that successful efforts at school reform will entail a substantially deeper analysis of schools and their relationships to communities and teachers than has thus far been undertaken.

To try to do justice to the aspirations of the national educational reform movement, I will try to make a sympathetic presentation of its arguments. I start with the acknowledgement that there is a sense of sweet reason to the arguments that the reformers have made. After all, with standards we will know where we are heading. We can return rigor to schooling; we can inform students, parents, and teachers of what we expect; we can have a common basis for appraising student performance; and we can, at last, employ an important lever for educational reform. Without standards, we are condemned to an unbroken journey into the abyss of mediocrity; we will remain a nation at risk.

In addition, the task of formulating standards is salutary for teachers and others involved in curriculum planning. By establishing national goals for each subject that schools teach, we will be able to achieve professional consensus that will give us a unified and educationally solid view of what students are expected to learn. By trying to define standards for each field, a single vision of a subject will be created, teachers will have an opportunity to profit from the goals and standards formulated by their peers, and ambiguity will be diminished because teachers will know not only the direction their efforts are to take, but also the specific destinations toward which their students are headed. Furthermore, teachers will have something of a timetable to help determine not only whether, but when, they have arrived.

As if they had just taken a cold shower, a population of sometimes lethargic and burned-out teachers will be reawakened and become alert. Our nation will, at last, have a national educational agenda, something that it has never possessed. Ultimately, such resources and the approach to education that these resources reflect will help us regain our competitive edge in the global economy. Parents will be satisfied, students will know what is expected of them, and the business community will have the employees it needs for America to become number one by the year 2000, not only in science and in math but in other fields as well. Our students and our schools will go for and get the gold at the educational Olympics in which we are competing. Our schools will become "world class."

An attractive vision? It seems so, yet a number of questions arise. You will recall that the standards about which reformers speak are national standards. The organizations – and there are dozens – that are engaged in formulating standards are doing so for the nation as a whole, not for some specific locality. Put another way, in a nation such as the United States in which 45 million students in 50 states go to approximately 108 000 schools overseen by some 15 000 school boards and in which 2.5 million teachers teach, there is a presumption that it makes good educational sense for there to be uniform expectations with respect to goals, content and levels of student achievement. I regard this assumption as questionable on at least two counts.

First, the educational uses of subjects are not singular. The social studies can be used to help students understand history, to help create a socially active citizenry, or to help students recognize the connection between culture and ideas. Biology can be used to help students learn to think like biologists, to understand the balance of nature, to appreciate the limits of science in establishing social policy, or to gain an appreciation of life. The language arts can be used to develop poetic forms of thought, to learn to appreciate great works of literary art, to acquire the mechanics of written and spoken language, to learn to appreciate forms of life that require literary rather than literal understanding. Mathematics can be taught to help students learn to compute, to understand the structure of mathematics, to solve mathematical problems, to cultivate forms of mathematical cognition, and to help students appreciate the beauty of structures in space. Where is it written that every subject has to be taught for the same reasons to 45 million students? Despite the effort to achieve professional consensus about the educational agendas of specific subjects, the virtue of uniformity is, to my mind, questionable.

Uniformity in curriculum content is a virtue *if* one's aim is to be able to compare students in one part of the country with students in others. Uniformity is a virtue when the aspiration is to compare the performance of American students with students in Korea, Japan, and Germany. But why should we wish to make such comparisons? To give up the idea that there needs to be one standard for all students in one field of study is not to give up the aspiration to seek high levels of educational quality in both pedagogical practices and educational outcomes. Together, the desire to compare and the recognition of individuality create one of the dilemmas of a social meritocracy: the richness of a culture rests not only on the prospect of cultivating a set of common commitments, but also on the prospect of cultivating those individual talents through which the culture at large is enriched.

A second problematic feature of the aspiration to adopt a common set of standards for all is a failure to recognize differences among students with whom we work. I am well aware of the fact that deleterious self-fulfilling prophecies can be generated when the judgments educators make are based on a limited appreciation of the potentialities of the students. This is a danger that requires our constant vigilance. However, the reality of differences – in region, in attitude, in interests, and in goals – suggests that it is reasonable that there be differences in programs.

The framers of the U.S. Constitution implicitly recognized the need for the localities they call states to develop educational programs that addressed the values and features of the populations in those states. We do not need the U.S. equivalent of a French Ministry of Education, prescribing a one-size-fits-all program. Ironically, at a time when the culture at large is recognizing the uniqueness of us all and cultivating our productive differences, the educational reform movement, in its anxiety about quality, wants to rein in our diversity, to reduce local discretion, and to give everybody the same target at which to aim.

Thus with respect to aspiration, I think there are fundamental problems with the concept of standards as applied to the nation as a whole. But there are other problems as well, and these problems relate to the concept of standards as it applies to the process of education and to what we know about normal patterns of human development.

You will remember that I referred to standards as units of measure that make possible the "objective" description of quantitative relationships. But there are qualitative standards as well. To have a *qualitative* standard you must create or select an icon, prototype, or what is sometimes called a benchmark against which the performance or products of students are matched. To have a *quantitative* standard you must specify the number or percentage of correct answers to pass a test or the number of allowable errors in a performance or product and to use that specification as the standard.

In each case, there is a fixed and relatively unambiguous unit of measurement. In the qualitative case, the task for both judge and performer is one of matching a performance with a model. This kind of matching is precisely what occurs in the Olympics. Olympic judges know what a particular dive should look like, and they compare a diver's performance to the model. The diver, too, knows what the model looks like and does his or her best to replicate the model.

With respect to the quantitative case, the application of the standard occurs in two different ways. The first has to do with determining the correctness of any individual response. An item response is judged correct if the appropriate bubble is filled in, or the appropriate selection is made, or if some other indication is given that the student has hit a prespecified mark. The prespecified correct response serves as a standard for each item. Once these item responses are summed, a determination is made as to whether the total number of correct responses meets a second standard, the standard specified as a passing grade by the test-maker or by some policy-making body.

Notice that in both cases innovation in response is not called for. The diver replicates a known model. The test-maker determines whether a student's score is acceptable, not by exercising judgment, but by counting which bubbles have been filled in and comparing the number of correct responses to a fixed predetermined standard.

There are, we must acknowledge, a number of important tasks that students must learn in school in which innovation is not useful. Learning how to spell correctly means knowing how to represent the known. The same holds true for what is taught in early arithmetic and in the language arts. There are many important tasks and skills that students need to learn – that is, conventions – that are necessary for doing more important work and that educational programs should help them learn. The more important work that I speak of is the work that makes it possible for students to think imaginatively about problems that matter to them, tasks that give them the opportunity to affix their own personal signature to their work, occasions to explore ideas and questions that have no correct answers, and projects in which they can reason and express their own ideas.

Learning to replicate known conventions is an important part of the *tactical outcomes* of education, but it is not adequate for achieving the *strategic aspirations* that we hold. These strategic aspirations require curricula and assessment policies that invite students to exercise judgment and create outcomes that are not identical with those of their peers. Again, the cultivation of productive idiosyncrasy ought to be one of the aims that matter in American schools, and, to my way of thinking, we ought to build programs that make the realization of such an outcome possible, even if it means that we will not find it easy to compare students. When we seek to measure such outcomes, we will not be able to use a fixed standard for scoring the work students have produced. We will have to rely on that most exquisite of human capacities – judgment.

Paradoxically, many of the groups that have been working diligently to formulate standards are not really formulating standards at all. They are formulating goals. Consider the following, all of which purport to be standards:

> • "Accomplished teachers work with families to achieve common goals for the education of their children"(Board for Professional Teaching Standards, 1994).
>
> • "Construct Personal Meaning from Nontraditional Dramatic Performances" (National Standards for Arts Education, 1994).
>
> • "How Progressives and Others Addressed Problems of Industrial Capitalism, Urbanization, and Political Corruption"(United States History: Exploring the American Experience, 1994).
>
> • "Folklore and Other Cultural Contributions from Various Regions of the United States and How They Help to Form a National Heritage" (United States History: Exploring the American Experience, 1994).

Such broad, general statements are aspirations that can function as criteria with which to interrogate the work students produce. But the criteria are not the same as standards. John Dewey described the difference in *Art as Experience*, one of his most important books, which is largely unread by educators.[6] In a telling chapter on the relationship of art criticism to perception, written when he was 75 years old, Dewey said that, in assessing works of art, standards are inappropriate; criteria are needed. Standards fix expectations; criteria are guidelines that enable one to search more efficiently for the qualities that might matter in any individual work. Describing the features of a standard, Dewey wrote:

> There are three characteristics of a standard. It is a particular physical thing existing under specified physical conditions; it is not a value. The yard is a yard-stick, and the meter is a bar deposited in Paris. In the second place, standards are measures of definite things, of lengths, weights, capacities. The things measured are not values, although it is of great social value to be able to measure them, since the properties of things in the way of size, volume,

weight, are important for commercial exchange. Finally, as standards of measure, standards define things with respect to quantity.[7]

Later, he went on to argue:

> Yet it does not follow because of absence of an uniform and publicly determined external object [a standard], that objective criticism of art is impossible. What follows is that criticism is judgment; that like every judgment it involves a venture, a hypothetical element; that it is directed to qualities which are nevertheless qualities of an *object*; and that it is concerned with an individual object, not with making comparisons by means of an external preestablished rule between different things.[8]

To say that by the end of a course students will be able to write a convincing essay on the competing interests of environmentalists and industrialists that marshals good arguments supported by relevant facts is to identify criteria that can be used to appraise the essay; it is not to provide a standard for measuring it. Regarding the meaning of criteria, Dewey wrote:

> If there are no standards for works of art and hence none for criticism (in the sense in which there are standards of measurement), there are nevertheless criteria in judgment. . . . But such criteria are not rules or prescriptions. They are the result of an endeavor to find out what a work of art is as an experience, the kind of experience which constitutes it.[9]

One might wonder whether it is appropriate to think about the appraisal of work produced by students at the elementary or secondary level as being comparable to the assessment of works of art. Aren't artworks objects in a different category? Criteria may be appropriate for paintings and poetry, but schoolwork requires the application of standards.

As plausible as this may seem at first glance, things are not so simple. The creation of conditions that allow students to display their creative and reasoning abilities in ways that are unique to their temperaments, their experience, and their aims is of fundamental importance in any educational enterprise – in contrast with one concerned with training. And, because such features are important, it is criteria that must be salient in our assessment.

Standards are appropriate for some kinds of tasks, but, as I argued above, those tasks are instrumental to larger and more important educational aims. We really don't need to erect a complex school system to teach the young how to read utility bills, how to do simple computation, or how to spell; they will learn those skills on their own. What we need to do is to teach them how to engage in higher order thinking, how to pose telling questions, how to solve complex problems that have more than one answer. When the concept of standards becomes salient in our discourse about educational expectations, it colors our view of what education can be and dilutes our conception of education's potential. Language matters, and the language of standards is by and large a limiting rather than a liberating language.

The qualities that define inventive work of any kind are qualities that by definition have both unique and useful features. The particular form those features take and what it is that makes them useful are not necessarily predictable, but sensitive critics – and sensitive teachers – are able to discover such properties in the work. Teachers who know the students they teach recognize the unique qualities in students' comments, in their paintings, in the essays they write, in the ways in which they relate to their peers. The challenge in teaching is to provide the conditions that will foster the growth of those personal characteristics that are socially important and, at the same time, personally satisfying to the student. The aim of education is not to train an army that marches to the same drummer, at the same pace, toward the same destination. Such an aim may be appropriate for totalitarian societies, but it is incompatible with democratic ideals.

If one used only philosophical grounds to raise questions about appropriateness of uniform national standards for students in American schools, there would still be questions enough to give one pause. But there are developmental grounds as well. The graded American public school system was built on an organizational theory that has little to do with the developmental characteristics of growing children. In the mid-19th century we thought it made very good sense for the school to be organized into grades and for there to be a body of content assigned to each grade.[10] Each grade was to be related to a specific age. The task of the student was to master the content taught at that grade as a precondition for promotion to the next grade. At the end of an eight- or 12- year period, it was assumed that, if the school and the teacher had done their jobs, everyone would come out at roughly the same place.

If you examine the patterns of human development for children from age 5 to age 18, you will find that, as children grow older, their rate of development is increasingly variable. Thus the range of variation among children of the same age increases with time.

For example, for ordinary, nonhomogeneous classes, the average range of reading achievement is roughly equal to the grade level; at the second grade there is, on average , a two-year spread in reading achievement. Some second-graders are reading at the first-grade level, and others are reading at the third-grade level. At the fourth grade the spread is about four years, and at the sixth grade, about six years. In the seventh grade the spread is about seven years; some children are reading at the fourth-grade level, and some are reading at the 10th-grade level.

What this means is that children develop at their own distinctive pace. The tidy structure that was developed in the 19th century to rationalize school organization may look wonderful on paper, but it belies what we know about the course of human development. Because we still operate with a developmentally insensitive organizational structure in our schools, the appeal of uniform standards by grade level or by outcome seems reasonable. It is not. Variability, not uniformity, is the hallmark of the human condition.

I do not want to overstate the idea. To be sure, humans are like all other humans, humans are like some other humans, and humans are like no other humans. All three claims are true. But we have become so preoccupied with remedying the perceived weaknesses of American schools that we have underestimated the diversity and hence the complexity that exists.

The varieties of unappreciated complexity are large. Let me suggest only a few. When evaluating students in the context of the classroom, the teacher – the person who has the widest variety of information about any particular student – takes into consideration much more than the specific features of a student's particular product. The age, grade, and developmental level of the student; the amount of progress the student has made; the degree of effort the student has expended; the amount of experience a student has had in a domain are all educationally relevant considerations that professionally competent teachers take into account when making judgments about a student's progress. Experienced teachers know in their bones that the student's work constitutes only one item in an array of educational values and that these values sometimes compete. There are times when it may be more important educationally for a teacher to publicly acknowledge the quality of a student's work than to criticize it, even when that work is below the class average.

Beyond the details of the classroom, there are more general questions having to do with the bases on which educational standards are formulated. Should educational standards be derived from the average level of performance of students in a school, in a school district, in a state, in a nation, *in the world*? How much talk have we heard of "*world class*" standards?

If national policy dictates that there will be uniform national standards for student performance, will there also be uniform national standards for the resources available to schools? To teachers? To administrators? Will the differences in performance between students living in well-heeled, upper-class suburbs and those living on the cusp of poverty in the nation's inner cities demonstrate the existing inequities in American education? Will they not merely confirm what we already know?

The socioeconomic level of the students and the resources available to them and their teachers in a school or school district do make a difference. If those urging standards on us believe that the use of standards will demonstrate inequities – and hence serve to alleviate them – why haven't these already painfully vivid inequities been effective in creating more equitable schools?

And, one might wonder, what would happen to standards in education if by some magic all students achieved them? Surely the standards would be considered too low. At first blush this doesn't sound like a bad thing. Shouldn't the bar always be higher than we can reach? Sounds reasonable. Yet such a view of the function of standards will ineluctably create groups of winners and losers. Can our education system flourish without losers? Is it possible for us to frame conceptions of education and society that rest on more generous assumptions? And consider the opposite. What will we do with those students who fail to meet the standards? Then what?

Perhaps one of the most important consequences of the preoccupation with national standards in education is that it distracts us from the deeper, seemingly intractable problems that beset our schools. It distracts us from paying attention to the importance of building a culture of schooling that is genuinely intellectual in character, that values questions and ideas at least as much as getting right answers. It distracts us from trying to understand how we can provide teachers the kind of professional opportunities that will afford the best among them opportunities to continue to grow through a lifetime of work. It distracts us from attending to the inevitable array of interactions between teaching, curriculum, evaluation, school organization, and the often deleterious expectations and pressures from universities.

How should these matters be addressed? Can schools and teachers and administrators afford the kind of risk-taking and exploratory activity that genuine inquiry in education requires?

Vitality within an organization is more likely when there are opportunities to pursue fresh possibilities, to exercise imagination, to try things out, and to relinquish the quest for certainty in either pedagogical method or educational outcome. Indeed, one of the important aims of education is to free the mind from the confines of certainty. Satisfaction, our children must learn, can come from the uncertainty of the journey, not just from the clarity of the destination.

I am not sure that American society is willing at this time to embrace so soft a set of values as I have described. We have become a tough-minded lot. We believe that we can solve the problems of crime by reopening the doors to the gas chamber and by building more prisons. But it's never been that simple. Nor is solving the problems of schooling as simple as having national educational standards.

And so I believe that we must invite our communities to join us in a conversation that deepens our understanding of the educational process and advances our appreciation of its possibilities. Genuine education reform is not about shallow efforts that inevitably fade into oblivion. It is about vision, conversation, and action designed to create a genuine and evolving educational culture. I hope we can resist the lure of slogans and the glitter of bandwagons and begin to talk seriously about education. That is one conversation in which we must play a leading role.

Notes

[1] The presence of subjectivity in scientific work has long been regarded as a source of bias. Most measurement procedures aspire to what is called "procedural objectivity," which represents a process in which the exercise of judgment is minimized. A competent 10-year-old can do as well as a Nobel Prize winner in measuring a room. Tasks that can be accomplished without appealing to human judgment can also be done by machine. Optical scanners can score multiple test forms more quickly and more accurately than humans. Some idealizations of science aspire to a pristine quantitative descriptive state that does not depend on human judgment or interpretation at all. For an extended discussion of the concept of "procedural objectivity," see Elliot W. Eisner, *The Enlightened Eye: Qualitative Inquiry and the Enhancement of Educational Practice* (New York: Macmillan, 1991).

[2] Robert Mager, *Preparing Instructional Objectives* (Palo Alto, CA: Fearon Publishers, 1962).

[3] Ibid.

[4] W. James Popham, "Must All Objectives Be Behavioral?," *Educational Leadership*, 1972: 605-608.

[5] Raymond Callahan, *Education and the Cult of Efficiency* (Chicago: University of Chicago Press, 1962).

[6] John Dewey, *Art as Experience* (New York: Minton, Balch, 1934).

[7] Ibid, 307.

[8] Ibid., 308.

[9] Ibid., 309.

[10] John I. Goodlad and Robert Anderson, *The Non-Graded Elementary School*, rev. ed. (New York: Teachers College Press, 1987).

24

How to Base Your Curriculum on Children's Interests

Charles Clark and P.S. Wilson

Carlson. I once taught a class whose educational activities were based entirely on the personal interests of the children.

Wick. I would have thought that children needed a basis of order. What drove you to that extreme?

Carlson. Desperation! In each of the urban schools in which I had hitherto taught, arrangements seemed intended more to restrict children than to help them learn. Stories were "done," "news" was written whether there was any or not, arithmetic was disposed of early in the morning, and the rest of the day slid slowly into "free choice," which was a euphemism for the condition where collective resistance finally overcame the institution and everyone enjoyed at last a kind of aimless dissipation or relief from what had gone before. To keep the whole thing going from day to day, various phony currencies were used such as stars, house points, shields, bursts of applause in Assembly, visits to "show the headmaster," "taking it home," "sticking it up," "going home early" and so on, plus certain nicely calculated bits of pain or unpleasantness such as "standing outside," "standing up," "keeping in," "putting hands on heads," "doing tables," "missing swimming" and similar things. To put it in a sentence, what these schools had was gross educational bankruptcy on the one hand and all the apparatus of inducements and deterrents, or pressure, on the other. Accordingly, I formed the desperate hypothesis that pressure was creating and perpetuating its own necessity, and therefore I decided to abolish the whole machinery and start again, *ex nihilo.*

Wick. But were the children's interests henceforth, then, to be the sole and only consideration guiding everything that went on?

Carlson. No, of course not. As in any community, social matters had to be regulated continually. Right from the start, one basic rule was repeatedly explained to the children, namely, that no child could be allowed to interfere with anyone else in the classroom, including the teacher, unless that person had been consulted about it and his or her provisional consent, or at least tolerance, gained. Without this rule, before long no one could have pursued his or her interests at all.

Wick. What a highly moral community!

Carlson. Not at all! I didn't say that this rule was actually adhered to in my class any more frequently than it is elsewhere. Disputes were quite common, as you can imagine, and when these occurred I sometimes intervened and always had to consider whether or not I ought to. For example, I had to insist that we were all responsible for our own mess. None of us, including me, could go home until the room was in reasonable order. The alternative was not to be allowed to do messy jobs.

Wick. But this is absurd! Children are capable of making any job whatsoever into a messy one! Your room must have been knee-deep in litter and abandoned projects half the time. And what about the noise?

Carlson. True, we were a noisy and messy class, but do you expect 40 children to work all day in the same room and leave it looking as if it had been unoccupied? Or to pursue their interests freely and at the same time look like a group of nuns at compline? In your obvious concern about noise and mess you are displaying exactly the preoccupations of my embattled colleagues who wished their classes to resemble geriatric wards because they wanted a quiet life. In my class, any noise or mess which was part of the job was not even commented on, unless it became generally disturbing. Noise generated by enthusiasm, in contrast to that arising from hostility and frustration, is rarely disturbing. Children just ignore it, in which case what does it matter?

Wick. All right, then. You are drawing a distinction between the pursuit of personal interests on the one hand and the requirements of social order on the other. How did you get these young children to grasp that you were giving them complete liberty in the former respect?

Carlson. Initially it was very difficult. After years of pressure, how could children possibly realize that the situation had changed overnight? In fact, they reprimanded me for my approach. "You're a teacher," they said. "You're supposed to make us do it." But the situation had indeed changed overnight, and they appreciated this slowly. They didn't suddenly become as articulate about the concept of interest as you or I, and of course I wasn't able to bring it home to them merely by telling them. Nevertheless, in every way I could think of, I tried to show them that pressure was no longer being applied and that, subject to the rule I've mentioned, they should choose their own activities. For instance, I continually showed them examples of the sort of thing I meant by "interesting activities."

Wick. But now you're making it sound as though you merely demonstrated to them some pre-selected range of "desirable activities" which you yourself were quite convinced that they jolly well ought to be interested in, even if in fact they weren't. Doesn't this take us back to the state of affairs which you thought you had abolished?

Carlson. No, you're confusing the issue. Certainly I picked out various activities to show them, but I chose these solely on the grounds of their possible interest, not because they were "desirable" on other grounds such as suiting the school's ethos or the current fashions in curriculum construction or the headteacher's tastes. In any case, the activities which I selected were only illustrations. I put no pressure on the children to do literally those things, rather than any others which they personally found more interesting. I was perfectly prepared for them to do nothing at all, if this was the only alternative to their doing something for its interest.

Wick. I'm still not clear about this. Did they start with their interests, or with yours?

Carlson. As long as they were taking an interest, what does its origin matter? It was made clear to them that they and only they were to decide what was interesting. The sources of the interest were of no consequence.

Wick. Tell me more, then, about these things which, for your part, you decided to introduce. Why did you choose just those things and not others?

Carlson. Well, I just chose the sorts of things which I thought the children might find interesting. We did a wide range of art and craft, such as collage, all sorts of painting, models, sculpture, printing, etc. We did a vast amount of work involving number and shape – in fact, in one form or another, this went on practically all the time. We read and wrote poetry and prose. We did dramatic work, including writing and producing our own plays and scenery. We engaged in a variety of scientific activities – physics, astronomy, zoology, etc., the last including the theory of evolution and some philosophy about the existence of God. We studied sex, history, geography, cookery . . . and so on and so on.

Wick. But this is just the ordinary junior school curriculum, more or less!

Carlson. That's what I thought you'd say.

Wick. But be realistic! Everyone knows that children are barbarians, culturally speaking. That's why they have to go to school. You can't seriously mean that your children were really interested in philosophy, science, poetry, art and all that stuff? I don't believe you!

Carlson. Strange as it may seem to you, yes, believe it or not, this is what I mean. My usual procedure was simply to make what I thought might be interesting suggestions for those who currently had nothing particular to do. Then, without any pressure from me to do what I'd suggested, we all went our various ways, my time being mostly spent in helping one child or another through any snags which he or she ran up against in pursuit of whatever had been chosen.

Wick. Incredible! You make it sound so easy!

Carlson. It wasn't easy at all.

Wick. But surely, in the absence of pressure to please you, the children would just have done whatever they liked – and I simply cannot see how their doing as they liked could possibly have given rise to the science, philosophy and so on which you mentioned. After all, children's likes are mostly indiscriminate and trivial. They are the product of every anti-educational influence to which they've ever been socially exposed. As is well known, they like to pick their noses, blow up frogs with bicycle pumps, bully smaller children, tease each other, and indulge in sex play in the Wendy house. If they were already interested in maths and history when they came to school, then no doubt you might have had a chance of succeeding in your plan. But, as a matter of fact, most children are not like that at all. You must have lured them into doing science by trading on their liking for flashes and bangs or cutting worms in half. I expect that you got them going on maths by offering them a rake-off of profits from the class "shop." Your discussions of sex and God were stimulated, I should think, by a prospect in the children's minds of forbidden thrills or of alarming their mums and dads. And the cookery, obviously, was motivated by plain greed, not by interest. What a fraud! Under the guise of letting them pursue their interests, you merely got them going on the traditional intellectual pursuits all over again. But educational disciplines such as science, history, even cookery, are not natural and inborn in children. These disciplines have taken mankind countless generations to develop. How could children possibly cotton on to them and engage in them straight away, just out of interest? They have to be made to understand them first, if they're even to have the chance of becoming interested in them eventually. Therefore, whatever you say you must have used pressure!

Carlson. What a peculiar and, if I may say so, depraved idea of humanity you conjure up! You imply that mankind can only become civilized as a result of pressure which, surely you can see, is itself barbaric and degrading! What is so striking about your view is its extreme pessimism. You seem firmly convinced that no one can possibly be interested in worthwhile activities willingly but, given half a chance, will prefer trivialities like wiggling ears or standing on one leg all day. Having assumed that culture, once identified, will be greeted by children with unequivocal hostility, you then construct oppressive machinery to deal with this "fact" and the result is that you create a stampede in the other direction – and so your machinery is necessary then, isn't it? If you are determined to stick to this fantasy of "human nature," then nothing I could ever say would convince you otherwise. There seem to be two additional reasons for your fixed opposition. One relates to your rigid and narrow views about the nature of "education" and of the worthwhile activities which comprise it, the other to your persistent misunderstanding of the notion of "interest."

Wick. Go on.

Carlson. In your mind, it seems to me, you have certain rigid paradigms of the sorts of activity which count as "science," "philosophy," and so on, ideas according to which the only activities which could conceivably be carried on under these grand titles are those of certain suitably accredited adults such as university dons, or perhaps A-level examiners. Inevitably, in this case, no child's activity could possibly count as "philosophy," etc. By contrast, all that I'm saying is that my unpressurized children did in fact engage with interest in activities which, according to my less rigid paradigms, were just as "historical," "mathematical," or whatever, at a child's level of understanding, as the activities of your dons and examiners are at theirs. We are looking at the same activities but from opposite ends of a spectrum, I from a child's end and you from an adult's. The only difference between us is that I see it as a continuum, but you refuse to admit that such continuity is even conceivable. Of course, then, children appear to you to be barbarians faced with an unbridgeable abyss across which they have to make a forced march into a state of civilization. But when you say that "therefore" pressure must be applied, the necessity which you feel derives from this mistake of yours and not from what children "as a matter of fact" are like. A child doesn't have to understand subject-matter in its adult form, before he or she can be interested in it. Any child can be interested in "science," I would say, so long as he or she has some grasp of the empirical or "real" as opposed to the fantastic ("weird," "way-out"), the fictitious ("far away," "long ago," "made up," "story time,") and the illusory or delusive ("seeing things," "mad," "nuts," "bananas"). As a basis for "mathematics," all I need is that the child has a grasp of the concept of some physical entity or other sufficient for him or her to be able to see where one example of its kind ends and another begins, plus an ability to handle simple logical connectives such as "and," "or," and "not." To get into what "history" is about, some conception of the past (e.g., yesterday) is needed, plus some understanding of the motives of others (e.g., "Are you getting up for breakfast?"). The beginnings of "aesthetic" appraisal are to be found in an interest in tastes, colours, pattern, balances, rhythms, and so on. Can you imagine what a human child would look like, who had none of these capacities? He or she could scarcely have any kind of "mind" at all!

Wick. So, contrary to what I was arguing earlier, on your view disciplines or "forms of knowledge" are natural and inborn in children already, then, are they?

Carlson. That's a very misleading way of talking. What I am saying is that if we assume that children have minds or indeed "know" anything at all, then it follows that anything which they knowingly choose to do must (logically) fall inside one or more of the "forms" of knowledge. Anything which could not be so characterized, such as fetishism and other compulsive preoccupations, would fall into categories of morbidity such as "neurotic" and "psychotic," meriting therapy not teaching, since they would represent points at which individuals' educational development had for the time being become impossible. I am saying, in other words, that certain pursuits such as science, etc. are epistemologically compulsory and that this makes psychological compulsion redundant.

Wick. I still don't see what you mean.

Carlson. Well, each time that I identified the kind of activity (e.g., scientific) which I thought that my children were interested in, then, with no implications that they had to listen to me (since in fact I might have got it quite wrong), I asked the children questions and set them problems about the kind of activity in which, so it seemed to me, they were engaged. These questions and problems, by specifying in the relevant language the sorts of things which might count as answers, in effect taught the children some of the implications (scientific, mathematical, or whatever) of what they were doing. If I was wrong about the kind of activity that it was and therefore about the kind of questions and problems that were relevant to it, then the children would simply stop doing it, or they would go on doing it but without paying any further attention to me. There was no pressure, then, because pressure was neither relevant nor needed.

Wick. But I still cannot see how the children's interests, alone, could sustain the development of their understanding in the directions which you describe. Surely, children's interests are often not only trivial and indiscriminate but also fleeting, fragmentary, and at times immoral and downright dangerous?

Carlson. This brings me to the second of your two errors, namely, your distorted view of "interest." You keep thinking of nose-picking, ear-wagging, frog-inflating, and so on as though these were paradigms of children's interests. Thus, you fail to discriminate between the things which children are interested in and the things which they like doing. But to say that I like my dinner, for example, is not the same as saying that I am interested in it. I like it, for instance, when it has an agreeable taste or when it suits me to have it, but this implies nothing about my interest in anything at all. On the other hand, a professor of dietetics, a forensic scientist, an anthropologist, a cannibal, or a baby of two could be very interested in my dinner without liking it at all. Interests have different objects from likings, and "doing what interests me" is a different sort of activity from "doing what I like." When I like my dinner, it is the potatoes, meat and gravy which I like, and the appropriate activity is eating them – because, if I like my dinner, I want to eat it. But when I am interested in my dinner, it is the food qua subject-matter that engages me, and the appropriate activity is investigation – that is, I want to learn more about it. No doubt (to take another example) Lord Longford was interested in pornography while not liking it in the least.

Wick. So what about the ear-wagging, frog-inflating, and frolics in the Wendy house which you say I'm hung up on? Are these likings? Or are they interests?

Carlson. They could be either, depending on whether children were investigating these things or just indulging in them. A zoologist who was interested in experimenting with frogs might heartily dislike doing it. By contrast, a child repeatedly blowing frogs up with a pump or something but without showing any concern for getting a further understanding of what was going on in this activity, would no more be doing it for its interest than I would be showing interest in marmalade by repeatedly eating it. Mere engagement in an activity implies nothing about the nature of one's motive for engaging in it.

Wick. This seems to commit you to the view then, and indeed it is tautological on your view, that any interest at all has educational potential or in other words holds import of some scientific, philosophical, aesthetic, or other rational kind and is thus a means to children's further understanding of their experiences and activities, whatever these happen to be.

Carlson. That's what I've been saying all along.

Wick. Yes, I see that now, but I still can't believe that when it came to the crunch (as it must very frequently have done, I imagine) you actually practised this philosophy consistently from day to day. Were you really prepared to tolerate dangerous and immoral interests on educational grounds even though you found them intolerable on prudential or moral ones?

Carlson. Of course not. You're forgetting the ground rule which I told you about at the beginning. Anything which interfered with others' pursuits was always liable to be ruled out.

Wick. Well then, weren't there some interests which, although maybe they interfered with nobody, nevertheless were just too fleeting and short-lived to provide a basis for anything?

Carlson. It's perfectly true that there are innumerable activities so simple that it doesn't make much sense to talk about someone being interested in them for more than a moment or two; where the subject-matter has very little mileage, for example, and also tends to lack demanding standards of what is to count as success or failure in it or intelligent as opposed to unintelligent doing of it. But my argument is that in so far as subject-matter lacks mileage and standards and cannot be a subject of interest, children need to find out this for themselves in any particular case, and I would never dream of stopping them from doing so. When they have done so, they will stop the activity spontaneously, won't they? For example, all the kids for miles around came to raid my comics cupboard, but after the first flush my own class largely ignored them. The only occasion when a child is likely not to stop doing some fleetingly-interesting thing is when he or she knows that the only alternative waiting for him or her is some compulsory "worthwhile activity."

Wick. You're saying that your class quickly exhausted the interest of comics, are you?

Carlson. That's what it seemed like. But in any case, children aren't going to get educated just by taking things on our say-so. If you rule out all trash from your classroom, how are children going to learn to discriminate? Personally, I welcomed the trivial and the nugatory in my classroom, because of the visible contrast it provided to the worthwhile. I had every confidence that the contents of the children's library, as it slowly came to be investigated, would easily outdistance my pile of silly comics, so I allowed them to exist together. By contrast, you regard wisdom as being founded not upon some experience of excess or folly but upon the habit of obediently following someone else's good rule. Thus you imply that a teacher should be feeding children all the time with the right answers which, since the children are not supposed to be capable of seeing any good reason for them, you therefore have to insist upon coercively. In your view, it is from acquiring these good habits of answering that the children are supposed to become capable eventually of formulating sensible "questions" and thus of becoming "autonomous." But logically this could never happen, so long as you consistently conceal wrong answers from them or treat these merely as problems of control. If children are to learn to ask good questions and recognize good answers, then they must be able to get a clear view of what is worthless, and they can only have this if it exists openly and on equal terms all around them. You take the position of a person who wants to teach a child what "up" means while systematically concealing from him or her any reference to "down." But if you can't make such mistakes in school, where can you?

Wick. Well, that seems to dispose of my points about the triviality, folly and ephemerality of children's interests, I suppose. What about their fragmentariness, though? Education is not sustained by perpetual euphoria. A great deal of sweat, strain, and agony is involved in any intellectual pursuit taken to a worthwhile level. Therefore, I would still say that some external discipline or support is needed to keep kids at it.

Carlson. I had hoped that by now I had sufficiently explained that "interest" neither is, nor needs to be, some sort of maniacal excitement or euphoria. You are asking me to consider the possibility of a child who is interested but who, for some reason, cannot persist or keep his or her mind on the job. But if the child can't stop his or her mind wandering, how can it also be true that the child is "interested" or, in other words, wants to learn? What would it mean to say that a child was very "interested" in playing the piano, but couldn't ever be bothered to do any practice? Or that the child was "interested" in writing stories, but had never persisted with his or her writing long enough to finish a story yet? We would all like to achieve instant success without going through the necessary grind, but this is just day-dreaming. Interest is wanting to learn, not just dreaming about it. The children in the above examples might wish or dream that they possessed the accomplishments mentioned, but they could hardly be said to be interested in them or they would surely do something realistic about it.

Wick. I still think that some external pressure is needed to sustain the child's effort.

Carlson. Do you then expect your pressures to commend to the child the value of the activities in question and help him or her to master them? And do you think that your "external discipline" will somehow pass into the children, so that they eventually begin to pressurize themselves? Discipline to me means that someone submits to the demands of the subject-matter, not to the demands of someone whose "authority" consists in a legalized right to employ coercive powers. The desire to please or placate such "authorities," whether they are "internalized" or are still external, results only in people going through the motions of learning, thus making the whole educational process and indeed experience itself little more than a progressively elaborate series of pretences. This is why I abandoned the attempt to pressure children into "learning" in the first place.

Wick. But by "pressure" I don't mean necessarily coercing children physically. What about things such as team points? What's wrong with getting children going with incentives of this kind?

Carlson. You only need these extrinsic rewards to bridge the gap between what the children want to involve themselves in and what you want to involve them in, or in other words because you have already lost contact with the children's values or have no intention of taking them seriously. To the extent that standards are already implicit in interesting activities, then "doing well" and "getting things right" already gain a purchase on the person engaging in those activities. Doing well in what you want to do, already is rewarding. Extra inducements will neither make you want what you did not want before, nor will they teach you to do well what you have so far been doing poorly. It is only because you ignore or see no educational significance in children's interests that you are forced to tempt them or goad them into your valued pursuits with extrinsic inducements. You will then have to believe, won't you, that things such as an interest in poetry or in truth have to be "picked up" or "caught" from others somehow, because there's now no method left to you of explaining rationally how the gap between your values and the children's is to be closed? But if by contrast it is the children's values that you're educating, rather than your own which you're trying to throw out to them over the great divide, then the rewards of their activities will be internal to them and will take care of themselves. No inducements, and no tricks or magic, will be necessary to get someone interested in poetry or the truth of the matter. All that will be necessary will be to learn what these things really are.

Wick. That's all very well, but if you're constantly tagging along behind children, "educating their values" as you put it rather than getting them up to your own standards of truth and so on, how can you guarantee that your teaching will be sufficiently organized and systematic ever to achieve anything really worthwhile?

Carlson. I wonder what you mean by this term "systematic"? If you mean that all worthwhile subject-matter has its own logical and possibly hierarchical structure, then I would remind you that I have myself relied upon this point in saying that the subject-matter can quite safely be left to guide the children (and the teacher) without our having to stick any extra oars in. But there seems to be more to it than this. No doubt you think that my approach must produce a logical rag-bag in children's heads. But, first, at the very beginning of their lives I want children to sample as wide a variety of activities as possible. Hence the sheer plurality of children's interests doesn't worry me in the least. It's one of the things which makes education possible. Second, I cannot see any reason for thinking that the logical structures of subject-matter entail that there is only one psychological route to understanding something, namely, the route embodied in your "systematic" curriculum. There are some imperatives, of course. For example, I suppose that you cannot teach fractions to children who do not understand division or history to children who have no idea when "yesterday" was. But these restrictions really leave plenty of room for manoeuvre, don't they? Third, such systematization of knowledge as is necessary must be achieved concretely in the child, not just abstractly in a curriculum. I saw it as my job to ensure that there were no hang-ups in a child's mind caused by some "unsystematic" (i.e., illogical) way in which he or she was viewing the subject-matter, so far as I could make out what this was. If there were such hang-ups, I would fill in the gaps for the child by supplying missing information, correcting misunderstanding and so on. In other words, whereas you seem to be mainly interested in the systematic presentation of subject-matter, I was interested in its systematic acquisition. You seem to think that the former guarantees the latter. This is false.

Wick. You have now answered my objections to "interest" on the grounds of its ambiguity, its vagueness, its lack of connection with activities such as science and history which are "educational" in the conventional sense, its dangerousness, morbidity, immorality, triviality, ephemerality, multifariousness, and lack of system. For the moment, I have no more to say.

Carlson. But I have . . . Underlying every one of your questions throughout this conversation has been your assumption that education is impossible without compulsion or pressure. Now, first, I can think of only two different social contexts for the use of this term. Sometimes you can gain leverage or exert pressure because you can depend upon the individual's identifying with the institution which you represent and with various "authority" figures of which you are probably one. Thus, when told to do things in such situations, children just acquiesce and allow themselves to be coerced. When being caned, for example, they obligingly "hold their hand out" or "bend over." Here, pressure does not produce identification; it depends on it. In the other type of pressure situation, however, there exists by contrast no identification at all. Here, children refuse to hold their hand out or bend over. They swear at you and, if that produces no results, they either get a gang up or run home. In this situation, then, actual and literal (not symbolic) force is needed in order to be able to coerce and pressurize the children, and the children have to fear the threat of this force or the coercion will be ineffective. Let's not be squeamish about saying this. "Pressure" here is a euphemism for force and fear. Thus, you are in a dilemma.

Wick. Really?

Carlson. You rely on pressure to produce identification, but it is in fact the prior existence of identification which makes the application of pressure possible. It follows, in that case, that the only resource open to you, then, is to apply literal force, and your "pressure" must be this dressed up. A second significant point is that when you claim that education can be initiated and sustained by "pressure," what you are in fact asserting is that such pressure, whether symbolic or literal, can be a way (and is perhaps the only way apart from chance) of establishing interest in or rational concern for subject-matter. But, since every interest has standards which are internal to it, it follows that children who are acting under pressure must actually be trying to measure up to two sets of standards at once, first the standards implicit in the subject-matter, second the standards of whoever is applying the pressure. If they are being pressurized to do math, say, first they are supposed to be doing math properly, but second they are also trying to do what you (the pressurizer) say, trying to please you, placate you, avoid your penalties, etc. Thus there arises a systematic confusion, generated by you, between what counts as good math and what counts as pleasing you. Nor does this confusion apply just to math or some other particular subject-matter. Ultimately, all subject-matter whatever goes under the same blanket in the child's mind, namely, "what pleases teacher" or "what teacher tells me." Thus, not only have you obscured from the child the distinctive nature of mathematical truth; you've now concealed from him or her the distinctive nature of everything else, except what pleases you. Children under your scheme are never really doing math at all. It is some hybrid of math on the one hand and your predilections on the other. They are doing math in much the same way that children forced to stand with their hands together are praying. If this is how you educate, how would you produce sycophants? If this is how you help children to understand things, then how would you set about mystifying them? And if your pressurizing is thus concealing the distinctive characteristics of subject-matter, then how at the same time can it be generating interest in that subject-matter? The most it can be generating is double standards and confusion.

Wick. Good heavens!

Carlson. And there is a third crucial point. Not only do you produce double standards and confusion in math and other subject-matters, this spreads into morals as well. By the superimposition of your approval, you have made children's participation in your curriculum a moral matter. If children do not "do their work," they are made to feel guilty and ashamed, as if they had been immoral. But why should they feel like this? Whatever the differences (which I remarked upon earlier) between "interests" and "likes," they are identical at least in sharing a common point of contrast with universalizable notions such as "true" and "good," namely that you cannot argue people into them, since they cannot be justified by appeal to reasons of any kind. There is no moral sense in which one can argue to children that they "ought" to be interested in math, etc., any more than it would make moral sense to argue to people in general that there are certain things (e.g., eating plum jam or climbing Everest) which they "ought" to like. The fact that a person, whoever he or she is, happens to like something, or happens to find it interesting, implies nothing at all about what "ought" (morally) to be liked, or to be found interesting, by children or anyone else. This is why I was content to show my children the interest of various things and then leave the choice of activities up to them, and this is why your attempt to produce interest by pressure is so profoundly misconceived, not only educationally but also morally – and you're the moralist, remember! If someone asks you why you are interested in poetry or mathematics, the only true answer is to say, "Because I am . . ." After that, you might go on to try to show him or her what poetry, or mathematics, is really like. The children still might not be interested, but that would be up to them. By contrast, the most that some application of pressure to them could conceivably do would be to make them go through the motions of being interested, and perhaps feel a bit ashamed or at least worried by the fact that they weren't "really" interested like you.

Wick. I cannot see that as a philosopher you have any right to make allegations such as these. What right have you, sitting here in your conceptual armchair, to make predictions about what children will or will not do or feel? These are empirical points, not philosophical ones. How do you know that if I got the children's heads down to some experiments or something they might not become interested in it eventually, given enough time? Who's to say? Who are you to make moralistic pronouncements about the matter? This is something for teachers to find out for themselves.

Carlson. All right, I'll get out of my conceptual armchair, as you call it – though as a matter of fact I was the one who did the teaching, remember, not you. But O.K., if you still think that this is not a conceptual matter and, moreover, if you think that therefore it is empirically possible and even likely that interest can be the outcome of pressure, then let's try it now! I can test it at once on you! I will keep you here in the staff room, by force, until you agree that you should start taking my arguments seriously. You might start understanding them a bit better, then, mightn't you? You might start finding a bit more interest in them than you're doing at the moment, don't you think?

Wick. Words fail me . . .

25

Indoctrination and Parental Rights

Eamon Callan

It is commonly assumed that parents have extensive moral rights in the formation of their children's moral and religious beliefs. I shall argue that whatever these rights may be, they do not entitle one to treat one's children in ways which disable or even disincline them from seriously questioning the ground of parental values or from seriously entertaining the possibility that other values might be preferable. The concept of *serious* questioning and reflection is one that undoubtedly deserves close analysis which it will not receive in this paper,[1] but I think there is enough agreement in how we ordinarily apply the concept for me to use it here without inviting misunderstanding on any matter of importance to my argument. We could all agree, surely, that I am not seriously questioning my ideals if I treat arguments deployed against them merely as obstacles to the making of converts or as a threat to my own peace of mind, and we could agree to this even if I displayed considerable ingenuity in how I dealt with these arguments. Of course, there are cases where just what counts as serious questioning or reflection is unclear, but such cases arise in the use of just about any important concept and so their occurrence provides no argument against the importance of any concept.

If one were to instil moral or religious beliefs in one's children in such a way that they become unable or disinclined to engage in serious thought about their validity, then one is guilty of indoctrination. There are very many experiences which children are subjected to in our culture, at the discretion of their parents, which appear to carry at least a grave risk of inculcating this kind of disability or disinclination. Among these experiences are being coaxed or compelled to engage in religious rituals, being denied access to scientific or artistic material merely on the grounds that it conflicts with parental ideals, and being made to attend denominational schools. There is some room for disagreement about which practices really do carry a grave risk of indoctrination, and only extensive and complex empirical inquiries could decisively resolve many such disputes. But even where the risk is indisputable we are often prepared not only to tolerate the practice, but also to defend it as a legitimate exercise of parents' moral rights. In Western societies there is a widely acknowledged moral right to send one's children to denominational schools. The substantive implications of the right have always been controversial, but few would claim that the right fails to apply to a school just because it strongly discourages students from ever seriously examining the grounds of the religion prescribed by their parents. In other words, few would claim that there is no parental right to send one's children to schools which clearly attempt to indoctrinate them. So long as my efforts to shape my child's values are made within humane limits and do not pose any substantial threat to the public interest, I am morally entitled to do as I please, or so the morality of commonsense would suggest.

There are considerations pertaining to the child's interests which give some semblance of justification to this state of affairs. (I use the word "interest" here and throughout the remainder of the paper in its normative sense to pick out things which ensure some fundamental good for the individual.) The mere fact that children in the conventional nuclear family are in constant intimate contact with one or two adults whom they will naturally love and admire creates a powerful tendency to identify with their values. In order to control filial identification, it would be necessary to curb intimate contact or else make the adults behave in a way which discourages identification, and neither option is an attractive one since both threaten the capacity of the family to provide the love and attention which children need. Moreover, if children are to be subject to massive adult influence in the formation of their values, then parents may seem to be the best candidates for controlling that influence. The great love which a father and mother ordinarily feel for their child make them far more likely to act in the child's best interests than others might be. If greater control over children's lives were given to others, the risk of indoctrination or other wrongs being done might well increase rather than diminish.

It is true that so long as we have intimate relationships between parents and children a strong tendency for filial identification is inevitable, but the practices which are at issue extend far beyond what is inevitable in such relationships. If Jones is a passionate Marxist her son is undoubtedly far more unlikely to become a disciple of Milton Friedman than he otherwise might be, but this surely does not entail that she has a right to bombard him with Marxist propaganda or that she is entitled to send him to a school with the express purpose of producing devout Marxists. The same point applies, *mutatis mutandis,* to parents who entertain passionate religious commitments. Undoubtedly, there are many adults whose relations with their children would become tainted with frustration and disappointment if they were not free to instil uncritical allegiance to some creed in the minds of their children. It might be advisable to grant such parents much of the freedom they demand so that their children continue to receive the love and attention they need. However, if such a policy is justified only because it is the best feasible one for the child, it surely does not follow that all parents, or even all parents with a powerful proclivity for indoctrination, have a moral right to the freedom we should grant them in these special circumstances. If Callan Senior is inclined to inflict a serious evil upon Callan Junior and any attempt you might make to curb Senior's inclination would merely bring about an even greater evil for the unfortunate Junior, then you should refrain from interfering, other things being equal; but it would be absurd to infer that Senior has a moral right to act upon his wicked inclination. To be indoctrinated on matters as important as moral and religious issues is to suffer a serious evil, even though being deprived of parental love and attention during childhood is ordinarily a greater evil. This may mean that we should permit parents to indoctrinate their children in certain situations but a moral right for parents to do so is another matter entirely.

One might object that it is mere philosophical quibbling to deny that the alleged right exists in these situations if the same policy of non-interference turns out to be justifiable, whether it does or does not exist. In fact, it makes a great practical difference whether indoctrination is seen as a moral right or as an evil which is sometimes to be reluctantly permitted to avert even greater evils, such as a loss of parental love for emotionally dependent children. If we take the latter course our reluctance to interfere will properly diminish as the child achieves emotional independence. On the other hand, given that parents do possess a right to indoctrinate, it is not clear that their entitlement would weaken at all merely because the child's emotional need of them decreases. Furthermore, there might be much that could be done to curtail parentally approved or initiated indoctrination, where even very young children are the victims, which would not imperil the child's interest in familial intimacy. A prohibition against sending one's children to schools where a particular religion is indoctrinated would doubtless elicit howls of protest from certain quarters, but it is at least doubtful that it would provoke any immediate and harmful estrangement between younger students and their parents.

Arguments concerning the child's need for love and attention within the family cannot establish any parental right to indoctrinate and neither can arguments about the love and goodwill which parents naturally display towards their children. First, even if parents were apt to be more concerned about protecting the interests of the child than others, that would establish only a presumption in favor of parental control over children's lives – a far cry from a right to indoctrinate. Second, it is plausible to say that the love I bear other persons may even incline me to act *against* their interests in certain situations. In intimate relationships between adults, for example, there is often difficulty in maintaining due respect for the interest which the other has in self-determination. There may be a temptation to foist one's ideals and aspirations upon the other, a temptation which would not ordinarily arise in less emotionally intense relationships. The desire to mold the loved one in one's own image is extremely prominent in the way we deal with our children and though acting upon it may be innocuous in many situations it is also, quite obviously, the motivational source of much indoctrination, and indoctrination is at least *prima facie* the same evil whether it is perpetrated by Big Brother or one's dear parents.

The alleged parental rights to indoctrinate, however, cannot be dismissed so easily. So far I have focused exclusively upon considerations pertaining to the interests of the child, thereby discounting the possibility that the right in question is one we should recognize partly for the sake of parents rather than merely for the sake of children. If my argument is to be successful I must consider the possibility that parents may sometimes have a right to indoctrinate which holds in virtue of *their* legitimate interests. In particular, it may be possible to argue that the right to self-determination which all sane adults possess includes a right to indoctrinate one's children. Charles Fried has recently maintained that "the right to form one's child's values, one's child's life-plan and the right to lavish attention on the child are extensions of the basic right not to be interfered with in doing these things for oneself."[2] A person has a general right to shape his or her own life as he or she sees fit (within certain limits) and this entails being entitled to a vast array of options with respect to the pursuit of religious or ethical ideals. My right to self-determination does not evaporate merely because my allegiance to some ideal is wholly uncritical or because I insulate my mind from the appeal of competing values. The respect we are due as self-determining agents is not contingent on our being paragons of open-mindedness. Therefore, if one thinks of children as extensions of the lives of their parents it is natural to suppose that the right of adults to pursue their own ideals uncritically or even fanatically implies a right to inculcate the same kind of commitment in the minds of their children.

I would suggest that this line of reasoning is needed to explain, even if it fails to justify, some widely held beliefs about what parents are entitled to do. For instance, it is common to claim that as self-determining agents all sane adults are entitled to religious liberty and this includes a right to send one's children to denominational schools which instil one's own faith. Now since it is the control of children's spiritual lives which is at stake here, it is surely *their* religious liberty which should be of paramount concern, and it is by no means clear that the best way of safeguarding their liberty is by allowing their parents to send them to denominational schools. This objection can only be circumvented by maintaining that children do not really have independent spiritual lives because as children they are really extensions of the lives of their parents, and so no defensible distinction can be drawn between their religious liberty and that of their parents.

The question which now arises is whether or not children can properly be regarded as extensions of their parents' lives. William Ruddick has suggested that even in adolescence it might be permissible to regard the individual in this light:

> We have no criteria, apart from legal convention, for deciding when in pregnancy there are two human bodies rather than just one or when in adolescence there are two distinct lives, that of the "child" and that of the parent(s), independently pursuable.[3]

Ruddick is talking about having a life in the biographical sense rather than being alive in the merely biological sense. Any normal adult has a life which is constituted by plans and ideals and the attempt to shape his or her experience according to them, and it is certainly true of infants, say, that they do not possess anything remotely resembling lives in this sense. It would be ludicrous to speak of a newborn feeling hope for the future, taking pride in successes, or feeling shame at failures because these various states of mind presuppose having a life and not merely being alive. Ruddick's doubts about adolescents having distinct lives are plainly extravagant, but we need not pursue that point here. For it is obvious that even in the case of the newborn, who clearly has no life in the relevant sense, it is profoundly wrong to regard the child *merely* as an extension of her parents' lives. Suppose an adult's religious convictions led her to inflict some serious physical hardship upon herself. She could argue cogently against those who tried to interfere by pointing out that it was *her* life in which they were meddling and since she was causing harm to no one else forbearance could be reasonably demanded of them. But if her faith led her to inflict the same severe hardship upon her infant, she could not convincingly demand forbearance on the same grounds. If she tried to do so we could reply that in these circumstances her life is not the only thing at stake because harm inflicted by a parent upon an infant is patently not self-inflicted harm. Even a newborn's experience of physical suffering is independent of his or her parents' experience, and to that extent at least, viewing the child as a mere extension of his or her parents' lives is morally unacceptable. But if it is necessary to regard even the youngest child as a being with distinct moral claims when her interest in avoiding physical suffering is threatened, why is it permissible to regard her as a mere appendage to the lives of her parents when her interest in not being indoctrinated is threatened? Those who wish to defend the right to indoctrinate as a matter of parental self-determination appear to face a serious difficulty here. On the one hand, they hardly wish to embrace the view that children are just appendages to their parents' lives, without any legitimate moral claims in their own right. This would put them in the same camp as the Roman *paterfamilias,* who claimed the right to dispose of his children as if they were mere private property. Alternatively, if children are recognized as distinct objects of moral concern, it is difficult to see how the interest in not being indoctrinated can be denied on the grounds that in some areas, and this one in particular, children *are* mere extensions to their parents' lives.

The defender of parental indoctrination might try to avoid these difficulties by taking a slightly different line. One could try to establish that children have no general interest in not being indoctrinated--and *a fortiori* no moral right not to be indoctrinated – on grounds that have nothing to do with claims about the inseparableness of parents' and children's lives. If this could be established it would be possible to sketch a plausible argument in defense of the parental right to indoctrinate, an argument which would affirm that right as an aspect of self-determination. Suppose that whatever rights parents have over their children are circumscribed by the obligation they have to show due regard for the interests each child bears as a distinct object of moral concern. Showing "due regard" in this context does not entail relentless self-sacrifice or always being the perfect mother or father. I am obliged to provide my child with an adequate education, but I have no duty to secure the best possible education. Thus although the interests of the child constrain the behavior of parents in important ways, they nonetheless leave an enormous area of latitude for parental decision-making. Interference in this area of discretion by non-parents could not be justified as an attempt to ensure due regard for the child's interests, because parental decisions which fail to show such regard fall outside the area of discretion, and so any interference that is justifiable would have to avert some substantial threat to the public interest. We may safely assume that threats of this sort will normally be rare where parental obligations to the child are being conscientiously fulfilled. Now imagine a situation where someone gratuitously intrudes into the area of parental discretion. This particular intrusion does not harm or demean the child in any way, but let us suppose that some plan for their child which the parents had long cherished is destroyed. The outrage which a mother or father might feel in this situation could not be justified in terms of the child's welfare or dignity, because the particular intrusion does not damage either, but outrage might be warranted nonetheless. So long as parents act with sufficient regard for the child's interests it is at least plausible to say that they have a right to non-interference, a right that is their due as self-determining agents. To gratuitously interfere in parents' decisions about their children is to disrupt, for no good reason, what the parents are likely to regard as one of the most precious undertakings of their lives. It is appropriate to regard arbitrary interference in other such undertakings, such as the conduct of one's sexual relationships or the practice of one's religion, as a gross violation of the right to self-determination and so it is natural to view this case in the same light. Indeed, if this is true there would appear to be no moral objection to viewing children as extensions of their parents' lives within limits set by the parental obligation to show due regard for children's interests. These limits guarantee respect for the child's status as a distinct object of moral concern, but the wide area of discretion which parents are nonetheless left with when they have met their obligation might help to explain why they could claim the right to many decisions about child-rearing as a matter of their *own* self-determination. In this way one might avoid the excesses of the Roman *paterfamilias* while retaining the commonsense view that parents, as self-determining agents, have a substantial though not unlimited right to rear their own children as they see fit.

Whether or not the argument I have just sketched can support a parental right to indoctrinate depends on whether children have a general interest in not being indoctrinated which parents are obliged to respect. If children have that interest then indoctrination does not fall within the area of parental discretion and so it cannot be defended as a legitimate exercise of the right to self-determination. That is the possibility which we must now consider.

For those who are passionately committed to some moral or religious ideal it will appear that one of the greatest benefits they could bestow upon another human being is the same passionate commitment which gives meaning to their own lives, and if indoctrination is a price that has to be paid to ensure that commitment in the lives of their children, that may seem to be a price worth paying. After all, a closed mind is not incontestably an evil if it merely shuts the mind off to voices which might lead one to abandon what is true and ultimately important. One might argue that indoctrination practised in support of the right values is a sensible protective measure, a way of safeguarding the loyalties of one's children against the temptations of the world. If indoctrination is a defensible means of ensuring a secure allegiance to the right values then the child can have no general interest in not being subjected to the practice. For reasons which will become immediately clear I shall call this "the fanatic's argument."

Taken just as it stands this argument obviously cannot help to justify the right to indoctrinate as an aspect of one's right to self-determination. For the proponents of the argument can only countenance the right to indoctrinate when it is employed in defense of their *own* values. Their position hinges on the assumption that their values are uniquely important for human beings and that all rival positions are sources of temptation from which children must be carefully shielded. Therefore, parents who adhere to rival views may not claim any right to indoctrinate their children. In fact, given the fanatic's argument, there is at least a *prima facie* case for taking the children of infidels away from their parents in order to protect them from evil influences. Clearly, this is a line of reasoning which does not consort well with claims about what all sane and conscientious parents are entitled to as self-determining agents.

Nevertheless, the fanatic's argument does make explicit a point which may be of cardinal relevance to the problems we are now considering. Parents who indoctrinate are likely to feel that the values they are attempting to instil in the minds of their children are essential to the very meaning of their own lives, and if the attempts they make are successful their children may well find a similar degree of fulfilment in these values. I suggested earlier that moral and religious indoctrination are serious evils, but this appears somewhat doubtful in light of the fact that it may lead to the adoption of beliefs which deeply enhance the individual's personal fulfilment. Things do not always work out so well. Neurosis and misery may often be the results of indoctrination, but it would be rash to suppose *a priori* that these are the inevitable or even the usual consequences. Moreover, the right to indoctrinate one's children, which a sensible person might claim, would not be a licence to do whatever one pleases in order to pass on one's values. I have already noted that what our conventional morality appears to acknowledge is a right which only applies when the child is treated humanely and when due regard is shown for the public interest. It could be argued that indoctrination practised within these limits would not infringe upon any interest of the child because it would not, at least in the ordinary course of events, bring any psychological harm in its wake. In many instances it might even enhance the child's personal fulfillment. Therefore, parents who practise indoctrination may be showing due regard for the interests of their children, and if that were the case their actions would fall within that area of discretion in child-rearing where the parental right to self-determination holds sway.

This argument may be attractive not only to parents who wish to indoctrinate their children but also to many who have no such desire. Ronald Dworkin has recently argued that liberalism rests upon a neutral conception of the good. The truly liberal state is one in which no one conception of the good is preferred to any other in the making of policy "either because the officials believe one is intrinsically superior or because one is held by the more numerous or more powerful group."[4] Dworkin has also suggested that liberal neutrality derives from the principle of respect for the "independence" of person,[5] and presumably what he has in mind by this is respect for persons as self-determining agents. Thus, liberal political morality may appear to support the argument which has just been presented. Parents who indoctrinate their children pass on a form of life which they find deeply fulfilling to others who may also come to find it deeply fulfilling. The fact that these parents may belong to a politically powerless minority gives us no right to impose our conception of the good upon them, nor can we assume that our conception of the good is intrinsically superior to theirs. Admittedly, there are some issues on the current liberal agenda which fit rather badly with this line of reasoning. If liberals must respect the parental right to indoctrinate when it is exercised in support of the values of religious minorities, say, they must also support it when it is used to perpetuate current gender norms. Liberals who have feminist sympathies will be uncomfortable with this implication of the argument, but if the argument is sound they will just have to live with their discomfort.

However, the argument contains a fatal defect which is easily identified. Indoctrination is a serious impediment to the victim's attempts to achieve self-determination, and this is true even of situations where it enhances one's sense of personal fulfilment. The position we are considering is that the right to self-determination which parents possess is vitally important and must not be invaded just because parents want to indoctrinate their children; but indoctrination on moral or religious matters impedes the child from becoming a genuinely self-determining agent in two central areas of human experience. I assume that whatever right parents have in matters pertaining to moral and religious socialization must be circumscribed by the interest which children have in becoming adults who can exercise self-determination in matters pertaining to morality and religion. Therefore, the parental right to self-determination cannot include any right to indoctrinate one's children. And if liberalism entails respect for the individual as a self-determining agent then it cannot be strictly neutral with regard to conceptions of the good because some conceptions involve treating one's children in ways which will undermine their capacity for self-determination.

This does not presuppose the controversial position that children already have a full-blown right to self-determination. The point is rather that since a child's experience is continuous with that of the adult he or she will eventually become, the child should not be treated in ways which vitiate those rights he or she will eventually come to possess. The right not to be indoctrinated is one of what Joel Feinberg has aptly called the "anticipatory autonomy rights." Feinberg accurately describes the nature of the wrong which is suffered when a right in this category is violated:

> The violating conduct guarantees *now* that when the child is an autonomous adult certain key options will already be closed to him. His right while he is still a child is to have these future options kept open until he is a fully formed self-determining adult capable of deciding among them.[6]

Feinberg does not make any dubious assumptions here about children possessing the *same* rights as adults. He is merely pointing to the fact that the rights of adults may be violated by what happens to them as children, and so if we wish to uphold the rights of adults it follows that children are entitled not to be treated in ways which involve such violations.

368 Standards and Rights: Whose Values?

It may not be obvious that indoctrination does interfere with self-determination so I had better explain just why it does. The paradigm case of interference with self-determination, of course, is external compulsion – the use of force or threats to constrain the conduct of another person. Compulsion interferes with self-determination because it closes or makes less eligible options which the individual might choose to take in shaping the course of his or her life. If legal penalties are attached to the practice of a particular religion then its practice becomes a less eligible option to everyone who might want to practise it, and so the self-determination of everyone is invaded by these penalties. Indoctrination curtails self-determination for precisely the same reasons. If a child has been reared in such a way that he or she has been made unable to seriously consider the possibility that any religious ideals might be worth embracing then the option of religious practice has been just as effectively closed for him or her as it would be if he or she lived in a society where severe legal penalties were inflicted upon anyone who tried to practise a religion. There is no relevant difference between indoctrination and external compulsion with respect to their impact upon self-determination

The arguments I have considered in defense of the parental right to indoctrinate do not exhaust all possible ways of constructing a defence, but at least it should be clear that no such argument can be taken seriously so long as the right to self-determination is taken seriously.

Notes

[1]The concept of seriousness is discussed in John Wilson, *Preface to Philosophy of Education* (London: Routledge & Kegan Paul, 1979), 163-193.

[2]Charles Fried, *Right and Wrong* (Cambridge: Harvard University Press, 1978), 152.

[3]William Ruddick, "Parents and Life Prospects," in Onora O'Neill and William Ruddick (eds.), *Having Children* (Oxford: Oxford University Press, 1979), 124.

[4]Ronald Dworkin, "Liberalism," in Stuart Hampshire (ed.), *Public and Private Morality (Cambridge: Cambridge University Press, 1978), 127.*

[5]Ronald Dworkin, *Taking Rights Seriously* (Cambridge: Cambridge University Press, 1978), 263.

[6]Joel Feinberg, "The Child's Right to an Open Future," in William Aiken and Hugh Lafollette (eds.), *Whose Child?* (Totowa, NJ: Rowman and Littlefield, 1980), p. 126.

26

Should We Teach Students to Resist?

Joyce Bellous

Introduction

To respond to the question, "Should we teach students to resist?" two dimensions of the term 'teach' are important, namely its formal and informal aspects.[1] Its formal aspect refers to what we consciously or intentionally (programatically) set out to do; that is, we teach something to someone so that our selected educational aims can be realized. The second aspect includes those practices that characterize our teaching; on the basis of these practices students pick up certain ideas along with formal instruction. As an example, our students may pick up the idea that we like them and care that they learn what we intend to teach them. The information that we like and care for students is not part of the program that we outline when we consciously consider teaching mathematics or English. Rather, it is what students pick up by being in our presence. It is not always easy for them to identify why they believe their teacher likes them and cares that they learn, but students seem particularly adept at garnering these messages.[2] It is common to think of the expression the 'hidden curriculum' when problems of this sort are described, but I am not at present interested in making relations between the practices I pick out and the notion of hidden curriculum except to note that these practices have to do with enculturated and unreflective ways of exercising power as much as they have to do with domination and the resistance that domination inevitably calls forth.

I propose that both the formal and informal aspects of teaching *should* inspire students to practice resistance that is directed towards the development of authenticity and agency. I will first identify and discuss reasons to support the proposal and then spell out a relationship between resistance and a concept of voice that is central to the empowerment of authentic participation in democratic cultures. Finally, I examine three types of practice that shape the exercise of power. The motivation for the proposal that effective teaching should inspire a particular kind of resistance comes from the confidence that teachers can and must learn to pay attention to the ways they open or close up the possibilities for democratic participation and practice in the classroom.

369

Resistance and Integrity

I have two reasons for saying that the formal and informal dimensions of teaching should educate students to resist. I shall discuss the first of these reasons in this section and the second in the section that follows. The first reason is that our pedagogic practices should support rather than contradict our formal assertions about what we value in the teaching/learning relation. By this I mean, we should *do* what we *say*. It is possible to take one of two paths to maintain educative integrity. Teachers could set out to promote student participation and their classroom practices could support this formal assertion. Resistance would take the form of reminding a professor or teacher when teaching practices were dismissive of student participation and perspective. In this instance, resistance would be carried out in league with a professor's or teacher's formal position on the value of student participation. Students would participate in keeping us on the straight and narrow, for it is certainly the case that their participation is a constraint on doing what we singlemindedly want to do as teachers. The issue here is whether we think of students as a distraction from, or the main point of our educational efforts. The second path teachers might take is to assert that student involvement is not permitted, giving students their reasons, and informal teaching practices would support non-participation. In this approach we would be doing what we say, but with respect to its legitimacy, I assume that the development of democratic skills requires practice in participation so that reasons given would have to be credible in the context of Canadian political culture, which requires democratic participation from its citizens eventually. Democratic skills rely on a developed capacity for involvement in public conversation. Despite our beliefs about Canadian society and the teaching environment, I suggest it is common for students to experience a failure of pedagogic integrity, i.e., the pedagogic hypocrisy of saying one thing and doing another, and common for educational institutions to practice the unimportance of student participation in Canadian schools, while giving students no good reasons for silencing them. Pedagogic hypocrisy opens to the door to a "culture of silence," as described by Paulo Freire and Ira Shor; this is a culture that works against the development of skill in democratic conversation.[3] At university, as an example, students are very good at sensing whether professors mean it when they say that classroom discussion is an important part of the course experience. We all remember classes in which we quickly realized that a professor did not want to be interrupted by our questions. While we may have misled ourselves about a professor's motives for silencing us, in those classes we learned to sit still and say nothing. When we consider resistance, the passivity and submissiveness that is exemplified by the university classroom example matters a great deal. How is it that one person, who says that classroom discussion is important, can silence a group of 10, 20, 30 or more students through the deployment of practices that students recognize as a signal to sit still and say nothing?

I want to look more closely at ways of maintaining pedagogic integrity and at the same time *working with* student resistance. I am assuming that student resistance is more educative than passivity because passivity stifles democratic participation and conversation. Passivity locks us into immaturity and, as a way of responding to someone who knows more than the student knows, can stick with people for life. In order to explicate its benefits, the educational dimension of resistance needs to be distinguished from its merely political aspects. Political resistance has drawn on practices that seem necessary in the face of an exercise of social power that limits people's maturity in ways they find insupportable. That is, there is a relationship between a particular exercise of power and the response of resistance. Throughout his analysis of modern power relations, Michel Foucault argues that domination, the exercise of power that reduces the one dominated to a thing, an object,[4] calls forth resistance. But he goes on to assert, *contra* Sartre, that the exercise of power is not automatically evil. To Foucault, power is a strategic game. He uses the example of the pedagogic institution and says:

> I don't see where the evil is in the practice of someone who, in a given game of truth, knowing more than another, tells him what he must do, teaches him, transmits knowledge to him, communicates skills to him. The problem is rather to know how you are to avoid in these practices – where power *cannot not play* and where it is not evil in itself – the effects of domination which will make a child subject to the arbitrary and useless authority of a teacher, or put a student under the power of an abusively authoritarian professor.[5]

Foucault suggests that the possibility of domination is a constant threat to the well-being of the teaching/learning relation, but that power can be exercised according to practices of freedom that limit domination. I agree with Foucault at this point. Yet the practical problem we have with the idea of resistance is due to the models we typically use to describe liberation. For example, Foucault posits that liberation on the model of the colonizer/colonized relationship does not serve as a generalizable model for resistance. Frantz Fanon spells out the colonial relation and posits the need for violence in the act of liberation.[6] He puts forward a position that influenced Paulo Freire's thinking as well. In this view, liberation requires violent opposition because the colonial relation originates in, and is sustained by, violence. Violence calls forth violence. The colonizer must be eradicated and replaced. In Freire's work, there is an oppositional relationship between the oppressor and the oppressed in which the oppressed must liberate themselves and their oppressors through an act of love; although Freire leaves open the possibility for violence.[7] Violence also grounds the model that Ira Shor uses when he describes classroom realities as he sees them. He asserts that:

There is a 'symbolic violence' in school and society which imposes silence on students. It is symbolic because it is in the very order of things, not an actual physical beating, but an environment of rules, curriculum, tests, punishments, requirements, correction, remediation, and standard English, which establishes the authorities as the ones in charge. The environment is symbolically violent because it is based in manipulation and subordination. It openly declares itself 'democratic' while actually constructing and reproducing inequality. . . . For individual students, it becomes hard to see alternatives to 'the way things are and have to be'.[8]

Shor's point about passivity and submissiveness is similar to Foucault's analysis of schooling in *Discipline and Punish* (1979), where Foucault places so much emphasis on the exercise of power in practices that constitute our experience.[9] But later, in 1984, Foucault says that the model of political liberation does not serve us adequately when we are trying to figure out how to live well with the freedom that liberation secures for us.[10]

I would say that if we picture resistance as constituted in an atmosphere of violence, we cannot make good *educational* use of its practices. Empowerment provides a better model for teaching, because empowerment is grounded on a view of power that suggests models for power relations that have everything to do with maturity and partnership.[11] Models for resistance that are grounded in violence remain within what I call a dominator paradigm for power relations; within this view an essential antagonism structures the pedagogic relationship, an antagonism that Foucault celebrates rather than eradicates but which Freire tries to eliminate through the loving opposition that the oppressed must engage in.[12] Models for resistance which remain within a dominator paradigm for power describe social relations in terms of violence and perpetuate the project of overwhelming the dominator, who is perceived as less than human and deserving of replacement. While this description of the oppressor is important to make and accurate, I suggest that the project of replacement is insupportable under the conditions of an empowering partnership model for power relations and under the conditions that inhere in trying to live well with freedom once it is founded.

In order to distinguish between resistance grounded in violence and resistance as a companion to empowerment, we must pick out the differences between power and empowerment. Although both terms, power and empowerment, seem to rely on the same root word, the practices associated with each are incompatible. If we use the term power in its traditional sense, power is grounded in an *economism* that operates on the basis of a commodity model so that power refers to *zero-sum* games in which one individual or group loses something while another individual or group gains something. What is lost or gained is power, sometimes expressed as a gain or loss of position, privilege or status. I suggest that what is lost may be more importantly conceived as a loss of confidence and self-knowledge; a loss that is best spelled out as a failure of *personal power*. *Personal power* refers to the feeling/belief that I am someone who can say and do those things that are congruent with the conception I have of myself. If power is thought of as a commodity, the individuals or groups who gain something in an exercise of power do not gain in *personal power*, as it is spelled out above; rather they gain a double portion of power as commodity that amounts to the ability to get their own way at the expense of others whose *personal power* is depleted or not developed in the first place. The reason that someone's *personal power* is not developed in the first place can only be understood in terms of the socially-constituted vulnerability that characterizes some people's lives due to conditions associated with gender, race, and poverty. In addition, on the view of power as commodity, resources may be scarce. Since power is a scarce resource, distributions of power must be passed among some individuals and exclude others. These distributions have typically coincided with divisions between gender (male versus female), race (white versus non-white), and money (those who have it and those who do not). In each case, power as commodity benefits those indicated by the first term in each bracketed pair.

When we use the term empowerment, its root word picks out an entirely different exercise of power in social relations. Here power is not a scarce material resource, nor is it the redistribution of a commodity that leaves some people out. Power is a kind of social energy which has no limit and is relational not material. If A empowers B, then *personal power* is created in B and is neither diminished nor exaggerated in A. The creation of power is not an *ex nihilo* act but is rather the excavating of the *personal power* that rightly should inhere in B's capacity to be human from the layers and layers of disabling social experience under which B's attempts to exercise power is buried. This assertion picks up Ira Shor's belief that passivity is not natural. When passivity characterizes people it is as a result of practices that constitute their social vulnerability and pin them to passivity. To suggest that resistance is related to democratic competencies is to distinguish this aspect of resistance from resistance that is primarily negative and frequently aggressive. Again, aggression is "inevitable because passivity is *not* a natural condition of childhood or adulthood."[13] In terms of negative resistance, student aggression may be effective at sabotaging the ease teachers have in using power to silence, but students are not able to use negative aggression to "change education in favor of their constructive freedom."[14] That is, aggressive efforts to resist the culture of silence are self-defeating for students in the long run because this resistance is grounded on a traditional view of power as the capacity to invade and take away, to destroy or get, without regard for the other. Power in this form does not provide young people with the skills they need to live well with the adult freedoms and responsibilities associated with democracy; and it is a response that should not be necessary in a democratic society.[15] Additionally, in passive or aggressive resistance, mistrust is ubiquitous and inevitable. In summary, our educational intentions and practices should unite to permit and affirm resistance that is aimed at exercising the democratic competencies that are necessary for the development of personal and political voice in future citizens.

Resistance and Trust

The second reason that formal and informal aspects of teaching should teach students to resist is connected to the building of trust that becomes possible in pedagogic integrity, i.e., the congruence between what we say and do as teachers. If students learn to resist in the context of pedagogic integrity, they can trust that what we say is what they will get in formal pedagogic programs as well as in informal classroom practices. Resistance would be motivated by a democratic urge to be mature, participating citizens. Under these conditions, resistance takes the form of posing authentic questions; in addition, resistance is free to take the form of listening to reasons given and assessing these reasons by the light of democratic ideals and challenging these reasons openly when they do not match up with the knowledge and perspective of the learner in the teaching/learning relation. I am not assuming that students will be good at these question-posing, listening, and assessing skills at first; rather, it is what they have to learn through practice. Their skill at contributing to the educative teaching/learning relation is influenced by the practices that have already shaped them, and I will say more of this shortly. Regardless of their skill, trust in the context of pedagogic integrity produces an environment in which resistance can come to be educative because it is exercised *with* rather than *over or against* others. Educative resistance can only take place in the absence of oppression and in the presence of an empowering teaching/learning relation. While trust, which must flow from students to teacher as well as from teacher to students, is not the only characteristic of an empowering pedagogic relationship, it is at its core. An empowering pedagogic relationship also is directed towards the development of human maturity and focuses on the development of the creative individual. Two-way trust is central to both these projects. Passivity and submissiveness in the presence of hypocrisy and oppression do not foster creativity and they frustrate the development of trust and human maturity.

The aim of resistance, in the context of trust, is toward developing maturity in students through the recognition by both teacher and students that a teacher's perspective is learned and authentic rather than authoritarian and is situated within a horizon of significance that may not be the same as the students'.[16] Students must come to realize (bring into being) their own thoughts and reflectively constituted perspectives, and speak and act from within these perspectives. In this way, a student's unique personal capacities are enlivened through the teaching/learning relation. This is a highly complex educational task. At this point I only want to pick out the role that resistance and empowerment play in its realization.

Resistance and the Art of Voice

The central and unifying aim of empowerment is human maturity. The goal of empowerment is the realization of the mature, creative individual who practices *personal power* and encourages *personal power* in others; the development of human agency and authenticity is central to maturity, partnership and participatory democracy. Resistance in this view does not presuppose the eradication of hitherto powerful members of society through oppositional practices to unseat them from their position; rather, this view assumes that human maturity is distorted in all such members of society and human power is misunderstood by them. Cooperational practices are directed by the determination to uncover self-knowledge through articulating agency and authenticity in a persistent and resilient exercise of *personal power*. The resiliency of *personal power* is expressed in the concept of voice.

Voice refers to the articulation of critical opinion aimed at making our legitimate interests known; voice is direct and straightforward as opposed to protest that is a private, secret vote.[17] Voice refers to any attempt to change, rather than escape from, an objectionable state of affairs, through working collectively or individually.[18] Voice implies being able to sense and say what we want and to provide others with our reasons. In terms of *personal power*, the art of voice conveys to others the plans and purposes we have for ourselves. If voice is related to empowerment, then the capacity to speak our identity clearly and to object to what is objectionable is not grounded in mere self-interest but our voice is related to the interests of others. Voice is an economic concept that has been applied to other contexts as well.[19] On this view, there is a complex relationship between voice and escape or exit such that the art of voice does not develop if exit is either too easy or too costly. There is a relationship between voice and escape or exit if it is applied to the classroom setting. In the classroom, physical exit is costly. Students are generally in classrooms out of necessity or compulsion. If a culture of silence predominates in North American classrooms, an art of voice is not likely to develop in students. The art of voice implies discernment that comes through practice; an art of voice is not stubborn or short-sighted; neither is it negatively or passively aggressive. Voice develops in a context in which educational practices permit students to understand and value what is going on in order to provide the teacher with insights about how the teaching/learning relation affects them. An art of voice enables us to sense, address, and resolve the conflict that will inevitably come up if we take seriously the dialogical aspect of the teaching/learning relation. Each time conflict crops up, the exercise of power in the teaching/learning relation is capable of silencing or instilling the art of voice.

Practising Education

In order to distinguish the oppositional practices that seem necessary in the face of domination and violence from the cooperational practices that are possible in an empowering pedagogic relationship (in which we express resistance to secure authenticity and agency) I want to identify three types of school and home practices that are influential in determining how students turn out. These practices may be coercive, laissez-faire, or empowering. In making distinctions between these three, it is important to note that these practices are embedded in the informal dimension of teaching. Teachers would not express formally the beliefs about the teaching/learning relation that are exemplified in the first two types of practice. We must listen to Canadian students, so well-tuned to the informal aspect, and examine their subjectivities in order to judge which of these practices have predominated in their schooling.

Coercive practices can be identified by their characteristic dependence on force, whether this is epistemological force, through deception, psychological force, through threatening talk or behavior, or physical force, through violence.[20] In analyzing coercive practices in the pedagogic situation, adults (parent, teacher, professor) exercise power on the assumptions that they do and should have all the power, students or the young should and do have none, and that power is a commodity that resides in their age or position which may be passed out or withheld at will. If students operate on these same assumptions, the outcome of coercive practices is demonstrated in their docility and utility and the young become useful for the purposes of others: those who are coerced become either passive and aggressive or passive and inaccessible. As an example, students' work may be used by professors with little recourse on the part of students and teachers may use students in a variety of ways, which include taking sexual advantage. The net result of these practices is an exercise of power which becomes an end in itself. In a coercive practice, the adult struggles for power in such a way that all other ends become secondary or are eclipsed entirely. As Simone Weil observes:

> power-seeking, owing to its essential incapacity to seize hold of its object, rules out all consideration of an end, and finally comes, through an inevitable reversal, to take the place of all ends. It is this reversal of the relationship between means and end, it is this fundamental folly that accounts for all that is senseless and bloody right through history.[21]

What must be picked out is that for Weil, as well as for Foucault, the exercise of power is never complete or absolute. Always there is the possibility of resistance or escape on the part of the one being dominated. But the resistance and/or escape is shaped by the coercive practices themselves. That is, students' possibilities for resistance are directed through these coercive practices so that they come to resist in ways which are self-defeating with the result that they do not acquire authentic self-knowledge and a capacity for cooperation. In addition, they have difficulty imagining a world different from the coercive one in which their experience has been constituted. That is, students engage in passive or aggressive resistance, mentioned earlier. The outcome of this kind of resistance in the context of coercive practices is students who procrastinate or oppose, who are hard to draw out or hard to guide, and feel worthless and unloved (perhaps unlovable). In short, they do not have a developed sense of *personal power*; they have no voice.

Laissez-faire practices are sometimes taken up by those who are appalled by coercive practices but who have not been sufficiently reflective about the limitations inherent in the practices they feel compelled to use. In laissez-faire practices students are given all the power and the adult abnegates his or her right to exercise power over students, a pattern which may also structure the relationship between parents and children. That is, power is conceived by the adult as evil and its use is abhorred. Oddly, the adult sees no problem in permitting power to be exercised in an unrestrained fashion by children or adolescents; although both teachers and parents may come to express fear of the young. What is lost in laissez-faire practices is the developed ability in the young to feel and show respect for others. At the core of laissez-faire practices is a neglect of adult responsibility to exercise power in the inevitable but temporary asymmetrical relationship that exists between adult, child, and adolescent. This inevitable but temporary asymmetry is picked out in Foucault's example, provided earlier, in which he asserts that in the pedagogic relation, the exercise of power is not necessarily evil in itself. Typically, good parents are sensitive to the need to gradually transfer power over to their children in an appropriate and measured way. In laissez-faire practices, domination from above is avoided at all costs, but the price we all pay for our failure to guide the young towards attitudes and practices of respect and cooperation is immeasurable. The offspring of laissez-faire practices cannot respect others and do not understand themselves and their own compulsive need for control and things. They cannot bear to have people say no to them. They become people who cannot find a sense of place in community with others. They are persistently marginalized because of this incapacity. In them, *personal power* is distorted. In terms of the resistance that is possible for them, blind resistance becomes the emblem of all social interactions. If children and students who suffer coercive practices are hard to draw out, children subjected to laissez-faire practices are impossible to control and perhaps impossible to be with at all, even with themselves. The laissez-faire child's incapacity to respect others is a burden that can last a life-time. At bottom, the neglect of adult responsibility that inheres in laissez-faire practices misdirects the child's sense of personal worth. The inability to be at peace in the presence of others conveys to this child just how unlovable he or she must be. The art of voice cannot grow or flourish in a vacuum of respect for others; these young people do not find an articulate voice.

In contrast to the first two types, empowering practices can lead children and students into mature, responsible, and responsive relationships with their social world. Empowerment results in the development of *personal power* and is grounded in reciprocity and respect. If coercive practices have force at their core, and if laissez-faire practices have neglect at their core, attentiveness is at the core of empowering practices. Attentiveness is that pedagogic stance in which the teacher/adult is engrossed in the other in such a way that the one attended to is capable of sensing his or her own abilities, interests, responsibilities, and inclinations in a context of care, respect, fairness, and eventual partnership.[22] Self-knowledge is made possible through attentiveness conveyed through a reflectively constituted world view inclusive of a world openness that is capable of prizing the authentic differences expressed in the child or student. That is, attentiveness is directed towards perceiving and prizing genuine and salient differences in the child's perspective. The child's resistance is educative because it is directed towards the development of agency and authenticity in the context of a coherent and plausible reality that at the same time is capable of countenancing these differences. Additionally, in empowering relationships, power is neither finite nor fixed in either player in the social relation; it is not hidden, as it is in Rousseau's *Emile*: power is not manipulative; the adult speaks clearly, confidently, personally, and directly. Unlike Rousseau's insistence that we must never make a mistake when we interact with the young or the entire relation is lost (a recipe for guilt), the empowered and empowering adult admits mistakes and works out conflict and is reflective in practice so that many mistakes are seen in advance. In general, nothing of force grounded in violence, nor neglect, is found in empowering relationships;

resistance is understood to contribute to the development of authentic differences between adults and youth so that participation in civil partnerships becomes possible.

In summary, the resistant response is ambiguous. At bottom, to resist is to say no; but if we listen to those who resist, we may hear, absolutely no, not now, not me, not this way, not according to my experience or knowledge. All these responses are potential expressions of agency and authenticity. The virtue of empowering educative resistance is grounded in a student's ability to sense and articulate good reasons for resisting something. For example, suppose a grade one child is told by a teacher that a tomato is a fruit.[23] In the child's experience tomatoes have been treated as vegetables. The child resists the category that the teacher puts forward. Perhaps the child argues with the teacher. Empowering teachers listen for the type of resistance that the child is expressing and they ask: What does this child know? What does this child want? What is this child feeling and thinking? Empowering teachers find a way to ask the child these questions to draw out their perceptions because they do not presume to know the child's answers in advance. A bureaucratic teacher will not attempt to decode this resistance but will try to find a way to manage it so that the child's resistance is snuffed out. If this happens, the child's experience is excluded from the classroom and does not become part of the information that the child uses in developing the critical reasoning necessary for the art of voice.

Students who enjoy empowering pedagogic relationships are capable of respecting others and themselves and develop skills necessary to participatory democracy. Such students would be good at resisting bureaucratic practices that promote passivity and submissiveness to the will of others in the absence of any good reasons. It is entirely possible that the partial resistance inherent in empowerment would be a nuisance in bureaucratic schools. So much the better for education.

Notes

[1]A version of this paper was presented at the Learned Society Conference, June 1993, at Carleton University, Ottawa. I appreciated the comments and questions of Evelina Orteza y Miranda, William Hare and John Portelli.

[2]I am not suggesting these messages cannot be consciously considered, but that they often are not.

[3]Ira Shor and Paulo Freire, *A Pedagogy of Liberation: Dialogues on Transforming Education* (New York: Bergin & Garvey, 1987), 121-141.

[4]Michel Foucault, "The Ethic of Care for the Self as a Practice of Freedom," In James Berbauer and David Rasmussen (eds.), *The Final Foucault* (Cambridge, MA: The MIT Press, 1988), 12.

[5]M. Foucault, *The Final Foucault,* 18-19. Italics mine.

[6]Frantz Fanon, *Black Skin, White Masks* (London: Pluto Press, 1967); Fanon, *The Wretched of the Earth* (New York: Grove Press Inc., 1968).

[7]Paulo Freire, *Pedagogy of the Oppressed* (New York: Continuum, 1988), 42.

[8]I. Shor and P. Freire, *A Pedagogy of Liberation*, 123.

[9]I explore Foucault's contribution to our understanding of power and experience more fully in J. E. Bellous, *Empowerment, Power and Education*, Ph.D. Dissertation, University of Alberta, 1993.

[10]M. Foucault, *The Final Foucault*, 3.

[11]Joyce Bellous and Allen Pearson, "Empowerment and Teacher Education," *Studies in Philosophy and Education*, 14, 1995: 49-62.

[12]Violence is a deeply problematic response in minority experience. The passivity that typifies, for example, the colonial relation is only ended when the oppressed become enraged enough to end their passive tolerance of harm to themselves; this rage seems to me to be a crucial step in articulating self-worth. It is an anger that shouts: "This is enough. I am no longer to be spoken to this way or treated in this manner." This anger, which moves those who are deeply disprivileged to prize their human dignity, is appropriate anger. If the structures that perpetuate and benefit from oppression do not recognize the legitimacy of this anger, violence appears as the only possibility to make the minority point. Since those who are in positions of privilege are numb to the acts or threats of violence that secure their position, they can be oblivious to the meaning of this anger.

[13]I. Shor and P. Freire, *A Pedagogy of Liberation*, 123.

[14]Ibid., 125.

[15]The point is examined carefully in Paul Willis, *Learning to Labour* (Farnborough, Hants.: Saxon House, 1977), especially pages 119-137. As Willis spells out, students' conception of the future is instrumental in the way they reproduce their past. In addition to thinking about our concept of democracy, we need to pay attention to how our students think about their own future.

[16]Charles Taylor, *The Malaise of Modernity* (Concord, Ont.: Anansi, 1991), 31-41.

[17]Albert O. Hirschman, *Exit, Voice and Loyalty: Responses to Decline in Firms, Organizations, and States* (Cambridge, MA: Harvard University Press, 1970), 15.

[18]Ibid., 30.

[19]Carol Gilligan explores the idea in *In a Different Voice* (Cambridge, MA: Harvard University Press, 1982) and in *Mapping the Moral Domain* (Cambridge, MA: Harvard University Press, 1988); as does Susan Moller Okin in *Justice, Gender and the Family* (New York: Basic Books, 1989); Elisabeth J. Porter, *Women and Moral Identity* (North Sydney: Allen & Unwin, 1991); and George Fletcher, *Loyalty* (New York: Oxford University Press, 1993).

[20]J.E. Bellous, *Towards a Philosophy of Multicultural Education*, Masters Dissertation, University of Calgary, 1988, 27.

[21]Lawrence A. Blum and Victor J. Seidler, *A Truer Liberty: Simone Weil and Marxism* (New York: Routledge, 1989), 194.

[22]I am not suggesting a model for the pedagogic relation in which the child has equal power to the teacher. See for example, Jesse Goodman, *Elementary Schooling for Critical Democracy* (Albany, NY: State University of New York Press, 1992). I agree with the position taken here that "teachers and students should not be 'equals' within elementary schools," 106. The trick is to lead children toward adult participation

eventually and to decipher the patterns of power exchange that contribute to that development.

[23]This example was given to me by John Portelli and I believe his child's experience is common if not characteristic of schooling. I know of a young women whose parents were employed in a third world country where orange trees grew. They returned to Canada so that their daughter could attend primary school. When the child was asked to color a picture that had oranges in it, she colored the skins green. The teacher corrected her and made her color the orange skins orange. In fact, in the country of her pre-school years, the oranges on the trees did have green skins. Yet her first-hand knowledge was dismissed as impertinent resistance.